GW00634430

THE GUIN
AMERICAN FOOTBALL
FACT BOOK

THE GUINNESS AMERICAN FOOTBALL FACT BOOK

Ian Morrison

GUINNESS PUBLISHING

Published in Great Britain by Guinness Publishing
Ltd, 33 London Road, Enfield, Middlesex

Cover design by Ad Vantage Studios
Text design and layout by Steve Leaning

Cover illustrations: Ottis Anderson (New York
Giants), Joe Montana (San Francisco 49ers), Super
Bowl XXVI, Larry Kennan (London Monarchs).
Courtesy of Allsport UK Ltd.

Typeset by Ace Filmsetting Ltd, Frome, Somerset

Printed and bound in Great Britain by
The Bath Press, Bath

A catalogue record for this book is available from
the British Library.

ISBN 0–85112–536–0

CONTENTS

ACKNOWLEDGEMENTS FOR ILLUSTRATIONS

Allsport/Shaun Botterill p 188
Allsport/David Cannon pp 110, 147
Allsport/Rich Clarkson pp 12 (top), 58
Allsport/Jim Commentuci p 168
Allsport/Jonathan Daniel pp 99, 124–5
Allsport/Tim Defrisco p 108
Allsport/Tony Duffy pp 43, 78–9
Allsport/Ken Levine p 159
Allsport/Mike Powell pp 52, 81, 86 (bottom), 91 (right), 107, 123, 157, 163, 172, 180
Allsport/Rick Stewart pp 86 (top), 89
Allsport/Damian Strohmeyer p 93

Fotosports International pp 57, 91 (left), 95, 130, 135, 139, 140, 141, 143, 154, 156 (both), 173, 177

NFL Photos pp 7, 8, 10, 23, 28, 167, 184 (right), 185 (left)
NFL Photos/Charles Aqua Viva pp 30, 33
NFL Photos/Alex Barkoff p 161
NFL Photos/John Biever p 153
NFL Photos/Vernon Biever pp 31, 35, 115, 128
NFL Photos/David Boss pp 171, 178, 181
NFL Photos/Thomas Croke p 49
NFL Photos/Dave Cross p 31
NFL Photos/Malcolm Emmons p 170
NFL Photos/Nate Fine p 164
NFL Photos/James Flores p 39
NFL Photos/George Gellatly p 186 (bottom)

NFL Photos/Richard Gentile p 72 (bottom)
NFL Photos/Hall of Fame pp 9, 20, 184 (left), 185 (right), 186 (top)
NFL Photos/Fred Kaplan p 96
NFL Photos/Al Messerschmidt pp 72 (top), 90 (right)
NFL Photos/Darryl Norenberg pp 111, 133
NFL Photos/Peter Read Miller p 90 (left)
NFL Photos/Frank Rippon p 12 (bottom)
NFL Photos/Dan Rubin p 187
NFL Photos/Robert Shaver p 120
NFL Photos/Vic Stein p 25
NFL Photos/Tony Tomsic p 102
NFL Photos/Corky Trewin p 183
NFL Photos/UPI p 18
NFL Photos/Herb Weitman pp 45, 105, 121, 149
NFL Photos/Lou Witt pp 116–17

Colour section
Allsport/Shaun Botterill pp 6 (both), 7 (top left and bottom)
Allsport/Howard Boylan p 7 (top right)
Allsport/Ron Chenoy p 4 (top)
Allsport/Rich Clarkson p 1
Allsport/Mike Powell pp 2 (top), 3 (bottom), 4 (bottom), 5 (bottom left and right)
Allsport/Rick Stewart p 2 (bottom)
Allsport/Damian Strohmeyer p 3 (top)
Fotosports International pp 5 (top), 8

ABBREVIATIONS

Field positions

FB	Full Back	E	End
HB	Half Back	DE	Defensive End
LB	Line Backer	G	Guard
QB	Quarter Back	WR	Wide Receiver
RB	Running Back	T	Tackle
C	Center	DT	Defensive Tackle

AUTHOR'S ACKNOWLEDGEMENTS

The author would like to thank the NFL Media Office for their help, and those teams who responded to his questionnaire. Thanks also to Steve Corten, formerly of the Gwent Mustangs and now of Mallorca, for his help in reading through the manuscript.

ORIGINS AND DEVELOPMENT

American Football regards 6 November 1869 as the date when the sport was 'born', because it was then that Rutgers beat Princeton 6–4 at New Brunswick in what is regarded as the first ever match, between two teams who were pioneering their own versions of 'American Football' rules.

Their sets of rules were a modification of those of the London Football Association, the 'soccer' code which most forms of football in the United States had followed since the game was introduced by English settlers at the turn of the 17th century.

It took more than 200 years for the 'round ball' game to reach the American colleges and the first rules of 'American Football' were drawn up at Princeton College in 1867. These rules were a simple modification of English soccer with an increase in the number of players to 25 being the major difference.

At about the same time, Rutgers also drew up a set of their own rules which was also for a 25-a-side game, played on a pitch measuring 120 yards (110 metres) by 75 (69m). But their rules contained a more significant departure from the London code: the ball could be

'batted' with the hand as well as kicked (although throwing of the ball or running with it was not allowed). The first break from soccer rules had been made as the Americans set about devising their own brand of football.

That historic first match in 1869 was played under Rutgers rules and their 6–4 win stemmed from the fact that their rules made the first team to score six goals the winners. When the teams met a fortnight later they played to Princeton rules and Princeton won 8–0 (first to eight goals the winner). One other main difference between the two

American football in the 19th century – a game takes place at Latrobe, once thought to be the birthplace of professional football in the US.

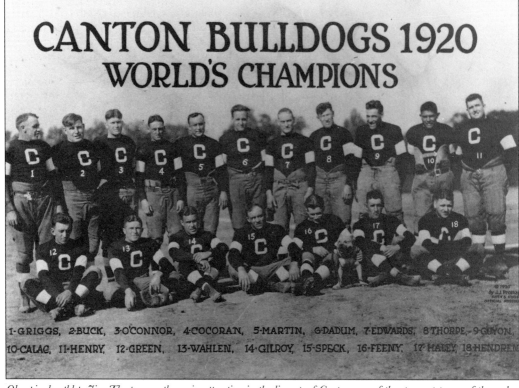

CANTON BULLDOGS 1920
WORLD'S CHAMPIONS

1-GRIGGS, 2-BUCK, 3-O'CONNOR, 4-COCORAN, 5-MARTIN, 6-DADUM, 7-EDWARDS, 8-THORPE, 9-GUYON, 10-CALAC, 11-HENRY, 12-GREEN, 13-WAHLEN, 14-GILROY, 15-SPECK, 16-FEENY, 17-HALEY, 18-HENDREN

Olympic decathlete Jim Thorpe was the main attraction in the line-up of Canton, one of the strongest teams of the early 1920s.

sets of rules was that Princeton's allowed a free kick at goal by any player making a clean catch of the ball.

Other colleges now adopted the new modified game with Columbia and Yale soon introducing it, and when Harvard revived the game of football in 1871 they played what was known as the Boston Game, in which a player could pick up the ball and run with it. American Football was now turning into a cross between soccer and rugby.

After playing the McGill University Football Club of Montreal at rugby in 1874, Harvard were so impressed with the game that they called a meeting, attended by Columbia, Princeton and Yale colleges, and tried to formulate amended rules based on rugby. In 1876 the Intercollegiate Football Association was duly formed with modified English rugby rules being adopted as their code.

Walter Chauncey Camp of Yale, who became known as the 'Father of American Football', decided that sweeping changes were needed to give the American game originality and in 1880 he changed the number of players from 15 to 11, abolished the scrummage and replaced it with the scrimmage, and introduced the now standard team line-up of seven linemen, two halfbacks, a fullback and a quarterback.

With Camp's changes the game had certainly taken on a distinctive look. The one thing that was lacking was the famous gridiron pitch, but that wasn't far away. In 1882 Camp introduced the 'downs' rule with five yards having to be achieved in three downs (it is now ten yards in four downs, of course). Because of this rule, it became necessary to be able to establish exactly how far the ball had travelled during each play and Camp was responsible for coming up with the idea of drawing a series of parallel lines across the pitch at five-yard intervals to help establish the distance of each play. American Football had become 'Gridiron' football, by which name it is popularly known.

With scoring possible from a touchdown (effectively a try from the old rugby days), a 'point after' (conversion) and a field goal (penalty kick) it was necessary to draw up a scoring system and that was also left in Camp's capable hands. The new scoring system was adopted in 1883, with five points for a field goal and four for a touchdown.

By now all traces of the London Football Association game had gone and American Football was also beginning to establish its own identity away from the rugby code. However, with more teams taking up the sport things became more competitive, and with tackling playing a major part in the game it got rough at times, to say the least. While such tactics fell within the laws of the game, various bodies felt it was necessary to try and curtail the 'rough stuff', and at a meeting of the major colleges in 1894 they introduced a rule which outlawed the 'mass play', which often resulted in several players, in a battery formation, taking an opposing player out of the game. The meeting also reduced playing time from 90 to 70 minutes.

Despite attempts to make the game safer and less brutal, teams like Pennsylvania, who won 65 of 66 games between 1894 and 1898 with their so-called 'Guards Back' strategy, still used strong-arm tactics. As the game went into the 20th century it remained potentially very dangerous and in 1905 there were a staggering 18 deaths as a result of injuries sustained in American Football games. This led President Theodore (Teddy) Roosevelt to intervene and he called together a meeting with representatives from Harvard, Yale and Princeton and told them the brutality had to stop or he would outlaw the game completely.

Captain Pierce of West Point presided over a meeting in December 1905 attended by representatives from more than 60 college teams as they sought to change the rules in order to protect their game as per the President's ultimatum. The meeting saw the formation of the Intercollegiate Association of the United States – it became the National Collegiate Athletic Association (NCAA) in 1910 – and they set about making sweeping changes in an attempt to make it a safer game.

Playing time was reduced even further, this time to 60 minutes. The forward pass was introduced, as was a neutral zone between the lines of scrimmage. The number of yards needed in the three downs was increased from five to ten. However, interlocked interference remained – and it was this that was potentially the most dangerous aspect of the game. But in 1910 it was completely outlawed, along with pulling and pushing of the ball carrier.

The game certainly became safer but the new target of ten yards in three downs resulted in it becoming more defensive and in 1912 the number of downs was increased to four. At the same time the length of the pitch was reduced to 100 yards (91m) and end zones were intro-

The traditional Thanksgiving game between the two Chicago teams in 1925 saw 36 000 turn out for the debut of Harold 'Red' Grange for the Bears.

duced. Other changes saw the lifting of the 20-yard maximum distance the ball could be thrown forward and the points for a touchdown increased from five to six – it had been increased from four to five in 1898, while the field goal had been reduced to four in 1904 and to its present value of three points in 1909. American Football's development was complete. The game now resembled that which is played worldwide today and there have been few changes since those last major ones in 1912.

Professionalism first crept into the game in 1892 when the Allegheny Athletic Association paid the former Yale guard 'Pudge' Heffelfinger to appear in a game against the Pittsburgh Athletic Club. The investment paid off as he scored the only points of the game in a 4–0 win for the AAA.

Several teams were soon fielding all-professional squads and when baseball clubs Philadelphia Athletics and Philadelphia Phillies formed football teams they joined with the Pittsburgh Stars in an attempt to form the first professional league, the National Football League in 1902.

Their efforts to start a national league were not successful but regional leagues soon developed as the professional game started to gain in popularity with players and fans. The Ohio League was the best known, and one of America's best track and field athletes, the decathlete Jim Thorpe, appeared in the league for Canton, one of the most successful teams during the First World War. However, by the end of the war the professional game was in a state of chaos. Not surprisingly, money was the cause of most of the problems. Players were moving from

team to team at random, depending on who would pay the highest price, and rising salaries meant some teams were struggling. A major review of the professional game had to be made and in 1920 a meeting was called at Canton, Ohio on 20 August, with a view to dealing with these problems and formulating rules to which all teams had to adhere in order to make the game fair for all. The rules on the pitch had long been sorted out. Now it was time to get the off-the-field problems put right.

The Canton meeting resulted in the formation of the American Professional Football Conference but at a second meeting a month later its name was changed to the American Professional Football Association (APFA) and Jim Thorpe was elected president. Fixtures were drawn up and within a month the first games in the new league

The first NFL Championship Game in 1933: Chicago's Bill Hewitt sets up the winning touchdown for Bill Karr. The Bears beat the New York Giants 23–21.

were played. On 3 October 1920 Dayton beat Columbus 14–0 in the first game between two APFA teams, with Lou Partlow scoring the first touchdown.

By the beginning of December, however, many teams had given up hope of winning the championship and several either failed to fulfil fixtures or simply folded. The Akron Pros won the first championship with an 8–0–3 record, but reorganisation was clearly necessary and in 1921 Joe Carr of the Columbus Panhandles was made League president. He moved the headquarters to Columbus and it changed its name to the National Football League (NFL) on 24 June 1922. Canton became the first NFL champions.

The Chicago Bears with their new recruit, the All-American halfback 'Red' Grange, helped to popularise the professional game in the mid-1920s and their game with the Giants in New York in December 1925 attracted a staggering crowd of 73 000. When they moved to the opposite coast a crowd of 75 000 watched them play in Los Angeles. The razzmatazz of the gridiron game had arrived.

In 1926 Red Grange's manager CC Pyle formed a breakaway American Football League with his team, the New York Yankees, and eight others. It lasted one season. The NFL consisted of 22 teams in 1926 but many of the teams were financially weak and at a meeting in April 1927, the League president set about getting rid of those teams. The NFL was reduced to 12 teams that season, and the following season there were only 10 teams.

The League's membership dropped to an all-time low eight teams in 1932, which was also the first season that official records were kept. The Bears and the Portsmouth Spartans

finished level at the top of the table and for the first time a play-off game decided the championship. The Bears won 9–0 and the match counted towards the regular season records of the two teams. Consequently, the records show that the Spartans finished *third* in the final table!

There were major changes on and off the field in 1933. The inbounds lines (hashmarks) were introduced and the goalposts brought forward to the goal line. Off the field a proposal was passed dividing the NFL into two divisions, Eastern and Western, with the respective champions meeting in a single game to decide the NFL champions: the Bears beat the Giants 23–21 at Wrigley Field for the title. There was also another attempt to form a rival league. Again it was called the American League, and again it was short-lived. It survived just two seasons with the Boston Shamrocks being the first champions.

For the first time in 1936 all NFL teams played the same number of games. That year was also significant because it saw the college draft introduced and there were no franchise changes for the first time since the NFL was formed. The NFL president Joe Carr died in 1939 and was succeeded by Carl Storck. Despite its having only 10 teams, the aggregate attendances for all League games in 1939 exceeded one million for the first time.

Yet another rival American League was formed in 1940 with six teams; the Columbus Bullies won its title. The Bears, with their famous 'T' formation, won the NFL Championship Game by a record 73–0 margin over the Washington Redskins.

The NFL headquarters were moved to Chicago in 1941. Storck resigned as acting president and an NFL commissioner

was appointed for the first time, Elmer Layden taking up the post. Columbus won the American Football League for the second and last time – its attempts to oust the NFL had, like its predecessors', failed. Undaunted, another rival league, the All-American Football Conference (AAFC) was formed in 1945 and the Cleveland Browns, coached by Paul Brown, won the first AAFC championship game the following year. The Browns went on to win four successive championships before the AAFC came to an end with the announcement that there would be a merger with the NFL. Three AAFC franchises – Cleveland, San Francisco and Baltimore – joined the NFL.

The NFL duly started the 1950 season as the National–American Football League, but reverted to its original name after three months. However, the old Eastern and Western Divisions were replaced by the American and National Conferences. The Browns carried on where they had finished off in the AAFC and lifted the NFL championship in their first season. The American and National Conferences became the Eastern and Western Conferences in 1953.

In 1959 plans were announced for yet another rival league, but this time it was a serious challenger to the NFL's standing as the professional game's senior body. Lamar Hunt of Dallas announced his new American Football League and in 1960 it got under way with eight teams; the NFL had 13 at the time. The Denver Broncos beat the Boston Patriots 13–10 in the first AFL regular season game but the first AFL championship went to the Houston Oilers who beat the Los Angeles Chargers 24–16.

By 1966 it was obvious that the AFL was strong and was

there to stay. Moves took place to merge the two leagues and after secret meetings between Lamar Hunt and Tex Schramm of the NFL it was announced on 8 June that the two would indeed merge into a single league with 24 teams, to be expanded to 26 in 1968 and to 28 by 1970 when the merger would be finally completed.

In the meantime the two leagues would remain autonomous but working in conjunction with each other, and an agreement was made that the AFL and NFL champions would meet in an end-of-season game to find the overall champions of the two leagues in January 1967. This was the birth of the Super Bowl. Green Bay of the NFL beat Kansas City of the AFL 35–10 in front of 69000 fans at Los Angeles to win Super Bowl I. It was an instant success and the people of American benefited from the merger between the two leagues.

Pete Rozelle was named as commissioner of the newly-

Pete Rozelle and Lamar Hunt (right) pictured before the start of Super Bowl I.

expanded league which saw AFL and NFL teams sharing the draft and playing pre-season games against each other. The NFL's Eastern and Western Conferences were divided from 1967–9 with Capitol and Century Divisions forming the Eastern Conference and Coastal and Central Divisions making up the Western Conference. How-

ever, with the merger between the AFL and NFL being complete in 1970 the League took on its present-day look with two Conferences, American and National, each being divided into Eastern, Central and Western Divisions.

The League format has remained unaltered since 1970. Players' strikes have threatened to disrupt the League, while the formation of yet another breakaway league, the United States Football League, failed to shake the solid foundations of the NFL. It has spread its wings beyond its traditional American bases and taken the game to Britain and other European countries, which have revelled in the skills and excitement of the game in recent years. The NFL has enjoyed Super Bowl XXVI and there are still many more to come as 'Gridiron' remains one of the big three sports in the United States and continues to gain in popularity worldwide.

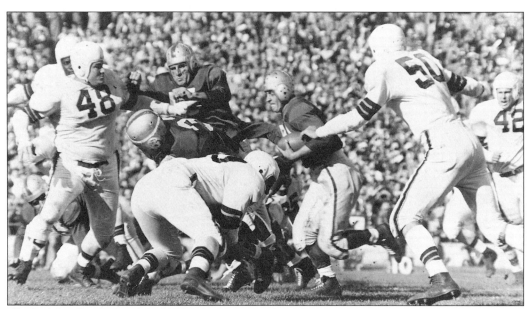

Cleveland, in white, dominated the AAFC before joining the NFL. They were well beaten in this 1949 game, however, 56–28 at San Francisco.

THE NFL SEASON: YEAR-BY-YEAR

1920

Following the formation of the American Professional Football Association (APFA) at a meeting on 17 September at Canton, Ohio, the new national league got under way.

The first game to feature an APFA team was on 26 September at Douglas Park, Rock Island, when a crowd of just 800 watched the Rock Island Independents beat non-APFA members St Paul's Ideals 48–0.

The following week, on 3 October, the first game between two APFA teams took place at Triangle Park, Dayton, with the home team beating Columbus 14–0 and Lou Partlow making history as the first man to score a touchdown in the League.

The organising of fixtures was left to the individual teams and it led to chaos, with some teams playing more matches than others. The Muncie Flyers, for example, lost 45–0 to Rock Island on the opening day of the season – it was their only match.

The Chicago Tigers and Detroit Heralds disbanded their teams upon completing their fixtures. The Akron Pros, who played 11 games, came through the inaugural season undefeated to capture the first title.

FINAL STANDINGS

	W	L	T	%
Akron Pros	8	0	3	1.000
Decatur Staleys	10	1	2	.909
Buffalo All-Americans	9	1	1	.900
Chicago Cardinals	6	2	2	.750
Rock Island Independents	6	2	2	.750
Dayton Triangles	5	2	2	.714
Rochester Jeffersons	6	3	2	.667
Canton Bulldogs	7	4	2	.636
Detroit Heralds	2	3	3	.400
Cleveland Tigers	2	4	2	.333
Chicago Tigers	2	5	1	.286
Hammond Pros	2	5	0	.286
Columbus Panhandles	2	6	2	.250
Muncie Flyers	0	1	0	.000

W=Wins   L=Losses   T=Ties   %=Percentile
PF=Points for   PA=Points against

1921

Membership increased to 21 teams with the Acme Packing Company being granted a franchise and they played as the Green Bay Packers. The Decatur Staleys, runners-up in the first season, were given over to player-coach George Halas who moved the team to Chicago and changed the name to the Chicago Staleys.

The move, and change of name, did them good because they won the title with only one defeat. The Buffalo All-Americans had a similar record, nine wins and one defeat, but they drew two matches to Chicago's one and the title was awarded to the Staleys after a ruling by the new APFA president Joe Carr.

FINAL STANDINGS

	W	L	T	%
Chicago Staleys	9	1	1	.900
Buffalo All-Americans	9	1	2	.900
Akron Pros	8	3	1	.727
Canton Bulldogs	5	2	3	.714
Rock Island Independents	4	2	1	.667
Evansville Crimson Giants	3	2	0	.600
Green Bay Packers	3	2	1	.600
Dayton Triangles	4	4	1	.500
Chicago Cardinals	3	3	2	.500
Rochester Jeffersons	2	3	0	.400
Cleveland Indians	3	5	0	.375
Washington Senators	1	2	0	.333
Cincinnati Celts	1	3	0	.250
Hammond Pros	1	3	1	.250
Minneapolis Marines	1	3	1	.250
Detroit Heralds	1	5	1	.167
Columbus Panhandles	1	8	0	.111
Tonawanda Kardex	0	1	0	.000
Muncie Flyers	0	2	0	.000
Louisville Brecks	0	2	0	.000
New York Giants	0	2	0	.000

1922

George Halas changed Chicago's name to the Chicago Bears. He also suggested a change of name for the League from the APFA to the National Football League (NFL). His suggestion was adopted at a meeting on 24 June.

The League consisted of 18 teams including the interestingly named Oorang Indians from Marion, Ohio. Theirs was an all-Indian team which included Olympic decathlete Jim Thorpe. The team was so named because of a sponsorship deal with the Oorang dog kennels.

The Canton Bulldogs captured their first title with a 10–0–2 record, player-coach Guy Chamberlin being the inspiration behind the team. When Rock Island beat Evansville 60–0 on 15 October, they became the first team to score sixty points in an NFL game.

FINAL STANDINGS

	W	L	T	%
Canton Bulldogs	10	0	2	1.000
Chicago Bears	9	3	0	.750
Chicago Cardinals	8	3	0	.727
Toledo Maroons	5	2	2	.714
Rock Island Independents	4	2	1	.667
Racine Legion	6	4	1	.600
Dayton Triangles	4	3	1	.571
Green Bay Packers	4	3	3	.571
Buffalo All-Americans	5	4	1	.556
Akron Pros	3	5	2	.375
Milwaukee Badgers	2	4	3	.333
Oorang Indians	2	6	0	.250
Minneapolis Marines	1	3	0	.250
Louisville Brecks	1	3	0	.250
Evansville Crimson Giants	0	3	0	.000
Rochester Jeffersons	0	4	1	.000
Hammond Pros	0	5	1	.000
Columbus Panhandles	0	7	0	.000

1923

Canton remained undefeated for the second successive season to retain the title with the Bears in second place. Oorang, who finished the season with ten defeats, folded after their brief existence. Jim Thorpe moved on to the Toledo Maroons mid-season. The Packers came close to folding after a financial crisis but were rescued by Andrew Turnbull, publisher of the *Green Bay Press Gazette*. He mobilised public support and the club was saved.

FINAL STANDINGS

	W	L	T	%
Canton Bulldogs	11	0	1	1.000
Chicago Bears	9	2	1	.818
Green Bay Packers	7	2	1	.778
Milwaukee Badgers	7	2	3	.778
Cleveland Indians	3	1	3	.750
Chicago Cardinals	8	4	0	.667

Duluth Kelleys	4	3	0	.571
Columbus Tigers	5	4	1	.556
Buffalo All-Americans	4	4	3	.500
Racine Legion	4	4	2	.500
Toledo Maroons	2	3	2	.400
Rock Island Independents	2	3	3	.400
Minneapolis Marines	2	5	2	.286
St Louis All-Stars	1	4	2	.200
Hammond Pros	1	5	1	.167
Dayton Triangles	1	6	1	.143
Akron Indians	1	6	0	.143
Oorang Indians	1	10	0	.091
Rochester Jeffersons	0	2	0	.000
Louisville Brecks	0	3	0	.000

1924

Despite their success on the field, Canton had been struggling to get fans through the gate and were forced to sell out to the owner of the Cleveland franchise who changed the name to Cleveland Bulldogs. They still won their third successive title with a 7–1–1 record. There were new franchises in Kansas City, Kenosha, and Frankford, Philadelphia.

FINAL STANDINGS

	W	L	T	%
Cleveland Bulldogs	7	1	1	.875
Chicago Bears	6	1	4	.857
Frankford Yellow Jackets	11	2	1	.846
Duluth Kelleys	5	1	0	.833
Rock Island Independents	6	2	2	.750
Green Bay Packers	7	4	0	.636
Racine Legion	4	3	3	.571
Chicago Cardinals	5	4	1	.556
Buffalo Bisons	6	5	0	.545
Columbus Tigers	4	4	0	.500
Hammond Pros	2	2	1	.500
Milwaukee Badgers	5	8	0	.385
Akron Indians	2	6	0	.333
Dayton Triangles	2	6	0	.333
Kansas City Blues	2	7	0	.222
Kenosha Maroons	0	5	1	.000
Minneapolis Marines	0	6	0	.000
Rochester Jeffersons	0	7	0	.000

1925

The Canton Bulldogs returned in 1925 as one of five new franchises. The others were awarded to the New York Giants, Detroit Panthers, Providence Steam and Pottsville Maroons.

The NFL received a tremendous boost when the All-American half back Harold 'Red' Grange joined the Chicago Bears after the University of Illinois finished its season. His arrival in the professional game aroused interest and boosted attendances and when the Bears played the Cardinals at Wrigley Field on Thanksgiving Day, an NFL record crowd of 36 000 turned out to see him play. But there was even more to come; 73 000 turned out to watch the Bears at the Polo Grounds against the Giants and when they played at the Los Angeles Coliseum, a staggering 75 000 fans were at the game.

The race for the title, however, was between the Cardinals and the Pottsville Maroons. When the Maroons won a late-season meeting 21–7 they looked to have the title sewn up but the Chicago team scraped it with an 11–2–1 record to Pottsville's 10–2–0.

FINAL STANDINGS

	W	L	T	%
Chicago Cardinals	11	2	1	.846
Pottsville Maroons	10	2	0	.833
Detroit Panthers	8	2	2	.800
New York Giants	8	4	0	.667
Akron Indians	4	2	2	.667
Frankford Yellow Jackets	13	7	0	.650
Chicago Bears	9	5	3	.643
Rock Island Independents	5	3	3	.625
Green Bay Packers	8	5	0	.615
Providence Steam Roller	6	5	1	.545
Canton Bulldogs	4	4	0	.500
Cleveland Bulldogs	5	8	1	.385
Kansas City Cowboys	2	5	1	.286
Hammond Pros	1	4	0	.250
Buffalo Bisons	1	6	2	.143
Duluth Kelleys	0	3	0	.000
Rochester Jeffersons	0	6	1	.000
Milwaukee Badgers	0	6	0	.000
Dayton Triangles	0	7	1	.000
Columbus Tigers	0	9	0	.000

1926

'Red' Grange did not play in the NFL in 1926; he played for the New York Yankees in the new rival American Football League which was formed by Grange's manager CC Pyle. He took Grange out of the NFL after Chicago refused to give him a five-figure salary and a third share of the franchise.

Philadelphia Quakers won the nine-team AFL while the Frankford Yellow Jackets captured the NFL title. They beat the Bears 7–6 late in the season by scoring in the closing minutes. The win took them above the Chicago team and on to the title.

Making their debut in this season were the Duluth Eskimos who included the latest All-American fullback Ernie Nevers in their line-up. He proved to be the star attraction to replace Grange.

FINAL STANDINGS

	W	L	T	%
Frankford Yellow Jackets	14	1	1	.933
Chicago Bears	12	1	3	.923
Pottsville Maroons	10	2	1	.833
Kansas City Cowboys	8	3	0	.727
Green Bay Packers	7	3	3	.700
Los Angeles Buccaneers	6	3	1	.667
New York Giants	8	4	1	.667
Duluth Eskimos	6	5	3	.545
Buffalo Rangers	4	4	2	.500
Chicago Cardinals	5	6	1	.455
Providence Steam Roller	5	7	1	.417
Detroit Panthers	4	6	2	.400
Hartford Blues	3	7	0	.300
Brooklyn Lions	3	8	0	.273
Milwaukee Badgers	2	7	0	.222
Akron Pros	1	4	3	.200
Dayton Triangles	1	4	1	.200
Racine Tornadoes	1	4	0	.200
Columbus Tigers	1	6	0	.143
Canton Bulldogs	1	9	3	.100
Hammond Pros	0	4	0	.000
Louisville Colonels	0	4	0	.000

1927

The League was drastically reduced from 22 to 12 teams after president Joe Carr decided it was time to get rid of those teams not financially strong enough to withstand the strains of running an NFL franchise. Grange's New York Yankees were granted a franchise but an injury to their star player resulted in them finishing in a mid-table position while their city rivals, the Giants, captured the title thanks to 10 shutouts in 13 games.

FINAL STANDINGS

	W	L	T	%
New York Giants	11	1	1	.917
Green Bay Packers	7	2	1	.778
Chicago Bears	9	3	2	.750
Cleveland Bulldogs	8	4	1	.667
Providence Steam Roller	8	5	1	.615
New York Yankees	7	8	1	.467
Frankford Yellow Jackets	6	9	3	.400
Pottsville Maroons	5	8	0	.385
Chicago Cardinals	3	7	1	.300
Dayton Triangles	1	6	1	.143

Duluth Eskimos	1	8	0	.111
Buffalo Bisons	0	5	0	.000

1928

The League was reduced to ten teams in 1928 and Red Grange and Ernie Nevers both announced their retirements. Grange went into the movies and vaudeville. The Providence Steam Roller won the title with an 8–1–2 record. They used to play their home matches in the local Cycledrome, built specially for cycle races.

FINAL STANDINGS

	W	L	T	%
Providence Steam Roller	8	1	2	.889
Frankford Yellow Jackets	11	3	2	.786
Detroit Wolverines	7	2	1	.778
Green Bay Packers	6	4	3	.600
Chicago Bears	7	5	1	.583
New York Giants	4	7	2	.364
New York Yankees	4	8	1	.333
Pottsville Maroons	2	8	0	.200
Chicago Cardinals	1	5	0	.167
Dayton Triangles	0	7	0	.000

1929

Grange and Nevers made comebacks and on 28 November they faced each other as Nevers' Chicago Cardinals team trounced the Bears 40–6 with Nevers scoring all 40 points, which remains an NFL record. His six touchdowns is also an NFL record which still stands.

The defending champions Providence made history by becoming the first team to play an NFL game under floodlights when they entertained the Cardinals on 3 November. Cal Hubbard and Johnny Blood added extra fire to the Green Bay team and they captured the first of three successive titles.

Dayton played its last season in the League. The last of the founder members, it was sold to John Dwyer who moved the franchise to Brooklyn and renamed the team the Dodgers.

FINAL STANDINGS

	W	L	T	%
Green Bay Packers	12	0	1	1.000
New York Giants	13	1	1	.929
Frankford Yellow Jackets	9	4	5	.692
Chicago Cardinals	6	6	1	.500
Boston Bulldogs	4	4	0	.500

Orange Tornadoes	3	4	4	.429
Staten Island Stapletons	3	4	3	.429
Providence Steam Roller	4	6	2	.400
Chicago Bears	4	9	2	.308
Buffalo Bisons	1	7	1	.125
Minneapolis Red Jackets	1	9	0	.100
Dayton Triangles	0	6	0	.000

1930

To make up for the loss of Ohio's Dayton team, the Portsmouth Spartans carried the state flag and became members of the NFL for the 1930 season. The Packers again just pipped the Giants for the title, but it was the attacking line-up of the Bears with their revolutionary 'T' formation which attracted a lot of attention as they improved from ninth in 1929 to third in 1930.

FINAL STANDINGS

	W	L	T	%
Green Bay Packers	10	3	1	.769
New York Giants	13	4	0	.765
Chicago Bears	9	4	1	.692
Brooklyn Dodgers	7	4	1	.636
Providence Steam Roller	6	4	1	.600
Staten Island Stapletons	5	5	2	.500
Chicago Cardinals	5	6	2	.455
Portsmouth Spartans	5	6	3	.455
Frankford Yellow Jackets	4	13	1	.222
Minneapolis Red Jackets	1	7	1	.125
Newark Tornadoes	1	10	1	.091

1931

Green Bay won their third successive title. They beat the Portsmouth Spartans into second place. The Spartans, who fielded rookie backs 'Dutch' Clark and Glenn Presnell were fined $1000 by League president Carr for using players who had not graduated from college. The Bears and the Packers were also fined similar sums for the same offence. The Frankford Yellow Jackets, who three years earlier had come close to winning the title, folded midway through the season

FINAL STANDINGS

	W	L	T	%
Green Bay Packers	12	2	0	.857
Portsmouth Spartans	11	3	0	.786
Chicago Bears	8	5	0	.615
Chicago Cardinals	5	4	0	.556
New York Giants	7	6	1	.538

	W	L	T	%
Providence Steam Roller	4	4	3	.500
Staten Island Stapletons	4	6	1	.400
Cleveland Indians	2	8	0	.200
Brooklyn Dodgers	2	12	0	.143
Frankford Yellow Jackets	1	6	1	.143

1932

Only eight teams contested the 1932 championship, the lowest number in the League's history. A newcomer was the Boston Braves team, named after the city's baseball team because they shared the same stadium.

At the end of the season the Chicago Bears and Portsmouth Spartans both had 6–1 win/loss records and for the first time a play-off game was required to decide the champions. Because of the cold weather the game was moved indoors and played in the Chicago Stadium. The pitch was very small, only 80 yards in length, and the walls around it made it potentially dangerous. The Bears won 9–0 with Red Grange scoring the only touchdown of the game. The Spartans protested against the legality of the pass to Grange made by Nagurski but the touchdown stood. If only they had had the slow-motion action replay facilities of today!

The 1932 season was the first for which official NFL records were kept.

FINAL STANDINGS

	W	L	T	%
Chicago Bears	7	1	6	.875
Green Bay Packers	10	3	1	.769
Portsmouth Spartans	6	2	4	.750
Boston Braves	4	4	2	.500
New York Giants	4	6	2	.400
Brooklyn Dodgers	3	9	0	.250
Chicago Cardinals	2	6	2	.250
Staten Island Stapletons	2	7	3	.222

Chicago Bears and Portsmouth Spartans finished the season tied for first place after each having 6–1 records. In a play-off the Bears won 9–0 and the result counted towards the final standings which resulted in Portsmouth dropping to third in the final table

1933

A motion was passed in July which divided the League into two divisions, Eastern and Western, with five teams in each.

Three new franchises were granted, to the Pittsburgh Pirates, Philadelphia Eagles and Cincinnati Reds. The Boston Braves became the Redskins, and the Staten Island Stapletons took a year off. But as it turned out they never returned to the NFL.

George Halas became the sole owner of the Chicago Bears and reinstated himself as team coach. It worked; the Bears won the Western Division and then beat the Giants 23–21 in the first ever Championship Game between divisional winners.

EASTERN DIVISION

	W	L	T	%	PF	PA
New York Giants	11	3	0	.786	244	101
Brooklyn Dodgers	5	4	1	.556	93	54
Boston Redskins	5	5	2	.500	103	97
Philadelphia Eagles	3	5	1	.375	77	158
Pittsburgh Pirates	3	6	2	.333	67	208

WESTERN DIVISION

	W	L	T	%	PF	PA
Chicago Bears	10	2	1	.833	133	82
Portsmouth Spartans	5	5	0	.545	128	87
Green Bay Packers	5	7	1	.417	170	107
Cincinnati Reds	3	6	1	.333	38	110
Chicago Cardinals	1	9	1	.100	52	101

CHAMPIONSHIP GAME

17 Dec *26 000*
CHICAGO BEARS 23   New York 21

1934

The Portsmouth Spartans were sold and the new owner, Dick Richards, took the franchise to Detroit where he renamed them the Detroit Lions.

There were several 'firsts' in 1934. The Thanksgiving Day game between the Bears and the Lions was the first NFL game to be broadcast nationally, with CBS radio commentator Graham McNamee behind the microphone; Beattie Feathers of the Bears became the first rusher to gain 1000 yards in a season; and the first Chicago All-Star game between the defending NFL champions, the Bears, and the best of the college footballers, attracted a crowd of 79 432 to Soldier Field. The game ended scoreless.

The Giants and Bears played out the Championship Game for the second successive season but this time it was sweet revenge for the Giants. They trailed 13–3 in the third quarter but a change of footwear to basketball shoes for the

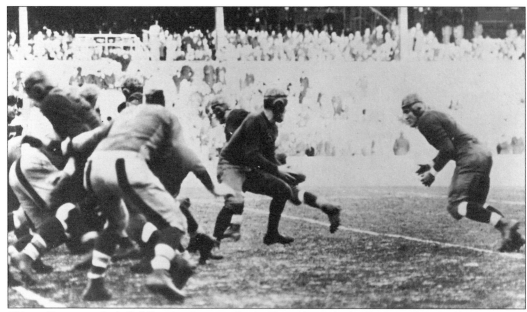

Chicago Bears quarterback Carl Brumbaugh sets up Bronko Nagurski early in the 'Sneakers' Championship Game won by the New York Giants.

final quarter, in the hope of getting a better grip in the freezing conditions, paid dividends as they ran out 30–13 winners in what became known as the 'Sneakers Championship Game'.

Jack Manders of the Bears created a record by scoring a record 79 points in the season.

EASTERN DIVISION

	W	L	T	%	PF	PA
New York Giants	8	5	0	.615	147	107
Boston Redskins	6	6	0	.500	107	94
Brooklyn Dodgers	4	7	0	.364	61	153
Philadelphia Eagles	4	7	0	.364	127	85
Pittsburgh Pirates	2	10	0	.167	51	206

WESTERN DIVISION

	W	L	T	%	PF	PA
Chicago Bears	13	0	0	1.000	286	86
Detroit Lions	10	3	0	.769	238	59
Green Bay Packers	7	6	0	.538	156	122
Chicago Cardinals	5	6	0	.455	80	84
St Louis Gunners	1	2	0	.333	27	61
Cincinnati Reds	0	8	0	.000	10	273

Reds suspended from League and replaced by the independent team St Louis Gunners for the last 3 games of the season

CHAMPIONSHIP GAME

9 Dec *35 059*
NEW YORK 30 Chicago Bears 13

1935

A fairly uneventful season saw the Giants win the Eastern Division despite three losses while Detroit also lost three games in winning the Western Division. In the battle for the championship on 15 December, Detroit beat the Giants, who were playing in their third successive Championship Game, by 26–7.

EASTERN DIVISION

	W	L	T	%	PF	PA
New York Giants	9	3	0	.750	180	96
Brooklyn Dodgers	5	6	1	.455	90	141
Pittsburgh Pirates	4	8	0	.333	100	209
Boston Redskins	2	8	1	.200	65	123
Philadelphia Eagles	2	9	0	.182	60	179

WESTERN DIVISION

	W	L	T	%	PF	PA
Detroit Lions	7	3	2	.700	191	111
Green Bay Packers	8	4	0	.667	181	96
Chicago Bears	6	4	2	.600	192	106
Chicago Cardinals	6	4	2	.500	99	97

CHAMPIONSHIP GAME

15 Dec *15 000*
DETROIT 26 New York 7

1936

For the first time the college draft was introduced, with the previous season's bottom team, Philadelphia, having the first pick of the college players. They chose the University of Chicago halfback and Heisman Trophy winner Jay Berwanger who thus became the first college player ever to be selected in the draft. However, the Eagles traded his rights to the Bears and Berwanger never actually played pro football.

Another rival league, again called the American Football League, was formed, the Boston Shamrocks winning its first title. The Boston Braves and Green Bay contested the NFL Championship Game and despite having home advantage, Boston moved the game to the New York Polo Grounds in the hope of boosting the attendance which in the event was nearly 30 000. However, the change of venue did Boston's chances little good and Green Bay took the championship. Green Bay's Arnie Herber became the first man to obtain 1000 yards passing in a season.

EASTERN DIVISION

	W	L	T	%	PF	PA
Boston Redskins	7	5	0	.583	149	110
Pittsburgh Pirates	6	6	0	.500	98	187
New York Giants	5	6	1	.455	115	163
Brooklyn Dodgers	3	8	1	.273	92	161
Philadelphia Eagles	1	11	0	.083	51	206

WESTERN DIVISION

	W	L	T	%	PF	PA
Green Bay Packers	10	1	1	.909	248	118
Chicago Bears	9	3	0	.750	222	94
Detroit Lions	8	4	0	.667	235	102
Chicago Cardinals	3	8	1	.273	74	143

CHAMPIONSHIP GAME

13 Dec *29 545 at Polo Grounds, New York*
GREEN BAY 21 Boston 6

1937

The Redskins moved to Washington and a Cleveland team returned to the NFL with the Rams making their debut in 1937. The Los Angeles Bulldogs won the second and last AFL title. The Redskins captured the NFL championship by beating the Bears 28–21 with rookie tailback Sammy Waugh starring for Washington.

EASTERN DIVISION

	W	L	T	%	PF	PA
Washington Redskins	8	3	0	.727	195	120
New York Giants	6	3	2	.667	128	109
Pittsburgh Pirates	4	7	0	.364	122	145
Brooklyn Dodgers	3	7	1	.300	82	174
Philadelphia Eagles	2	8	1	.200	86	177

WESTERN DIVISION

	W	L	T	%	PF	PA
Chicago Bears	9	1	1	.900	201	100
Green Bay Packers	7	4	0	.636	220	122
Detroit Lions	7	4	0	.636	180	105
Chicago Cardinals	5	5	1	.500	135	165
Cleveland Rams	1	10	0	.091	75	207

CHAMPIONSHIP GAME

12 Dec *15 870*
Chicago Bears 21 WASHINGTON 28

1938

George Marshall, Bill Henry of the *Los Angeles Times* and promoter Tom Gallery launched the Pro Bowl to be played by the season's NFL champions and a team of all-star players from the rest of the League. The Giants, who beat Green Bay 23–17 to capture the championship on 11 December, then beat the All-Star team 13–10 at Wrigley Field a month later.

EASTERN DIVISION

	W	L	T	%	PF	PA
New York Giants	8	2	1	.800	194	79
Washington Redskins	6	3	2	.667	148	154
Brooklyn Dodgers	4	4	3	.500	131	161
Philadelphia Eagles	5	6	0	.455	154	164
Pittsburgh Pirates	2	9	0	.182	79	169

WESTERN DIVISION

	W	L	T	%	PF	PA
Green Bay Packers	8	3	0	.727	223	118
Detroit Lions	7	4	0	.636	119	108
Chicago Bears	6	5	0	.545	194	148
Cleveland Rams	4	7	0	.364	131	215
Chicago Cardinals	2	9	0	.182	111	168

CHAMPIONSHIP GAME

11 Dec *48 120*
NEW YORK 23 Green Bay 17

1939

It was a sad year because Joe Carr, League president since 1921, died on 20 May. His place as acting president was taken by Carl Storck. The Brooklyn Dodgers–Philadelphia Eagles game made history by being the first NFL game to be televised. About one thousand people with television sets in New York managed to pick up the game. Crowds topped one million for the first time in NFL history as the average attendance rose to 19476. Green Bay avenged their defeat of a year earlier by beating the Giants 27–0 in the Championship Game at Milwaukee.

EASTERN DIVISION

	W	L	T	%	PF	PA
New York Giants	9	1	1	.900	168	85
Washington Redskins	8	2	1	.800	242	94
Brooklyn Dodgers	4	6	1	.400	108	219
Philadelphia Eagles	1	9	1	.100	105	200
Pittsburgh Pirates	1	9	1	.100	114	216

WESTERN DIVISION

	W	L	T	%	PF	PA
Green Bay Packers	9	2	0	.818	233	153
Chicago Bears	8	3	0	.727	298	157
Detroit Lions	6	5	0	.545	145	150
Cleveland Rams	5	5	1	.500	195	164
Chicago Cardinals	1	10	0	.091	84	254

CHAMPIONSHIP GAME

10 Dec *32279*
GREEN BAY 27 New York 0

1940

Yet another American Football League sprang up in 1940. Yet again, it didn't last long. The first champions of the six-team league were the Columbus Bullies. In the NFL the Pittsburgh Pirates changed their name to the Steelers.

The NFL season belonged to the Chicago Bears whose famous 'T' formation carried them to the Western Division title and then in the Championship Game was at its most effective as the Bears destroyed the Redskins with a performance that saw them win with a record 73–0 scoreline. It was the first Championship Game to be broadcast on national network radio. Sammy Baugh of Washington improved the NFL record for the most yards gained passing with a new record of 1367 yards.

EASTERN DIVISION

	W	L	T	%	PF	PA
Washington Redskins	9	2	0	.818	245	142
Brooklyn Dodgers	8	3	0	.727	186	120
New York Giants	6	4	1	.600	131	133
Pittsburgh Pirates	2	7	2	.222	60	178
Philadelphia Eagles	1	10	0	.091	111	221

WESTERN DIVISION

	W	L	T	%	PF	PA
Chicago Bears	8	3	0	.727	238	152
Green Bay Packers	6	4	1	.600	238	155
Detroit Lions	5	5	1	.500	138	153
Cleveland Rams	4	6	1	.400	171	191
Chicago Cardinals	2	7	2	.222	139	222

Bill Osmanski runs in from 68 yards to begin the Chicago Bears' 73–0 rout of the Washington Redskins.

CHAMPIONSHIP GAME

8 Dec *36 034*
Washington 0 CHICAGO BEARS 73

1941

Carl Storck, the acting president of the League, resigned a month after the NFL announced the appointment of its first commissioner, Elmer Layden. Columbus won the second and last of the 'new' American Football League titles. The Bears and the Packers finished level at the top of the NFL Western Division and so there was the first ever divisional play-off in NFL history which the Bears won 33–14. They went on to beat the Giants 37–9 to win their third championship.

EASTERN DIVISION

	W	L	T	%	PF	PA
New York Giants	8	3	0	.727	238	114
Brooklyn Dodgers	7	4	0	.636	158	127
Washington Redskins	6	5	0	.545	176	174
Philadelphia Eagles	2	8	1	.200	119	218
Pittsburgh Steelers	1	9	1	.100	103	276

WESTERN DIVISION

	W	L	T	%	PF	PA
Chicago Bears	10	1	0	.909	396	147
Green Bay Packers	10	1	0	.909	258	120
Detroit Lions	4	6	1	.400	121	195
Chicago Cardinals	3	7	1	.300	127	197
Cleveland Rams	2	9	0	.182	116	244

Divisional Play-off
14 Dec *43 425* CHICAGO BEARS 33 Green Bay 14

CHAMPIONSHIP GAME

21 Dec *13 341*
CHICAGO BEARS 37 New York 9

1942

The war deprived the NFL of some of its star players as team rosters were badly depleted. Nevertheless, it was action as usual during the hostilities. The Bears, despite being without George Halas for part of the season because of military duties, managed to record a 100 per cent record with 11 wins from 11 games only to lose surprisingly to the Redskins 14–6 in the Championship Game.

Don Hutson of Green Bay became the first man to score 100 points in an NFL regular season when he scored 138 and team-mate Cecil Isbell became the first man to pass for more than 2000 yards in a season as he increased his own NFL record by more than 500 yards.

EASTERN DIVISION

	W	L	T	%	PF	PA
Washington Redskins	10	1	0	.909	227	102
Pittsburgh Steelers	7	4	0	.636	167	119
New York Giants	5	5	1	.500	155	139
Brooklyn Dodgers	3	8	0	.273	100	168
Philadelphia Eagles	2	9	0	.182	134	239

WESTERN DIVISION

	W	L	T	%	PF	PA
Chicago Bears	11	0	0	1.000	376	84
Green Bay Packers	8	2	1	.800	300	215
Cleveland Rams	5	6	0	.455	150	207
Chicago Cardinals	3	8	0	.273	98	209
Detroit Lions	0	11	0	.000	38	263

CHAMPIONSHIP GAME

13 Dec *36 006*
WASHINGTON 14 Chicago Bears 6

1943

A revised 10-game schedule for all teams was announced for 1943 and that same season the wearing of helmets became compulsory. Philadelphia and Pittsburgh were allowed to merge for one season – the fans renamed the new amalgamated team the 'Steagles'. The Redskins, led by Sammy Baugh, the season's leader in passing, interceptions and punting, tied with the Giants in the Eastern Division but won the divisional play-off 28–0. However, they lost 41–21 to the Bears in the Championship Game on 26 December.

EASTERN DIVISION

	W	L	T	%	PF	PA
Washington Redskins	6	3	1	.667	229	137
New York Giants	6	3	1	.667	197	170
Phil-Pitt	5	4	1	.556	225	230
Brooklyn Dodgers	2	8	0	.200	65	234

Divisional Play-off
19 Dec *42 800* New York 0 WASHINGTON 28

WESTERN DIVISION

	W	L	T	%	PF	PA
Chicago Bears	8	1	1	.889	303	157

	W	L	T	%	PF	PA
Green Bay Packers	7	2	1	.778	264	172
Detroit Lions	3	6	1	.333	178	218
Chicago Cardinals	0	10	0	.000	95	238

CHAMPIONSHIP GAME

26 Dec *34 320*
CHICAGO BEARS 41 Washington 21

1944

The Boston Yanks made their debut while Cleveland resumed after a year out of the NFL. The Brooklyn Dodgers became the Brooklyn Tigers. The Pittsburgh–Philadelphia merger ended and the Eagles resumed duties under their own name. However, the Steelers merged with the Cardinals and played under the name of Card-Pitt. The Green Bay Packers won their third Championship Game when they beat the Giants 14–7.

EASTERN DIVISION

	W	L	T	%	PF	PA
New York Giants	8	1	1	.889	206	75
Philadelphia Eagles	7	1	2	.875	267	131
Washington Redskins	6	3	1	.667	169	180
Boston Yanks	2	8	0	.200	82	233
Brooklyn Tigers	0	10	0	.000	69	166

WESTERN DIVISION

	W	L	T	%	PF	PA
Green Bay Packers	8	2	0	.800	238	141
Chicago Bears	6	3	1	.667	258	172
Detroit Lions	6	3	1	.667	216	151
Cleveland Rams	4	6	0	.400	188	224
Card-Pitt	0	10	0	.000	108	328

CHAMPIONSHIP GAME

17 Dec *46 016*
New York 7 GREEN BAY 14

1945

The Cardinals–Pittsburgh merger was dissolved at the end of the previous season but another merger in 1945 saw Brooklyn and Boston merge to become the Boston Yanks. However, at the end of the season Brooklyn withdrew from the NFL to join to the new All-American Football Conference in 1946.

George Halas returned to the Bears after military duties, but sadly 21 NFL players were killed in action during the war.

Philadelphia's Steve Van Buren was the 'man of the season', topping the League in scoring, rushing and kick-off returns. But it was rookie quarterback Bob Waterfield who led Cleveland to a 15–14 championship victory over Washington.

EASTERN DIVISION

	W	L	T	%	PF	PA
Washington Redskins	8	2	0	.800	209	121
Philadelphia Eagles	7	3	0	.700	272	133
New York Giants	3	6	1	.333	179	198
Boston Yanks	3	6	1	.333	123	211
Pittsburgh Steelers	2	8	0	.200	79	220

WESTERN DIVISION

	W	L	T	%	PF	PA
Cleveland Rams	9	1	0	.900	244	136
Detroit Lions	7	3	0	.700	195	194
Green Bay Packers	6	4	0	.600	258	173
Chicago Bears	3	7	0	.300	192	235
Chicago Cardinals	1	9	0	.100	98	228

CHAMPIONSHIP GAME

16 Dec *32 178*
CLEVELAND 15 Washington 14

1946

Bert Bell, one of the co-owners of the Steelers, replaced Layden as commissioner and moved the League headquarters from Chicago to a suburb of Philadelphia. The reigning champions, the Cleveland Rams, moved to Los Angeles, but the Cleveland Browns kept football in the city and they captured the inaugural AAFC championship by beating the Yankees 14–9.

In the NFL Bill Dudley of the Steelers won the Most Valuable Player of the Year award; hardly surprising because he led the League in rushing, interceptions and punt returns. The Bears beat the Giants 24–14 to win the championship. It was the fourth time these two teams had met in the Championship Game since its launch in 1933.

EASTERN DIVISION

	W	L	T	%	PF	PA
New York Giants	7	3	1	.700	236	162
Philadelphia Eagles	6	5	0	.545	231	220
Washington Redskins	5	5	1	.500	171	191
Pittsburgh Steelers	5	5	1	.500	136	117
Boston Yanks	2	8	1	.200	189	273

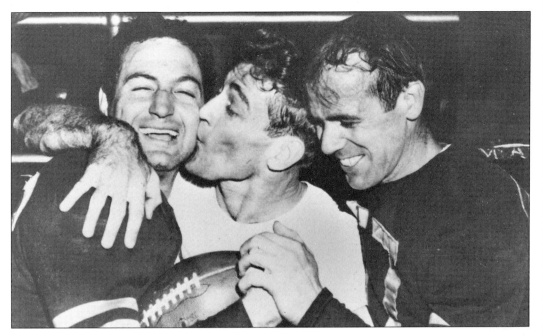

More joy for the Bears, after the 1946 Championship Game. Left to right: Sid Luckman, George McAfee, Ray McLean.

WESTERN DIVISION

	W	L	T	%	PF	PA
Chicago Bears	8	2	1	.800	289	193
Los Angeles Rams	6	4	1	.600	277	257
Green Bay Packers	6	5	0	.545	148	158
Chicago Cardinals	6	5	0	.545	260	198
Detroit Lions	1	10	0	.091	142	310

CHAMPIONSHIP GAME

15 Dec *58 346*
New York 14 CHICAGO BEARS 24

EASTERN DIVISION

	W	L	T	%	PF	PA
Philadelphia Eagles	8	4	0	.667	308	242
Pittsburgh Steelers	8	4	0	.667	240	259
Boston Yanks	4	7	1	.364	168	256
Washington Redskins	4	8	0	.333	295	367
New York Giants	2	8	2	.200	190	309

Divisional play-off
21 Dec *35 729* Pittsburgh 0 PHILADELPHIA 21

WESTERN DIVISION

	W	L	T	%	PF	PA
Chicago Cardinals	9	3	0	.750	306	231
Chicago Bears	8	4	0	.667	363	241
Green Bay Packers	6	5	1	.545	274	210
Los Angeles Rams	6	6	0	.500	259	214
Detroit Lions	3	9	0	.250	231	305

CHAMPIONSHIP GAME

28 Dec *30 759*
CHICAGO CARDINALS 28 Philadelphia 21

1947

Philadelphia and Pittsburgh, who had played as one team just four years earlier, shared the Eastern Division title, which Philadelphia subsequently captured with a 21–0 play-off victory. However, they lost the Championship Game 28–21 to the Chicago Cardinals who just pipped their local rivals, the Bears, to the Western divisional title. The Cardinals' win made up for the loss of their owner Charles Bidwell senior, who died a few months before the start of the season. However, his family kept control of the team. The Cleveland Browns retained the AAFC title, and Philadelphia's Steve Van Buren became the second man to rush for more than 1000 yards in a regular season.

1948

The Browns won their third successive AAFC title after a season that saw them win 14 games and lose none. They beat the Buffalo Bills 49–7 in the AAFC Championship Game. The new league was posing the first serious threat to the NFL, where in a repeat of the previous year's Championship Game, the Philadelphia Eagles gained revenge over the Cardinals by winning 7–0 in a game played in a blizzard.

EASTERN DIVISION

	W	L	T	%	PF	PA
Philadelphia Eagles	9	2	1	.818	376	156
Washington Redskins	7	5	0	.583	291	287
New York Giants	4	8	0	.333	297	388
Pittsburgh Steelers	4	8	0	.333	200	243
Boston Yanks	3	9	0	.250	174	372

WESTERN DIVISION

	W	L	T	%	PF	PA
Chicago Cardinals	11	1	0	.917	395	226
Chicago Bears	10	2	0	.833	375	151
Los Angeles Rams	6	5	1	.545	327	269
Green Bay Packers	3	9	0	.250	154	290
Detroit Lions	2	10	0	.167	200	407

CHAMPIONSHIP GAME

19 Dec *36 309*
PHILADELPHIA 7 Chicago Cardinals 0

1949

The Boston Yanks became the New York Bulldogs and shared the Polo Grounds with the Giants. Steve Van Buren of Philadelphia and Green Bay's Tony Canadeo both rushed for over 1000 yards with Van Buren increasing his own record to 1146 yards.

The Browns won their fourth consecutive AAFC title and on 9 December it was announced that Cleveland, San Francisco and Baltimore of the AAFC would be joining the NFL for 1950 in a merger deal.

Again the NFL Championship Game was played in dreadful conditions. This time it was in heavy rain as the Philadelphia Eagles beat the Los Angeles Rams 14–0

EASTERN DIVISION

	W	L	T	%	PF	PA
Philadelphia Eagles	11	1	0	.917	364	134
Pittsburgh Steelers	6	5	1	.545	224	214
New York Giants	6	6	0	.500	287	298
Washington Redskins	4	7	1	.364	268	339
New York Bulldogs	1	10	1	.091	153	365

WESTERN DIVISION

	W	L	T	%	PF	PA
Los Angeles Rams	8	2	2	.800	360	239
Chicago Bears	9	3	0	.750	332	218
Chicago Cardinals	6	5	1	.545	360	301
Detroit Lions	4	8	0	.333	237	259
Green Bay Packers	2	10	0	.167	114	329

CHAMPIONSHIP GAME

18 Dec *27 980*
Los Angeles 0 PHILADELPHIA 14

1950

As a result of the merger between some AAFC teams into the NFL the two divisions changed their names from Eastern and Western Divisions to the American and National Conferences. The New York Bulldogs became the Yanks.

The first game of the season paired the AAFC champions Cleveland with NFL champions Philadelphia, the Browns winning 35–10. Remarkably both conferences required play-offs to decide their respective champions. The Cleveland Browns beat the New York Giants to win the American Conference and the Los Angeles Rams, who had all their games throughout the season televised, beat the Chicago Bears 24–14 to win the National Conference.

In the Championship Game, the Browns continued their winning ways from their AAFC days and beat the Rams 30–28 in a close and exciting game. The Rams had set a regular season record and become the first team to score seventy points in a match when they beat Baltimore 70–27 on 22 October.

AMERICAN CONFERENCE

	W	L	T	%	PF	PA
Cleveland Browns	10	2	0	.833	310	144
New York Giants	10	2	0	.833	268	150
Philadelphia Eagles	6	6	0	.500	254	141
Pittsburgh Steelers	6	6	0	.500	180	195
Chicago Cardinals	5	7	0	.417	233	287
Washington Redskins	3	9	0	.250	232	326

Divisional play-off
17 Dec *33 054* CLEVELAND 8 New York Giants 3

NATIONAL CONFERENCE

	W	L	T	%	PF	PA
Los Angeles Rams	9	3	0	.750	466	309
Chicago Bears	9	3	0	.750	279	207
New York Yankees	7	5	0	.583	366	367
Detroit Lions	6	6	0	.500	321	285
Green Bay Packers	3	9	0	.250	244	406
San Francisco 49ers	3	9	0	.250	213	300
Baltimore Colts	1	11	0	.083	213	462

Divisional play-off
17 Dec *83 501* LOS ANGELES 24 Chicago Bears 14

CHAMPIONSHIP GAME

24 Dec *29 751*
CLEVELAND 30 Los Angeles 28

1951

For the first time the Championship Game was televised all over America as a result of the DuMont Network paying $75 000 for the rights. The Rams defeated the Browns 24–17 as the championship went to Los Angeles for the first time.

The Pro Bowl game was revived after an absence of nine years and became a game between all-star teams from the two Conferences.

Playing for Los Angeles against the New York Giants on 28 September, Norm Van Brocklin passed for 554 yards, a record which still stood at the end of the 1991 season.

Action from the Los Angeles Rams versus Chicago Cardinals game in the 1951 regular season, won 45–21 by the Rams on their way to the Championship.

AMERICAN CONFERENCE

	W	L	T	%	PF	PA
Cleveland Browns	11	1	0	.917	331	152
New York Giants	9	2	1	.818	254	161
Washington Redskins	5	7	0	.417	183	296
Pittsburgh Steelers	4	7	1	.364	183	235
Philadelphia Eagles	4	8	0	.333	234	264
Chicago Cardinals	3	9	0	.250	210	287

NATIONAL CONFERENCE

	W	L	T	%	PF	PA
Los Angeles Rams	8	4	0	.667	392	261
Detroit Lions	7	4	1	.636	336	259
San Francisco 49ers	7	4	1	.636	255	205
Chicago Bears	7	5	0	.583	286	282
Green Bay Packers	3	9	0	.250	254	375
New York Yanks	1	9	2	.100	241	382

CHAMPIONSHIP GAME

23 Dec *57 522*
LOS ANGELES 24 Cleveland 17

1952

The New York Yanks handed in their franchise which was sold to a group of Texas businessmen who moved the team to Dallas and renamed them the Dallas Texans. However, the new owners handed the team back to the NFL in mid-season and for the last five games of the season the team was run by the NFL with its home base at Hershey, Pennsylvania. They ended the season with a 1–11–0 record and the franchise was cancelled. To date they are the last team to fail mid-season.

The Detroit Lions won their first championship since 1935 when they beat the Browns, appearing in their third successive Championship Game, by 17–7. The season's aggregate attendances topped two million for the first time at an average of 28 502.

AMERICAN CONFERENCE

	W	L	T	%	PF	PA
Cleveland Browns	8	4	0	.667	310	213
New York Giants	7	5	0	.583	234	231
Philadelphia Eagles	7	5	0	.583	252	271
Pittsburgh Steelers	5	7	0	.417	300	273
Chicago Cardinals	4	8	0	.333	172	221
Washington Redskins	4	8	0	.333	240	287

NATIONAL CONFERENCE

	W	L	T	%	PF	PA
Detroit Lions	9	3	0	.750	344	192
Los Angeles Rams	9	3	0	.750	349	234
San Francisco 49ers	7	5	0	.583	285	221
Green Bay Packers	6	6	0	.500	295	312
Chicago Bears	5	7	0	.417	245	326
Dallas Texans	1	11	0	.083	182	427

Divisional Play-off
21 Dec *47 645* DETROIT 31 Los Angeles 21

CHAMPIONSHIP GAME

28 Dec *50 934*
Cleveland 7 DETROIT 17

1953

The American and National Conferences became the Eastern and Western Conferences in 1953 and a new team emerged from the old Dallas set-up when the Baltimore Colts joined the league. The Lions again beat the Browns in the Championship Game which was a thrilling affair with Detroit capturing their second successive title 17–16.

EASTERN CONFERENCE

	W	L	T	%	PF	PA
Cleveland Browns	11	1	0	.917	348	162
Philadelphia Eagles	7	4	1	.636	352	215
Washington Redskins	6	5	1	.545	208	215
Pittsburgh Steelers	6	6	0	.500	211	263
New York Giants	3	9	0	.250	179	277
Chicago Cardinals	1	10	1	.091	190	337

WESTERN CONFERENCE

	W	L	T	%	PF	PA
Detroit Lions	10	2	0	.833	271	205
San Francisco 49ers	9	3	0	.750	372	237
Los Angeles Rams	8	3	1	.727	366	236
Chicago Bears	3	8	1	.273	218	262
Baltimore Colts	3	9	0	.250	182	350
Green Bay Packers	2	9	1	.182	200	338

CHAMPIONSHIP GAME

27 Dec *54 577*
DETROIT 17 Cleveland 16

1954

Joe Perry of the San Francisco 49ers created history by becoming the first man in League history to gain 1000 yards rushing in consecutive seasons. The Championship Game, the fifth in succession which featured the Browns since they joined the NFL from the AAFC, saw them make amends for three successive defeats with a decisive 56–10 revenge win over the Detroit Lions.

EASTERN CONFERENCE

	W	L	T	%	PF	PA
Cleveland Browns	9	3	0	.750	336	162
Philadelphia Eagles	7	4	1	.636	284	230
New York Giants	7	5	0	.583	293	184
Pittsburgh Steelers	5	7	0	.417	219	263
Washington Redskins	3	9	0	.250	207	432
Chicago Cardinals	2	10	0	.167	183	347

WESTERN CONFERENCE

	W	L	T	%	PF	PA
Detroit Lions	9	2	1	.818	337	189
Chicago Bears	8	4	0	.667	301	279
San Francisco 49ers	7	4	1	.636	313	251
Los Angeles Rams	6	5	1	.545	314	285
Green Bay Packers	4	8	0	.333	234	251
Baltimore Colts	3	9	0	.250	131	279

CHAMPIONSHIP GAME

26 Dec *43827*
CLEVELAND 56 Detroit 10

1955

The sudden-death overtime rule was inaugurated in 1955 as an experiment in pre-season games and the first time it was used was in a game between the Rams and Giants which the Rams won 23–17 with a touchdown three minutes into overtime. The Browns appeared in their tenth consecutive Championship Game (including AAFC) and their quarterback in all ten games had been Otto Graham. He bowed out a winner after the Browns 38–14 defeat of the Rams to capture the 1955 championship. Off the field, one of the most significant moves of the year was NBC's capture of the NFL television rights, their $100 000 outbidding DuMont.

EASTERN CONFERENCE

	W	L	T	%	PF	PA
Cleveland Browns	9	2	1	.818	349	218
Washington Redskins	8	4	0	.667	246	222
New York Giants	6	5	1	.545	267	223
Chicago Cardinals	4	7	1	.364	224	252
Philadelphia Eagles	4	7	1	.364	248	231
Pittsburgh Steelers	4	8	0	.333	195	285

WESTERN CONFERENCE

	W	L	T	%	PF	PA
Los Angeles Rams	8	3	1	.727	260	231
Chicago Bears	8	4	0	.667	294	251
Green Bay Packers	6	6	0	.500	258	276
Baltimore Colts	5	6	1	.455	214	239
San Francisco 49ers	4	8	0	.333	216	298
Detroit Lions	3	9	0	.250	230	275

CHAMPIONSHIP GAME

26 Dec *85693*
Los Angeles 14 CLEVELAND 38

1956

George Halas retired as the Chicago Bears head coach after first taking up the post in 1920 (he would return to the post in 1958). The Giants moved their home to the Yankee Stadium and they went on to capture the Eastern Conference. In the Championship Game they destroyed the Bears and ran out comfortable 47–7 winners. It was their first championship since 1938.

EASTERN CONFERENCE

	W	L	T	%	PF	PA
New York Giants	8	3	1	.727	264	197
Chicago Cardinals	7	5	0	.583	240	182
Washington Redskins	6	6	0	.500	183	225
Cleveland Browns	5	7	0	.417	167	177
Pittsburgh Steelers	5	7	0	.417	217	250
Philadelphia Eagles	3	8	1	.273	143	215

WESTERN CONFERENCE

	W	L	T	%	PF	PA
Chicago Bears	9	2	1	.818	363	246
Detroit Lions	9	3	0	.750	300	188
San Francisco 49ers	5	6	1	.455	233	284
Baltimore Colts	5	7	0	.417	270	322
Green Bay Packers	4	8	0	.333	264	342
Los Angeles Rams	4	8	0	.333	291	307

CHAMPIONSHIP GAME

30 Dec *56863*
NEW YORK 47 Chicago Bears 7

1957

At the Los Angeles Memorial Coliseum on 10 November, an all-time regular season record crowd of 102368 saw the San Francisco 49ers play the Los Angeles Rams. Two weeks earlier Anthony J Morabito, founder and co-owner of the 49ers, had died of a heart attack whilst watching a game against the Chicago Bears at the Kezar Stadium. The 49ers shared the Western Conference with Detroit, the Lions winning the play-off 31–27, coming from 20 points behind to snatch victory. A week later the Lions captured the championship by beating the Browns 59–14.

WESTERN CONFERENCE

	W	L	T	%	PF	PA
Detroit Lions	8	4	0	.667	251	231
San Francisco 49ers	8	4	0	.667	260	264
Baltimore Colts	7	5	0	.583	303	235
Los Angeles Rams	6	6	0	.500	307	278
Chicago Bears	5	7	0	.417	203	211
Green Bay Packers	3	9	0	.250	218	311

Divisional play-off
22 Dec *60 118* San Francisco 27 DETROIT 31

CHAMPIONSHIP GAME

29 Dec *55 263*
DETROIT 59 Cleveland 14

EASTERN CONFERENCE

	W	L	T	%	PF	PA
Cleveland Browns	9	2	1	.818	269	172
New York Giants	7	5	0	.583	254	211
Pittsburgh Steelers	6	6	0	.500	161	178
Washington Redskins	5	6	1	.455	251	230
Philadelphia Eagles	4	8	0	.333	173	230
Chicago Cardinals	3	9	0	.250	200	299

1958

George Halas was back in charge of the Bears after their first losing season for five years in 1957. Jim Brown (Cleveland) established an NFL record by rushing 1527 yards, the first time any man had surpassed 1500 yards in a season.

Baltimore's Alan Ameche (centre) dives in for the winning touchdown in the 1958 Championship Game, the first to go into overtime.

However, in the divisional play-off with the Giants he was held to a mere eight yards by the Giants defense as New York won 10–0. They then lost 23–17 to Baltimore in the first Championship Game to go into sudden-death overtime. Colts fullback Alan Ameche scored the winning touchdown after a one-yard run eight minutes and 15 seconds into overtime. The season's aggregate attendances topped three million for the first time at an average of 41 752.

EASTERN CONFERENCE

	W	L	T	%	PF	PA
New York Giants	9	3	0	.750	246	183
Cleveland Browns	9	3	0	.750	302	217
Pittsburgh Steelers	7	4	1	.636	261	230
Washington Redskins	4	7	1	.364	214	268
Chicago Cardinals	2	9	1	.182	261	356
Philadelphia Eagles	2	9	1	.182	235	306

Divisional play-off
21 Dec *61 274* NEW YORK 10 Cleveland 0

WESTERN CONFERENCE

	W	L	T	%	PF	PA
Baltimore Colts	9	3	0	.750	381	203
Chicago Bears	8	4	0	.667	298	230
Los Angeles Rams	8	4	0	.667	344	278
San Francisco 49ers	6	6	0	.500	257	324
Detroit Lions	4	7	1	.364	261	276
Green Bay Packers	1	10	1	.091	193	382

CHAMPIONSHIP GAME

28 Dec *64 185*
New York 17 BALTIMORE 23 (OT)

OT=Overtime

1959

This was an important year in American Football history. Vince Lombardi, one of the best known names in the sport, was appointed coach to the Green Bay Packers at the beginning of the year; then in August, Lamar Hunt called a meeting of a proposed new American Football League . . . only this time Lamar's set-up was to prove a serious threat to the NFL. By the end of the year eight strong franchises had been signed up with a view to starting the new League in 1960.

NFL commissioner Bell died in October after suffering a heart attack in the closing minutes of the Eagles–Steelers game. The Giants and Colts were the respective Conference winners and for the second successive year the championship went to Baltimore who won with considerably more ease than in the previous year, 31–16.

EASTERN CONFERENCE

	W	L	T	%	PF	PA
New York Giants	10	2	0	.833	284	170
Cleveland Browns	7	5	0	.583	268	278
Philadelphia Eagles	7	5	0	.583	270	214
Pittsburgh Steelers	6	5	1	.545	257	216
Washington Redskins	3	9	0	.250	185	350
Chicago Cardinals	2	10	0	.167	234	324

WESTERN CONFERENCE

	W	L	T	%	PF	PA
Baltimore Colts	9	3	0	.750	374	251
Chicago Bears	8	4	0	.667	252	196
Green Bay Packers	7	5	0	.583	248	246
San Francisco 49ers	7	5	0	.583	255	237
Detroit Lions	3	8	1	.273	203	275
Los Angeles Rams	2	10	0	.167	242	315

CHAMPIONSHIP GAME

27 Dec *57 545*
BALTIMORE 31 New York 16

1960

The NFL headquarters moved to New York after Pete Rozelle was named the new commissioner following Bell's death. The AFL got under way with eight teams while the NFL had 13.

The Chicago Cardinals moved to St Louis before the start of the season and Dallas returned to NFL action as the Cowboys, but their debut season saw them finish with a 0–11–1 record in the Western Conference. Green Bay took the Western title while the Philadelphia Eagles won the Eastern Conference, the Eagles going on to win the championship with a 17–13 win.

The first regular season AFL game saw the Denver Broncos beat the Boston Patriots 13–10 on 9 September, but it was the Houston Oilers who became the first AFL champions when they beat the Los Angeles Chargers 24–16. The average attendance for all AFL games was 16 538 compared to 40 106 in the NFL.

Paul Hornung increased the all-time scoring record in a season by 38 points when he scored 176 for Green Bay. The record still stands. Jack Kemp of the Los Angeles Chargers passed for 3018 yards to become the first man to throw for 3000 yards in a season.

NFL

Eastern Conference

	W	L	T	%	PF	PA
Philadelphia Eagles	10	2	0	.833	321	246
Cleveland Browns	8	3	1	.727	362	217
New York Giants	6	4	2	.600	271	261
St Louis Cardinals	6	5	1	.545	288	230
Pittsburgh Steelers	5	6	1	.455	240	275
Washington Redskins	1	9	2	.100	178	309

Western Conference

	W	L	T	%	PF	PA
Green Bay Packers	8	4	0	.667	332	209
Detroit Lions	7	5	0	.583	239	212
San Francisco 49ers	7	5	0	.583	208	205
Baltimore Colts	6	6	0	.500	288	234
Chicago Bears	5	6	1	.455	194	299
Los Angeles Rams	4	7	1	.367	265	297
Dallas Cowboys	0	11	1	.000	177	369

AFL

Eastern Conference

	W	L	T	%	PF	PA
Houston Oilers	10	4	0	.714	379	285
New York Titans	7	7	0	.500	382	399
Buffalo Bills	5	8	1	.385	296	303
Boston Patriots	5	9	0	.357	286	349

Western Conference

	W	L	T	%	PF	PA
Los Angeles Chargers	10	4	0	.714	373	336
Dallas Texans	8	6	0	.571	362	253
Oakland Raiders	6	8	0	.429	319	388
Denver Broncos	4	9	1	.308	309	393

CHAMPIONSHIP GAMES

NFL 26 Dec *67325* PHILADELPHIA 17 Green Bay 13
AFL 1 Jan *32183* HOUSTON 24 LA Chargers 16

Charley Tolar (right) makes ground for Houston during their AFL Championship win over San Diego in 1961.

1961

Willard Dewveall moved from the Chicago Bears to the Houston Oilers and he became the first player purposely to move from the NFL to the AFL. The Los Angeles Chargers of the AFL moved to San Diego. The move did them no harm as they again won the AFL Western Division but they lost 10–3 to Houston in the Championship Game.

In the NFL Green Bay won their first championship for 17 years by defeating the Giants 37–0. George Blanda of Houston increased Jack Kemp's year-old record for most yards passed when he completed 3330 yards. Houston became the first team to score 500 points in a season when their regular season yielded 513.

NFL

Eastern Conference

	W	L	T	%	PF	PA
New York Giants	10	3	1	.769	368	220
Philadelphia Eagles	10	4	0	.714	361	297
Cleveland Browns	8	5	1	.615	319	270
St Louis Cardinals	7	7	0	.500	279	267
Pittsburgh Steelers	6	8	0	.429	295	287
Dallas Cowboys	4	9	1	.308	236	380
Washington Redskins	1	12	1	.077	174	392

Western Conference

	W	L	T	%	PF	PA
Green Bay Packers	11	3	0	.786	391	223
Detroit Lions	8	5	1	.615	270	258
Baltimore Colts	8	6	0	.571	302	307
Chicago Bears	8	6	0	.571	326	302
San Francisco 49ers	7	6	1	.538	346	272
Los Angeles Rams	4	10	0	.286	263	333
Minnesota Vikings	3	11	0	.214	285	407

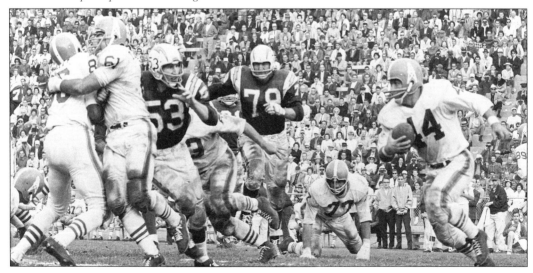

AFL

Eastern Division	W	L	T	%	PF	PA
Houston Oilers	10	3	1	.769	513	242
Boston Patriots	9	4	1	.692	413	313
New York Titans	7	7	0	.500	301	390
Buffalo Bills	6	8	0	.429	294	342
Western Division						
San Diego Chargers	12	2	0	.857	396	219
Dallas Texans	6	8	0	.429	334	343
Denver Broncos	3	11	0	.214	251	432
Oakland Raiders	2	12	0	.143	237	458

CHAMPIONSHIP GAMES

NFL 31 Dec *39 029* GREEN BAY 37 New York Giants 0
AFL 24 Dec *29 566* San Diego 3 HOUSTON 10

1962

Off the field, the courts ruled against the AFL in its charge of monopoly and conspiracy against the NFL. The case had lasted two and a half years. On the field, the AFL championship was resolved after a record 17 minutes and 54 seconds overtime when Tommy Brooker kicked a 25-yard field goal to give the Dallas Texans a 20–17 victory over the Houston Oilers. The Green Bay Packers, without a championship since 1944 prior to 1961, made it two in a row when they beat the Giants 16–7 to take the NFL title.

NFL

Eastern Conference	W	L	T	%	PF	PA
New York Giants	12	2	0	.857	398	283
Pittsburgh Steelers	9	5	0	.643	312	363
Cleveland Browns	7	6	1	.538	291	257
Washington Redskins	5	7	2	.417	305	376
Dallas Cowboys	5	8	1	.385	398	402
St Louis Cardinals	4	9	1	.308	287	361
Philadelphia Eagles	3	10	1	.231	282	356
Western Conference						
Green Bay Packers	13	1	0	.929	415	148
Detroit Lions	11	3	0	.786	315	177
Chicago Bears	9	5	0	.643	321	287
Baltimore Colts	7	7	0	.500	293	288
San Francisco 49ers	6	8	0	.429	282	331
Minnesota Vikings	2	11	1	.154	254	410
Los Angeles Rams	1	12	1	.077	220	334

AFL

Eastern Division	W	L	T	%	PF	PA
Houston Oilers	11	3	0	.786	387	270
Boston Patriots	9	4	1	.692	346	295

The Green Bay defense shuts out the Bears during their 1962 Championship season.

Buffalo Bills	7	6	1	.538	309	272
New York Titans	5	9	0	.357	278	423
Western Division						
Dallas Texans	11	3	0	.786	389	233
Denver Broncos	7	7	0	.500	353	334
San Diego Chargers	4	10	0	.286	314	392
Oakland Raiders	1	13	0	.071	213	370

CHAMPIONSHIP GAMES

NFL 30 Dec *64 892* N.Y. Giants 7 GREEN BAY 16
AFL 23 Dec *37 981* Houston 17 DALLAS TEXANS 20 (OT)

1963

The New York Titans became the Jets after being sold to a five-man syndicate and the Dallas Texans moved to Kansas City where they became the Chiefs. Don Shula, who went on to become one of the game's greatest coaches, was appointed the Colts head coach in succession to Weeb Ewbank. The Pro Football Hall of Fame was inducted at Canton, Ohio on 7 September, Canton being the birthplace of the League back in 1920.

Cleveland's Jim Brown set a season record by rushing for 1863 yards, but the Browns were pipped for the NFL Eastern Conference title by the Giants, who were then beaten 14–10 by the Chicago Bears in the Championship Game. It was the Bears' sixth title under George Hallas, who first took charge of the team in 1920. The Chargers beat the Patriots 51–10 to win their first AFL title.

NFL

Eastern Conference	W	L	T	%	PF	PA
New York Giants	11	3	0	.786	448	280
Cleveland Browns	10	4	0	.714	343	262
St Louis Cardinals	9	5	0	.643	341	283
Pittsburgh Steelers	7	4	3	.636	321	295
Dallas Cowboys	4	10	0	.286	305	378
Washington Redskins	3	11	0	.214	279	398
Philadelphia Eagles	2	10	2	.167	242	381

Western Conference	W	L	T	%	PF	PA
Chicago Bears	11	1	2	.917	301	144
Green Bay Packers	11	2	1	.846	369	206
Baltimore Colts	8	6	0	.571	316	285
Detroit Lions	5	8	1	.385	326	265
Minnesota Vikings	5	8	1	.385	309	390
Los Angeles Rams	5	9	0	.357	210	350
San Francisco 49ers	2	12	0	.143	198	391

AFL

Eastern Division	W	L	T	%	PF	PA
Boston Patriots	7	6	1	.538	327	257
Buffalo Bills	7	6	1	.538	304	291
Houston Oilers	6	8	0	.429	302	372
New York Jets	5	8	1	.385	249	399

Divisional Play-off
AFL 28 Dec *33044* Buffalo 8 BOSTON 26

Western Division	W	L	T	%	PF	PA
San Diego Chargers	11	3	0	.786	399	256
Oakland Raiders	10	4	0	.714	363	288
Kansas City Chiefs	5	7	2	.417	347	263
Denver Broncos	2	11	1	.154	301	473

CHAMPIONSHIP GAMES

NFL 29 Dec *45801* CHICAGO 14 New York Giants 10
AFL 5 Jan *30127* SAN DIEGO 51 Boston 10

1964

Paul Hornung of Green Bay and Alex Karras of Detroit were reinstated after being suspended indefinitely the previous season for placing bets on their own teams' results, as well as the outcome of other NFL games. Despite their return, neither team figured prominently in the NFL championship race which was dominated by Cleveland and Baltimore. In the Championship Game the Browns gained a convincing 27–0 win, a first-season success for their new coach Blanton Collier, replacing Paul Brown who had held the post for 17 years. The AFL title went to Buffalo, clearly the best team in the League, who beat San Diego 20–7.

NFL

Eastern Conference	W	L	T	%	PF	PA
Cleveland Browns	10	3	1	.769	415	293
St Louis Cardinals	9	3	2	.750	357	331
Philadelphia Eagles	6	8	0	.429	312	313
Washington Redskins	6	8	0	.429	307	305
Dallas Cowboys	5	8	1	.385	250	289
Pittsburgh Steelers	5	9	0	.357	253	315
New York Giants	2	10	2	.167	241	399

Western Conference	W	L	T	%	PF	PA
Baltimore Colts	12	2	0	.857	428	225
Green Bay Packers	8	5	1	.615	342	245
Minnesota Vikings	8	5	1	.615	355	296
Detroit Lions	7	5	2	.583	280	260
Los Angeles Rams	5	7	2	.417	283	339
Chicago Bears	5	9	0	.357	260	379
San Francisco 49ers	4	10	0	.286	236	330

AFL

Eastern Division	W	L	T	%	PF	PA
Buffalo Bills	12	2	0	.857	400	242
Boston Patriots	10	3	1	.769	365	297
New York Jets	5	8	1	.385	278	315
Houston Oilers	4	10	0	.286	310	355

Western Division	W	L	T	%	PF	PA
San Diego Chargers	8	5	1	.615	341	300
Kansas City Chiefs	7	7	0	.500	366	306
Oakland Raiders	5	7	2	.417	303	350
Denver Broncos	2	11	1	.154	240	438

CHAMPIONSHIP GAMES

NFL 27 Dec *79544* CLEVELAND 27 Baltimore 0
AFL 26 Dec *40242* BUFFALO 20 San Diego 7

1965

Cleveland comfortably won the NFL Eastern Conference but Green Bay and Baltimore were locked at the top of the Western Conference. It was just as close when they met in the play-off game, which was resolved 13 minutes and 39 seconds into overtime when Don Chandler kicked a 25-yard field goal to give the Packers victory. They went on to beat the Cleveland Browns 23–12 to win the NFL championship. The Bills beat the Chargers 23–0 in a repeat of the 1964 AFL Championship Game.

NFL

Eastern Conference	W	L	T	%	PF	PA
Cleveland Browns	11	3	0	.786	363	325
Dallas Cowboys	7	7	0	.500	325	280
New York Giants	7	7	0	.500	270	338
Washington Redskins	6	8	0	.429	257	301
Philadelphia Eagles	5	9	0	.357	363	359
St Louis Cardinals	5	9	0	.357	296	309
Pittsburgh Steelers	2	12	0	.143	202	397

Western Conference

	W	L	T	%	PF	PA
Green Bay Packers	10	3	1	.769	316	224
Baltimore Colts	10	3	1	.769	389	284
Chicago Bears	9	5	0	.643	409	275
San Francisco 49ers	7	6	1	.538	421	402
Minnesota Vikings	7	7	0	.500	383	403
Detroit Lions	6	7	1	.462	257	295
Los Angeles Rams	4	10	0	.286	269	328

Divisional Play-off

26 Dec *50 484* GREEN BAY 13 Baltimore 10 (OT)

AFL

Eastern Division	W	L	T	%	PF	PA
Buffalo Bills	10	3	1	.769	313	226
New York Jets	5	8	1	.385	285	303
Boston Patriots	4	8	2	.333	244	302
Houston Oilers	4	10	0	.286	298	429

Western Division

	W	L	T	%	PF	PA
San Diego Chargers	9	2	3	.818	340	227
Oakland Raiders	8	5	1	.615	298	239
Kansas City Chiefs	7	5	2	.583	322	285
Denver Broncos	4	10	0	.286	303	392

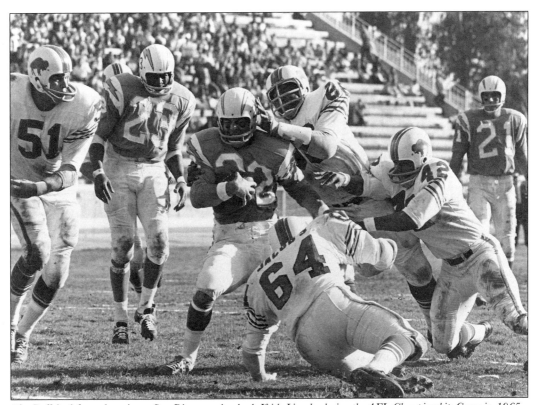

The Buffalo defense closes in on San Diego running back Keith Lincoln during the AFL Championship Game in 1965, comfortably won by the Bills.

CHAMPIONSHIP GAMES

NFL 2 Jan *50777* GREEN BAY 23 Cleveland 12
AFL 26 Dec *30361* San Diego 0 BUFFALO 23

1966

The five-year battle between the AFL and NFL eventually ended when, following secret meetings between Lamar Hunt and Tex Schramm of Dallas, Pete Rozelle announced on 8 June that the two Leagues would merge and an enlarged League of 24 teams formed. While it was agreed that the two Leagues would continue to run as separate entities until the end of the 1969 season, it was decided that there should be a Championship Game between the AFL and NFL champions. This game would be played each January and so was born the Super Bowl, although it would be a couple of years before the NFL actually named it as such; it was originally known as the AFL–NFL World Championship Game.

To help with the merger at the end of 1969 it was agreed that both Leagues would share the draft as from 1967 and that pre-season games would be allowed between teams from the two Leagues. All this was to be part of the 'courting' period before the 'marriage' in 1970 when one League with two Conferences was planned.

Atlanta made its NFL debut in 1966 while Miami appeared for the first time in the AFL. Neither enjoyed a particularly happy start; both finished with 3–11–0 records.

On 27 November the Washington Redskins beat the New York Giants 72–41. The Redskins' 72 points is the most by any one team in a regular season game and the 113 points aggregate represents the only occasion that 100 points have been scored in an NFL game.

Green Bay beat Dallas for the right to represent the NFL in the Super Bowl while on the same day Kansas City beat Buffalo to capture the AFL title. Green Bay went on to become the first winners of the 'Super Bowl' as nearly 62000 fans came to the Los Angeles Coliseum to witness the first game between NFL and AFL champions.

NFL

Eastern Conference	W	L	T	%	PF	PA
Dallas Cowboys	10	3	1	.769	445	239
Cleveland Browns	9	5	0	.643	403	259
Philadelphia Eagles	9	5	0	.643	326	340
St Louis Cardinals	8	5	1	.615	264	265
Washington Redskins	7	7	0	.500	351	355
Pittsburgh Steelers	5	8	1	.385	316	347
Atlanta Falcons	3	11	0	.214	204	437
New York Giants	1	12	1	.077	263	501

Western Conference						
Green Bay Packers	12	2	0	.857	335	163
Baltimore Colts	9	5	0	.643	314	216
Los Angeles Rams	8	6	0	.571	289	212
San Francisco 49ers	6	6	2	.500	320	325
Chicago Bears	5	7	2	.417	234	272
Detroit Lions	4	9	1	.308	206	317
Minnesota Vikings	4	9	1	.308	292	304

AFL

Eastern Division	W	L	T	%	PF	PA
Buffalo Bills	9	4	1	.692	358	255
Boston Patriots	8	4	2	.677	315	283
New York Jets	6	6	2	.500	322	312
Houston Oilers	3	11	0	.214	335	396
Miami Dolphins	3	11	0	.214	213	362

Western Division						
Kansas City Chiefs	11	2	1	.846	448	276
Oakland Raiders	8	5	1	.615	315	288
San Diego Chargers	7	6	1	.538	335	284
Denver Broncos	4	10	0	.286	196	381

CHAMPIONSHIP GAMES

NFL 1 Jan *74152* Dallas 27 GREEN BAY 34
AFL 1 Jan *42080* Buffalo 7 KANSAS CITY 31

SUPER BOWL

15 Jan *Los Angeles 61946*
GREEN BAY 35 Kansas City 10

1967

When Baltimore took Bubba Smith as their first choice in the draft on 14 March he became the first ever choice in the combined AFL/NFL draft. New Orleans made their debut in the NFL which now consisted of two conferences, each divided into two divisions. The Eastern Conference was split into Capitol and Century Divisions whilst the Western Conference was divided into Coastal and Central Divisions. Consequently it resulted in two Conference championship games before the winners met to decide which should represent the NFL in the Super Bowl.

That honour eventually went to Green Bay who beat Dallas with a one-yard sneak by quarterback Bart Starr in the last minute of the game, which was played in sub-zero temperatures at Green Bay. Oakland beat Houston 40–7 to win the AFL title but Green Bay went on to win their second successive Super Bowl.

Bart Starr, who led the Green Bay Packers to successive Super Bowl victories, is taken out during this Central Division clash with the Detroit Lions in 1967.

Houston won the AFL Eastern Division after finishing bottom of the division the previous season. They were the first team to perform this turnaround. Sonny Jurgensen of Washington established a new League record for the most yards passed in a season with 3747 yards.

NFL EASTERN CONFERENCE

Capitol Division	W	L	T	%	PF	PA
Dallas Cowboys	9	5	0	.643	342	268
Philadelphia Eagles	6	7	1	.462	351	409
Washington Redskins	5	6	3	.455	347	353
New Orleans Saints	3	11	0	.214	233	379

Century Division	W	L	T	%	PF	PA
Cleveland Browns	9	5	0	.643	334	297
New York Giants	7	7	0	.500	369	379
St Louis Cardinals	6	7	1	.462	333	356
Pittsburgh Steelers	4	9	1	.308	281	320

Conference Play-off
24 Dec *70 786* DALLAS 52 Cleveland 14

NFL WESTERN CONFERENCE

Coastal Division	W	L	T	%	PF	PA
Los Angeles Rams	11	1	2	.917	398	196
Baltimore Colts	11	1	2	.917	394	198
San Francisco 49ers	7	7	0	.500	273	337
Atlanta Falcons	1	12	1	.077	175	422

Central Division	W	L	T	%	PF	PA
Green Bay Packers	9	4	1	.692	332	209
Chicago Bears	7	6	1	.538	239	218
Detroit Lions	5	7	2	.417	260	259
Minnesota Vikings	3	8	3	.273	233	294

Conference Play-off
23 Dec *49 861* GREEN BAY 28 Los Angeles 7

AFL

Eastern Division	W	L	T	%	PF	PA
Houston Oilers	9	4	1	.692	258	199
New York Jets	8	5	1	.615	371	329
Buffalo Bills	4	10	0	.286	237	285
Miami Dolphins	4	10	0	.286	219	407
Boston Patriots	3	10	1	.231	280	389

Western Division

	W	L	T	%	PF	PA
Oakland Raiders	13	1	0	.929	468	233
Kansas City Chiefs	9	5	0	.643	408	254
San Diego Chargers	8	5	1	.615	360	352
Denver Broncos	3	11	0	.214	256	409

CHAMPIONSHIP GAMES

NFL 31 Dec *50861* GREEN BAY 21 Dallas 17
AFL 31 Dec *53330* OAKLAND 40 Houston 7

SUPER BOWL

14 Jan *Miami 75546*
GREEN BAY 33 Oakland 14

1968

Cincinnati joined the AFL but opened their League campaign by finishing bottom of the Western Division. George Halas retired for the last time as the Chicago Bears head coach. The Houston Oilers became the first team to play regularly indoors when they moved their base from the Rice Stadium to the Astrodome.

Weeb Ewbank made history when he took the Jets to the AFL championship, because he had already taken the Baltimore Colts to the NFL title. He was the first man to coach championship-winning teams in both leagues. Ewbank then went on to become the first coach of an AFL team to win the Super Bowl when he took the Jets to a 16–7 victory over his former team, the Colts. It was the first time that the NFL officially recognised the name Super Bowl for the AFL–NFL Championship Game.

NFL EASTERN CONFERENCE

Capitol Division	W	L	T	%	PF	PA
Dallas Cowboys	12	2	0	.857	431	186
New York Giants	7	7	0	.500	294	325
Washington Redskins	5	9	0	.357	249	358
Philadelphia Eagles	2	12	0	.143	202	351

Century Division						
Cleveland Browns	10	4	0	.714	394	273
St Louis Cardinals	9	4	1	.692	325	289
New Orleans Saints	4	9	1	.308	246	327
Pittsburgh Steelers	2	11	1	.154	244	397

Conference Play-off
21 Dec *81497* CLEVELAND 31 Dallas 20

NFL WESTERN CONFERENCE

Coastal Division	W	L	T	%	PF	PA
Baltimore Colts	13	1	0	.929	402	144
Los Angeles Rams	10	3	1	.769	312	200
San Francisco 49ers	7	6	1	.538	303	310
Atlanta Falcons	2	12	0	.143	170	389

Central Division						
Minnesota Vikings	8	6	0	.571	282	242
Chicago Bears	7	7	0	.500	250	333
Green Bay Packers	6	7	1	.462	281	227
Detroit Lions	4	8	2	.333	207	241

Conference Play-off
22 Dec *60238* BALTIMORE 24 Minnesota 14

AFL

Eastern Division	W	L	T	%	PF	PA
New York Jets	11	3	0	.786	419	280
Houston Oilers	7	7	0	.500	303	248
Miami Dolphins	5	8	1	.385	276	355
Boston Patriots	4	10	0	.286	229	406
Buffalo Bills	1	12	1	.077	199	367

Western Division						
Oakland Raiders	12	2	0	.857	453	233
Kansas City Chiefs	12	2	0	.857	371	170
San Diego Chargers	9	5	0	.643	382	310
Denver Broncos	5	9	0	.357	255	404
Cincinnati Bengals	3	11	0	.214	215	329

Divisional Play-off
22 Dec *53605* OAKLAND 41 Kansas City 6

CHAMPIONSHIP GAMES

NFL 29 Dec *78410* Cleveland 0 BALTIMORE 34
AFL 29 Dec *62627* NEW YORK JETS 27 Oakland 23

SUPER BOWL

12 Jan *Miami 75389*
NEW YORK JETS 16 Baltimore 7

1969

The AFL adopted a play-off system at the end of the season with the winner of one division playing the runner-up in the other and vice versa. Kansas City, who were second in the AFL Western Division with an 11–3–0 record, beat the Eastern Division champions New York Jets in the divisional play-off and then beat Oakland for the AFL championship. In the Super Bowl they beat the NFL champions Minnesota for an amazing success. In the last season of the two Leagues, the AFL's average attendance had crept up on the NFL's. It was 40620 to 54430.

NFL EASTERN CONFERENCE

Capitol Division	W	L	T	%	PF	PA
Dallas Cowboys	11	2	1	.846	369	223
Washington Redskins	7	5	2	.583	307	319
New Orleans Saints	5	9	0	.357	311	393
Philadelphia Eagles	4	9	1	.308	279	377

Century Division	W	L	T	%	PF	PA
Cleveland Browns	10	3	1	.769	351	300
New York Giants	6	8	0	.429	264	298
St Louis Cardinals	4	9	1	.308	314	389
Pittsburgh Steelers	1	13	0	.071	218	404

Conference Play-off
28 Dec *69321* Dallas 14 CLEVELAND 38

NFL WESTERN CONFERENCE

Coastal Division	W	L	T	%	PF	PA
Los Angeles Rams	11	3	0	.786	320	243
Baltimore Colts	8	5	1	.615	279	268
Atlanta Falcons	6	8	0	.429	276	268
San Francisco 49ers	4	8	2	.333	277	319

Central Division	W	L	T	%	PF	PA
Minnesota Vikings	12	2	0	.857	379	133
Detroit Lions	9	4	1	.692	259	188
Green Bay Packers	8	6	0	.571	269	221
Chicago Bears	1	13	0	.071	210	339

Conference Play-off
27 Dec *47900* MINNESOTA 23 Los Angeles 20

AFL

Eastern Division	W	L	T	%	PF	PA
New York Jets	10	4	0	.714	353	269
Houston Oilers	6	6	2	.500	278	279
Boston Patriots	4	10	0	.286	266	316
Buffalo Bills	4	10	0	.286	230	359
Miami Dolphins	3	10	1	.231	233	332

Western Division	W	L	T	%	PF	PA
Oakland Raiders	12	1	1	.923	377	242
Kansas City Chiefs	11	3	0	.786	359	177
San Diego Chargers	8	6	0	.571	288	276
Denver Broncos	5	8	1	.385	297	344
Cincinnati Bengals	4	9	1	.308	280	367

Divisional Play-offs
20 Dec *62977* New York Jets 6 KANSAS CITY 13
21 Dec *53539* OAKLAND 56 Houston 7

CHAMPIONSHIP GAMES

NFL 4 Jan *46503* MINNESOTA 27 Cleveland 7
AFL 4 Jan *53564* Oakland 7 KANSAS CITY 17

SUPER BOWL

11 Jan *New Orleans 80562*
KANSAS CITY 23 Minnesota 7

1970

This was the first season that the two Leagues were totally integrated with the formation of two Conferences, each containing three divisions; Eastern, Central and Western. The number of teams remained at 26 despite previous plans to increase it to 28 by 1970. The three divisional champions, plus the best runner-up in each Conference, became eligible for the divisional play-offs at the end of the season.

There were a couple of ground moves before the start of the season: the Steelers moved to the Three Rivers Stadium while the Cincinnati Bengals moved to the Riverfront Stadium. The start of the season was marred by the death of Vince Lombardi, the man who led the Green Bay Packers to the first Super Bowl, The Super Bowl trophy is now named in his honour.

Against Detroit on 8 November, Tom Dempsey won the game for New Orleans with a record 63-yard field goal. Dallas and Baltimore won the respective AFC and NFC titles with Baltimore capturing Super Bowl V thanks to a Jim O'Brien 32-yard field goal with five seconds remaining. It gave the Colts a 16–13 victory.

AMERICAN CONFERENCE

Eastern Division	W	L	T	%	PF	PA
Baltimore Colts	11	2	1	.846	321	234
Miami Dolphins*	10	4	0	.714	297	228
New York Jets	4	10	0	.286	255	286
Buffalo Bills	3	10	1	.231	204	337
Boston Patriots	2	12	0	.143	149	361

Central Division	W	L	T	%	PF	PA
Cincinnati Bengals	8	6	9	.571	312	255
Cleveland Browns	7	7	0	.500	286	265
Pittsburgh Steelers	5	9	0	.357	210	272
Houston Oilers	3	10	1	.231	217	352

Western Division	W	L	T	%	PF	PA
Oakland Raiders	8	4	2	.667	300	293
Kansas City Chiefs	7	5	2	.583	272	244
San Diego Chargers	5	6	3	.455	282	278
Denver Broncos	5	8	1	.385	253	264

* indicates wild-card entry to play-offs in tables following

NATIONAL CONFERENCE

Eastern Division	W	L	T	%	PF	PA
Dallas Cowboys	10	4	0	.714	299	221
New York Giants	9	5	0	.643	301	270
St Louis Cardinals	8	5	1	.615	325	228
Washington Redskins	6	8	0	.429	297	314
Philadelphia Eagles	3	10	1	.231	241	332

Central Division						
Minnesota Vikings	12	2	0	.857	335	143
Detroit Lions*	10	4	0	.714	347	202
Chicago Bears	6	8	0	.429	256	261
Green Bay Packers	6	8	0	.429	196	293

Western Division						
San Francisco 49ers	10	3	1	.769	352	267
Los Angeles Rams	9	4	1	.692	325	202
Atlanta Falcons	4	8	2	.333	206	261
New Orleans Saints	2	11	1	.154	172	347

DIVISIONAL PLAY-OFFS

NFC 26 Dec *69 613* DALLAS 5 Detroit 0
AFC 26 Dec *49 694* BALTIMORE 17 Cincinnati 0
NFC 27 Dec *45 103* Minnesota 14 SAN FRANCISCO 17
AFC 27 Dec *52 594* OAKLAND 21 Miami 14

CHAMPIONSHIP GAMES

NFC 3 Jan *59 364* San Francisco 10 DALLAS 17
AFC 3 Jan *55 799* BALTIMORE 27 Oakland 17

SUPER BOWL

11 Jan *Miami 79 204*
BALTIMORE 16 Dallas 13

1971

The year started with the first Pro Bowl between the AFC and NFC. The NFC won 27–6 at Los Angeles. The Boston Pirates moved to the new Schaefer Stadium and became the New England Patriots, while the Philadelphia Eagles also moved to their new Veterans Stadium and the 49ers from Kezar Stadium to Candlestick Park. After the season started the Dallas Cowboys were also on the move, from the Cotton Bowl to Texas Stadium.

Miami beat Kansas City 27–24 in the AFC divisional play-offs after 22 minutes and 40 seconds of overtime, the longest ever game in NFL history. Garo Yepremian ended the deadlock with a 37-yard field goal. Miami eventually beat Baltimore 21–0 for the AFC championship but succumbed to Dallas 24–3 in the Super Bowl.

AMERICAN CONFERENCE

Eastern Division	W	L	T	%	PF	PA
Miami Dolphins	10	3	1	.769	315	174
Baltimore Colts*	10	4	0	.714	313	140
New England Patriots	6	8	0	.429	238	325
New York Jets	6	8	0	.429	212	299
Buffalo Bills	1	13	0	.071	184	394

Central Division						
Cleveland Browns	9	5	0	.643	285	273
Pittsburgh Steelers	6	8	0	.429	246	292
Houston Oilers	4	9	1	.308	251	330
Cincinnati Bengals	4	10	0	.286	284	265

Western Division						
Kansas City Chiefs	10	3	1	.769	302	208
Oakland Raiders	8	4	2	.667	344	278
San Diego Chargers	6	8	0	.429	311	341
Denver Broncos	4	9	1	.308	203	275

NATIONAL CONFERENCE

Eastern Division	W	L	T	%	PF	PA
Dallas Cowboys	11	3	0	.786	406	222
Washington Redskins*	9	4	1	.692	276	190
Philadelphia Eagles	6	7	1	.462	221	302
St Louis Cardinals	4	9	1	.308	231	279
New York Giants	4	10	0	.286	228	362

Central Division						
Minnesota Vikings	11	3	0	.786	245	139
Detroit Lions	7	6	1	.538	341	286
Chicago Bears	6	8	0	.429	185	276
Green Bay Packers	4	8	2	.333	274	298

Western Division						
San Francisco 49ers	9	5	0	.643	300	216
Los Angeles Rams	8	5	1	.615	313	260
Atlanta Falcons	7	6	1	.538	274	277
New Orleans Saints	4	8	2	.333	266	347

DIVISONAL PLAY-OFFS

NFC 25 Dec *47 307* Minnesota 12 DALLAS 20
AFC 25 Dec *45 822* Kansas City 24 MIAMI 27 (OT)
NFC 26 Dec *45 327* SAN FRANCISCO 24 Washington 20
AFC 26 Dec *70 734* Cleveland 3 BALTIMORE 20

CHAMPIONSHIP GAMES

NFC 2 Jan *63 409* DALLAS 14 San Francisco 3
AFC 2 Jan *76 622* MIAMI 21 Baltimore 0

SUPER BOWL

16 Jan *New Orleans 81 203*
DALLAS 24 Miami 3

1972

No changes of names or venues in 1972 but there was a change in the rules concerning tied regular season games. Previously they did not count in the final standings but now for the first time a tied game was regarded as a half-win (and half-loss).

The regular season belonged to Miami who had a 14–0–0 record. The Pittsburgh Steelers

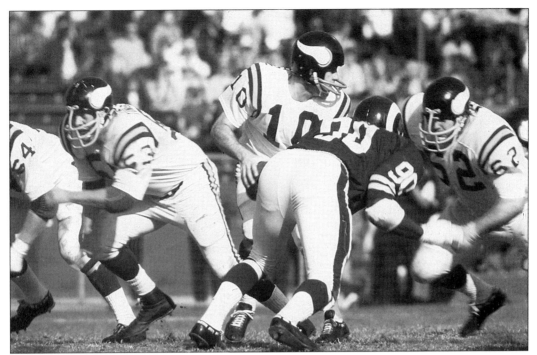

Minnesota Vikings quarterback Fran Tarkenton in the thick of the action. The Vikings enjoyed consistent regular season success in the 1970s but no Super Bowl triumph.

beat the Oakland Raiders 13–7 in the AFC divisional play-offs for their first ever post-season win, but Miami beat them to capture the AFC championship and in the Super Bowl they made up for the previous year's disappointment when they beat Washington 14–7 in front of 90 000 fans at Los Angeles. Miami ended the season with 17 wins from 17 matches to become the first team to remain undefeated through the regular and post-seasons.

AMERICAN CONFERENCE

Eastern Division	W	L	T	%	PF	PA
Miami Dolphins	14	0	0	1.000	385	171
New York Jets	7	7	0	.500	367	324
Baltimore Colts	5	9	0	.357	235	252
Buffalo Bills	4	9	1	.321	257	377
New England Patriots	3	11	0	.214	192	446

Central Division	W	L	T	%	PF	PA
Pittsburgh Steelers	11	3	0	.786	343	175
Cleveland Browns*	10	4	0	.714	268	249
Cincinnati Bengals	8	6	0	.571	299	229
Houston Oilers	1	13	0	.071	164	380

Western Division	W	L	T	%	PF	PA
Oakland Raiders	10	3	1	.750	365	248
Kansas City Chiefs	8	6	0	.571	287	254
Denver Broncos	5	9	0	.357	325	350
San Diego Chargers	4	9	1	.321	264	344

NATIONAL CONFERENCE

Eastern Division	W	L	T	%	PF	PA
Washington Redskins	11	3	0	.786	336	218
Dallas Cowboys*	10	4	0	.714	319	240
New York Giants	8	6	0	.571	331	247
St Louis Cardinals	4	9	1	.321	193	303
Philadelphia Eagles	2	11	1	.179	145	352

Central Division	W	L	T	%	PF	PA
Green Bay Packers	10	4	0	.714	304	226
Detroit Lions	8	5	1	.607	339	290
Minnesota Vikings	7	7	0	.500	301	252
Chicago Bears	4	9	1	.321	225	275

Western Division	W	L	T	%	PF	PA
San Francisco 49ers	8	5	1	.607	353	249
Atlanta Falcons	7	7	0	.500	269	274
Los Angeles Rams	6	7	1	.464	291	286
New Orleans Saints	2	11	1	.179	215	361

DIVISIONAL PLAY-OFFS

NFC 23 Dec *59 746* San Francisco 28 DALLAS 30
AFC 23 Dec *50 327* PITTSBURGH 13 Oakland 7
NFC 24 Dec *52 321* WASHINGTON 16 Green Bay 3
AFC 24 Dec *78 916* MIAMI 20 Cleveland 14

CHAMPIONSHIP GAMES

NFC 31 Dec *53 129* WASHINGTON 26 Dallas 3
AFC 31 Dec *50 845* Pittsburgh 17 MIAMI 21

SUPER BOWL

14 Jan *Los Angeles 90 182*
MIAMI 14 Washington 7

1973

The current jersey-numbering system was adopted in 1973. However, those players in the NFL in 1972 were allowed to retain their old numbers. There were a couple of moves in 1973: the Buffalo Bills moved to Rich Stadium in Orchard Park while the Giants' tie with the Eagles on 23 September was their last game in the Yankee Stadium before their move to the Yale Bowl at New Haven, Connecticut. The NFL was hit with the announcement that another rival League, the World Football League, would be starting in 1974.

The Bills' OJ Simpson made League history by becoming the first man to rush for 2000 yards in a season. Miami won the AFC with a 12–2–0 record and went on to win their second successive Super Bowl by beating the Minnesota Vikings 24–7 at Houston. By winning their first game of the season Miami extended their run of regular-season wins to an all-time record 16.

AMERICAN CONFERENCE

Eastern Division	W	L	T	%	PF	PA
Miami Dolphins	12	2	0	.857	343	150
Buffalo Bills	9	5	0	.643	259	230
New England Patriots	5	9	0	.357	258	300
Baltimore Colts	4	10	0	.286	226	341
New York Jets	4	10	0	.286	240	306
Central Division						
Cincinnati Bengals	10	4	0	.714	286	231
Pittsburgh Steelers*	10	4	0	.714	347	210
Cleveland Browns	7	5	2	.571	234	255
Houston Oilers	1	13	0	.071	199	447
Western Division						
Oakland Raiders	9	4	1	.679	292	175
Denver Broncos	7	5	2	.571	354	296
Kansas City Chiefs	7	5	2	.571	231	192
San Diego Chargers	2	11	1	.179	188	386

NATIONAL CONFERENCE

Eastern Division	W	L	T	%	PF	PA
Dallas Cowboys	10	4	0	.714	382	203
Washington Redskins*	10	4	0	.714	325	198
Philadelphia Eagles	5	8	1	.393	310	393
St Louis Cardinals	4	9	1	.321	286	365
New York Giants	2	11	1	.179	226	362
Central Division						
Minnesota Vikings	12	2	0	.857	296	168
Detroit Lions	6	7	1	.464	271	247
Green Bay Packers	5	7	2	.429	202	259
Chicago Bears	3	11	0	.214	195	334
Western Division						
Los Angeles Rams	12	2	0	.857	388	178
Atlanta Falcons	9	5	0	.643	318	224
New Orleans Saints	5	9	0	.357	163	312
San Francisco 49ers	5	9	0	.357	262	319

DIVISONAL PLAY-OFFS

NFC 22 Dec *48 040* MINNESOTA 27 Washington 20
AFC 22 Dec *52 646* OAKLAND 33 Pittsburgh 14
NFC 23 Dec *63 272* DALLAS 27 Los Angeles 16
AFC 23 Dec *78 928* MIAMI 34 Cincinnati 16

CHAMPIONSHIP GAMES

NFC 30 Dec *64 422* Dallas 10 MINNESOTA 27
AFC 30 Dec *79 325* MIAMI 27 Oakland 10

SUPER BOWL

13 Jan *Houston 71 882*
MIAMI 24 Minnesota 7

1974

There were several rule changes in 1974. Amongst them was the moving of the goal posts from the goal line to the end line, and for regular season games one period of overtime was now allowed – previously overtime was only permitted in pre- and post-season games.

In the new rival league, the WFL, the Birmingham Americans beat the Florida Blazers 22–21 in the World Bowl, and in the NFL Oakland of the American Conference had the best regular season record, 12–2–0. But their chances of a Super Bowl appearance were thwarted in the AFC Championship Game by Pittsburgh who won 24–13 at Oakland. Pittsburgh then went on to inflict a second successive Super Bowl defeat on Minnesota with a 16–6 win. It was the Steelers' first championship win since they joined the League in 1933.

AMERICAN CONFERENCE

Eastern Division

	W	L	T	%	PF	PA
Miami Dolphins	11	3	0	.786	327	216
Buffalo Bills*	9	5	0	.643	264	244
New England Patriots	7	7	0	.500	348	289
New York Jets	7	7	0	.500	279	300
Baltimore Colts	2	12	0	.143	190	329

Central Division

	W	L	T	%	PF	PA
Pittsburgh Steelers	10	3	1	.750	305	189
Cincinnati Bengals	7	7	0	.500	283	259
Houston Oilers	7	7	0	.500	236	282
Cleveland Browns	4	10	0	.286	251	344

Western Division

	W	L	T	%	PF	PA
Oakland Raiders	12	2	0	.857	355	228
Denver Broncos	7	6	1	.536	302	294
Kansas City Chiefs	5	9	0	.357	233	293
San Diego Chargers	5	9	0	.357	212	285

NATIONAL CONFERENCE

Eastern Division

	W	L	T	%	PF	PA
St Louis Cardinals	10	4	0	.714	285	218
Washington Redskins*	10	4	0	.714	320	196
Dallas Cowboys	8	6	0	.571	297	235
Philadelphia Eagles	7	7	0	.500	242	217
New York Giants	2	12	0	.143	195	299

Central Division

	W	L	T	%	PF	PA
Minnesota Vikings	10	4	0	.714	310	195
Detroit Lions	7	7	0	.500	256	270
Green Bay Packers	6	8	0	.429	210	206
Chicago Bears	4	10	0	.286	152	279

Western Division

	W	L	T	%	PF	PA
Los Angeles Rams	10	4	0	.714	263	181
San Francisco 49ers	6	8	0	.429	226	236
New Orleans Saints	5	9	0	.357	166	263
Atlanta Falcons	3	11	0	.214	111	271

DIVISIONAL PLAY-OFFS

NFC 21 Dec *48 150* MINNESOTA 30 St Louis 14
AFC 21 Dec *53 023* OAKLAND 28 Miami 26
NFC 22 Dec *77 925* LOS ANGELES 19 Washington 10
AFC 22 Dec *49 841* PITTSBURGH 32 Buffalo 14

CHAMPIONSHIP GAMES

NFC 29 Dec *48 444* MINNESOTA 14 Los Angeles 10
AFC 29 Dec *53 800* Oakland 13 PITTSBURGH 24

SUPER BOWL

12 Jan *New Orleans 80 997*
PITTSBURGH 16 Minnesota 6

1975

There was an innovative move in 1975 when referees were equipped with wireless microphones so they could announce their decisions over the tannoy system. The Detroit Lions moved home to the new Pontiac Silverdome in this year, the Giants played their home matches in the Shea Stadium and the Saints moved to the Louisiana Superdome. The World Football League ceased to be a rival when it folded in October.

Dallas finished their regular season with a 10–4–0 record and made the play-offs as a wild card team. They then proceeded to beat Central Division champions Minnesota 17–14 in the divisional play-offs and the Rams 37–7 in the Championship Game before losing to Pittsburgh in the Super Bowl. Nevertheless, they made history as the first wild card team to reach the Super Bowl. Pittsburgh joined Green Bay and Miami as two-time winners of the Super Bowl. Eighty million people, then the largest audience in television history, watched the game.

AMERICAN CONFERENCE

Eastern Division

	W	L	T	%	PF	PA
Baltimore Colts	10	4	0	.714	395	269
Miami Dolphins	10	4	0	.714	357	222
Buffalo Bills	8	6	0	.571	420	355
New England Patriots	3	11	0	.214	258	358
New York Jets	3	11	0	.214	258	433

Central Division

	W	L	T	%	PF	PA
Pittsburgh Steelers	12	2	0	.857	373	162
Cincinnati Bengals*	11	3	0	.786	340	246
Houston Oilers	10	4	0	.714	293	226
Cleveland Browns	3	11	0	.214	218	372

Western Division

	W	L	T	%	PF	PA
Oakland Raiders	11	3	0	.786	375	255
Denver Broncos	6	8	0	.429	254	307
Kansas City Chiefs	5	9	0	.357	282	341
San Diego Chargers	2	12	0	.143	189	345

NATIONAL CONFERENCE

Eastern Division

	W	L	T	%	PF	PA
St Louis Cardinals	11	3	0	.786	356	276
Dallas Cowboys*	10	4	0	.714	350	268
Washington Redskins	8	6	0	.571	325	276
New York Giants	5	9	0	.357	216	306
Philadelphia Eagles	4	10	0	.286	225	302

Central Division

	W	L	T	%	PF	PA
Minnesota Vikings	12	2	0	.857	377	180
Detroit Lions	7	7	0	.500	245	262
Chicago Bears	4	10	0	.286	191	379
Green Bay Packers	4	10	0	.286	226	285

Western Division

Los Angeles Rams	12	2	0	.857	312	135
San Francisco 49ers	5	9	0	.357	255	286
Atlanta Falcons	4	10	0	.286	240	289
New Orleans Saints	2	12	0	.143	165	360

DIVISONAL PLAY-OFFS

NFC 27 Dec *73459* LOS ANGELES 35 St Louis 23
AFC 27 Dec *49557* PITTSBURGH 28 Baltimore 10
NFC 28 Dec *48050* Minnesota 14 DALLAS 17
AFC 28 Dec *53030* OAKLAND 31 Cincinnati 28

CHAMPIONSHIP GAMES

NFC 4 Jan *88919* Los Angeles 7 DALLAS 37
AFC 4 Jan *50609* PITTSBURGH 16 Oakland 10

SUPER BOWL

18 Jan *Miami 80197*
PITTSBURGH 21 Dallas 17

1976

Tampa Bay Buccaneers made their debut in the NFL . . . and ended their first season in the AFC Western Division with a 0–14–0 record. Seattle also made their debut; they finished bottom of the NFC Western Division but at least managed two wins out of their 14 games.

The Giants eventually moved to a new permanent home, Giants Stadium at East Rutherford, New Jersey. St Louis and San Diego made history when they played the first NFL game outside North America, a pre-season encounter in front of 38000 fans in Tokyo. Nobody dominated the regular season and the championships were wide open. Pittsburgh seemed to be heading for their third successive Super Bowl but their ambitions were ended by a 24–7 defeat at Oakland. The Raiders then went on to maintain the AFC's record of five straight Super Bowl successes when they beat Minnesota 32–14 in front of a massive 100421 fans (although the paying attendance was 103438) at the Rose Bowl, Pasadena, to win their first Super Bowl.

AMERICAN CONFERENCE

Eastern Division	W	L	T	%	PF	PA
Baltimore Colts	11	3	0	.786	417	246
New England Patriots*	11	3	0	.786	376	236
Miami Dolphins	6	8	0	.429	263	264
New York Jets	3	11	0	.214	169	383
Buffalo Bills	2	12	0	.143	245	363

Central Division

Pittsburgh Steelers	10	4	0	.714	342	138
Cincinnati Bengals	10	4	0	.714	335	210
Cleveland Browns	9	5	0	.643	267	287
Houston Oilers	5	9	0	.357	222	273

Western Division

Oakland Raiders	13	1	0	.929	350	237
Denver Broncos	9	5	0	.643	315	206
San Diego Chargers	6	8	0	.429	248	285
Kansas City Chiefs	5	9	0	.357	290	376
Tampa Bay Buccaneers	0	14	0	.000	125	412

NATIONAL CONFERENCE

Eastern Division	W	L	T	%	PF	PA
Dallas Cowboys	11	3	0	.786	296	194
Washington Redskins*	10	4	0	.714	291	217
St Louis Cardinals	10	4	0	.714	309	267
Philadelphia Eagles	4	10	0	.286	165	286
New York Giants	3	11	0	.214	170	250

Central Division

Minnesota Vikings	11	2	1	.821	305	176
Chicago Bears	7	7	0	.500	253	216
Detroit Lions	6	8	0	.429	262	220
Green Bay Packers	5	9	0	.357	218	299

Western Division

Los Angeles Rams	10	3	1	.750	351	190
San Francisco 49ers	8	6	0	.571	270	190
Atlanta Falcons	4	10	0	.286	172	312
New Orleans Saints	4	10	0	.286	253	346
Seattle Seahawks	2	12	0	.143	229	429

DIVISONAL PLAY-OFFS

NFC 18 Dec *41466* MINNESOTA 35 Washington 20
AFC 18 Dec *53050* OAKLAND 24 New England 21
NFC 19 Dec *63283* Dallas 12 LOS ANGELES 14
AFC 19 Dec *59296* Baltimore 14 PITTSBURGH 40

CHAMPIONSHIP GAMES

NFC 26 Dec *48379* MINNESOTA 24 Los Angeles 13
AFC 26 Dec *53821* OAKLAND 24 Pittsburgh 7

SUPER BOWL

9 Jan *Pasadena 103438*
OAKLAND 32 Minnesota 14

1977

Walter Payton of the Chicago Bears set the current NFL record for a single game when he rushed for 275 yards against Minnesota. The Bears made the play-offs courtesy of a wild card but were beaten by the eventual Super Bowl winners Dallas in the NFC divisional play-offs.

Ken 'The Snake' Stabler throws for the Raiders against Green Bay in 1976. The Raiders suffered just one regular season loss and went on to win the Super Bowl.

Dallas ended the AFC's recent monopoly of the Super Bowl with a 27–10 win over Denver at the Louisiana Superdome, the first time the Super Bowl had been played indoors. The game was watched by more than 100 million people on television, making it the most watched show in television history.

AMERICAN CONFERENCE

Eastern Division	W	L	T	%	PF	PA
Baltimore Colts	10	4	0	.714	295	221
Miami Dolphins	10	4	0	.714	313	197
New England Patriots	9	5	0	.643	278	217
New York Jets	3	11	0	.214	191	300
Buffalo Bills	3	11	0	.214	160	313

Central Division						
Pittsburgh Steelers	9	5	0	.643	283	243
Houston Oilers	8	6	0	.571	299	230
Cincinnati Bengals	8	6	0	.571	238	235
Cleveland Browns	6	8	0	.429	269	267

Western Division						
Denver Broncos	12	2	0	.857	274	148
Oakland Raiders*	11	3	0	.786	351	230
San Diego Chargers	7	7	0	.500	222	205
Seattle Seahawks	5	9	0	.357	282	373
Kansas City Chiefs	2	12	0	.143	225	349

NATIONAL CONFERENCE

Eastern Division	W	L	T	%	PF	PA
Dallas Cowboys	12	2	0	.857	345	212
Washington Redskins	9	5	0	.643	196	189
St Louis Cardinals	7	7	0	.500	272	287
Philadelphia Eagles	5	9	0	.357	220	207
New York Giants	5	9	9	.357	181	265

Central Division						
Minnesota Vikings	9	5	0	.643	231	227
Chicago Bears*	9	5	0	.643	255	253
Detroit Lions	6	8	0	.429	183	252
Green Bay Packers	4	10	0	.286	134	219
Tampa Bay Buccaneers	2	12	0	.143	103	223

Western Division

Los Angeles Rams	10	4	0	.714	302	146
Atlanta Falcons	7	7	0	.500	179	129
San Francisco 49ers	5	9	0	.357	220	260
New Orleans Saints	3	11	0	.214	232	336

DIVISIONAL PLAY-OFFS

AFC 24 Dec *75 059* DENVER 34 Pittsburgh 21
AFC 24 Dec *59 925* Baltimore 31 OAKLAND 37 (OT)
NFC 26 Dec *70 203* Los Angeles 7 MINNESOTA 14
NFC 26 Dec *63 260* DALLAS 37 Chicago 7

CHAMPIONSHIP GAMES

NFC 1 Jan *64 293* DALLAS 23 Minnesota 6
AFC 1 Jan *75 044* DENVER 20 Oakland 17

SUPER BOWL

15 Jan *New Orleans 75 538*
DALLAS 27 Denver 10

1978

The current format of a 4-game pre-season and 16-game regular season was adopted for the first time. A second wild card into the play-offs was also allowed for the first time, with the two wild card teams playing each other and the winners advancing to the divisional play-offs.

The NFL rolled into Mexico City for a pre-season game between the Saints and the Eagles. The increase in the regular season games meant attendances increased beyond the 12 million mark for the regular season at an average of 57 017.

Pittsburgh went into the play-offs as favourites to capture the Super Bowl after a 14–2–0 regular season record. They confirmed their standing as after beating Denver and Houston they beat Dallas 35–31 in a thrilling climax to the season and became the first team to win three Super Bowls.

AMERICAN CONFERENCE

Eastern Division	W	L	T	%	PF	PA
New England Patriots	11	5	0	.688	358	286
Miami Dolphins*	11	5	0	.688	372	254
New York Jets	8	8	0	.500	359	364
Buffalo Bills	5	11	0	.313	302	354
Baltimore Colts	5	11	0	.313	239	421

Central Division						
Pittsburgh Steelers	14	2	0	.875	356	195
Houston Oilers*	10	6	0	.625	283	298
Cleveland Browns	8	8	0	.500	334	356

Cincinnati Bengals	4	12	0	.250	252	284

Western Division						
Denver Broncos	10	6	0	.625	282	198
Oakland Raiders	9	7	0	.563	311	283
Seattle Seahawks	9	7	0	.563	345	358
San Diego Chargers	9	7	0	.563	355	309
Kansas City Chiefs	4	12	0	.250	243	327

NATIONAL CONFERENCE

Eastern Division	W	L	T	%	PF	PA
Dallas Cowboys	12	4	0	.750	384	208
Philadelphia Eagles*	9	7	0	.563	270	250
Washington Redskins	8	8	0	.500	273	283
St Louis Cardinals	6	10	0	.375	248	296
New York Giants	6	10	0	.375	264	298

Central Division						
Minnesota Vikings	8	7	1	.531	294	306
Green Bay Packers	8	7	1	.531	249	269
Detroit Lions	7	9	0	.438	290	300
Chicago Bears	7	9	0	.438	253	274
Tampa Bay Buccaneers	5	11	0	.313	241	259

Western Division						
Los Angeles Rams	12	4	0	.750	316	245
Atlanta Falcons*	9	7	0	.563	240	290
New Orleans Saints	7	9	0	.438	281	298
San Francisco 49ers	2	14	0	.125	219	350

WILD CARD GAMES

NFC 24 Dec *59 403* ATLANTA 14 Philadelphia 13
AFC 24 Dec *72 445* Miami 9 HOUSTON 17

DIVISIONAL PLAY-OFFS

NFC 30 Dec *63 406* DALLAS 27 Atlanta 20
AFC 30 Dec *50 230* PITTSBURGH 33 Denver 10
NFC 31 Dec *70 436* LOS ANGELES 34 Minnesota 10
AFC 31 Dec *60 735* New England 14 HOUSTON 31

CHAMPIONSHIP GAMES

NFC 7 Jan *71 086* Los Angeles 0 DALLAS 28
AFC 7 Jan *50 725* PITTSBURGH 34 Houston 5

SUPER BOWL

21 Jan *Miami 79 484*
PITTSBURGH 35 Dallas 31

Right *Preston Pearson charges through for Dallas despite the efforts of the St Louis Cardinals defense.*

1979

Pittsburgh went on to win their fourth Super Bowl in 1979. San Diego suffered a surprise home defeat by wild card entry Houston in the AFC divisional play-offs, but Pittsburgh, after easily disposing of Miami and Houston, had little trouble in overcoming Los Angeles in the Super Bowl in front of 103 985 at Pasadena. Dan Fouts of San Diego established the record for the most yards passed in a season when he became the first man to throw for 4000 yards (4082).

AMERICAN CONFERENCE

Eastern Division	W	L	T	%	PF	PA
Miami Dolphins	10	6	0	.625	341	257
New England Patriots	9	7	0	.563	411	326
New York Jets	8	8	0	.500	337	383
Buffalo Bills	7	9	0	.438	268	279
Baltimore Colts	5	11	0	.313	271	351

Central Division	W	L	T	%	PF	PA
Pittsburgh Steelers	12	4	0	.750	416	262
Houston Oilers*	11	5	0	.688	362	331
Cleveland Browns	9	7	0	.563	359	352
Cincinnati Bengals	4	12	0	.250	337	421

Western Division	W	L	T	%	PF	PA
San Diego Chargers	12	4	0	.750	411	246
Denver Broncos*	10	6	0	.625	289	262
Seattle Seahawks	9	7	0	.563	378	372
Oakland Raiders	9	7	0	.563	365	337
Kansas City Chiefs	7	9	0	.438	238	262

NATIONAL CONFERENCE

Eastern Division	W	L	T	%	PF	PA
Dallas Cowboys	11	5	0	.688	371	313
Philadelphia Eagles*	11	5	0	.688	339	282
Washington Redskins	10	6	0	.625	348	295
New York Giants	6	10	0	.375	237	323
St Louis Cardinals	5	11	0	.313	307	358

Central Division	W	L	T	%	PF	PA
Tampa Bay Buccaneers	10	6	0	.625	273	237
Chicago Bears*	10	6	0	.625	306	249
Minnesota Vikings	7	9	0	.438	259	337
Green Bay Packers	5	11	0	.313	246	316
Detroit Lions	2	14	0	.125	219	365

Western Division	W	L	T	%	PF	PA
Los Angeles Rams	9	7	0	.563	323	309
New Orleans Saints	8	8	0	.500	370	360
Atlanta Falcons	6	10	0	.375	300	388
San Francisco 49ers	2	14	0	.125	308	416

WILD CARD GAMES

NFC 23 Dec *69 397* PHILADELPHIA 27 Chicago 17
AFC 23 Dec *48 776* HOUSTON 13 Denver 7

DIVISIONAL PLAY-OFFS

NFC 29 Dec *71 402* TAMPA BAY 24 Philadelphia 17
AFC 29 Dec *51 192* San Diego 14 HOUSTON 17
NFC 30 Dec *64 792* Dallas 19 LOS ANGELES 21
AFC 30 Dec *50 214* PITTSBURGH 34 Miami 14

CHAMPIONSHIP GAMES

NFC 6 Jan *72 033* Tampa Bay 0 LOS ANGELES 9
AFC 6 Jan *50 475* PITTSBURGH 27 Houston 13

SUPER BOWL

20 Jan *Pasadena 103 985*
PITTSBURGH 31 Los Angeles 19

1980

The AFC–NFC Pro Bowl was played at the Aloha Stadium, Honolulu, the first time the Pro Bowl had been played in a city not holding an NFL franchise. However, the venue proved popular and it became the permanent home of the Bowl. The Rams moved home in 1980, basing themselves at the Anaheim Stadium in Orange County. NFL attendances totalled more than 13 million for the second successive regular season, with the average crowd of 59 787 setting a new record.

Oakland, who were just pipped for the AFC Western Division title by San Diego, made history by becoming the first wild card team to go on and win the Super Bowl. They beat Houston and Cleveland before gaining revenge over San Diego in the AFC Championship Game. In the Super Bowl they beat Philadelphia 27–10 to win their second title.

Against New Orleans on 7 December the 49ers came from 35–7 behind at the end of the second quarter to win 38–35, the biggest comeback in NFL history. Brian Snipe of Cleveland wiped out Dan Fouts' twelve month old record when he passed for a new record 4132 yards.

AMERICAN CONFERENCE

Eastern Division	W	L	T	%	PF	PA
Buffalo Bills	11	5	0	.688	320	260
New England Patriots	10	6	0	.625	441	325
Miami Dolphins	8	8	0	.500	266	305
Baltimore Colts	7	9	0	.438	355	387
New York Jets	4	12	0	.250	302	395

Central Division

	W	L	T	%	PF	PA
Cleveland Browns	11	5	0	.688	357	310
Houston Oilers*	11	5	0	.688	295	251
Pittsburgh Steelers	9	7	0	.563	352	313
Cincinnati Bengals	6	10	0	.375	244	312

Western Division

	W	L	T	%	PF	PA
San Diego Chargers	11	5	0	.688	418	327
Oakland Raiders*	11	5	0	.688	364	306
Kansas City Chiefs	8	8	0	.500	319	336
Denver Broncos	8	8	0	.500	310	323
Seattle Seahawks	4	12	0	.250	291	408

NATIONAL CONFERENCE

Eastern Division

	W	L	T	%	PF	PA
Philadelphia Eagles	12	4	0	.750	384	222
Dallas Cowboys*	12	4	0	.750	454	311
Washington Redskins	6	10	0	.375	261	293
St Louis Cardinals	5	11	0	.313	299	350
New York Giants	4	12	0	.250	249	425

Central Division

Minnesota Vikings	9	7	0	.563	317	308
Detroit Lions	9	7	0	.563	334	272
Chicago Bears	7	9	0	.438	304	264
Tampa Bay Buccaneers	5	10	1	.344	271	341
Green Bay Packers	5	10	1	.344	231	371

Western Division

Atlanta Falcons	12	4	0	.750	405	272
Los Angeles Rams*	11	5	0	.688	424	289
San Francisco 49ers	6	10	0	.375	320	415
New Orleans Saints	1	15	0	.063	291	487

WILD CARD GAMES

NFC 28 Dec *63052* DALLAS 34 Los Angeles 13
AFC 28 Dec *53333* OAKLAND 27 Houston 7

DIVISIONAL PLAY-OFFS

NFC 3 Jan *70178* PHILADELPHIA 31 Minnesota 16
AFC 3 Jan *52253* SAN DIEGO 20 Buffalo 14
NFC 4 Jan *59793* Atlanta 27 DALLAS 30
AFC 4 Jan *78245* Cleveland 12 OAKLAND 14

CHAMPIONSHIP GAMES

NFC 11 Jan *71522* PHILADELPHIA 20 Dallas 7
AFC 11 Jan *52675* San Diego 27 OAKLAND 34

SUPER BOWL

25 Jan *New Orleans 76 135*
OAKLAND 27 Philadelphia 10

1981

Attendances were up again as polls showed that football was gaining in popularity and more American sports fans followed football than baseball. This was reflected when average gates topped 60 000 for the first time. Further confirmation came when more than 110 million people watched the Super Bowl on television.

There was to be no repeat of the previous season, with all wild card teams being eliminated by the end of the divisional play-offs. The 49ers were clear favourites for the Super Bowl after an impressive 13–3–0 regular season. San Diego sneaked past Miami in the AFC divisional play-off with a 29-yard field goal 13 minutes and 52 seconds into overtime to win 41–38 in the fourth longest post-season game in NFL history.

San Francisco were given a fright by Dallas in the NFC Championship Game but managed to win 28–27. And in the Super Bowl, the first to be played in the North of America, at the Pontiac Silverdome, the 49ers were again pushed but hung on for a 26–21 win against Cincinnati.

AMERICAN CONFERENCE

Eastern Division

	W	L	T	%	PF	PA
Miami Dolphins	11	4	1	.719	345	275
New York Jets*	10	5	1	.656	355	287
Buffalo Bills*	10	6	0	.625	311	276
Baltimore Colts	2	14	0	.125	259	533
New England Patriots	2	14	0	.125	322	370

Central Division

Cincinnati Bengals	12	4	0	.750	421	304
Pittsburgh Steelers	8	8	0	.500	356	297
Houston Oilers	7	9	0	.438	281	355
Cleveland Browns	5	11	0	.313	276	375

Western Division

San Diego Chargers	10	6	0	.625	478	390
Denver Broncos	10	6	0	.625	321	289
Kansas City Chiefs	9	7	0	.563	343	290
Oakland Raiders	7	9	0	.438	273	343
Seattle Seahawks	6	10	0	.375	322	388

NATIONAL CONFERENCE

Eastern Division

	W	L	T	%	PF	PA
Dallas Cowboys	12	4	0	.750	367	277
Philadelphia Eagles*	10	6	0	.625	368	221
New York Giants*	9	7	0	.563	295	257
Washington Redskins	8	8	0	.500	347	349
St Louis Cardinals	7	9	0	.438	315	408

Central Division

Tampa Bay Buccaneers	9	7	0	.563	315	268
Detroit Lions	8	8	0	.500	397	322

Green Bay Packers	8	8	0	.500	324	361
Minnesota Vikings	7	9	0	.438	325	369
Chicago Bears	6	10	0	.375	253	324

Western Division

San Francisco 49ers	13	3	0	.813	357	250
Atlanta Falcons	7	9	0	.438	426	355
Los Angeles Rams	6	10	0	.375	303	351
New Orleans Saints	4	12	0	.250	207	378

WILD CARD GAMES

NFC 27 Dec *71611* Philadelphia 21 NEW YORK GIANTS 27
AFC 27 Dec *57050* N.Y. Jets 27 BUFFALO 31

DIVISIONAL PLAY-OFFS

NFC 2 Jan *64848* DALLAS 38 Tampa Bay 0
AFC 2 Jan *73735* Miami 38 SAN DIEGO 41 (OT)
NFC 3 Jan *58630* SAN FRANCISCO 38 NY Giants 24
AFC 3 Jan *55420* CINCINNATI 28 Buffalo 21

CHAMPIONSHIP GAMES

NFC 10 Jan *60525* SAN FRANCISCO 28 Dallas 27
AFC 10 Jan *46302* CINCINNATI 27 San Diego 7

SUPER BOWL

24 Jan *Pontiac 81270*
SAN FRANCISCO 26 Cincinnati 21

1982

Oakland Raiders, after taking legal action against the NFL, were allowed by the courts to move their base to Los Angeles where they became the Los Angeles Raiders. They went on to finish top of the American Conference in a season reduced to just nine matches after a 57-day players' strike.

Because of the strike action, all teams in the AFC and NFC were graded 1–14 according to their records after nine games and the top eight from each Conference engaged in a knockout competition to find the respective Conference champions. Miami, second to the Raiders, captured the AFC crown while Washington, who finished top of the NFC 'League Table' went on to beat second-placed Dallas in the Championship Game.

Another six-figure crowd watched the Super Bowl, which was again played in Pasadena, and they saw Washington beat Miami 27–17. The game was beamed to 40 million homes across the United States.

AMERICAN CONFERENCE

	W	L	T	%	PF	PA
Los Angeles Raiders	8	1	0	.889	260	200
Miami Dolphins	7	2	0	.778	198	131
Cincinnati Bengals	7	2	0	.778	232	177
Pittsburgh Steelers	6	3	0	.667	204	146
San Diego Chargers	6	3	0	.667	288	221
New York Jets	6	3	0	.667	245	166
New England Patriots	5	4	0	.556	143	157
Cleveland Browns	4	5	0	.444	140	182
Buffalo Bills	4	5	0	.444	150	154
Seattle Seahawks	4	5	0	.444	127	147
Kansas City Chiefs	3	6	0	.333	176	184
Denver Broncos	2	7	0	.222	148	226
Houston Oilers	1	8	0	.111	136	245
Baltimore Colts	0	8	1	.056	113	236

NATIONAL CONFERENCE

	W	L	T	%	PF	PA
Washington Redskins	8	1	0	.889	190	128
Dallas Cowboys	6	3	0	.667	226	145
Green Bay Packers	5	3	1	.611	226	169
Minnesota Vikings	5	4	0	.556	187	198
Atlanta Falcons	5	4	0	.556	183	199
St Louis Cardinals	5	4	0	.556	135	170
Tampa Bay Buccaneers	5	4	0	.556	158	178
Detroit Lions	4	5	0	.444	181	176
New Orleans Saints	4	5	0	.444	129	160
New York Giants	4	5	0	.444	164	160
San Francisco 49ers	3	6	0	.333	209	206
Chicago Bears	3	6	0	.333	141	174
Philadelphia Eagles	3	6	0	.333	191	195
Los Angeles Rams	2	7	0	.222	200	250

Season reduced to nine games because of 57-day players' strike. Top eight teams in each Conference played-off to decide Conference champions

FIRST ROUND PLAY-OFFS

NFC 8 Jan *55045* WASHINGTON 31 Detroit 7
NFC 8 Jan *54282* GREEN BAY 41 St Louis 16
AFC 8 Jan *68842* MIAMI 28 New England 13
AFC 8 Jan *56555* L.A. RAIDERS 27 Cleveland 10
NFC 9 Jan *60560* MINNESOTA 30 Atlanta 24
NFC 9 Jan *65042* DALLAS 30 Tampa Bay 17
AFC 9 Jan *53546* Pittsburgh 28 SAN DIEGO 31
AFC 9 Jan *57560* Cincinnati 17 NEW YORK JETS 44

SECOND ROUND PLAY-OFFS

NFC 15 Jan *54593* WASHINGTON 21 Minnesota 7
AFC 15 Jan *90038* L.A. Raiders 14 NEW YORK JETS 17
NFC 16 Jan *63927* DALLAS 37 Green Bay 26
AFC 16 Jan *71383* MIAMI 34 San Diego 13

CHAMPIONSHIP GAMES

NFC 22 Jan *55045* WASHINGTON 31 Dallas 17
AFC 23 Jan *67396* MIAMI 14 New York Jets 0

SUPER BOWL

30 Jan *Pasadena 103667*
WASHINGTON 27 Miami 17

1983

The seventh weekend of the season (October 16–17) saw an NFL record 761 points scored. Washington won the NFC Eastern Division with the best regular season record (14–2–0) and with an NFL record 541 points, and when they beat wild card entrants the Rams 51–7 in the divisional play-off, they looked very much the likely Super Bowl winners. A 24–21 win over the 49ers secured the NFC Championship and it put them in their second successive Super Bowl. But they were well beaten by the Los Angeles Raiders who captured their third title.

AMERICAN CONFERENCE

Eastern Division	W	L	T	%	PF	PA
Miami Dolphins	12	4	0	.750	389	250
New England Patriots	8	8	0	.500	274	289
Buffalo Bills	8	8	0	.500	283	351
Baltimore Colts	7	9	0	.438	264	354
New York Jets	7	9	0	.438	313	331

Central Division						
Pittsburgh Steelers	10	6	0	.625	355	303
Cleveland Browns	9	7	0	.563	356	342
Cincinnati Bengals	7	9	0	.438	346	302
Houston Oilers	2	14	0	.125	288	460

Western Division						
Los Angeles Raiders	12	4	0	.750	442	338
Seattle Seahawks*	9	7	0	.563	403	397
Denver Broncos*	9	7	0	.563	302	327
San Diego Chargers	6	10	0	.375	358	462
Kansas City Chiefs	6	10	0	.375	386	367

NATIONAL CONFERENCE

Eastern Division	W	L	T	%	PF	PA
Washington Redskins	14	2	0	.875	541	332
Dallas Cowboys*	12	4	0	.750	479	360
St Louis Cardinals	8	7	1	.531	374	428
Philadelphia Eagles	5	11	0	.313	233	322
New York Giants	3	12	1	.219	267	347

Central Division						
Detroit Lions	9	7	0	.563	347	286
Green Bay Packers	8	8	0	.500	429	439
Chicago Bears	8	8	0	.500	311	301
Minnesota Vikings	8	8	0	.500	316	348
Tampa Bay Buccaneers	2	14	0	.125	241	380

Western Division						
San Francisco 49ers	10	6	0	.625	432	293
Los Angeles Rams*	9	7	0	.563	361	344
New Orleans Saints	8	8	0	.500	319	337
Atlanta Falcons	7	9	0	.438	370	389

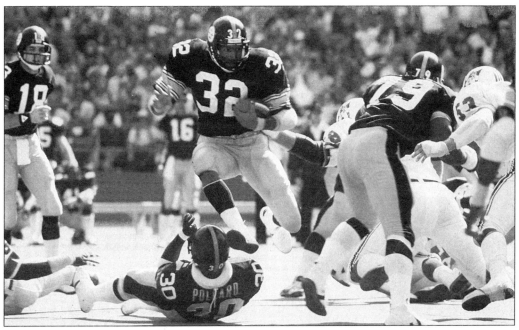

Franco Harris leads the Pittsburgh offense.

WILD CARD GAMES

AFC 24 Dec *64275* SEATTLE 31 Denver 7
NFC 24 Dec *62118* Dallas 17 LOS ANGELES RAMS 24

DIVISIONAL PLAY-OFFS

NFC 31 Dec *59979* SAN FRANCISCO 24 Detroit 23
AFC 31 Dec *74136* Miami 20 SEATTLE 27
NFC 1 Jan *54440* WASHINGTON 51 L.A. Rams 7
AFC 1 Jan *90380* L.A. RAIDERS 38 Pittsburgh 10

CHAMPIONSHIP GAMES

NFC 8 Jan *55363* WASHINGTON 24 San Francisco 21
AFC 8 Jan *91445* L.A. RAIDERS 30 Seattle 14

SUPER BOWL

22 Jan *Tampa 72920*
LOS ANGELES RAIDERS 38 Washington 9

1984

The Jets left their Shea Stadium home to share with the Giants at East Rutherford. Miami were the AFC's top team with an excellent 14–2–0 regular season record but they were upstaged by the San Francisco 49ers who won the NFC Western Division with a 15–1–0 record, the best since the 16-game schedule was launched.

Hardly surprisingly, Miami and the 49ers both reached the Super Bowl with Joe Montana's San Francisco team taking the honours for the first time with a convincing 38–16 win. Nearly 116 million watched the game on television in America with an additional six million watching it in Great Britain.

Houston and Pittsburgh shared in a piece of NFL history in 1984 when they engaged in the 100th overtime game in regular season matches since it was introduced into the regular season in 1974. Houston went on to win 23–20. Dan Marino of the Miami Dolphins passed for a record 5084 yards. It is the only time any quarterback has thrown passes for five thousand yards in a season and is nearly one thousand yards better than the next best figure.

Eric Dickerson of the Rams rushed for the present-day record 2105 yards, and to add further to the record-breaking season Walter Payton of the Bears broke Jim Brown's all-time career rushing record and Art Monk of Washington caught a record 106 passes in the season. Miami equalled their own record winning streak when they won the first 11 regular season games to extend their run to 16 consecutive wins.

AMERICAN CONFERENCE

Eastern Division	W	L	T	%	PF	PA
Miami Dolphins	14	2	0	.875	513	298
New England Patriots	9	7	0	.563	362	352
New York Jets	7	9	0	.438	332	364
Indianapolis Colts	4	12	0	.250	239	414
Buffalo Bills	2	14	0	.125	250	454

Central Division	W	L	T	%	PF	PA
Pittsburgh Steelers	9	7	0	.563	387	310
Cincinnati Bengals	8	8	0	.500	339	339
Cleveland Browns	5	11	0	.313	250	297
Houston Oilers	3	13	0	.188	240	437

Western Division	W	L	T	%	PF	PA
Denver Broncos	13	3	0	.813	353	241
Seattle Seahawks*	12	4	0	.750	418	282
Los Angeles Raiders*	11	5	0	.688	368	278
Kansas City Chiefs	8	8	0	.500	314	324
San Diego Chargers	7	9	0	.438	394	413

NATIONAL CONFERENCE

Eastern Division	W	L	T	%	PF	PA
Washington Redskins	11	5	0	.688	426	310
New York Giants*	9	7	0	.563	299	301
St Louis Cardinals	9	7	0	.563	423	345
Dallas Cowboys	9	7	0	.563	308	308
Philadelphia Eagles	6	9	1	.406	278	320

Central Division	W	L	T	%	PF	PA
Chicago Bears	10	6	0	.625	325	248
Green Bay Packers	8	8	0	.500	390	309
Tampa Bay Buccaneers	6	10	0	.375	335	380
Detroit Lions	4	11	1	.281	283	408
Minnesota Vikings	3	13	0	.188	276	484

Western Division	W	L	T	%	PF	PA
San Francisco 49ers	15	1	0	.938	475	227
Los Angeles Rams*	10	6	0	.625	346	316
New Orleans Saints	7	9	0	.438	298	361
Atlanta Falcons	4	12	0	.250	281	382

WILD CARD GAMES

AFC 22 Dec *62049* SEATTLE 13 Los Angeles Raiders 7
NFC 22 Dec *67037* L.A. Rams 13 NEW YORK GIANTS 16

DIVISIONAL PLAY-OFFS

NFC 29 Dec *60303* SAN FRANCISCO 21 N.Y.Giants 10
AFC 29 Dec *73469* MIAMI 31 Seattle 10
NFC 30 Dec *55431* Washington 19 CHICAGO 23
AFC 30 Dec *74981* Denver 17 PITTSBURGH 24

CHAMPIONSHIP GAMES

NFC 6 Jan *61336* SAN FRANCISCO 23 Chicago 0
AFC 6 Jan *76029* MIAMI 45 Pittsburgh 28

SUPER BOWL

20 Jan *Stanford 84059*
SAN FRANCISCO 38 Miami 16

1985

Record crowds still continued to attend NFL games and on the weekend of October 27–28 a single weekend record of 902657 acquired tickets for the 14 matches. In beating Atlanta in overtime on 10 November, Ron Jaworski threw a massive 99-yard pass to Mike Quick to win the game for Philadelphia.

The Bears equalled the 49ers regular season record of the previous year by winning 15 of their 16 games, and their passage to their first Super Bowl was a fairly easy one. They beat the Giants 21–0 in a divisional play-off game, and then the Rams with another shutout in the NFC Championship Game. In Super Bowl XX they played the New England Patriots who had reached the Bowl as a wild card team and had to play all three post-season games away from home. However, the Pats were no match for the Bears who won a one-sided final that was watched by a television audience of 127 million which thereby ousted the final episode of *M*A*S*H* as the most watched single television programme in the United States. The Bowl was beamed live to 59 countries, by satellite to the *QEII* and was watched by an estimated 300 million Chinese the following day!

AMERICAN CONFERENCE

Eastern Division	W	L	T	%	PF	PA
Miami Dolphins	12	4	0	.750	428	320
New York Jets*	11	5	0	.688	393	264
New England Patriots*	11	5	0	.688	362	290
Indianapolis Colts	5	11	0	.313	320	386
Buffalo Bills	2	14	0	.125	200	381

Central Division	W	L	T	%	PF	PA
Cleveland Browns	8	8	0	.500	287	294
Cincinnati Bengals	7	9	0	.438	441	437
Pittsburgh Steelers	7	9	0	.438	379	355
Houston Oilers	5	11	0	.313	284	412

Western Division	W	L	T	%	PF	PA
Los Angeles Raiders	12	4	0	.750	354	308
Denver Broncos	11	5	0	.688	380	329
Seattle Seahawks	8	8	0	.500	349	303
San Diego Chargers	8	8	0	.500	467	435
Kansas City Chiefs	6	10	0	.375	317	360

NATIONAL CONFERENCE

Eastern Division	W	L	T	%	PF	PA
Dallas Cowboys	10	6	0	.625	357	333
New York Giants*	10	6	0	.625	399	283
Washington Redskins	10	6	0	.625	297	312
Philadelphia Eagles	7	9	0	.438	286	310
St Louis Cardinals	5	11	0	.313	278	414

Central Division	W	L	T	%	PF	PA
Chicago Bears	15	1	0	.938	456	198
Green Bay Packers	8	8	0	.500	337	355
Minnesota Vikings	7	9	0	.438	346	359
Detroit Lions	7	9	0	.438	307	366
Tampa Bay Buccaneers	2	14	0	.125	294	448

Western Division	W	L	T	%	PF	PA
Los Angeles Rams	11	5	0	.688	340	277
San Francisco 49ers*	10	6	0	.625	411	263
New Orleans Saints	5	11	0	.313	294	401
Atlanta Falcons	4	12	0	.250	282	452

WILD CARD GAMES

AFC 28 Dec *75945* New York Jets 14 NEW ENGLAND 26
NFC 29 Dec *75131* N.Y. GIANTS 17 San Francisco 3

DIVISIONAL PLAY-OFFS

NFC 4 Jan *66581* L.A. RAMS 20 Dallas 0
AFC 4 Jan *74667* MIAMI 24 Cleveland 21
NFC 5 Jan *65670* CHICAGO 21 New York Giants 0
AFC 5 Jan *87163* L.A. Raiders 20 NEW ENGLAND 27

CHAMPIONSHIP GAMES

NFC 12 Jan *66030* CHICAGO 24 Los Angeles Rams 0
AFC 12 Jan *75662* Miami 14 NEW ENGLAND 31

SUPER BOWL

26 Jan *New Orleans 73818*
CHICAGO 46 New England 10

1986

The NFL roadshow moved on to London in 1986 with the Bears beating the Cowboys 17–6 in front of over 82000 fans at Wembley Stadium in the first American Bowl. The limited use of instant replays to assist officials came into force and during the regular season 38 decisions were reversed as a result of looking at the action replay evidence.

The Giants and the Bears had identical regular season records, 14–2–0, but the Bears fell at the first hurdle in the post-season games with a home defeat by Washington, one of the NFC wild card entries. Cleveland required overtime to beat the

Chicago Bears quarterback Jim McMahon looks for his receivers – he ran in for two touchdowns himself in Super Bowl XX.

Jets in their divisional play-off in the third longest ever NFL game at 77 minutes two seconds, and in the AFC Championship Game at home to Denver they were involved in another overtime game, only this time they were on the losing end.

Denver lost to the New York Giants in the Super Bowl by 39 points to 20 in a game watched by another six-figure crowd at the Rose Bowl, Pasadena. The victory gave the Giants their first NFL title since 1956. Average attendances topped 60 000 for the second time and attendances in all games, pre-season, regular and post-season, reached 17 million.

AMERICAN CONFERENCE

Eastern Division

	W	L	T	%	PF	PA
New England Patriots	11	5	0	.688	412	307
New York Jets*	10	6	0	.625	364	386
Miami Dolphins	8	8	0	.500	430	405
Buffalo Bills	4	12	0	.250	287	348
Indianapolis Colts	3	13	0	.188	229	400

Central Division

	W	L	T	%	PF	PA
Cleveland Browns	12	4	0	.750	391	310
Cincinnati Bengals	10	6	0	.625	409	394
Pittsburgh Steelers	6	10	0	.375	307	336
Houston Oilers	5	11	0	.313	274	329

Western Division

	W	L	T	%	PF	PA
Denver Broncos	11	5	0	.688	378	327
Kansas City Chiefs*	10	6	0	.625	358	326
Seattle Seahawks	10	6	0	.625	366	293
Los Angeles Raiders	8	8	0	.500	323	346
San Diego Chargers	4	12	0	.250	335	396

NATIONAL CONFERENCE

Eastern Division

	W	L	T	%	PF	PA
New York Giants	14	2	0	.875	371	236
Washington Redskins*	12	4	0	.750	368	296
Dallas Cowboys	7	9	0	.438	346	337
Philadelphia Eagles	5	10	1	.344	256	312
St Louis Cardinals	4	11	1	.281	218	351

Central Division

	W	L	T	%	PF	PA
Chicago Bears	14	2	0	.875	352	187
Minnesota Vikings	9	7	0	.563	398	273
Detroit Lions	5	11	0	.313	277	326
Green Bay Packers	4	12	0	.250	254	418
Tampa Bay Buccaneers	2	14	0	.125	239	473

Western Division

	W	L	T	%	PF	PA
San Francisco 49ers	10	5	1	.656	374	247
Los Angeles Rams*	10	6	0	.625	309	267
Atlanta Falcons	7	8	1	.469	280	280
New Orleans Saints	7	9	0	.438	288	287

WILD CARD GAMES

NFC 28 Dec *54567* WASHINGTON 19 L.A. Rams 7
AFC 28 Dec *75210* NEW YORK JETS 35 Kansas City 15

DIVISIONAL PLAY-OFFS

NFC 3 Jan *65524* Chicago 13 WASHINGTON 27
AFC 3 Jan *79720* CLEVELAND 23 New York Jets 20 (OT)
NFC 4 Jan *75691* N.Y. GIANTS 49 San Francisco 3
AFC 4 Jan *75262* DENVER 22 New England 17

CHAMPIONSHIP GAMES

NFC 11 Jan *76891* N.Y. GIANTS 17 Washington 0
AFC 11 Jan *79973* Cleveland 20 DENVER 23 (OT)

SUPER BOWL

25 Jan *Pasadena 101063*
NEW YORK GIANTS 39 Denver 20

1987

The regular season was reduced from 16 to 15 games as a result of a 24-day players' strike. The games scheduled for the third weekend were cancelled but the show continued over the next three weeks with replacement teams, before regular members returned after their dispute for week seven. The 49ers won their division with a 13–2–0 record and scored 459 points, only to be humbled by wild card team Minnesota in their divisional play-off game. The Washington Redskins clinched a fourth Super Bowl appearance and when they beat Denver 42–10 in another one-sided match, they captured their second title. The Jack Murphy Stadium at San Diego played host to its first Super Bowl.

AMERICAN CONFERENCE

Eastern Division

	W	L	T	%	PF	PA
Indianapolis Colts	9	6	0	.600	300	238
New England Patriots	8	7	0	.533	320	293
Miami Dolphins	8	7	0	.533	362	335
Buffalo Bills	7	8	0	.467	270	305
New York Jets	6	9	0	.400	334	360

Central Division

	W	L	T	%	PF	PA
Cleveland Browns	10	5	0	.667	390	239
Houston Oilers*	9	6	0	.600	345	349
Pittsburgh Steelers	8	7	0	.533	285	299
Cincinnati Bengals	4	11	0	.267	285	370

Western Division

	W	L	T	%	PF	PA
Denver Broncos	10	4	1	.700	379	288
Seattle Seahawks*	9	6	0	.600	371	314
San Diego Chargers	8	7	0	.533	253	317
Los Angeles Raiders	5	10	0	.333	301	289
Kansas City Chiefs	4	11	0	.267	273	388

NATIONAL CONFERENCE

Eastern Division

	W	L	T	%	PF	PA
Washington Redskins	11	4	0	.733	379	285
Dallas Cowboys	7	8	0	.467	340	348
St Louis Cardinals	7	8	0	.467	362	368
Philadelphia Eagles	7	8	0	.467	337	380
New York Giants	6	9	0	.400	280	312

Central Division

	W	L	T	%	PF	PA
Chicago Bears	11	4	0	.733	356	282
Minnesota Vikings*	8	7	0	.533	336	335
Green Bay Packers	5	9	1	.367	255	300

	W	L	T	%	PF	PA
Tampa Bay Buccaneers	4	11	0	.267	286	360
Detroit Lions	4	11	0	.267	269	384

Western Division

	W	L	T	%	PF	PA
San Francisco 49ers	13	2	0	.867	459	253
New Orleans Saints*	12	3	0	.800	422	283
Los Angeles Rams	6	9	0	.400	317	361
Atlanta Falcons	3	12	0	.200	205	436

Regular season reduced to 15 because of players strike

WILD CARD GAMES

NFC 3 Jan *68546* New Orleans 10 MINNESOTA 44
AFC 3 Jan *50519* HOUSTON 23 Seattle 20 (OT)

DIVISIONAL PLAY-OFFS

NFC 9 Jan *63008* San Francisco 24 MINNESOTA 36
AFC 9 Jan *79372* CLEVELAND 38 Indianapolis 21
NFC 10 Jan *65268* Chicago 17 WASHINGTON 21
AFC 10 Jan *75440* DENVER 34 Houston 10

CHAMPIONSHIP GAMES

NFC 17 Jan *55212* WASHINGTON 17 Minnesota 10
AFC 17 Jan *76197* DENVER 38 Cleveland 33

SUPER BOWL

31 Jan *San Diego 73302*
WASHINGTON 42 Denver 10

1988

St Louis became the last team to move its franchise when the Cardinals became known as the Phoenix Cardinals after a move to Arizona. Sweden played host to its first NFL pre-season game as Minnesota beat Chicago 28–21, and the sport's popularity at home was again highlighted when the weekend of October 16–17 drew a record 934 271 spectators at an average of 66 734 for the weekend's 14 games. Buffalo's 622 793 aggregate crowd for their eight home matches also set an NFL record, representing an average of 77 849.

The regular season gave no clues as to the eventual champions but after beating Minnesota 34–9 in their NFC divisional play-off, the 49ers emerged as the likely champions, and so they were, after beating Cincinnati 20–16 in one of the closer Super Bowls of recent years. Super Bowl XXII was the first to be played in Miami's Joe Robbie Stadium. Cincinnati had reversed a previous season 4–11 record to win their division with a 12–4 record. It is the biggest reversal by a team finishing bottom of their division one season and top the next.

AMERICAN CONFERENCE

Eastern Division	W	L	T	%	PF	PA
Buffalo Bills	12	4	0	.750	329	237
Indianapolis Colts	9	7	0	.563	354	315
New England Patriots	9	7	0	.563	250	284
New York Jets	8	7	1	.531	372	354
Miami Dolphins	6	10	0	.375	319	380

Central Division	W	L	T	%	PF	PA
Cincinnati Bengals	12	4	0	.750	448	329
Cleveland Browns*	10	6	0	.625	304	288
Houston Oilers*	10	6	0	.625	424	365
Pittsburgh Steelers	5	11	0	.313	336	421

Western Division	W	L	T	%	PF	PA
Seattle Seahawks	9	7	0	.563	339	329
Denver Broncos	8	8	0	.500	327	352
Los Angeles Raiders	7	9	0	.438	325	369
San Diego Chargers	6	10	0	.375	231	332
Kansas City Chiefs	4	11	1	.281	254	320

NATIONAL CONFERENCE

Eastern Division	W	L	T	%	PF	PA
Philadelphia Eagles	10	6	0	.625	379	319
New York Giants	10	6	0	.625	359	304
Washington Redskins	7	9	0	.438	345	387
Phoenix Cardinals	7	9	0	.438	344	398
Dallas Cowboys	3	13	0	.188	265	381

Central Division	W	L	T	%	PF	PA
Chicago Bears	12	4	0	.750	312	215
Minnesota Vikings*	11	5	0	.688	406	233
Tampa Bay Buccaneers	5	11	0	.313	261	350
Detroit Lions	4	12	0	.250	220	313
Green Bay Packers	4	12	0	.250	240	315

Western Division	W	L	T	%	PF	PA
San Francisco 49ers	10	6	0	.625	369	294
Los Angeles Rams*	10	6	0	.625	407	293
New Orleans Saints	10	6	0	.625	312	283
Atlanta Falcons	5	11	0	.313	244	315

WILD CARD GAMES

NFC 26 Dec *61204* MINNESOTA 28 Los Angeles Rams 17
AFC 26 Dec *75896* Cleveland 23 HOUSTON 24

DIVISIONAL PLAY-OFFS

NFC 31 Dec *65534* CHICAGO 20 Philadelphia 12
AFC 31 Dec *58560* CINCINNATI 21 Seattle 13
NFC 1 Jan *61848* SAN FRANCISCO 34 Minnesota 9
AFC 1 Jan *79532* BUFFALO 17 Houston 10

CHAMPIONSHIP GAMES

NFC 8 Jan *66946* Chicago 3 SAN FRANCISCO 28
AFC 8 Jan *59747* CINCINNATI 21 Buffalo 10

SUPER BOWL

22 Jan *Miami 75 129*
SAN FRANCISCO 20 Cincinnati 16

1989

Pete Rozelle, the NFL commissioner since 1960, announced in March that he was stepping down and eight months later Paul Tagliabue was installed as the League's new commissioner. The Los Angeles Raiders appointed Art Shell as their head coach on 3 October. Shell became the first black head coach in the NFL since Fritz Pollard of the Akron Pros in 1921. Aggregate attendances for the regular season reached a record 13 652 662 at an average of 60 829, also a record. The ten post-season games were watched by average crowds of more than 68 000.

The 49ers were clearly the League's outstanding team and after a 14–2–0 regular season they steamrollered their way to their second successive Super Bowl by beating Minnesota 41–13 and the Rams 30–3 in the Championship Game. The Super Bowl was an even more one-sided affair as they beat Denver 55–10 and became the first team to score fifty points in a Super Bowl. They joined Pittsburgh as the only four-times winners of the championship.

AMERICAN CONFERENCE

Eastern Division	W	L	T	%	PF	PA
Buffalo Bills	9	7	0	.563	409	317
Indianapolis Colts	8	8	0	.500	298	301
Miami Dolphins	8	8	0	.500	331	379
New England Patriots	5	11	0	.313	297	391
New York Jets	4	12	0	.250	253	411

Central Division	W	L	T	%	PF	PA
Cleveland Browns	9	6	1	.594	334	254
Houston Oilers*	9	7	0	.563	365	412
Pittsburgh Steelers*	9	7	0	.563	265	326
Cincinnati Bengals	8	8	0	.500	404	285

Western Division	W	L	T	%	PF	PA
Denver Broncos	11	5	0	.688	362	226
Kansas City Chiefs	8	7	1	.531	318	286
Los Angeles Raiders	8	8	0	.500	315	297
Seattle Seahawks	7	9	0	.438	241	327
San Diego Chargers	6	10	0	.375	266	290

NATIONAL CONFERENCE

Eastern Division	W	L	T	%	PF	PA
New York Giants	12	4	0	.750	348	252
Philadelphia Eagles*	11	5	0	.688	342	274
Washington Redskins	10	6	0	.625	386	308
Phoenix Cardinals	5	11	0	.313	258	377
Dallas Cowboys	1	15	0	.063	204	393

Central Division	W	L	T	%	PF	PA
Minnesota Vikings	10	6	0	.625	351	275
Green Bay Packers	10	6	0	.625	362	356
Detroit Lions	7	9	0	.438	312	364
Chicago Bears	6	10	0	.375	358	377
Tampa Bay Buccaneers	5	11	0	.313	320	419

Western Division	W	L	T	%	PF	PA
San Francisco 49ers	14	2	0	.875	442	253
Los Angeles Rams*	11	5	0	.688	426	344
New Orleans Saints	9	7	0	.563	386	301
Atlanta Falcons	3	13	0	.188	279	437

WILD CARD GAMES

NFC 31 Dec *65 479* Philadelphia 7 L.A. RAMS 21
AFC 31 Dec *59 406* Houston 23 PITTSBURGH 26 (OT)

DIVISIONAL PLAY-OFFS

NFC 6 Jan *64 918* SAN FRANCISCO 41 Minnesota 13
AFC 6 Jan *78 291* CLEVELAND 34 Buffalo 30
NFC 7 Jan *76 256* New York Giants 13 L.A. RAMS 19 (OT)
AFC 7 Jan *75 477* DENVER 24 Pittsburgh 23

CHAMPIONSHIP GAMES

NFC 14 Jan *65 634* SAN FRANCISCO 30 L.A. Rams 3
AFC 14 Jan *76 046* DENVER 37 Cleveland 21

SUPER BOWL

28 Jan *New Orleans 72 919*
SAN FRANCISCO 55 Denver 10

1990

A change in format allowed two extra wild card teams in the play-offs from each Conference. They were joined in the first round play-offs by the divisional champions with the worst records. The Rams and Kansas City played the first ever NFL pre-season game in Germany.

San Francisco again ended their regular season with a 14–2–0 record and after four games every team had won at least one game. The last time that had happened was in 1957. The aggregate regular season attendance rose to another record, 13 959 896, at an average of 62 321.

Despite their impressive record and being hot favourites for the title, the 49ers came unstuck in the NFC Championship Game at home to the

Giants with the New Yorkers winning 15–13. Buffalo, who notched up some high scores in their post-season games including a 51–3 AFC Championship Game win over the Raiders, were beaten in a thrilling Super Bowl which saw their kicker Scott Norwood miss a field goal in the dying seconds that would have given them victory. The Giants won the closest Super Bowl ever by 20 points to 19.

AMERICAN CONFERENCE

Eastern Division	W	L	T	%	PF	PA
Buffalo Bills	13	3	0	.813	428	263
Miami Dolphins*	12	4	0	.750	336	242
Indianapolis Colts	7	9	0	.438	281	353
New York Jets	6	10	0	.375	295	345
New England Patriots	1	15	0	.063	181	446

Central Division	W	L	T	%	PF	PA
Cincinnati Bengals	9	7	0	.563	360	352
Houston Oilers*	9	7	0	.563	405	307
Pittsburgh Steelers	9	7	0	.563	292	240
Cleveland Browns	3	13	0	.188	228	462

Western Division	W	L	T	%	PF	PA
Los Angeles Raiders	12	4	0	.750	337	268
Kansas City Chiefs*	11	5	0	.688	369	257
Seattle Seahawks	9	7	0	.563	306	286
San Diego Chargers	6	10	0	.375	315	281
Denver Broncos	5	11	0	.313	331	374

NATIONAL CONFERENCE

Eastern Division	W	L	T	%	PF	PA
New York Giants	13	3	0	.813	335	211
Philadelphia Eagles*	10	6	0	.625	396	299
Washington Redskins*	10	6	0	.625	381	301
Dallas Cowboys	7	9	0	.438	244	308
Phoenix Cardinals	5	11	0	.313	268	396

Central Division	W	L	T	%	PF	PA
Chicago Bears	11	5	0	.688	348	280
Tampa Bay Buccaneers	6	10	0	.375	264	367
Detroit Lions	6	10	0	.375	373	413
Green Bay Packers	6	10	0	.375	271	347
Minnesota Vikings	6	10	0	.375	351	326

Western Division	W	L	T	%	PF	PA
San Francisco 49ers	14	2	0	.875	353	239
New Orleans Saints*	8	8	0	.500	274	275
Los Angeles Rams	5	11	0	.313	345	412
Atlanta Falcons	5	11	0	.313	348	365

FIRST ROUND PLAY-OFFS

NFC 5 Jan *65 287* Philadelphia 6 WASHINGTON 20
AFC 5 Jan *67 276* MIAMI 17 Kansas City 16
NFC 6 Jan *60 767* CHICAGO 15 New Orleans 6
AFC 6 Jan *60 012* CINCINNATI 41 Houston 14

SECOND ROUND PLAY-OFFS

NFC 12 Jan *65 292* SAN FRANCISCO 28 Washington 10
AFC 12 Jan *77 087* BUFFALO 44 Miami 34
NFC 13 Jan *77 025* N.Y. GIANTS 31 Chicago 3
AFC 13 Jan *92 045* L.A. RAIDERS 20 Cincinnati 10

CHAMPIONSHIP GAMES

NFC 20 Jan *65 750* San Francisco 13 N.Y. GIANTS 15
AFC 20 Jan *80 325* BUFFALO 51 L.A. Raiders 3

SUPER BOWL

27 Jan *Tampa 73 813*
NEW YORK GIANTS 20 Buffalo 19

1991

The NFL branched out from its traditional American roots with the launch of its World League of American Football on 23 March. As well as its US bases, the game was played in Frankfurt, London and Barcelona, and the London Monarchs captured the first title.

When the Miami Dolphins beat Green Bay 16–13 on 22 September it gave Don Shula his 300th win as a coach and he became only the second man after George Halas (Chicago) to register 300 wins.

The Washington Redskins had the best regular season record (14–2–0) in capturing the NFC Eastern title. Buffalo had the next best record (13–3–0) in taking the AFC Eastern title and both teams continued their winning ways through the play-offs before meeting in Super Bowl XXVI watched by an estimated television audience of 120 million and 63 130 fans at the Minneapolis Metrodome. Washington won 37–24 after a scoreless first quarter. Their 17 points in the second quarter set up their third title.

AMERICAN CONFERENCE

Eastern Division	W	L	T	%	PF	PA
Buffalo Bills	13	3	0	.813	458	318
New York Jets*	8	8	0	.500	314	293
Miami Dolphins	8	8	0	.500	343	349
New England Patriots	6	10	0	.375	211	305
Indianapolis Colts	1	15	0	.063	143	381

Central Division	W	L	T	%	PF	PA
Houston Oilers	11	5	0	.688	386	251
Pittsburgh Steelers	7	9	0	.438	292	344
Cleveland Browns	6	10	0	.375	293	298
Cincinnati Bengals	3	13	0	.188	263	435

Western Division

	W	L	T	%	PF	PA
Denver Broncos	12	4	0	.750	304	235
Kansas City Chiefs*	10	6	0	.625	322	252
Los Angeles Raiders*	9	7	0	.563	298	297
Seattle Seahawks	7	9	0	.438	276	261
San Diego Chargers	4	12	0	.250	274	342

NATIONAL CONFERENCE

Eastern Division	W	L	T	%	PF	PA
Washington Redskins	14	2	0	.875	485	224
Dallas Cowboys*	11	5	0	.688	342	310
Philadelphia Eagles	10	6	0	.625	285	244
New York Giants	8	8	0	.500	281	297
Phoenix Cardinals	4	12	0	.250	196	344

Central Division						
Detroit Lions	12	4	0	.750	339	295
Chicago Bears*	11	5	0	.688	299	269
Minnesota Vikings	8	8	0	.500	301	306
Green Bay Packers	4	12	0	.250	273	313
Tampa Bay Buccaneers	3	13	0	.188	199	365

Western Division						
New Orleans Saints	11	5	0	.688	341	211
Atlanta Falcons*	10	6	0	.625	361	338
San Francisco 49ers	10	6	0	.625	393	239
Los Angeles Rams	3	13	0	.188	234	390

FIRST ROUND PLAY-OFFS

AFC 28 Dec *75827* KANSAS CITY 10 L.A. Raiders 6
NFC 28 Dec *68794* New Orleans 20 ATLANTA 27
AFC 29 Dec *61485* HOUSTON 17 New York Jets 10
NFC 29 Dec *62594* Chicago 13 DALLAS 17

DIVISIONAL PLAY-OFFS

AFC 4 Jan *75301* DENVER 26 Houston 24
NFC 4 Jan *55181* WASHINGTON 24 Atlanta 7
AFC 5 Jan *80182* BUFFALO 37 Kansas City 14
NFC 5 Jan *79835* DETROIT 38 Dallas 6

CHAMPIONSHIP GAMES

AFC 12 Jan *80272* BUFFALO 10 Denver 7
NFC 12 Jan *55585* WASHINGTON 41 Detroit 10

SUPER BOWL

26 Jan *Minneapolis 63130*
WASHINGTON 37 Buffalo 24

Below *Quarterback Jim Kelly's outstanding form in 1991 helped Buffalo to another Super Bowl only to desert him in Minneapolis.*

THE SUPER BOWL

The Super Bowl was inaugurated in 1967 when it was decided that the winners of the NFL championship would meet the AFL champions in what the NFL labelled the World Championship of Professional Football. Lamar Hunt, the Kansas City Chiefs' owner, and various sections of the media immediately dubbed it the Super Bowl, but it was a couple of years before the NFL officially recognised this as the game's title.

The Super Bowl is held at the end of January each year and the winning team receive a copy of the Vince Lombardi Trophy which they are allowed to retain. The trophy, named after the coach of the first champions, Green Bay, is made of sterling silver, stands 20 inches high and weighs approximately seven pounds. It depicts a regulation size football. Winning players receive rings instead of medals as presented in most other sports. A Super Bowl ring is the sport's most cherished possession.

1967

SUPER BOWL I
15 January
Memorial Coliseum,
Los Angeles
61 946
MVP: Bart Starr
(Green Bay / quarterback)

On a warm January Los Angeles day, teams from the AFL and NFL met for the first time to do battle for the first World Championship of Professional Football. It seemed strange at first seeing teams from two opposing leagues facing each other but the 61 000 fans soon put that out of their minds as battle commenced.

Max McGee opened the scoring for Green Bay, the favourites, as he took a 37-yard pass from MVP Bart Starr. McGee came into the side as a replacement for the injured Boyd Dowler and during the regular season took only three passes. Now he had opened the scoring in the first Super Bowl and, furthermore, he was to go on and make seven successful catches.

The Packers finished the first quarter 7–0 in front and seemed to be well on their way to a big victory, such was their superiority. But the Chiefs were not overawed and came back thanks to quarterback Dawson who pierced the Packers' defense to put McClinton in for the equalising touchdown. Green Bay reasserted their advantage with a Taylor touchdown after a 14-yard rush before Mercer's 31-yard field goal brought it back to 14–10 at half-time.

But that was it as far as the Chiefs were concerned. And

when Willie Wood returned 50 yards on an interception to set up Elijah Pitts' five-yard rush for another touchdown, it was all over. McGee and Pitts each scored further touchdowns as the Packers ran out comfortable 35–10 winners.

Left *Action from the first ever Super Bowl – over 60 000 attended but the Coliseum was just two-thirds full.*

THE TEAMS

GREEN BAY PACKERS (NFL)
35 – 7 7 14 7
T: McGee 2, Pitts 2, Taylor
PA: Chandler 5
Starting Line Up:
OFFENSE: Curry, Dale, Dowler, Fleming, Gregg, Kramer, E Pitts, Skoronski, Starr, J Taylor, Thurston
Substitutes: B Anderson, D Anderson, Bowman, Bratkowski, Gillingham, Grabowski, Long, Mack, McGee, Vandersea, Wright
DEFENSE: Adderley, Aldridge, T Brown, Coffey, Davis, Jeter, Jordan, Kostelnik, Nitschke, D Robinson, Wood
Substitutes: B Brown, Crutcher, Hart, Heathcock, Weatherwax
KICKER: Chandler

KANSAS CITY CHIEFS (AFL)
10 – 0 10 0 0
T: McClinton
FG: Mercer
PA: Mercer
Starting Line Up:
OFFENSE: Arbanas, Budde, Burford, Dawson, Frazier, Garrett, Hill, McClinton, Merz, O Taylor, Tyrer
Substitutes: Beathard, Biodrowski, Carolan, Coan, DiMidio, Gilliam, F Pitts, Reynolds, G Thomas
DEFENSE: Bell, Buchanan, Headrick, Holub, Hunt, Hurston, Mays, Mitchell, Rice, J Robinson, Williamson
Substitutes: Abell, A Brown, Corey, Ply, Smith, Stover, E Thomas
KICKERS: Mercer, Wilson

PLAYERS' STATISTICS

Kansas City   Green Bay

RUSHING

	No	Yds	Avge		No	Yds	Avge
Dawson	3	24	8.0	Taylor	16	53	3.3
Garrett	6	17	2.8	Pitts	11	45	4.1
McClinton	6	16	2.7	D Anderson	4	30	7.5
Beathard	1	14	14.0	Grabowski	2	2	1.0
Coan	3	1	0.3				

RECEIVING

	No	Yds	Avge		No	Yds	Avge
Burford	4	67	16.8	McGee	7	138	19.7
Taylor	4	57	14.3	Dale	4	59	14.8
Garrett	3	28	9.3	Pitts	2	32	16.0
McClinton	2	34	17.0	Fleming	2	22	11.0
Arbanas	2	30	15.0	Taylor	1	−1	−1.0
Carolan	1	7	7.0				
Coan	1	5	5.0				

PASSING

	Att	Comp	Comp %	Yds	Yds Int	Yds Att.	Yds Comp.
Kansas City							
Dawson	27	16	59.3	211	1	7.8	13.2
Beathard	5	1	20.0	17	0	3.4	17.0
Green Bay							
Starr	23	16	69.6	250	1	10.9	15.6
Bratkowski	1	0	0.0	0	0	–	–

Key *T=Touchdown PA=Point After FG= Field Goal No=Number Att=Attempts Comp=Completions Int=Intercepted Yds Att.=Yards average per attempt Yds Comp.=Yards average per completion*

1968

SUPER BOWL II
14 January
Orange Bowl, Miami
75 546
MVP: Bart Starr
(Green Bay/quarterback)

Super Bowl II was Vince Lombardi's last game as the Packers coach and the players wanted to give him the send-off he deserved. After all, in the nine years he had been in charge he had turned Green Bay from annual losers into the most feared team in the NFL.

The Raiders started the game looking stiffer opponents than Kansas City a year earlier, particularly after their thrashing of Houston for the AFL title. But in the Super Bowl they made too many basic errors and Green Bay capitalised. However, the only score of the first quarter was Don Chandler's 39-yard field goal.

The Packers went 6–0 ahead after a further Chandler field goal in the second quarter but then the Raiders made their first major mistake when their defense left Boyd Dowler unmarked and he took a 62-yard Starr pass for a touchdown. Chandler made the kick and the Packers had a 13–0 lead. Daryle Lamonica found Bill Miller with a 25-yard touchdown pass to give Oakland their first score but another Chandler field goal gave the Packers a 16–7 halftime lead.

A two-yard rush by Anderson then increased Green Bay's lead still further and Chandler's fourth field goal saw the Packers go into the final quarter with a healthy 26–7 lead. They sealed it when Herb Adderley returned a 60-yard interception for a touchdown. Miller scored a consolation touchdown for Oakland. Bart Starr, who completed 13 of 24 passes for 202 yards, was again the MVP as he and his colleagues made sure Vince Lombardi went out of the game on a winning note.

THE TEAMS

GREEN BAY PACKERS (NFL)
33 – 3 13 10 7
T: Dowler, Anderson, Adderley
FG: Chandler 4
PA: Chandler 3
Starting Line Up:
OFFENSE: Anderson, Bowman, Dale, Dowler, Fleming, Gregg, Gillingham, Kramer, Skoronski, Starr, Wilson
Substitutes: Bratkowski, Capp, Hyland, Long, McGee, Mercein, Thurston, T Williams
DEFENSE: Adderley, Aldridge, T Brown, Caffey, Davis, Jeter, Jordan, Kostelnik, Nitschke, Robinson, Wood
Substitutes: B Brown, Crutcher, Flanigan, Hart, Rowser, Weatherwax
KICKER: Chandler

OAKLAND RAIDERS (AFL)
14 – 0 7 0 7
T: Miller 2
PA: Blander 2
Starting Line Up:
OFFENSE: Banaszak, Biletnikoff, Cannon, Dixon, Hawkins, Lamonica, Miller, J Otto, Schuh, Svihus, Upshaw
Substitutes: Archer, Hagberg, Harvey, Herock, Kocourek, Kruse, Todd, Wells
DEFENSE: Birdwell, W Brown, Connors, Davidson, Keating, Lassiter, Laskey, McCloughan, G Otto, Powers, H Williams
Substitutes: Bird, Benson, Budness, Grayson, Oates, Sligh, Williamson
KICKERS: Blander, Eischeid

PLAYERS' STATISTICS

Green Bay   **Oakland**

RUSHING

	No	Yds	Avge		No	Yds	Avge
Wilson	17	62	3.6	Dixon	12	54	4.5
Anderson	14	48	3.4	Todd	2	37	18.5
Williams	8	36	4.5	Banaszak	6	16	2.7
Starr	1	14	14.0				
Mercein	1	0	0.0				

RECEIVING

	No	Yds	Avge		No	Yds	Avge
Dale	4	43	10.8	Miller	5	84	16.8
Fleming	4	35	8.8	Banaszak	4	69	17.3
Dowler	2	71	35.5	Cannon	2	25	12.5
Anderson	2	18	9.0	Biletnikoff	2	10	5.0
McGee	1	35	35.0	Wells	1	17	17.0
				Dixon	1	3	3.0

PASSING

	Att	Comp	Comp %	Yds	Int	Yds Att.	Yds Comp.
Green Bay							
Starr	24	13	54.2	202	0	8.4	15.5
Oakland							
Lamonica	34	15	44.1	208	1	6.1	13.9

1969

SUPER BOWL III
12 January
Orange Bowl, Miami
75 389
MVP: Joe Namath
(New York Jets/quarterback)

With the NFL having won the first two Super Bowls, there was little to suggest that the Baltimore Colts would not make it three in a row in 1969. But when New York Jets quarterback Joe Namath announced on the Thursday before the game, 'I think we'll win it; in fact I'll guarantee it,' football fans stopped and wondered.

The Colts, coached by Don Shula, had a well-marshalled defense, and with Earl Morrall coming in as mid-season quarterback for the injured Johnny Unitas, their offense was quite capable of overcoming the best that could be thrown at it and they had lost just once in 16 games all season.

The Colts had the better of the first quarter but did everything except score. Even Lou Michaels missed a close-range field goal. Their frustration got worse in the second quarter when Morrall missed the opportunity of throwing a touchdown pass to Jimmy Orr in the end zone. Not seeing him, he threw a pass to New York's Jim Hudson instead.

Namath, on the other hand, was the inspiration behind the Jets' plays and he led them on an 80-yard drive in 12 plays which resulted in Snell carrying the ball into the end zone for the opening score. Turner kicked the point after. Two Turner field goals for the Jets were the only third-quarter scores as Namath continued to grind the Colts defense down.

A third Turner field goal after one minute 34 seconds of the final quarter put the Jets in front by 16 points to nil. With a little over three minutes of the match remaining Baltimore's Hill went in for a one-yard rush after Unitas, on for the last quarter, tried to get the Colts back into the game. But it was too late; the AFL registered their first Super Bowl win.

THE TEAMS

NEW YORK JETS (AFL)
16 – 0 7 6 3
T: Snell
FG: Turner 3
PA: Turner
Starting Line Up:
OFFENSE: Boozer, Herman, W Hill, Lammons, Maynard, Namath, Rasmussen, Sauer, Schmitt, Snell, Talamini
Substitutes: Crane, Mathis, Parilli, Rademacher, J Richardson, Smolinski, B Turner, Walton
DEFENSE: Atkinson, Baird, Baker, Beverly, Biggs, Elliot, Grantham, Hudson, Philbin, Rochester, Sample
Substitutes: Christy, D'Amato, Dockery, Gordon, McAdams, Neidert, Richards, Thompson
KICKERS: Johnson, J Turner

BALTIMORE COLTS (NFL)
7 – 0 0 0 7
T: Hill
PA: Michaels
Starting Line Up:
OFFENSE: Ball, Curry, J Hill, Mackey, Matte, Morrall, Orr, Ressler, W Richardson, Sullivan, Vogel
Substitutes: Brown, Cole, Hawkins, Johnson, Mitchell, Pearson, Perkins, Szymanski, Unitas, J Williams
DEFENSE: Boyd, Braase, Curtis, Gaubatz, Logan, Lyles, Miller, Shinnick, B Smith, BR Smith, Volk
Substitutes: Austin, Hilton, Michaels, Porter, Stukes, S Williams
KICKER: Lee

PLAYERS' STATISTICS

New York Jets   Baltimore

RUSHING

	No	Yds	Avge		No	Yds	Avge
Snell	30	121	4.0	Matte	11	116	10.5
Boozer	10	19	1.9	Hill	9	29	3.2
Mathis	3	2	0.7	Unitas	1	0	0.0
				Morrall	2	−2	−1.0

RECEIVING

	No	Yds	Avge		No	Yds	Avge
Sauer	8	133	16.6	Richardson	6	58	9.7
Snell	4	40	10.0	Orr	3	42	14.0
Mathis	3	20	6.7	Mackey	3	35	11.7
Lammons	2	13	6.5	Matte	2	30	15.0
				Hill	2	1	0.5
				Mitchell	1	15	15.0

PASSING

New York Jets	Att	Comp	Comp %	Yds	Int	Yds Att.	Yds Comp.
Namath	28	17	60.7	206	0	7.4	12.1
Parilli	1	0	0.0	0	0	–	–
Baltimore							
Morrall	17	6	35.3	71	3	4.2	11.8
Unitas	24	11	45.8	110	1	4.6	10.0

1970

SUPER BOWL IV
11 January
Tulane Stadium,
New Orleans
80 562
MVP: Len Dawson
(Kansas City / quarterback)

This game effectively was the last between AFL and NFL teams because the following season the two leagues would be integrated as one. And the Chiefs, beaten in Super Bowl I, took the AFL out in style with an easy win over Minnesota who had started as the favourites to take the title back for the NFL. Their defense had steamrollered its way to the NFL title but the Chiefs were not going to succumb like Minnesota's other opponents.

Kansas City's 'I' formation posed the Vikings problems right from the start and the Kansas City defense pressurised the Vikings' quarterback Joe Kapp. The only score of the first quarter came from the Chiefs from Jan Stenerud's 48-yard field goal. Two more field goals from the boot of Stenerud and a Garrett touchdown from a five-yard rush, successfully kicked by Stenerud, gave the Chiefs a 16–0 lead at the interval.

The Vikings started the second half with a new found determination and Kapp led them on a 69-yard drive which resulted in Osborn scoring their first touchdown. However, they were struggling to gain yardage with their rushes and compared to their 222 yards in the Championship Game against Cleveland, they could now manage only 67. They failed to add to their score after Cox's point after, and Otis Taylor scored a touchdown for the Chiefs by taking a 46-yard pass from Dawson. He became the fourth consecutive quarterback to win the MVP award as Kansas City ran out the winners and levelled the series for the AFL.

THE TEAMS

KANSAS CITY CHIEFS (AFL)
23 – 3 13 7 0
T: Garrett, Taylor
FG: Stenerud 3
PA: Stenerud 2
Starting Line Up:
OFFENSE: Arbanas, Budde, Dawson, Garrett, Hill, Holmes, Holub, Moorman, Pitts, Taylor, Tyrer
Substitutes: Daney, Hayes, Livingston, McClinton, McVea, Podalak, Prudhomme, Richardson
DEFENSE: Bell, A Brown, Buchanan, Culp, Kearney, Lanier, Lynch, Marsalis, Mays, Robinson, Thomas
Substitutes: Belser, Hurston, Lothamer, Mitchell, Sellers, Stein, Trosch
KICKERS: Stenerud, Wilson

MINNESOTA VIKINGS (NFL)
7 – 0 0 7 0
T: Osborn
PA: Cox
Starting Line Up:
OFFENSE: Alderman, Beasley, B Brown, Henderson, Kapp, Osborn, Sunde, Tingelhoff, Vellone, Washington, Yary
Substitutes: Cuozzo, Grim, Harris, Jones, Kramer, Lee, Lindsey, Reed, Smith, White
DEFENSE: Eller, Hilgenberg, Kassulke, Krause, Larsen, Mackbee, Marshall, Page, Sharockman, Winston, Warwick
Substitutes: Dickson, Hackbart, Hargrove, McGill, West
KICKER: Cox

PLAYERS' STATISTICS

Kansas City   **Minnesota**

RUSHING

	No	Yds	Avge		No	Yds	Avge
Garrett	11	39	3.5	Brown	6	26	4.3
Pitts	3	37	12.3	Reed	4	17	4.3
Hayes	8	31	3.9	Osborn	7	15	2.1
McVea	12	26	2.2	Kapp	2	9	4.5
Dawson	3	11	3.7				
Holmes	5	7	1.4				

RECEIVING

	No	Yds	Avge		No	Yds	Avge
Taylor	6	81	3.5	Henderson	7	111	15.9
Pitts	3	33	11.0	Brown	3	11	3.7
Garrett	2	25	12.5	Beasley	2	41	20.5
Hayes	1	3	3.0	Reed	2	16	8.0
				Osborn	2	11	5.5
				Washington	1	9	9.0

PASSING

Kansas City	Att	Comp	Comp %	Yds	Int	Yds Att.	Yds Comp.
Dawson	17	12	70.6	142	1	8.4	11.8
Minnesota							
Kapp	25	16	64.0	183	2	7.3	11.4
Cuozzo	3	1	33.3	16	1	5.3	16.0

1971

SUPER BOWL V
17 January
Orange Bowl, Miami
79 204
MVP: Chuck Howley
(Dallas/linebacker)

This was the first Super Bowl after the merger of the AFL and NFL and what drama it produced. Both sides endured a series of turnovers during the 60 minutes play, but the eventual outcome made it the closest Super Bowl thus far.

The defenses dominated the first quarter with a Mike Clark 14-yard field goal for Dallas being the only score. A 30-yarder from Clark made it 6–0 before Mackey took a 75-yard pass from Unitas to bring the Colts level. O'Brien's kick was blocked.

Johnny Unitas was put out of the game on Baltimore's next offensive run after fumbling on his own 29-yard line. Bruised ribs resulted and he had to leave the field. From that Duane Thomas took a seven-yard pass from Dallas quarterback Craig Morton, who continued playing despite a sore arm, as the Cowboys regained the lead.

The third quarter remained scoreless as the so called 'comedy of errors' continued with firstly Jim Duncan and then Duane Thomas fumbling. As the game went into the final eight minutes the Cowboys still held their 13–6 lead, but then a pass from Dallas quarterback Morton bounced off the fingers of fullback Garrison and into the hands of the Colts' safety Rick Volk. His return led to Tom Nowatzke rushing into the end zone from two yards. O'Brien made the kick and suddenly the scores were level, 13–13.

With overtime looming an-

THE TEAMS

BALTIMORE COLTS (AFC)
16 – 0 6 0 10
T: Mackey, Nowatzke
FG: O'Brien
PA: O'Brien
Starting Line Up:
OFFENSE: Bulaich, Curry, Hinton, Jefferson, Mackey, Nowatzke, Ressler, Sullivan, Unitas, Vogle, Williams
Substitutes: Bell, Goode, Havrilak, J Hill, Johnson, Maitland, Mitchell, Morrall, Perkins
DEFENSE: Curtis, Duncan, Hendricks, Hilton, Logan, May, Miller, B Smith, BR Smith, Stukes, Volk
Substitutes: Gardin, Grant, Maxwell, Newsome, Nichols
KICKERS: O'Brien, Lee

DALLAS COWBOYS (NFC)
13 – 3 10 0 0
T: Thomas
FG: Clark 2
PA: Clark
Starting Line Up:
OFFENSE: Garrison, Hayes, Manders, Morton, Neely, Niland, Norman, Nye, Rucker, Thomas, Wright
Substitutes: Asher, Ditka, C Hill, Homan, Reeves, Welch
DEFENSE: Adderley, Andrie, Cole, Edwards, Green, Howley, Jordan, Lilly, Pugh, Renfro, Waters
Substitutes: East, Flowers, Harris, Kiner, Lewis, Stincic, Toomay, Washington
KICKERS: Clark, Widby

PLAYERS' STATISTICS

Baltimore   Dallas

RUSHING

	No	Yds	Avge		No	Yds	Avge
Nowatzke	10	33	3.3	Garrison	12	65	5.4
Bulaich	18	28	1.6	Thomas	18	35	1.9
Unitas	1	4	4.0	Morton	1	2	2.0
Havrilak	1	3	3.0				
Morrall	1	1	1.0				

RECEIVING

	No	Yds	Avge		No	Yds	Avge
Jefferson	3	52	17.3	Reeves	5	46	9.2
Mackey	2	80	40.0	Thomas	4	21	5.3
Hinton	2	51	25.5	Garrison	2	19	9.5
Havrilak	2	27	13.5	Hayes	1	41	41.0
Nowatzke	1	45	45.0				
Bulaich	1	5	5.0				

PASSING

Baltimore	Att	Comp	Comp %	Yds	Int	Yds Att.	Yds Comp.
Morrall	15	7	46.7	147	1	9.8	21.0
Unitas	9	3	33.3	88	2	9.8	29.3
Havrilak	1	1	100.0	25	0	25.0	25.0
Dallas							
Morton	26	12	46.2	127	3	4.9	10.6

other Morton pass was intercepted by Mike Curtis on the 41-yard line with one minute nine seconds remaining. Curtis returned it to the 28 and after two running plays brought the clock down, Baltimore's rookie kicker Jim O'Brien converted a 32-yard field goal and secured victory by 16 points to 13. Chuck Howley, who intercepted two passes, became the first defensive player, and the first from a losing team, to win the MVP award.

1972

SUPER BOWL VI
16 January
Tulane Stadium,
New Orleans
81023
*MVP: Roger Staubach
(Dallas/ quarterback)*

Since Roger Staubach replaced Craig Morton midway through the 1971 season, the Cowboys had gone seven regular season and two post-season games without defeat. They were therefore confident of avenging their defeat in Super Bowl V.

Facing Dallas were Don Shula's young Miami Dolphins team and their inexperience showed in the first quarter when fullback Larry Csonka made a mess of a hand-off from quarterback Bob Griese. The error eventually led to the first quarter's opening score, a field goal from Dallas kicker Mike Clark.

The Cowboys increased their lead when Lance Alworth took a seven-yard touchdown pass from Staubach after a long drive. Clark kicked for the extra point before Garo Yepremian reduced the arrears close to half-time with a 31-yard field goal.

The Cowboys managed to retain possession cleverly from the second half kick-off and it resulted in a three-yard run by Duane Thomas for a touchdown after a 71-yard drive. Clark again made the kick and it was the only score of the third quarter.

It was a similar story in the final quarter with Staubach throwing a seven-yard pass to Mike Ditka in the end zone.

Clark made the extra point and Dallas ran out 24–3 winners. The Cowboys set a Super Bowl record by rushing for 252 yards.

In their 69 plays, Dallas ran for 352 yards while Miami made a Super Bowl low 185 yards from their 44 plays.

THE TEAMS

DALLAS COWBOYS (NFC)
24 – 3 7 7 7
T: Alworth, D Thomas, Ditka
FG: Clark
PA: Clark 3
Starting Line Up:
OFFENSE: Alworth, Ditka, Garrison, Hayes, Liscio, Manders, Niland, Nye, Staubach, D Thomas, Wright
Substitutes: Fitzgerald, Hill, Reeves, Truax, Welch, Williams
DEFENSE: Adderley, Andrie, L Cole, Edwards, Green, Harris, Harley, Jordan, Lillie, Pugh, Renfro
Substitutes: Gregory, Lewis, Smith, Stincic, I Thomas, Toomay, Waters
KICKERS: Clark, Widby

MIAMI DOLPHINS (AFC)
3 – 0 3 0 0
FG: Yepremian
Starting Line Up:
OFFENSE: Csonka, Crusan, DeMarco, Evans, Fleming, Griese, Kiick, Kuechenberg, Little, Twilley, Warfield
Substitutes: T Cole, Ginn, Langer, Mandich, Moore, Morris, Noonan, Stowe
DEFENSE: Anderson, Buoniconti, Fernandez, Foley, Heinz, Johnson, Kolen, Riley, Scott, Stanfill, Swift
Substitutes: Cornish, Den Herder, Matheson, Mumphord, Petrella, Powell
KICKERS: Yepremian, Seiple

PLAYERS' STATISTICS

Dallas | | | | Miami | | |

RUSHING

	No	Yds	Avge		No	Yds	Avge
D Thomas	19	95	5.0	Csonka	9	40	4.4
Garrison	14	74	5.3	Kiick	10	40	4.0
Hill	7	25	3.6	Griese	1	0	0.0
Staubach	5	18	3.6				
Ditka	1	17	17.0				
Hayes	1	16	16.0				
Reeves	1	7	7.0				

RECEIVING

	No	Yds	Avge		No	Yds	Avge
D Thomas	3	17	5.7	Warfield	4	39	9.8
Alworth	2	28	14.0	Kiick	3	21	7.0
Ditka	2	28	14.0	Csonka	2	18	9.0
Hayes	2	23	11.5	Fleming	1	27	27.0
Garrison	2	11	5.5	Twilley	1	20	20.0
Hill	1	12	12.0	Mandich	1	9	9.0

PASSING

Dallas	Att	Comp	Comp %	Yds	Int	Yds Att.	Yds Comp.
Staubach	19	12	63.2	119	0	6.3	9.9
Miami							
Griese	23	12	52.2	134	1	5.8	11.2

1973

SUPER BOWL VII
14 January
Memorial Coliseum,
Los Angeles
90 182
MVP: Jake Scott (Miami/ safety)

Miami went into their second successive Super Bowl having won all 14 regular season games and both their post-season games. They were keen to end the season with a 17–0–0 record and only the Washington Redskins stood between them and that goal. Don Shula's team had matured vastly in the 12 months since their defeat in Super Bowl VI, and had well drilled teams in both offense and defense.

It was the defense which thwarted the Washington running-plays right from the start. The opening score came late in the first period when Howard Twilley took a 28-yard pass from Bob Griese to put Miami on the scoreboard first. Garo Yepremian made the kick and the Dolphins led 7–0 after the first quarter. They added another seven points late in the second quarter, when Jim Kiick wound up a long drive by going over from one yard. Yepremian made the kick again and at half-time the Dolphins led 14–0.

Washington had the most possession at the start of the second half and were gradually getting into the game. But when Curt Knight missed a relatively easy 32-yard field goal, the Dolphins regained possession. There was no scoring in the third quarter and the final quarter looked like going the same way.

But with two minutes of the game left, Miami's Yepremian attempted a 42-yard field goal. His kick was blocked, and when the ball bounced back to him he didn't know what to do with it and his attempted pass was intercepted by Mike Bass who ran over from 49 yards for the Redskins only touchdown, Knight making the point after. But the scoring ended there and the Dolphins achieved their aim of going through the season with a one hundred per cent record.

THE TEAMS

MIAMI DOLPHINS (AFC)
14 – 7 7 0 0
T: Twilley, Kiick
PA: Yepremian 2
Starting Line Up:
OFFENSE: Csonka, Evans, Fleming, Griese, Kiick, Kuechenberg, Langer, Little, W Moore, Twilley, Warfield
Substitutes: Briscoe, Crusan, Ginn, Jenkins, Kindig, Leigh, Mandich, Morrall, Morris
DEFENSE: Anderson, Buoniconti, Den Herder, Fernandez, Heinz, Johnson, Kolen, Mumphord, Scott, Stanfill, Swift
Substitutes: Babb, Ball, Matheson, M Moore, Powell, Stuckey
KICKERS: Seiple, Yepremian

WASHINGTON REDSKINS (NFC)
7 – 0 0 0 7
T: Bass
PA: Knight
Starting Line Up:
OFFENSE: Brown, Harraway, Hauss, Hermeling, Jefferson, Kilmer, Laaveg, Rock, Smith, C Taylor, Wilbur
Substitutes: Alston, Brunet, Burman, Hull, McNeil, Mul-Key, Wyche
DEFENSE: Bass, Biggs, Brundige, Fischer, Hanburger, McDole, Owens, Pardee, Pottios, Talbert, R Taylor
Substitutes: Fanucci, Haymond, Jaqua, McLinton, Severson, Sistrunk, Tillman, Vactor
KICKERS: Bragg, Knight

PLAYERS' STATISTICS

Miami   Washington

RUSHING

	No	Yds	Avge		No	Yds	Avge
Csonka	15	112	7.5	Brown	22	72	3.3
Kiick	12	38	3.2	Harraway	10	37	3.7
Morris	10	34	3.4	Kilmer	2	18	9.0
				Taylor	1	8	8.0
				Smith	1	6	6.0

RECEIVING

	No	Yds	Avge		No	Yds	Avge
Warfield	3	36	12.0	Jefferson	5	50	10.0
Kiick	2	6	3.0	Brown	5	26	5.2
Twilley	1	28	28.0	Taylor	2	20	10.0
Mandich	1	19	19.0	Smith	1	11	11.0
Csonka	1	–1	–1.0	Harraway	1	–3	–3.0

PASSING

	Att	Comp	Comp %	Yds	Int	Yds Att.	Yds Comp.
Miami							
Griese	11	8	72.7	88	1	8.0	11.0
Washington							
Kilmer	28	14	50.0	104	3	3.7	7.4

1974

SUPER BOWL VIII
13 January
Rice Stadium, Houston
71882
*MVP: Larry Csonka
(Miami/running back)*

While it was not to be another unbeaten season, the Dolphins played as though they were invincible in their third successive Super Bowl as they emulated the Packers by winning it back-to-back.

They set up their victory with two touchdowns, after drives of 62 and 56 yards, in the first quarter. The first was scored by Larry Csonka, the game's MVP, who went over after a five-yard run, and the second by Jim Kiick, who scored from one yard out. It was Kiick's first score all season. The Minnesota quarterback Fran Tarkenton could make no impression against the strong Miami defense and the only score of the second quarter was Garo Yepremian's 28-yard field goal to increase the Dolphins' halfway lead to 17–0.

Midway through the third quarter the Dolphins scored their third touchdown when Csonka went over for the second time after a two-yard rush and Yepremian's kick gave them an unassailable 24–0 lead. Fran Tarkenton went over for the Vikings' only score, which Cox converted, but it was too late to prevent a second successive victory for Don Shula and his men. MVP Csonka rushed for a Super Bowl record 145 yards.

THE TEAMS

MIAMI DOLPHINS (AFC)
24 – 14 3 7 0
T: Csonka 2, Kiick
FG: Yepremian
PA: Yepremian 3
Starting Line Up:
OFFENSE: Briscoe, Csonka, Evans, Griese, Kuechenberg, Langer, Little, Mandich, W Moore, Morris, Warfield
Substitutes: Crusan, Fleming, Goode, Kiick, Morrall, Newman, Nottingham, Twilley
DEFENSE: Anderson, Buoniconti, Fernandez, Heinz, Den Herder, Johnson, Kolen, Mumphord, Scott, Stanfill, Swift
Substitutes: Babb, Ball, Bannon, Foley, Matheson, M Moore, Stuckey
KICKERS: Seiple, Yepremian

MINNESOTA VIKINGS (NFC)
7 – 0 0 0 7
T: Tarkenton
PA: Cox
Starting Line Up:
OFFENSE: Alderman, Dale, Foreman, Gallagher, Gilliam, Reed, Tarkenton, Tingelhoff, Voigt, White, Yary
Substitutes: B Brown, Goodrum, Kingsriter, Lash, Marinaro, Osborn
DEFENSE: Bryant, Eller, Hilgenberg, Krause, Larsen, Marshall, Page, Siemon, Winston, N Wright, J Wright
Substitutes: T Brown, Lurtsema, Martin, Porter, Sutherland, West
KICKERS: Cox, Eischeid

PLAYERS' STATISTICS

Miami   Minnesota

RUSHING

	No	Yds	Avge		No	Yds	Avge
Csonka	33	145	4.4	Reed	11	32	2.9
Morris	11	34	3.1	Foreman	7	18	2.6
Kiick	7	10	1.4	Tarkenton	4	17	4.3
Griese	2	7	3.5	Marinaro	1	3	3.0
				B Brown	1	2	2.0

RECEIVING

	No	Yds	Avge		No	Yds	Avge
Warfield	2	33	16.5	Foreman	5	27	5.4
Mandich	2	21	10.5	Gilliam	4	44	11.0
Briscoe	2	19	9.5	Voigt	3	46	15.3
				Marinaro	2	39	19.5
				B Brown	1	9	9.0
				Kingsriter	1	9	9.0
				Lash	1	9	9.0
				Reed	1	−1	−1.0

PASSING

	Att	Comp	Comp %	Yds	Int	Yds Att.	Yds Comp.
Miami							
Griese	7	6	85.7	73	0	10.4	12.2
Minnesota							
Tarkenton	28	18	64.3	182	1	6.5	10.1

1975

SUPER BOWL IX
12 January
Tulane Stadium,
New Orleans
80 997
*MVP: Franco Harris
(Pittsburgh/ running back)*

Super Bowl IX pitched the Vikings, making their third appearance, against the Pittsburgh Steelers, making their Super Bowl debut. The winners would be taking the title for the first time, and the Steelers were particularly keen to take the ultimate prize after capturing their first Conference title since 1933.

It was a rather dull affair with the first quarter being scoreless and the only score of the first half coming when Minnesota quarterback Fran Tarkenton made a mistake deep in his own territory and had to fall on the ball in the end zone for a safety, giving Pittsburgh a 2–0 half-time lead.

The lead did little justice to Pittsburgh's superiority in offense and defense and they increased their lead from the second half kick-off when Minnesota's Bill Brown fumbled and Marv Kellum recovered it on the 30-yard line. From there Franco Harris, the Pittsburgh running back, and MVP thanks to his record 158 yards rushing, led the drive before sweeping in for a nine-yard touchdown which Garela converted.

The Steelers held their 9–0 lead going into the final quarter but the Vikings came back strongly and after a series of fumbles and mistakes, Terry Brown fell on the ball in the end zone after Bobby Walden's punt had been blocked. The kick failed but the Steelers had been pulled back to 9–6. However,

THE TEAMS

PITTSBURGH STEELERS (AFC)
16 – 0 2 7 7
T: Harris, L Brown
PA: Gerela 2
Safety: 1
Starting Line Up:
OFFENSE: Bleier, Bradshaw, L Brown, Clack, Gravelle, Harris, Kolb, Lewis, Mansfield, Mullins, Shanklin
Substitutes: Sam Davis, Steve Davis, Druschel, Garrett, Grossman, Harrison, McMakin, Pearson, Reeves, Swann, Stallworth, Webster
DEFENSE: Blount, Edwards, Greenwood, Greene, Ham, Holmes, Lambert, Russell, Thomas, Wagner, White
Substitutes: Allen, Bradley, Conn, C Davis, Furness, Kellum, Shell, Toews
KICKERS: Gerela, Walden

MINNESOTA VIKINGS (NFC)
6 – 0 0 0 6
T: Brown T
Starting Line Up:
OFFENSE: Foreman, Gilliam, Goodrum, Lash, Maurer, Osborn, Tarkenton, Tingelhoff, Voigt, White, Yary
Substitutes: Alderman, Anderson, B Brown, Craig, Kingsriter, Lawson, Marinaro, McClanahan, McCullum, Reed, Sunde
DEFENSE: Eller, Hilgenberg, Krause, Marshall, Page, Siemon, Sutherland, Wallace, Winston, N Wright, J Wright
Substitutes: Blair, T Brown, Larsen, Lurtsema, Martin, McNeill, Poltl
KICKERS: Cox, Eischeid

PLAYERS' STATISTICS

Pittsburgh **Minnesota**

RUSHING

	No	Yds	Avge		No	Yds	Avge
Harris	34	158	4.6	Foreman	12	18	1.5
Bleier	17	65	3.8	Tarkenton	1	0	0.0
Bradshaw	5	33	6.6	Osborn	8	−1	−0.1
Swann	1	−7	−7.0				

RECEIVING

	No	Yds	Avge		No	Yds	Avge
T Brown	3	49	16.3	Foreman	5	50	10.0
Stallworth	3	24	8.0	Voigt	2	31	15.5
Bleier	2	11	5.5	Osborn	2	7	3.5
Lewis	1	12	12.0	Gilliam	1	16	16.0
				Reed	1	−2	−2.0

PASSING

Pittsburgh	Att	Comp	Comp %	Yds	Int	Yds Att.	Yds Comp.
Bradshaw	14	9	64.3	96	0	6.9	10.7
Minnesota							
Tarkenton	26	11	42.3	102	3	3.9	9.3

with three and a half minutes remaining a 65-yard Pittsburgh drive resulted in Larry Brown going over after a four-yard pass from Terry Bradshaw. Garela added the final point as the Steelers won on their Super Bowl debut. For the Vikings it was a third defeat in three appearances.

1976

SUPER BOWL X
18 January
Orange Bowl, Miami
80 187
MVP: Lynn Swann
(Pittsburgh/wide receiver)

The Steelers started as favourites against a Dallas team who made their way to the Super Bowl as a wild card entrant into the play-offs. However, the Cowboys held a surprise 10–7 lead going into the final, explosive quarter.

Drew Pearson had put Dallas in front after four minutes 36 seconds of the first quarter when he took a 29-yard pass from quarterback Roger Staubach. Pittsburgh levelled when Grossman took a seven-yard pass from Terry Bradshaw for a touchdown which Gerela converted. A 36-yard field goal by Fritsch was the only score of the second quarter as Dallas led 10–7 at the interval. The third quarter remained scoreless but how different the final quarter was.

After three minutes 32 seconds Pittsburgh's Reggie Harrison blocked a Mitch Hoopes punt. The ball bounced off Harrison's face mask and into the end zone for a two point safety. Pittsburgh went in front for the first time three minutes later when Roy Gerela kicked a 36-yard field goal and he added another three points two minutes later when he kicked from 18 yards. Pittsburgh had now taken a 15–10 lead and were getting on top. However, the game was won when their MVP Lynn Swann took a 59-yard pass from Terry Bradshaw and ran five yards into the end zone. Gerela failed with the kick and with just three minutes left on the clock the Steelers led 21–10.

The Cowboys then came back with an 80-yard drive in five plays which ended in Percy Howard taking a 34-yard pass from Staubach to reduce the arrears to four points with Fritsch's successful kick. But the final quarter glut of scoring ended there as the Steelers held on for a second successive victory. The game's turning point was the blocked punt, but a lot of credit for Pittsburgh's victory must go to Swann's handling. His four catches yielded a Super Bowl record 161 yards.

THE TEAMS

PITTSBURGH STEELERS (AFC)
21 – 7 0 0 14
T: Grossman, Swann
FG: Gerela 2
PA: Gerela
Safety: 1
Starting Line Up:
OFFENSE: Bleier, Bradshaw, L Brown, Clack, Gravelle, F Harris, Kolb, Mansfield, Mullins, Stallworth, Swann
Substitutes: Collier, S Davis, Fuqua, Garrett, Grossman, Hanratty, Harrison, Lewis, Reavis, Webster
DEFENSE: Blount, G Edwards, Greenwood, Green, Ham, Holmes, Lambert, Russell, Thomas, Wagner, D White
Substitutes: Allen, Banaszak, Bradley, D Brown, Furness, Kellum, Shell, Toews
KICKERS: Garela, Walden

DALLAS COWBOYS (NFC)
17 – 7 3 0 7
T: D Pearson, P Howard
FG: Fritsch
PA: Fritsch 2
Starting Line Up:
OFFENSE: Fitzgerald, Fugett, Lawless, Neely, Newhouse, Nye, D Pearson, P Pearson, Richards, Staubach, Wright
Substitutes: K Davis, Dennison, Donovan, DuPree, P Howard, R Howard, Scott, Young
DEFENSE: Cole, D Edwards, C Harris, Jones, Jordan, Lewis, Martin, Pugh, Renfro, Washington, Waters
Substitutes: Barnes, Breunig, Capone, Gregory, Henderson, Hughes, Peterson, R White, Woolsey
KICKERS: Fritsch, Hoopes

PLAYERS' STATISTICS

Pittsburgh				Dallas			

RUSHING

	No	Yds	Avge		No	Yds	Avge
F Harris	27	82	3.0	Newhouse	16	56	3.5
Bleier	15	51	3.4	Staubach	5	22	4.4
Bradshaw	4	16	4.0	Dennison	5	16	3.2
				P Pearson	5	14	2.8

RECEIVING

	No	Yds	Avge		No	Yds	Avge
Swann	4	161	40.3	P Pearson	5	53	10.6
Stallworth	2	8	4.0	Young	3	31	10.3
F Harris	1	26	26.0	D Pearson	2	59	29.5
L Brown	1	7	7.0	Newhouse	2	12	6.0
Grossman	1	7	7.0	P Howard	1	34	34.0
				Fugett	1	9	9.0
				Dennison	1	6	6.0

PASSING

Pittsburgh	Att	Comp	Comp %	Yds	Int	Yds Att.	Yds Comp.
Bradshaw	19	9	47.4	209	0	11.0	23.2
Dallas							
Staubach	24	15	62.5	204	3	8.5	13.6

1977

SUPER BOWL XI
9 January
Rose Bowl, Pasadena
103438
*MVP: Fred Biletnikoff
(Oakland/wide receiver)*

The Oakland Raiders were appearing in the first Super Bowl since being humbled by the Packers in Super Bowl II. For the Vikings it was their fourth appearance in eight years and they were still looking for their first win.

After a scoreless first quarter, any challenge the NFC champions posed to the Raiders evaporated in the second quarter when Oakland took the lead thanks to an Errol Mann field goal, a Casper touchdown from a Ken Stabler one-yard pass and another from a Pete Banaszak one-yard run. A 16–0 half-time lead put the AFC champions in confident mood and they went further ahead when Mann added another field goal nearly ten minutes into the third quarter, but Minnesota pulled back seven points when Tarkenton threw an eight-yard pass to Sammy White for a touchdown which was converted.

However, the Vikings' hopes disappeared midway through the final quarter when Banaszak went over for his second touchdown and two minutes later Brown intercepted a Fran Tarkenton pass and ran for 75 yards to make the touchdown and make the Raiders safe at 32–7. Bob Lee came on for Tarkenton and while he passed to Voigt for a second Minnesota touchdown, with less than 30 seconds remaining on the clock it was too late to get back into the game and the Vikings suffered their fourth Super Bowl defeat.

THE TEAMS

OAKLAND RAIDERS (AFC)
32 – 0 16 3 13
T: Banaszak 2, Casper, Brown
FG: Mann 2
PA: Mann 2
Starting Line Up:
OFFENSE: Biletnikoff, Branch, Buehler, Casper, Dalby, Davis, Stabler, Shell, Upshaw, van Eeghen, Vella
Substitutes: Banaszak, Bankston, Bradshaw, Garrett, Humm, Lawrence, Medlin, Moore, Rae, Siani, Sylvester
DEFENSE: Atkinson, Brown, Willie Hall, Hendricks, M Johnson, Matuzek, Rowe, Sistrunk, Tatum, Thomas, Villapiano
Substitutes: Barnes, Bonness, Colzie, Ginn, McMath, Phillips, Philyaw, Rice
KICKERS: Guy, Mann

MINNESOTA VIKINGS (NFC)
14 – 0 0 7 7
T: S White, Voigt
PA: Cox 2
Starting Line Up:
OFFENSE: Foreman, Goodrum, McClanahan, Rashad, Riley, Tarkenton, Tingelhoff, Voigt, E White, S White, Yary
Substitutes: Berry, Bueton, Craig, Dumler, Grim, Groce, Hamilton, S Johnson, Lee, Miller, Willis
DEFENSE: Blair, Bryant, Eller, Hilgenberg, Krause, Marshall, Page, Siemon, Sutherland, N Wright, J Wright
Substitutes: Allen, Beamon, Windlan Hall, Martin, McNeil, Mullaney, J White, Winston
KICKERS: Clabo, Cox

PLAYERS' STATISTICS

Oakland   **Minnesota**

RUSHING

	No	Yds	Avge		No	Yds	Avge
Davis	16	137	8.6	Foreman	17	44	2.6
van Eeghen	18	73	4.1	S Johnson	2	9	4.5
Garrett	4	19	4.8	S White	1	7	7.0
Banaszak	10	19	1.9	Lee	1	4	4.0
Ginn	2	9	4.5	Miller	2	4	2.0
Rae	2	9	4.5	McClanahan	3	3	1.0

RECEIVING

	No	Yds	Avge		No	Yds	Avge
Biletnikoff	4	79	19.8	S White	5	77	15.4
Casper	4	70	17.5	Foreman	5	62	12.4
Branch	3	20	6.7	Voigt	4	49	12.3
Garrett	1	11	11.0	Miller	4	19	4.8
				Rashad	3	53	17.7
				S Johnson	3	26	8.7

PASSING

Oakland	Att	Comp	Comp %	Yds	Int	Yds Att.	Yds Comp.
Stabler	19	12	63.2	180	0	9.5	15.0
Minnesota							
Tarkenton	35	17	48.6	205	2	5.9	12.1
Lee	9	7	77.8	81	0	9.0	11.6

1978

SUPER BOWL XII
15 January
Louisiana Superdome,
New Orleans
75 583
*MVPs: Harvey Martin (Dallas/
defensive end) and Randy White
(Dallas/ defensive tackle)*

The first Super Bowl to be played indoors saw the Denver Broncos making their Super Bowl debut. But poor throwing by quarterback Craig Morton, who made more passes to Dallas players than to his own, meant they trailed from the first quarter and never recovered. He had four passes intercepted in a game littered with errors – there were ten fumbles and a total of 20 penalties.

The first score followed a Morton error: Randy Hughes latched on to one of his passes and the outcome was a Tony Dorsett three-yard run for a touchdown. Efren Herrera made the kick and towards the end of the quarter he added another three points with a 35-yard field goal. The only points of the second quarter also came from Herrera's boot as Dallas went in at half-time with a 13–0 lead.

Jim Turner pulled three points back with a 47-yard field goal before Butch Johnson went over with a diving catch for Dallas' second touchdown eight minutes into the third quarter. With six minutes 40 seconds of the quarter remaining, Denver took off Morton and replaced him with Norris Weese whose presence added more mobility to their offense and he had been on the field barely a minute when Rob Lytle plunged over the line and reduced the score to 20–10.

But the Denver dream ended midway through the final quarter when Golden Richards took

THE TEAMS

DALLAS COWBOYS (NFC)
27 – 10 3 7 7
T: Dorsett, Johnson, Richards
FG: Herrera 2
PA: Herrera 3
Starting Line Up:
OFFENSE: Donovan, Dorsett, DuPree, Fitzgerald, Neely, Newhouse, D Pearson, Rafferty, Richards, Scott, Staubach
Substitutes: Brinson, Carano, Cooper, Dennison, Frederick, Hill, Johnson, Laidlaw, Lawless, P Pearson, Saldi, D White, R Wright
DEFENSE: Barnes, Bruenig, Harris, Henderson, Jones, Kyle, Lewis, Martin, Pugh, R White, Waters
Substitutes: Brown, Cole, Gregory, Hegman, Hughes, Huther, Renfro, Stalls, Washington
KICKER: Herrera

DENVER BRONCOS (AFC)
10 – 0 0 10 0
T: Lytle
FG: Turner
PA: Turner
Starting Line Up:
OFFENSE: Armstrong, Dolbin, Glassic, Howard, Keyworth, Maurer, Minor, Montier, Morton, Moses, Odoms
Substitutes: Allison, Egloff, Hyde, Jensen, Lytle, Maples, Penrose, Perrin, Schindler, Schultz, Upchurch, Weese
DEFENSE: Alzado, Carter, Chavous, Foley, Gradisher, I Jackson, T Jackson, Rizzo, Swenson, Thompson, L Wright
Substitutes: Evans, Grant, Jackson, Manor, Nairn, Poltl, Rich, Riley, Smith, Turk
KICKERS: Dilts, Turner

PLAYERS' STATISTICS

Dallas · **Denver**

RUSHING

	No	Yds	Avge		No	Yds	Avge
Dorsett	15	66	4.4	Lytle	10	35	3.5
Newhouse	14	55	3.9	Armstrong	7	27	3.9
D White	1	13	13.0	Weese	3	26	8.7
P Pearson	3	11	3.7	Jensen	1	16	16.0
Staubach	3	6	2.6	Keyworth	5	9	1.8
Laidlaw	1	1	1.0	Perrin	3	8	2.7
Johnson	1	–9	–9.0				

RECEIVING

	No	Yds	Avge		No	Yds	Avge
P Pearson	5	37	7.4	Dolbin	2	24	12.0
DuPree	4	66	16.5	Odoms	2	9	4.5
Newhouse	3	–1	–0.3	Moses	1	21	21.0
Johnson	2	53	26.5	Upchurch	1	9	9.0
Richards	2	38	19.0	Jensen	1	5	5.0
Dorsett	2	11	5.5	Perrin	1	–7	–7.0
D Pearson	1	13	13.0				

PASSING

Dallas	Att	Comp	Comp %	Yds	Int	Yds Att.	Yds Comp.
Staubach	25	17	68.0	183	0	7.5	10.8
D White	2	1	50.0	5	0	2.5	5.0
Newhouse	1	1	100.0	29	0	29.0	29.0
Denver							
Morton	15	4	26.7	39	4	2.6	9.8
Weese	10	4	40.0	22	0	2.2	5.5

a 29-yard pass over his head from Robert Newhouse for another Dallas six-pointer. Herrera made the kick and Dallas ran out winners by 27–10. For the first time in Super Bowl history the MVP award was shared.

1979

SUPER BOWL XIII
21 January
Orange Bowl, Miami
79484
MVP: Terry Bradshaw
(Pittsburgh/ quarterback)

The Steelers made history as the first team to win the Super Bowl three times, but the Cowboys gave them a fright after they had seemed to be coasting to the title.

The difference between the two teams was Pittsburgh's MVP Terry Bradshaw, who threw four touchdown passes and by half-time had surpassed Bart Starr's record of 250 yards passing. He went on to set a new record of 318 yards from 30 attempts, of which 17 were completed. Dallas quarterback Roger Staubach, despite being overshadowed by Bradshaw, still managed to throw for 228 yards.

John Stallworth took the first of Bradshaw's passes to land the first touchdown but a Bradshaw fumble resulted in Roger Staubach throwing 39 yards to Tony Hill three plays later to level the scores. Dallas went ahead for the first and only time early in the second quarter when Mike Hegman picked up another Bradshaw fumble and raced 37 yards. Two minutes later the Steelers were level again when John Stallworth crossed the line after a 75-yard run, and then a seven-yard pass from Bradshaw to Bleier restored the Steelers' seven point advantage at half-time.

Jackie Smith dropped a pass in the end zone for the Cowboys and the only score of the third quarter, therefore, was a Rafael Septien field goal from 27 yards and with 15 minutes remaining just four points separated the two teams.

Franco Harris increased Pitts-

THE TEAMS

PITTSBURGH STEELERS (AFC)
35 – 7 14 0 14
T: Stallworth 2, Bleier, Harris, Swann
PA: Gerela 5
Starting Line Up:
OFFENSE: Bradshaw, Bleier, Davis, Grossman, Harris, Kolb, Mullins, Pinney, Stallworth, Webster, Swann
Substitutes: Bell, Brown, Courson, Cunningham, Deloplaine, Kruczek, Mandich, Moser, Peterson, Smith, Stoudt, Thornton
DEFENSE: Banaszak, Blount, Furness, Greenwood, Greene, Ham, Johnson, Lambert, Shell, Toews, Wagner
Substitutes: F Anderson, L Anderson, Beasley, Cole, Dungy, Dunn, Oldham, White, Winston
KICKERS: Colquitt, Gerela

DALLAS COWBOYS (NHC)
31 – 7 7 3 14
T: Hill, Hegman, DuPree, B Johnson
FG: Septien
PA: Septien 4
Starting Line Up:
OFFENSE: Donovan, Dorsett, DuPree, Fitzgerald, Hill, Newhouse, D Pearson, Rafferty, Scott, Staubach, Wright
Substitutes: Blackwell, Brinson, Carano, Cooper, Frederick, Johnson, Laidlaw, Lawless, P Pearson, Randall, Smith, Steele, D White
DEFENSE: Barnes, Breunig, Cole, Harris, Henderson, Jones, Kyle, Lewis, Martin, Waters, R White
Substitutes: Bethea, Brown, Hegman, Hughes, Huther, Pugh, Stalls, Thurman, Washington
KICKER: Septien

PLAYERS' STATISTICS

Pittsburgh   Dallas

RUSHING

	No	Yds	Avge		No	Yds	Avge
Harris	20	68	3.4	Dorsett	16	96	6.0
Bleier	2	3	1.5	Staubach	4	37	9.3
Bradshaw	2	−5	−2.5	Laidlaw	3	12	4.0
				P Pearson	1	6	6.0
				Newhouse	8	3	0.4

RECEIVING

	No	Yds	Avge		No	Yds	Avge
Swann	7	124	17.7	Dorsett	5	44	8.8
Stallworth	3	115	38.3	D Pearson	4	73	18.3
Grossman	3	29	9.7	Hill	2	49	24.5
Bell	2	21	10.5	Johnson	2	30	15.0
Harris	1	22	22.0	DuPree	2	17	8.5
Bleier	1	7	7.0	P Pearson	2	15	7.5

PASSING

Pittsburgh	Att	Comp	Comp %	Yds	Int	Yds Att.	Yds Comp.
Bradshaw	30	17	56.7	318	1	10.6	18.7
Dallas							
Staubach	30	17	56.7	228	1	7.6	13.4

burgh's lead with a 22-yard rush and Swann increased it further, to 35–17, when he took an 18-yard pass from Bradshaw. But the Cowboys never gave up, despite only six minutes remaining. Staubach rallied his team to two touchdowns in the closing minutes but it was too late and the honour of being the first team to win the Super Bowl three times fell to Pittsburgh.

Left *Terry Bradshaw, the Steelers quarterback in four Super Bowls, and MVP in 1979 and 1980.*

Below *Vince Ferragamo aims long for the Los Angeles Rams in Super Bowl XIV but Pittsburgh prevailed for the fourth time.*

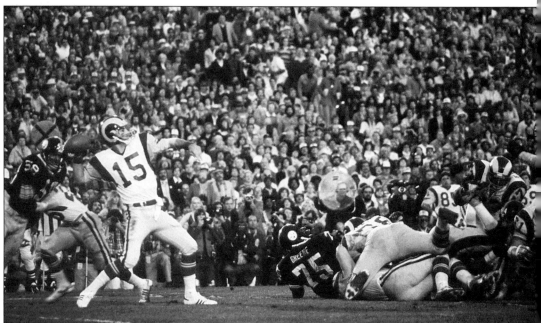

1980

SUPER BOWL XIV
20 January
Rose Bowl, Pasadena
103 985
*MVP: Terry Bradshaw
(Pittsburgh/ quarterback)*

Pittsburgh trailed at the end of each of the first three quarters before staging a final-quarter comeback to win the Super Bowl for the fourth time in four attempts. Again their hero was Terry Bradshaw, MVP for the second successive year, as he threw for another 309 yards and completed 14 of 21 passes.

The Rams were expected to be no match for the Steelers and when Pittsburgh scored with a Bahr 41-yard field goal during their first possession it seemed that would be the case. But the Los Angeles team had other things in store. Cullen Bryant rushed over for a touchdown which Frank Corral converted and at the end of the first quarter the Rams led 7–3. Pittsburgh retook the lead early in the second quarter when Franco Harris went over from one yard, but two field goals from Corral, from 31 and 45 yards, put the Rams back into the lead 13–10 at the interval.

Again Pittsburgh retook the lead early in the third quarter when Lynn Swann took a 47-yard pass from Bradshaw. But the Rams would not let the Steelers pull away and they restored their lead on the next play when Lawrence McCutcheon found Ron Smith with a 24-yard pass. After three quarters the Rams led 19–17, but the Steelers then played like the champions they were.

With just three minutes of the final quarter gone, Bradshaw threw a 73-yard bomb to John Stallworth as the Steelers went

THE TEAMS

PITTSBURGH STEELERS (AFC)
31 – 3 7 7 14
T: Harris 2, Swann, Stallworth
FG: Bahr
PA: Bahr 4
Starting Line Up:
OFFENSE: Bleier, Bradshaw, Brown, Cunningham, Davis, Kolb, Mullins, Stallworth, Webster, Swann, Harris
Substitutes: A Anderson, Bell, Courson, Dornbrook, Grossman, Hawthorne, Kruczek, Moser, Petersen, Smith, Stoudt, Thornton
DEFENSE: Banaszak, Blount, Cole, Dunn, Greenwood, Greene, Johnson, Lambert, Shell, Thomas, Winston
Substitutes: L Anderson, Beasley, Furness, Graves, Ham, Toews, Valentine, White, Woodruff
KICKERS: Bahr, Colquitt

LOS ANGELES RAMS (NFC)
19 – 7 6 6 0
T: Bryant, Smith
FG: Corral 2
PA: Corral
Starting Line Up:
OFFENSE: Bryant, Dennard, Ferragamo, France, Harrar, K Hill, Nelson, Saul, Slater, Tyler, Waddy
Substitutes: Bain, Gravelle, D Hill, E Hill, Jodat, Lee, McCutcheon, Rutledge, Ryczek, R Smith, Young
DEFENSE: Brooks, Brudzinski, Cromwell, Dryer, Elmendorf, Fanning, Perry, Reynolds, Thomas, Jack Youngblood, Jim Youngblood
Substitutes: Andrews, E Brown, Doss, Ellis, Harris, O'Steen, Sully, Wallace, Westbrooks, Wilkinson
KICKERS: Clark, Corral

PLAYERS' STATISTICS

Pittsburgh **Los Angeles**

RUSHING

	No	Yds	Avge		No	Yds	Avge
Harris	20	46	2.3	Tyler	17	60	3.5
Bleier	10	25	2.5	Bryant	6	30	5.0
Bradshaw	3	9	3.0	McCutcheon	5	10	2.0
Thornton	4	4	1.0	Ferragamo	1	7	7.0

RECEIVING

	No	Yds	Avge		No	Yds	Avge
Swann	5	79	15.8	Waddy	3	75	25.0
Stallworth	3	121	40.3	Bryant	3	21	7.0
Harris	3	66	22.0	Tyler	3	20	6.7
Cunningham	2	21	10.5	Dennard	2	32	16.0
Thornton	1	22	22.0	Nelson	2	20	10.0
				D Hill	1	28	28.0
				R Smith	1	24	24.0
				McCutcheon	1	16	16.0

PASSING

Pittsburgh	Att	Comp	Comp %	Yds	Int	Yds Att.	Yds Comp.
Bradshaw	21	14	66.7	309	3	14.7	22.1
Los Angeles							
Ferragamo	25	15	60.0	212	1	8.5	14.1
McCutcheon	1	1	100.0	24	0	24.0	24.0

back into the lead. By now Pittsburgh were doing most of the attacking and another long pass from Bradshaw to Stallworth ended with Franco Harris going over for a one-yard touchdown and that was the end of the Rams' brave challenge. Bradshaw took his career figures to nine touchdown passes and 932 yards passing, both Super Bowl records.

1981

SUPER BOWL XV
25 January
Louisiana Superdome,
New Orleans
76 135
*MVP: Jim Plunkett
(Oakland/quarterback)*

The Philadelphia Eagles started as slight favourites to win Super Bowl XV, but the Raiders, after coming through the post-season games as a wild card entry and reaching the Super Bowl, must have warranted some share of the betting; and they justified their backers by becoming the first wild card team to take the sport's ultimate prize.

Ron Jaworski's first pass of the day was intercepted by Rod Martin as the Raiders gained the early initiative. Midway through the first quarter they went 7–0 up when Cliff Branch took a two-yard pass from Jim Plunkett, and in the closing seconds of the quarter Plunkett's Super Bowl record 80-yard pass to Kenny King resulted in another touchdown for the Raiders. It was the longest play from a scrimmage in Super Bowl history.

A Tony Franklin field goal in the second quarter reduced the lead to 14–3 at half-time, but Oakland got on top again in the third quarter when Branch went over for his second touchdown after a 29-yard pass from Plunkett, and a 46-yard Bahr field goal saw the Raiders go into the final quarter 24–3 in front.

Ron Jaworski did his best to get the Eagles back into the game and while his 291 yards of passing went unrewarded most of the time, it resulted in the only touchdown of the final quarter when he threw an eight-yard pass to Keith Krepfle.

Another Bahr field goal rounded off the scoring as Oakland won 27–10, the first wild card winners of the Super Bowl.

THE TEAMS

OAKLAND RAIDERS (AFC)
27 – 14 0 10 3
T: Branch 2, King
FG: Bahr 2
PA: Bahr 3
Starting Line Up:
OFFENSE: Branch, Chandler, Chester, Dalby, King, Lawrence, Marvin, Plunkett, Shell, Upshaw, van Eeghen
Substitutes: Bradshaw, Christiansen, B Davis, Jensen, Martini, Mason, Matthews, Ramsey, Sylvester, Whittington, Wilson
DEFENSE: Browning, M Davis, Hayes, Hendricks, Kinlaw, Martin, Matuszak, Miller, Nelson, O'Steen, Owens
Substitutes: Barnes, Campbell, Celotto, Hardman, Jackson, Jones, McClanahan, McKinney, Moody, Pear
KICKERS: Guy, Bahr

PHILADELPHIA EAGLES (NFC)
10 – 0 3 0 7
T: Krepfle
FG: Franklin
PA: Franklin
Starting Line Up:
OFFENSE: Carmichael, Harris, Jaworski, Krepfle, Montgomery, Morriss, Peoples, Perot, Sisemore, Spagnola, Walters
Substitutes: Baker, Campfield, Giammona, Harrington, Henry, Hertel, Kenney, Parker, Pisarcik, Slater, Smith, Torrey
DEFENSE: Bergey, Bunting, Edwards, Hairston, Harrison, Johnson, LeMaster, Logan, Robinson, Wilson, Young
Substitutes: Blackmore, Brown, Chesley, Clarke, Henderson, Humphrey, Phillips, Sciarra, Wilkes
KICKERS: Franklin, Runager

PLAYERS' STATISTICS

Oakland | Philadelphia

RUSHING

	No	Yds	Avge		No	Yds	Avge
van Eeghen	19	80	4.2	Montgomery	16	44	2.8
King	6	18	3.0	Harris	7	14	2.0
Jensen	3	12	4.0	Giammona	1	7	7.0
Plunkett	3	9	3.0	Harrington	1	4	4.0
Whittington	3	−2	−0.7	Jaworski	1	0	0.0

RECEIVING

	No	Yds	Avge		No	Yds	Avge
Branch	5	67	13.4	Montgomery	6	91	15.2
Chandler	4	77	19.3	Carmichael	5	83	16.6
King	2	93	46.5	Krepfle	2	16	8.0
Chester	2	24	12.0	Smith	2	59	29.5
				Spagnola	1	22	22.0
				Parker	1	19	19.0
				Harris	1	1	1.0

PASSING

	Att	Comp	Comp %	Yds	Int	Yds Att.	Yds Comp.
Oakland							
Plunkett	21	13	61.9	261	0	12.4	20.1
Green Bay							
Jaworski	38	18	47.4	291	3	7.7	16.2

1982

SUPER BOWL XVI
24 January
Pontiac Silverdome, Pontiac
81 270
*MVP: Joe Montana
(San Francisco/quarterback)*

A 20–0 half-time lead was too much for the Cincinnati Bengals to overcome as the 49ers went on to win the first of their record-equalling four Super Bowls. As in all their other triumphs, the man at the heart of their offense was quarterback Joe Montana, the game's MVP.

After sacking Cincinnati's Ken Anderson, the 49ers pushed downfield and on their 11th play of the drive Montana dived over for the opening touchdown. A Montana pass of 11 yards to Cooper, with Ray Wersching converting again, increased San Francisco's lead to 14–0 after the longest drive, at 92 yards, in Super Bowl history. With only seconds of the half remaining Wersching put over a 22-yard field goal and then from the kick-off Archie Griffin fumbled. The 49ers recovered the ball and set up Wersching for another field goal, and suddenly they led 20–0 at the halfway stage.

The Bengals came out for the second half faced with the biggest deficit any team had had to overhaul at this stage of a Super Bowl. But they did their chances no harm from the kick-off when they drove for 83 yards, resulting in a Ken Anderson touchdown. That was the only score of the third quarter but when Dan Ross went over for a second touchdown in the fourth quarter the Bengals were back in the match at 20–14. But just as they seemed to be threatening, the 49ers defense shut them down and two more Wersching field goals, from 40 and 23

THE TEAMS

SAN FRANCISCO 49ers (NFC)
26 – 7 13 0 6
T: Montana, Cooper
FG: Wersching 4
PA: Wersching 2
Starting Line Up:
OFFENSE: Audick, Ayers, Clark, Cooper, Cross, Fahnhorst, Montana, Patton, Quillan, Solomon, Young
Substitutes: Benjamin, Choma, Davis, Downing, Easley, Elliott, Kennedy, Lawrence, Ramson, Ring, Schumann, Wilson
DEFENSE: Board, Harper, Hicks, Lott, Puki, Reese, Reynolds, Stuckey, Turner, Williamson, Wright
Substitutes: Bunz, Dean, Gervais, Harty, Leopold, Martin, McColl, Pillers, Thomas
KICKERS: Miller, Wersching

CINCINNATI BENGALS (AFC)
21 – 0 0 7 14
T: Ross 2, Anderson
PA: Breech 3
Starting Line Up:
OFFENSE: Alexander, Anderson, Bush, Collinsworth, Curtis, Johnson, Lapham, Mantoya, Munoz, Ross, Wilson
Substitutes: Bass, A Griffin, Hargrove, M Harris, Kreider, McInally, Moore, Obrovac, Schonert, Thompson, Verser
DEFENSE: Breeden, Browner, Cameron, B Harris, Hicks, Kemp, LeClair, Riley, St Clair, Whitley, Williams
Substitutes: Burley, Davis, Dinkel, Edwards, Frazier, Fuller, Horn, R Griffin, Razzano, Schuh, Simmons
KICKER: Breech

PLAYERS' STATISTICS

Cincinnati   San Francisco

RUSHING

	No	Yds	Avge		No	Yds	Avge
Johnson	14	36	2.6	Patton	17	55	3.2
Alexander	5	17	3.4	Cooper	9	34	3.8
Anderson	4	15	3.8	Montana	6	18	3.0
A Griffin	1	4	4.0	Ring	5	17	3.4
				Davis	2	5	2.5
				Clark	1	−2	−2.0

RECEIVING

	No	Yds	Avge		No	Yds	Avge
Ross	11	104	9.5	Solomon	4	52	13.0
Collinsworth	5	107	21.4	Clark	4	45	11.3
Curtis	3	42	14.0	Cooper	2	15	7.5
Kreider	2	36	18.0	Wilson	1	22	22.0
Johnson	2	8	4.0	Young	1	14	14.0
Alexander	2	3	1.5	Patton	1	6	6.0
				Ring	1	3	3.0

PASSING

	Att	Comp	Comp %	Yds	Int	Yds Att.	Yds Comp.
Cincinnatti							
Anderson	34	25	73.5	300	2	8.8	12.0
San Francisco							
Montana	22	14	63.6	157	0	7.1	11.2

yards, to equal the Super Bowl record of four, increased San Francisco's lead to 26–14.

A late touchdown by Ross, who set a Super Bowl record with 11 receptions for 104 yards, came too late as the 49ers ran out winners by five points. Despite the scoreline, Cincinnati gained more yards from the scrimmage, the first time a losing team had achieved this, and Anderson out-threw Montana 300 yards to 157 as he broke records for the most completions (25) and biggest completion percentage (73.5%).

1983

SUPER BOWL XVII
30 January
Rose Bowl, Pasadena
103 667
MVP: John Riggins
(Washington/ running back)

Super Bowl XVII was a re-run of Super Bowl VII but this time the outcome was reversed as Washington won their first championship since 1942. Neither team had figured as likely Super Bowl contenders at the start of the season but both defied the critics.

David Woodley split the Redskins defense with a 76-yard touchdown pass to Jimmy Cefalo in the first quarter, and in the second period Mark Moseley and Uwe von Schamann exchanged field goals before Washington levelled the scores after an 80-yard drive in 11 plays resulted in a short pass from Joe Theismann for Alvin Garrett to score. But Fulton Walker then restored the Dolphins seven-point lead when he returned for a record 98 yards from the kickoff.

Moseley reduced the arrears by three points, the third quarter's only score, as Washington trailed 17–13 with one quarter left. Early in the final quarter the Redskins went in front when Riggins went on a 43-yard run down the sideline to score. Washington had contained Miami by restricting them to just 34 yards in the second half and they sealed victory with a six-yard touchdown pass from Theismann to Charlie Brown with one minute 55 seconds left. Washington fullback John Riggins won the MVP award after setting a Super Bowl record 166 yards in 38 carries.

THE TEAMS

WASHINGTON REDSKINS (NFC)
27 – 0 10 3 14
T: Garrett, Riggins, Brown
FG: Moseley 2
PA: Moseley 3
Starting Line Up:
OFFENSE: Bostic, Brown, Dean, Garrett, Grimm, Jacoby, Riggins, Starke, Theismann, Walker, Warren
Substitutes: Caster, Didier, Giaquinto, Harmon, Holly, Jackson, Laster, May, Owen, Puetz, Seay, Washington, Wonsley
DEFENSE: Butz, Dean, Grant, Kaufman, Manley, Mendenhall, Milot, Murphy, Olkewicz, Peters, White
Substitutes: Brooks, Coleman, Cronan, Jordan, Kubin, Lavender, Liebenstein, Lowry, McDaniel, McGee, Nelms
KICKERS: Hayes, Moseley

MIAMI DOLPHINS (AFC)
17 – 7 10 0 0
T: Cefalo, Walker
FG: von Schamann
PA: von Schamann 2
Starting Line Up:
OFFENSE: Cefalo, Giesler, Franklin, Hardy, Harris, Laakso, Kuechenberg, Nathan, Stephenson, Toews, Woodley
Substitutes: Bennett, Dennard, Diana, Duper, Foster, Green, Heflin, Hill, Jensen, Lee, Moore, Rose, Strock, Vigorito
DEFENSE: Baumhower, Betters, G Blackwood, L Blackwood, Bokamper, Brudzinski, Duhe, Gordon, McNeal, Rhone, Small
Substitutes: Bishop, Bowser, Clark, Den Herder, Hester, Judson, Kozlowski, Lankford, Potter, Shull, Walker
KICKERS: Orosz, von Schamann

PLAYERS' STATISTICS

Washington   Miami

RUSHING

	No	Yds	Avge		No	Yds	Avge
Riggins	38	166	4.4	Franklin	16	49	3.1
Garrett	1	44	44.0	Nathan	7	26	3.7
Harmon	9	40	4.4	Woodley	4	16	4.0
Theismann	3	20	6.7	Vigorito	1	4	4.0
Walker	1	6	6.0	Harris	1	1	1.0

RECEIVING

	No	Yds	Avge		No	Yds	Avge
Brown	6	60	10.0	Cefalo	2	82	41.0
Warren	5	28	5.6	Harris	2	15	7.5
Garrett	2	13	6.5				
Walker	1	27	27.0				
Riggins	1	15	15.0				

PASSING

Washington	Att	Comp	Comp %	Yds	Int	Yds Att.	Yds Comp.
Theismann	23	15	65.2	143	2	6.2	9.5

Miami							
Woodley	14	4	28.6	97	1	6.9	24.3
Strock	3	0	0.0	0.0	0	0.0	0.0

1984

SUPER BOWL XVIII
22 January
Tampa Stadium, Tampa
72920
MVP: Marcus Allen
(LA Raiders/running back)

The Raiders, now playing out of Los Angeles, thwarted Washington's bid to win successive championships with an excellent show of defensive play. The pundits could not separate the teams before the match; both came to the Super Bowl with impeccable records.

The Raiders drew first blood after four minutes 52 seconds when Derrick Jensen blocked a Jeff Hayes punt and recovered the ball in the end zone. Mark Moseley missed the chance of pulling three points back when he missed with his 44-yard field goal and the Raiders held their seven-point lead at the end of the quarter.

The Los Angeles defense continued to contain Washington in the second quarter and the Raiders added another seven points early on when Branch went over the line after a Plunkett pass. Mark Moseley booted a 24-yard field goal for Washington at the end of a 13-play drive but the Raiders added a further seven points before the end of the quarter when, with 12 seconds left on the clock, a Washington pass deep in their own territory by Theismann was intercepted by Jack Squirek who had only five yards to run into the end zone.

Washington came out for the second half in determined mood and their first drive, of 70 yards, resulted in Riggins rushing over from one yard. But the Raiders reasserted their superiority when Marcus Allen drove in from five yards, and on the final play of the third period Allen ran for a record 74-yard touchdown. The final quarter was an anti-climax with a Bahr field goal being the only score as he extended the Raiders' margin of victory to 29 points. Marcus Allen won the MVP award having rushed for a Super Bowl record 191 yards in 20 carries.

THE TEAMS

LOS ANGELES RAIDERS (AFC)

38 – 7 14 14 3
T: Allen 2, Jensen, Branch, Squirek
FG: Bahr
PA: Bahr 5
Starting Line Up:
OFFENSE: Allen, Barnwell, Branch, Christensen, Dalby, Davis, Hannah, King, Lawrence, Marin, Plunkett
Substitutes: Hasselbeck, Hawkins, Humm, Jensen, S Jordon, Mosebar, Muhammad, Montgomery, Pruitt, Sylvester, D Williams, Willis, Wilson
DEFENSE: Alzado, Davis, Hayes, Haynes, Hendricks, Kinlaw, Long, McElroy, Martin, Millen, Nelson
Substitutes: Barnes, Byrd, Caldwell, Davis, Hill, McKinney, Pickel, Robinson, Squirek, Stalls, Townsend, Watts
KICKERS: Bahr, Guy

WASHINGTON REDSKINS (NFC)

9 – 0 3 6 0
T: Riggins
FG: Moseley
Starting Line Up:
OFFENSE: Bostic, Brown, Grimm, Jacoby, May, Monk, Riggins, Starke, Theismann, Walker, Warren
Substitutes: Didier, Evans, Garrett, Giaquinto, Holly, Huff, Kimball, Laufenberg, McGrath, Seay, Simons, Washington, J Williams, Wonsley
DEFENSE: Butz, Coffey, Grant, Green, Kaufman, Liebenstein, Manley, Milot, Murphy, Olkewicz, Washington
Substitutes: Anderson, Brooks, Carpenter, Coleman, Cronan, Dean, C Jordan, Kubin, Mann, McGee, G Williams
KICKERS: Hayes, Moseley

PLAYERS' STATISTICS

Los Angeles Raiders   **Washington**

RUSHING

	No	Yds	Avge		No	Yds	Avge
Allen	20	191	9.6	Riggins	26	64	2.5
Pruitt	5	17	3.4	Theismann	3	18	6.0
King	3	12	4.0	Washington	3	8	2.7
Willis	1	7	7.0				
Hawkins	3	6	2.0				
Plunkett	1	–2	–2.0				

RECEIVING

	No	Yds	Avge		No	Yds	Avge
Branch	6	94	15.7	Didier	5	65	13.0
Christensen	4	32	8.0	Brown	3	93	31.0
Hawkins	2	20	10.0	Washington	3	20	6.7
Allen	2	18	9.0	Giaquinto	2	21	10.5
King	2	8	4.0	Monk	1	26	26.0
				Garrett	1	17	17.0
				Riggins	1	1	1.0

PASSING

Los Angeles Raiders	Att	Comp	Comp %	Yds	Int	Yds Att.	Yds Comp.
Plunkett	25	16	64.0	172	0	6.9	10.8
Washington							
Theismann	35	16	45.7	243	2	6.9	15.2

1985

SUPER BOWL XIX
21 January
Stanford Stadium, Stanford
84059
*MVP: Joe Montana
(San Francisco/quarterback)*

Super Bowl XIX promised to be quite a contest for the 84 000 fans at Stanford with two of the game's finest quarterbacks, Dan Marino of Miami and Joe Montana of San Francisco, opposing each other. Montana got the better of their personal duel as his team went on to capture their second title, while Marino was sacked four times by the San Francisco defense.

In the first quarter, however, Marino completed nine of ten passes for 103 yards, and then a touchdown at the end of the half when his two-yard pass found Johnson gave the Dolphins a 10–7 lead. Uwe von Schamann had earlier kicked Miami in front with a 37-yard field goal before the 49ers took the lead when Monroe took a 33-yard touchdown pass from Montana.

The 49ers changed their defense in the second quarter and successfully curtailed Marino's activities as the San Francisco team dominated the quarter. Roger Craig scored the first of a record three touchdowns when he took an eight-yard pass from Montana and the 49ers quarterback went over himself from six yards to put his team 21–10 in front. A further seven points followed when Craig ran in from two yards and Wersching added his fourth point after. The Dolphins managed

THE TEAMS

SAN FRANCISCO 49ers (NFC)
38 – 7 21 10 0
T: Craig 3, Monroe, Montana
FG: Wersching
PA: Wersching 5
Starting Line Up:
OFFENSE: Ayers, Clark, Craig, Cross, Fahnhorst, Francis, Montana, Paris, Quillan, Solomon, Tyler
Substitutes: Cooper, Harmon, Monroe, Nehemiah, Ring, Wilson
DEFENSE: Board, Bunz, Ellison, Hicks, Lott, Pillers, Reynolds, Tuiasosopo, Turner, Williamson, Wright
Substitutes: Carter, Dean, Fuller, Holmoe, Johnson, Kelcher, Kennedy, McColl, McIntyre, McLemore, Montgomery, Shell, Shields, Stover, Stuckey, Walter
KICKERS: Runager, Wersching

MIAMI DOLPHINS (AFC)
16 – 10 6 0 0
T: D Johnson
FG: von Schamann 3
PA: von Schamann
Starting Line Up:
OFFENSE: Bennett, Clayton, Duper, Foster, Giesler, Green, Hardy, Marino, Nathan, Newman, Stephenson
Substitutes: Carter, Cefalo, Heflin, Jensen, D Johnson, Moore, Rose, Strock
DEFENSE: Betters, Baumhower, G Blackwood, L Blackwood, Bokamper, Brudzinski, Brophy, Brown, Bowser, Judson, McNeal
Substitutes: Barnett, Benson, B Brown, Charles, Clark, Duhe, Hill, Kozlowski, Lankford, Lee, Rhone, Shipp, Shiver, Sowell, Toews, Walker
KICKERS: Roby, von Schamann

At the bottom of the pile is Roger Craig, having run in for one of three touchdowns for the 49ers in Super Bowl XIX.

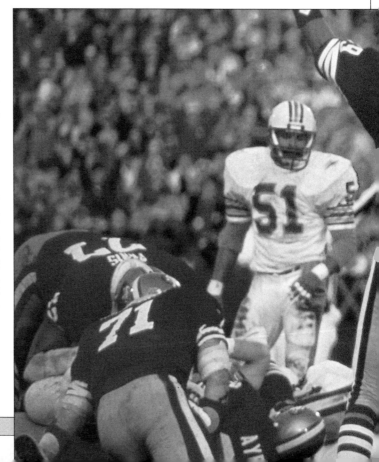

PLAYERS' STATISTICS

San Francisco   Miami

RUSHING

	No	Yds	Avge		No	Yds	Avge
Tyler	13	65	5.0	Nathan	5	18	3.6
Montana	5	59	11.8	Bennett	3	7	2.3
Craig	15	58	3.9	Marino	1	0	0.0
Harmon	5	20	4.0				
Solomon	1	5	5.0				
Cooper	1	4	4.0				

RECEIVING

	No	Yds	Avge		No	Yds	Avge
Craig	7	77	11.0	Nathan	10	83	8.3
D Clark	6	77	12.8	Clayton	6	92	15.3
Francis	5	60	12.0	Rose	6	73	12.2
Tyler	4	70	17.5	D Johnson	3	28	9.3
Monroe	1	33	33.0	Moore	2	17	8.5
Solomon	1	14	14.0	Cefalo	1	14	14.0
				Duper	1	11	11.0

PASSING

San Francisco	Att	Comp	Comp %	Yds	Int	Yds Att.	Yds Comp.
Montana	35	24	69	331	0	9.5	13.8
Miami							
Marino	50	29	58	318	2	6.4	11.0

two field goals in the last 22 seconds, both successfully kicked by von Schamann.

Any chance the Dolphins had of making a comeback disappeared when Marino was sacked three times early in the second half. A Wersching field goal (27 yards) and a third touchdown from Craig gave San Francisco a 38–16 lead with one quarter to go. The final quarter yielded no points and Marino was sacked again as the battle of the quarterbacks was easily won by Joe Montana, who won the MVP award and passed for a record 331 yards.

1986

SUPER BOWL XX
26 January
Louisiana Superdome,
New Orleans
73818
MVP: Richard Dent
(Chicago/ defensive end)

The 20th Super Bowl was a real David and Goliath clash, with the Chicago Bears playing the part of Goliath. They had a 15–1 regular season record and then had two post-season shutouts in capturing the NFC championship. The New England Patriots, on the other hand, had entered the play-offs as the second wild card team after an 11–5 regular season record.

The fairytale continued when their barefooted kicker Tony Franklin kicked a 36-yard field goal for the Pats in the opening seconds of the Super Bowl, but the Bears then took charge and dominated what became one of the most one-sided games in Super Bowl history. Kevin Butler kicked two field goals to give them the lead and an 11-yard rush from Matt Suhey gave them a 13–3 advantage after the first quarter.

Even now, after just 15 minutes, one sensed the game was over. Despite their early lead, the Patriots were making mistakes and were clearly overawed by the Bears and the occasion. Quarterback Jim McMahon ended a 59-yard drive by scoring from two yards and Butler added another field goal as the Bears added ten more points before half-time. In the first half the Bears had piled on 236 yards while the Patriots were on *minus* 14.

Third quarter touchdowns by McMahon, the first quarterback to rush for two touchdowns, reserve cornerback Reggie

THE TEAMS

CHICAGO BEARS (NFC)
46 – 13 10 21 2
T: McMahon 2, Suhey, Phillips, Perry
FG: Butler 3
PA: Butler 5
Safety: 1
Starting Line Up:
OFFENSE: Bortz, Covert, Gault, Hilgenberg, McKinnon, McMahon, Moorehead, Payton, Suhey, Thayer, Van Horne
Substitutes: Andrews, Frederick, Fuller, Gentry, Humphries, Margerum, Ortego, Sanders, Thomas, Tomczak, Wrightman
DEFENSE: Dent, Duerson, Fencik, Frazier, Hampton, McMichael, Marshall, Perry, Richardson, Singletary, Wilson
Substitutes: Cabral, Gayle, Hartenstine, Keys, Morrissey, Phillips, Rivera, Taylor, Thrift
KICKERS: Buford, Butler

NEW ENGLAND PATRIOTS (AFC)
10 – 3 0 0 7
T: Fryar
FG: Franklin
PA: Franklin
Starting Line Up:
OFFENSE: Brock, Collins, Dawson, Eason, Holloway, Hannah, James, Morgan, Moore, Starring, Wooten
Substitutes: Fairchild, Fryar, Grogan, Hawthorne, Jones, Morriss, Plunkett, Ramsey, Tatupu, Weathers
DEFENSE: Adams, Blackmon, Clayborn, James, Lippett, McGrew, Marion, Nelson, Tippett, Veris, Williams
Substitutes: Bowman, Creswell, Gibson, Ingram, McSwain, Owens, Ramsey, Rembert, Reynolds, Thomas, Williams
KICKERS: Camarillo, Franklin

PLAYERS' STATISTICS

Chicago | New England

RUSHING

	No	Yds	Avge		No	Yds	Avge
Payton	22	61	2.8	C James	5	1	0.2
Suhey	11	52	4.7	Collins	3	4	0.8
McMahon	5	14	2.8	Grogan	1	3	3.0
Sanders	4	15	3.8	Weathers	1	3	3.0
Gentry	3	15	5.0	Hawthorne	1	–4	–4.0
Thomas	2	8	4.0				
Fuller	1	1	1.0				
Perry	1	1	1.0				

RECEIVING

	No	Yds	Avge		No	Yds	Avge
Gault	4	129	32.3	Morgan	7	70	10.0
Gentry	2	41	20.5	Starring	2	39	19.5
Margerum	2	36	18.0	Fryar	2	24	12.0
Moorehead	2	22	11.0	Collins	2	19	9.5
Suhey	1	24	24.0	Ramsey	2	16	8.0
Thomas	1	4	4.0	C James	1	6	6.0
				Weathers	1	3	3.0

PASSING

Chicago	Att	Comp	Comp %	Yds	Int	Yds Att.	Yds Comp.
McMahon	20	12	60.0	256	0	12.8	21.3
Fuller	4	0	0.0	0	0	0.0	0.0
New England							
Grogan	30	17	56.7	177	2	5.9	10.4
Eason	6	0	0.0	0	0	0.0	0.0

Phillips, following an interception, and William Perry, who powered his way into the end zone from one yard, gave the Bears an invincible 44–3 lead. New England opened the scoring in the final quarter when a 76-yard drive ended with Irving Fryar taking an eight-yard pass from Grogan. But the Bears had the last word as they took their points tally to 46 when Henry Waechter tackled Grogan in the end zone for a safety.

Bears quarterback Jim McMahon dives in for a touchdown as Chicago cruise to victory in Super Bowl XX.

1987

SUPER BOWL XXI
25 January
Rose Bowl, Pasadena
101063
MVP: Phil Simms
(New York Giants/quarterback)

The Giants scored 30 points in the second half to win their first Super Bowl and their first championship in 30 years. Phil Simms of New York won the MVP award as he completed 22 of 25 passes for 268 yards, including three touchdowns. His 88% completion percentage was a post-season record.

Denver started the scoring with a Rich Karlis field goal on the opening play, his barefooted kick from 48 yards equalling the Super Bowl distance record. The Giants bounced right back to take the lead following a 78-yard drive when Simms threw a touchdown pass to Zeke Mowatt to finish the move. Denver then regained the lead when their quarterback John Elway ran in from four yards.

The only score of the second quarter was a safety when Elway was tackled in the end zone. Denver had a chance earlier to increase their lead but Karlis missed the shortest field goal in Super Bowl history when his 23-yard kick was off target. So Denver held just a narrow one-point lead going into the second half.

New York completed their first drive of the second half (63 yards) with a 13-yard touchdown pass from Simms to Mark Bavaro. Allegre then kicked a 21-yard field goal, and before the quarter was finished Joe Morris plunged over from one yard to make it 26–10.

The Giants extended that lead when McConkey took a six-yard touchdown pass from Simms. A Karlis field goal briefly reduced the Giants' lead before Ottis Anderson went over following a two-yard run. John Elway hit Vance Johnson with a 47-yard touchdown pass to give Denver a consolation score.

THE TEAMS

NEW YORK GIANTS (NFC)
39 – 7 2 17 13
T: Mowatt, Bavaro, Morris, McConkey, Anderson
FG: Allegre
PA: Allegre 4
Safety: 1
Starting Line Up:
OFFENSE: Ard, Bavaro, Benson, Carthon, Godfrey, Johnson, Morris, Nelson, Oates, Robinson, Simms
Substitutes: Anderson, Galbreath, B Johnson, Johnston, Manuel, McConkey, Miller, Mowatt, Roberts, Rouson, Rutledge
DEFENSE: Banks, Carson, Collins, Hill, Howard, Marshall, Martin, Reasons, Taylor, Welch, Williams
Substitutes: Burt, Collins, Dorsey, Flynn, Headen, Hunt, P Johnson, Jones, Lasker, Patterson, Sally
KICKERS: Allegre, Landeta

DENVER BRONCOS (AFC)
20 – 10 0 0 10
T: Elway, V Johnson
FG: Karlis 2
PA: Karlis 2
Starting Line Up:
OFFENSE: Bishop, Bryan, Elway, Howard, V Johnson, Lanier, Mobley, Studdard, Watson, Willhite, Winder
Substitutes: Bell, Bishop, Cooper, Freeman, Hackett, M Jackson, Kubiak, Lang, Micho, Remsberg, Sampson, Sewell
DEFENSE: Foley, Harden, Hunley, T Jackson, Jones, Kragen, Mecklenburg, Ryan, Smith, Townsend, Wright
Substitutes: Colorito, Comeaux, Dennison, Fletcher, Gilbert, Haynes, Lilly, Robinson, Wilson, Woodard
KICKERS: Horan, Karlis

PLAYERS' STATISTICS

New York Giants   **Denver**

RUSHING

	No	Yds	Avge		No	Yds	Avge
Morris	20	67	3.3	Elway	6	27	4.5
Simms	3	25	8.3	Willhite	4	19	4.8
Rouson	3	22	7.3	Sewell	3	4	1.3
Galbreath	4	17	4.3	Lang	2	2	1.0
Carthon	3	4	1.3	Winder	4	0	0.0
Anderson	2	1	0.5				
Rutledge	3	0	0.0				

RECEIVING

	No	Yds	Avge		No	Yds	Avge
Bavaro	4	51	12.8	V Johnson	5	121	24.2
Morris	4	20	5.0	Willhite	5	39	7.8
Carthon	4	13	3.3	Winder	4	34	8.5
Robinson	3	62	20.7	M Jackson	3	51	17.0
Manuel	3	43	14.3	Watson	2	54	27.0
McConkey	2	50	25.0	Sampson	2	20	10.0
Rouson	1	23	23.0	Mobley	2	17	8.5
Mowatt	1	6	6.0	Sewell	2	12	6.0
				Lang	1	4	4.0

PASSING

New York	Att	Comp	Comp %	Yds	Int	Yds Att.	Yds Comp.
Simms	25	22	88.0	268	0	10.7	12.2
Denver							
Elway	37	22	59.5	304	1	8.2	13.8
Kubiak	4	4	100.0	48	0	12.0	12.0

1988

SUPER BOWL XXII
31 January
Jack Murphy Stadium,
San Diego
73 302
*MVP: Doug Williams
(Washington / quarterback)*

Fifty-two points were scored in Super Bowl XXII and a record 35 of them came in one explosive quarter. The Broncos took the lead on their first play when John Elway threw a 56-yard touchdown pass to Ricky Nattiel. Karlis added a field goal as Denver took a 10–0 lead into the second quarter. But that was their moment over and they slipped to their second successive defeat as the Redskins scored a staggering five touchdowns on five successive possessions in the second quarter.

Four of their touchdowns came from passes by Doug Williams, the first black quarterback to start a Super Bowl, and MVP winner. Williams had in fact twisted his knee shortly before the end of the first quarter but came out, limping, for the second quarter. Remarkably Washington's five second-quarter touchdowns came from just 18 plays and during a possession period of only five minutes 47 seconds. It was an incredible scoring spree.

Ricky Sanders started it by taking a record-equalling 80-yard pass from Williams. The next came when Gary Clark took a 27-yard pass from Williams. Tim Smith ran in from 58 yards for the third, Sanders gathered a 50-yard pass from Williams for the fourth and the scoring was rounded off when Clint Didier took an eight-yarder from Williams. In their 18 plays, the Redskins totalled 356 yards.

The next quarter was an anti-

climax with neither team scoring, and in the final quarter the only score was yet another Redskins touchdown when Tim Smith ran in from four yards. All Washington's six touchdowns were successfully converted by

Haji-Sheikh who set a Super Bowl record, just one of many set in this remarkable game. Rookie Tim Smith, who had gained only 126 yards for the entire season, rushed for a record 204 yards.

THE TEAMS

WASHINGTON REDSKINS (NFC)
42 – 0 35 0 7
T: Sanders 2, Smith 2, Clark, Didier
PA: Haji-Sheikh 6
Starting Line Up:
OFFENSE: Bostic, Clark, Didier, Jacoby, McKenzie, May, Sanders, Smith, Thielemann, Warren, Williams
Substitutes: Branch, Bryant, Griffin, Grimm, Jones, Kehr, Monk, Orr, Rogers, Schroeder, Vaughn, Yarber
DEFENSE: Bowles, Butz, Coleman, Grant, Green, Kaufman, Mann, Manley, Olkewicz, Walton, Wilburn
Substitutes: Caldwell, Davis, Dean, Gouveai, Hamel, Hamilton, Koch, Milot, Woodberry
KICKERS: Cox, Haji-Sheikh

DENVER BRONCOS (AFC)
10 – 10 0 0 0
T: Nattiel
FG: Karlis
PA: Karlis
Starting Line Up:
OFFENSE: Bishop, Elway, Freeman, Humphries, Jackson, Kay, Lang, Lanier, Nattiel, Studdard, Winder
Substitutes: Bell, Boddie, Bowyer, Braxton, Johnson, Kartz, Kubiak, Micho, Mobley, Sewell, Watson
DEFENSE: Fletcher, Haynes, Hunley, Kragen, Jones, Lilly, Smith, Mecklenburg, Ryan, Townsend, Wilson
Substitutes: Brooks, Castille, Clark, Dennison, Fletcher, Gilbert, Klosterman, Lucas, Plummer, Robbins, Woodard
KICKERS: Horan, Karlis

PLAYERS' STATISTICS

Washington   **Denver**

RUSHING

	No	Yds	Avge		No	Yds	Avge
Smith	22	204	9.3	Lang	5	38	7.6
Bryant	8	38	4.8	Elway	3	32	10.7
Clark	1	25	25.0	Winder	8	30	3.8
Rogers	5	17	3.4	Sewell	1	–3	–3.0
Griffin	1	2	2.0				
Sanders	1	–4	–4.0				
Williams	2	–2	–2.0				

RECEIVING

	No	Yds	Avge		No	Yds	Avge
Sanders	9	193	21.4	Jackson	4	76	19.0
Clark	3	55	18.3	Sewell	4	41	10.3
Warren	2	15	7.5	Nattiel	2	69	24.5
Monk	1	40	40.0	Kay	2	38	19.0
Bryant	1	20	20.0	Winder	1	26	26.0
Smith	1	9	9.0	Elway	1	23	23.0
Didier	1	8	8.0	Lang	1	7	7.0

PASSING

Washington	Att	Comp	Comp %	Yds	Int	Yds Att.	Yds Comp.
Williams	29	18	62.1	340	1	11.7	18.9
Schroeder	1	0	0.0	0	0	0.0	0.0

Denver							
Elway	38	14	36.8	257	3	6.8	18.4
Sewell	1	1	100.0	23	0	23.0	23.0

1989

SUPER BOWL XXIII
22 January
Joe Robbie Stadium, Miami
75 129
MVP: Jerry Rice
(San Francisco/wide receiver)

San Francisco became the first NFC team to win three Super Bowls, but despite having an advantage of 453 yards to 229 they left it late before snatching victory from the Bengals.

At half-time the score was tied at 3–3 with Cofer (San Francisco) and Breech kicking field goals from 41 and 34 yards respectively. It was the first time in Super Bowl history there had been a tie at the halfway stage. Breech and Cofer again exchanged field goals in the third quarter before Stanford Jennings ran in a touchdown for Cincinnati on a 93-yard kick-off return in the dying seconds of the quarter. Breech made the kick and the Bengals led 13–6 at the start of the last period.

With less than a minute of the final quarter gone, the two sides were level again when the 49ers covered 85 yards in four plays which ended with Montana's 14-yard touchdown pass to MVP Jerry Rice, who caught 11 passes for a record 215 yards. But with three minutes 20 seconds remaining Jim Breech kicked his third field goal of the day, from 40 yards, to put Cincinnati in front 16–13.

The 49ers started their winning drive on their eight-yard line. Over the next 11 plays they covered the length of the field and the winning pass came 34 seconds from time when Montana threw 10 yards to match-winner John Taylor. Cofer made the kick and San Francisco won a dramatic match 20–16.

THE TEAMS

SAN FRANCISCO 49ers (NFC)
20 – 3 0 3 14
T: Rice, Taylor
FG: Cofer 2
PA: Cofer 2
Starting Line Up:
OFFENSE: Barton, Craig, Cross, Frank, McIntyre, Montana, Rathman, Rice, Sapolu, Taylor, Wallace
Substitutes: Collie, Flagler, Greer, Haller, B Jones, Paris, Pollard, Sydney, Thomas, Wilson, Young
DEFENSE: Carter, Fagan, Fahnhorst, Fuller, Griffin, Haley, Lott, McKyer, Roberts, Turner, Walter
Substitutes: Cox, Ellison, Kennedy, Kugler, Holmoe, Holt, Romanowski, Stover, Stubbs, Wright
KICKERS: Cofer, Helton

CINCINNATI BENGALS (AFC)
16 – 0 3 10 3
T: Jennings
FG: Breech 3
PA: Breech
Starting Line Up:
OFFENSE: Blados, Brooks, Brown, Esiason, Holman, Kozerski, McGee, Montoya, Munoz, Reimers, Woods
Substitutes: Collinsworth, Douglas, Hillary, Jennings, Logan, Norseth, Parker, Riggs, Rourke, D Smith, Schonert
DEFENSE: Billups, Buck, Fulcher, Kelly, Krumrie, Skow, Thomas, White, Wilcots, Williams, Zander
Substitutes: Barker, Brady, Bussey, Dixon, Edwards, Grant, Horton, King, McClendon, Smith
KICKERS: Breech, Johnson

PLAYERS' STATISTICS

San Francisco   Cincinnati

RUSHING

	No	Yds	Avge		No	Yds	Avge
Craig	17	74	4.4	Woods	20	79	4.0
Rathman	5	23	4.6	Brooks	6	24	4.0
Montana	5	9	1.8	Jennings	1	3	3.0
Rice	1	5	5.0	Esiason	1	0	0.0

RECEIVING

	No	Yds	Avge		No	Yds	Avge
Rice	11	215	19.6	Brown	4	44	11.0
Craig	5	101	20.2	Collinsworth	3	40	13.3
France	2	15	7.5	McGee	2	23	11.5
Rathman	1	16	16.0	Brooks	1	20	20.0
Taylor	1	10	10.0	Hillary	1	17	17.0

PASSING

San Francisco	Att	Comp	Comp %	Yds	Int	Yds Att.	Yds Comp.
Montana	36	23	63.9	357	0	9.9	15.5

Cincinnati							
Esiason	25	11	44.0	144	1	5.8	13.1

1990

SUPER BOWL XXIV
28 January
Louisiana Superdrome,
New Orleans
72919
*MVP: Joe Montana
(San Francisco/ quarterback)*

San Francisco joined the Pittsburgh Steelers as the Super Bowl's most successful team with their fourth win in four attempts. The Broncos, on the other hand, joined the Minnesota Vikings as four-time losers as they were trounced 55–10 in the most one-sided Super Bowl ever, and the highest scoring.

The 49ers notched up double figures in each quarter as Joe Montana led the side to victory and at the same time captured his third MVP award. He threw a record five touchdown passes, three to Jerry Rice. Montana completed 22 of 29 passes including a record 13 consecutive.

San Francisco scored touchdowns on four of their six first-half possessions. The first was in the opening quarter when Rice took a 20-yard touchdown pass from Montana. Treadwell kicked a 42-yard field goal for Denver but Jones scored a second touchdown as the 49ers led 13–3 at the end of the first quarter. A one-yard Rathman run and another Montana pass (38 yards) to Rice took the half-time score to 27–3 in San Francisco's favour.

Another Montana–Rice combination yielded their third touchdown in the third quarter and the 49ers ended the quarter 41–10 in front after Taylor took a 35-yard pass from Montana before John Elway scored Denver's only touchdown with a three-yard run. Two more touchdowns in the final quarter rounded off San Francisco's scoring; the first, a three-yard run

THE TEAMS

SAN FRANCISCO 49ers (NFC)
55 – 13 14 14 14
T: Rice 3, Rathman 2, Jones, Taylor, Craig
PA: Cofer 7
Starting Line Up:
OFFENSE: Barton, Collie, Craig, Jones, McIntyre, Montana, Paris, Rathman, Rice, Sapolu, Taylor
Substitutes: Flagler, Sherrard, Sydney, Tausch, Thomas, Wallace, Walls, Wilson, Young
DEFENSE: Brooks, Carter, Fagan, Griffin, Haley, Holt, Lott, Millen, Pollard, Turner, Walter
Substitutes: De Long, J Jackson, Kugler, McKyer, Roberts, Romanowski, Stubbs, Wright
KICKERS: Cofer, Helton

DENVER BRONCOS (AFC)
10 – 3 0 7 0
T: Elway
FG: Treadwell
PA: Treadwell
Starting Line Up:
OFFENSE: Bratton, Elway, Humphrey, M Jackson, Johnson, Juriga, Kartz, Kay, Lanier, Perry, Widell
Substitutes: Alexander, Bishop, Kubiak, Mobley, Nattiel, Ruether, Smith, Winder, Young
DEFENSE: Atwater, Braxton, Brooks, Carreker, Dennison, Fletcher, Henderson, Holmes, Kragen, Macklenburg, Smith
Substitutes: Carrington, Corrington, Dennison, Haynes, Henke, Klostermann, Lucas, Munford, Powers, Robbins, Townsend
KICKERS: Treadwell, Horan

PLAYERS' STATISTICS

San Francisco   Denver

RUSHING

	No	Yds	Avge		No	Yds	Avge
Craig	20	69	3.5	Humphrey	12	61	5.1
Rathman	11	38	3.5	Elway	4	8	2.0
Montana	2	15	7.5	Winder	1	–5	–5.0
Flagler	6	14	2.3				
Young	4	6	1.5				
Sydney	1	2	2.0				

RECEIVING

	No	Yds	Avge		No	Yds	Avge
Rice	7	148	21.1	Humphrey	3	38	12.7
Craig	5	34	6.8	Sewell	2	22	11.0
Rathman	4	43	10.8	Johnson	2	21	10.5
Taylor	3	49	16.3	Nattiel	1	28	28.0
Sherrard	1	13	13.0	Bratton	1	1	1.0
Walls	1	9	9.0	Winder	1	7	7.0
Jones	1	7	7.0	Kay	1	6	6.0
Williams	1	7	7.0				
Sydney	1	7	7.0				

PASSING

San Francisco	Att	Comp	Comp %	Yds	Int	Yds Att.	Yds Comp.
Montana	29	22	75.9	297	0	10.2	13.5
Young	3	2	66.7	20	0	6.7	10.0
Denver							
Elway	26	10	38.5	108	2	4.2	10.8
Kubiak	3	1	33.3	28	0	9.3	28.0

from Rathman, was followed by a one-yard run from Roger Craig as the rout of the Broncos was completed.

Left *Jerry Rice celebrates a San Francisco touchdown in the 49ers 55–10 crushing of the Denver Broncos.*

Below *Ottis Anderson rushed for 102 yards, ran in for a touchdown and was MVP as the New York Giants held out against Buffalo for a second Super Bowl success.*

1991

SUPER BOWL XXV
27 January
Tampa Stadium, Tampa
73813
MVP: Ottis Anderson
(New York Giants/running back)

If Super Bowl XXIV had been the most one-sided in Super Bowl history, Super Bowl XXV was the closest and most exciting as the Giants won for the second time in four years, beating Buffalo by a mere point. There was agony for the Bills' kicker Scott Norwood when his 47-yard field goal just eight seconds from time went wide of the posts.

The Bills had steamrollered their way to the Super Bowl by scoring 95 points in their previous two play-off games. The Giants decided the best way to prevent a repeat performance was to keep possession of the ball and they did that for a Super Bowl record 40 minutes and 33 seconds, confining the Bills to less than 20 minutes' possession. The Bills had the ball for less than eight minutes in the second half.

The only scores of the first quarter came from field goals from Matt Bahr (Giants) and Norwood. Don Smith ran in the first touchdown in the second quarter from one yard, Norwood made the point after and Buffalo led 10–3. They increased it to 12–3 midway through the quarter when New York quarterback Jeff Hostetler was tackled in the end zone by Bruce Smith for a safety. But Hostetler made amends by throwing a 14-yard touchdown pass to Stephen Baker which closed the gap to 12–10, with Bahr's kick, at the interval.

Ottis Anderson ran in from one yard and Bahr converted for the only score of the third

THE TEAMS

NEW YORK GIANTS (NFC)
20 – 3 7 7 3
T: Baker, Anderson
FG: Bahr 2
PA: Bahr 2
Starting Line Up:
OFFENSE: Anderson, Bavaro, Cross, Elliott, Hostetler, Ingram, Moore, Mrosko, Oates, Riesenberg, Roberts
Substitutes: Baker, Carton, Kratch, Kyles, Meggett, Robinson, Rouson, Tilman, Williams
DEFENSE: Banks, Collins, Guyton, Howard, G Jackson, Johnson, Marshall, Taylor, Thompson, Walls, Williams
Substitutes: Abrahams, Brown, Cavanagh, Cooks, DeOssie, Dorsey, Duerson, Fox, McGrew, Reasons, Washington, Whitmore
KICKERS: Bahr, Landeta

BUFFALO BILLS (AFC)
19 – 3 9 0 7
T: D Smith, Thomas
FG: Norwood
PA: Norwood 2
Safety: 1
Starting Line Up:
OFFENSE: Ballard, Davis, Edwards, Hull, Kelly, Lofton, McKeller, Reed, Ritcher, Thomas, Wolford
Substitutes: Davis, Frerotte, Gardner, Lingner, Metzelaars, Mueller, Parker, Rolle, Reich, Smith, Tasker
DEFENSE: Bennett, Bentley, Conlon, K Jackson, Kelso, Odomes, Seals, B Smith, L Smith, Talley, Wright
Substitutes: Bailey, Baldinger, Drane, Garner, Gilbert, Hagy, Hicks, Lodish, Pike, Williams
KICKERS: Norwood, Tuten

PLAYERS' STATISTICS

New York Giants   Buffalo

RUSHING

	No	Yds	Avge		No	Yds	Avge
Anderson	21	102	4.9	Thomas	15	135	9.0
Meggett	9	48	5.3	Kelly	6	23	3.8
Carthon	3	12	4.0	K Davis	2	4	2.0
Hostetler	6	10	1.7	Mueller	1	3	3.0
				D Smith	1	1	1.0

RECEIVING

	No	Yds	Avge		No	Yds	Avge
Ingram	5	74	14.8	Reed	8	62	7.8
Bavaro	5	50	10.0	Thomas	5	55	11.0
Cross	4	39	9.8	K Davis	2	23	11.5
Baker	2	31	15.5	McKeller	2	11	5.5
Meggett	2	18	9.0	Lofton	1	61	61.0
Anderson	1	7	7.0				
Carthon	1	3	3.0				

PASSING

	Att	Comp	Comp %	Yds	Int	Yds Att.	Yds Comp.
New York Giants							
Hostetler	32	20	62.5	222	0	6.9	11.1
Buffalo							
Kelly	30	18	60.0	212	0	7.1	11.8

quarter as the Giants retook the lead 17–12. Buffalo got the lead back on the first play of the final quarter when Thurman Thomas ran in from 31 yards for a touchdown. Norwood's kick made it 19–17. Then the Giants

regained the lead seven minutes 40 seconds from time with Matt Bahr's 21-yard field goal. There were no other scores, only that dramatic miss by Scott Norwood from 47 yards in the closing seconds.

1992

SUPER BOWL XXVI
26 January
Minneapolis Metrodome,
Minnesota
63 130

*MVP: Mark Rypien
(Washington/quarterback)*

The Redskins and Bills came to Minneapolis for Super Bowl XXVI with the season's two best regular season records: Washington were 14–2 and Buffalo 13–3. And it was Washington who confirmed their tag as favourites by taking the title.

The first quarter was scoreless for the fourth time in Super Bowl history but the second quarter came alive when Washington ran in two touchdowns to assert their superiority. Chip Lohmiller kicked a 34-yard field goal after one minute 58 seconds before Ernest Byner took a 10-yard pass from Mark Rypien for the game's first touchdown after five minutes. Gerald Riggs ran in the second from one yard less than three minutes later as Washington went 17–0 ahead.

They increased their lead to 24 points in the first couple of minutes of the third quarter when Riggs ran in from two yards for his second touchdown. Scott Norwood kicked a 21-yard field goal to give Buffalo their first score after three minutes of the quarter before Thomas ran in the Bills' first touchdown after nine minutes. But Gary Clark took a 30-yard touchdown pass from Rypien one and a half minutes from the end of the quarter to restore Washington's lead at 31–10.

Two field goals from Lohmiller in the first four minutes of the final quarter, the first after just six seconds following a fumble, put Washington further ahead at 37–10. All Buffalo could do was restore some pride with two touchdowns in the second part of the final quarter. Both passes came from Jim Kelly, the first a two-yarder to Pete Metzelaars and the second from four yards to Don Beebe. Kelly attempted a record 58 passes during the game. But it was all too late – Super Bowl XXVI had been won by Washington with that 17-point burst in the second quarter.

THE TEAMS

WASHINGTON REDSKINS (NFC)	**BUFFALO BILLS** (AFC)
37 – 0 17 14 6	24 – 0 0 10 14
T: Riggs 2, Byner, Clark	*T:* Thomas, Metzelaars, Beebe
FG: Lohmiller 3	*FG:* Norwood
PA: Lohmiller 4	*PA:* Norwood 3

Starting Line Up:

OFFENSE: Bostic, Byner, Clark, Jacoby, Lachey, McKenzie, Monk, Rypien, Sanders, Schlereth, Warren
Substitutes: Buck, Caldwell, Coleman, Geathers, AJ Johnson, S Johnson, Mays, Milien, Walton, Wilson
DEFENSE: Collins, Copeland, Edwards, Gouveia, Green, T Johnson, Mann, Marshall, Mayhew, Stokes, Williams
Substitutes: Adickes, Brandes, Ervins, Grimm, Hobbs, Humphries, Jenkins, Middleton, Mitchell, Orr, Riggs, Rutledge, Simmons
KICKERS: Lohmiller, Goodburn

Starting Line Up:

OFFENSE: Ballard, Frerotte, Gardner, Hull, Kelly, Lofton, McKeller, Reed, Ritcher, Thomas, Wolford
Substitutes: Beebe, Brennan, Davis, Edwards, Gilbert, Lingner, Metzelaars, Reich, Rolle, Staysniak, Tasker
DEFENSE: Bailey, Bennett, Conlan, Jackson, Kelso, Odomes, Seals, B Smith, L Smith, Talley, Wright
Substitutes: Bentley, Garner, Hansen, Hicks, Jones, Lodish, Patton, Pike, Taylor, Williams
KICKERS: Norwood, Mohr

PLAYERS' STATISTICS

Washington · Buffalo

RUSHING

	No	Yds	Avge		No	Yds	Avge
Ervins	13	72	5.5	Davis	4	17	4.3
Byner	14	49	3.5	Kelly	3	16	5.3
Riggs	5	7	1.4	Thomas	10	13	1.3
Sanders	1	1	1.0	Lofton	1	–3	–3.0
Rutledge	1	0	0.0				
Rypien	6	–4	–0.7				

RECEIVING

	No	Yds	Avge		No	Yds	Avge
Clark	7	114	16.3	Reed	5	34	6.8
Monk	7	113	16.1	Lofton	7	92	13.1
Byner	3	24	8.0	McKeller	2	29	14.5
Sanders	1	41	41.0	Thomas	4	27	6.8
				Beebe	4	61	15.3
				Kelly	1	–8	–8.0
				Edwards	1	11	11.0
				Davis	4	38	9.5
				Metzelaars	1	2	2.0

PASSING

Washington	Att	Comp	Comp %	Yds	Int	Yds Att.	Yds Comp.
Rypien	33	18	55.6	292	1	8.9	16.2
Buffalo							
Kelly	58	28	48.3	275	4	4.7	9.8
Reich	1	1	100.0	11	0	11.0	11.0

An impressive display from quarterback Mark Rypien saw the Washington Redskins run out comfortable winners over the Buffalo Bills in 1992.

SUPER BOWL RECORDS

MOST APPEARANCES

Players
5 Marv Fleming, Green Bay 1967–8, Miami 1972–4
5 Larry Cole, Dallas 1971–2, 1976, 1978–9
5 Cliff Harris, Dallas 1971–2, 1976, 1978–9
5 DD Lewis, Dallas 1971–2, 1976, 1978–9
5 Preston Pearson, Baltimore 1969, Pittsburgh 1975, Dallas 1976, 1978–9
5 Charlie Waters, Dallas 1971–2, 1976, 1978–9
5 Rayfield Wright, Dallas 1971–2, 1976, 1978–9
Coach
6 Don Shula, Baltimore 1969, Miami 1972–4, 1983, 1985

MOST GAMES FOR WINNING TEAM

Players
4 Many players have appeared on four winning teams
Coach
4 Chuck Noll, Pittsburgh 1975–6, 1979–80
Bud Grant (Minnesota 1970, 1974–5, 1977) and Don Shula (Baltimore 1969, Miami 1972, 1983, 1985) have both lost a record four games as coach

DD Lewis, one of five from the Dallas Cowboys team of the 1970s to claim a record five Super Bowl appearances.

Don Shula has a word with his quarterback Marino during the 1985 Super Bowl. It was Shula's fourth losing game in a record six appearances as coach.

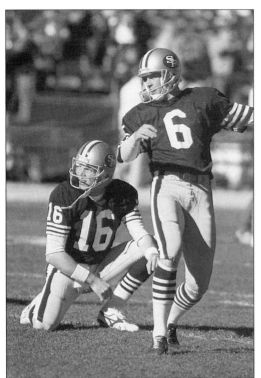

Mike Cofer (right) holds the record for the most Extra Points kicked in Super Bowls, seven of nine coming against Denver in 1990.

SCORING

Most Points
Career: 24 Franco Harris, Pittsburgh
24 Roger Craig, San Francisco
24 Jerry Rice, San Francisco
Game: 18 Roger Craig, San Francisco v Miami, 1985
18 Jerry Rice, San Francisco v Denver, 1990

Most Touchdowns
Career: 4 Franco Harris, Pittsburgh
4 Roger Craig, San Francisco
4 Jerry Rice, San Francisco
Game: 3 Roger Craig, San Francisco v Miami, 1985
3 Jerry Rice, San Francisco v Denver, 1990

Most Points After Touchdown
Career: 9 Mike Cofer, San Francisco
Game: 7 Mike Cofer, San Francisco v Denver, 1990

Most Field Goals Attempted
Career: 7 Roy Gerela, Pittsburgh
Game: 5 Jim Turner, NY Jets v Baltimore, 1969
5 Efren Herrera, Dallas v Denver, 1978

Most Field Goals Made
Career: 5 Ray Wersching, San Francisco
Game: 4 Don Chandler, Green Bay v Oakland, 1968
4 Ray Wersching, San Francisco v Cincinnati, 1982

Longest Field Goal
48 yds, Jan Stenerud, Kansas City v Minnesota, 1970
48 yds, Rich Karlis, Denver v NY Giants, 1987

RUSHING

Most Attempts
Career: 101 Franco Harris, Pittsburgh
Game: 38 John Riggins, Washington v Miami, 1983

Most Yards Gained
Career: 354 Franco Harris, Pittsburgh
Game: 204 Tim Smith, Washington v Denver, 1988

Longest Run from Scrimmage
Game: 74 yds, Marcus Allen, LA Raiders v Washington, 1984

Most Touchdowns
Career: 4 Franco Harris, Pittsburgh
Game: 2 Elijah Pitts, Green Bay v Kansas City, 1967
2 Larry Csonka, Miami v Minnesota, 1974
2 Pete Banaszak, Oakland v Minnesota, 1977
2 Franco Harris, Pittsburgh v LA Rams, 1980
2 Marcus Allen, LA Raiders v Washington, 1984
2 Jim McMahon, Chicago v New England, 1986
2 Tim Smith, Washington v Denver, 1988
2 Tom Rathman, San Francisco v Denver, 1990
2 Gerald Riggs, Washington v Buffalo, 1992

Highest Average Gain
Career: (Min. 20 attempts)
9.6 yds Marcus Allen, LA Raiders
Game: (Min. 10 attempts)
10.5 yds Tom Matte, Baltimore v NY Jets, 1969

Tim Smith rushed for 204 yards for Washington in their astonishing blitz on Denver in 1988.

PASSING

Most Attempts
Career: 122 Joe Montana, San Francisco
Game: 58 Jim Kelly, Buffalo v Washington, 1992
Completions
Career: 83 Joe Montana, San Francisco
Game: 29 Dan Marino, Miami v San Francisco, 1985
Most Consecutive Completions
Game: 13 Joe Montana, San Francisco v Denver, 1990
Highest Completion Percentage
Career: 68.0% Joe Montana, San Francisco
Game: 88.0% Phil Simms, NY Giants v Denver, 1987
Most Yards Gained
Career: 1142 Joe Montana, San Francisco
Game: 357 Joe Montana, San Francisco v Cincinnati, 1989
Most Touchdowns
Career: 11 Joe Montana, San Francisco
Game: 5 Joe Montana, San Francisco v Denver, 1990
Most Intercepted
Career: 7 Craig Morton, Dallas/Denver
Game: 4 Craig Morton, Denver v Dallas, 1978
4 Jim Kelly, Buffalo v Washington, 1992
Longest Completion
80 yds, Jim Plunkett (to Kenny King) Oakland v Philadelphia, 1981
80 yds, Doug Williams (to Ricky Sanders) Washington v Denver, 1988
Highest Average Gains
Career: (Min. 40 attempts)
11.10 yds (84 for 932) Terry Bradshaw, Pittsburgh
Game: (Min. 20 attempts)
14.71 yds (21 for 309) Terry Bradshaw, Pittsburgh v LA Rams, 1980
Most Touchdown Passes
Career: 11 Joe Montana, San Francisco
Game: 5 Joe Montana, San Francisco v Denver, 1990
Most Attempts Without Being Intercepted
Game: 36 Joe Montana, San Francisco v Cincinnati, 1989
Lowest Percentage of Passes Intercepted
Career: (Min. 40 attempts)
0.00% Jim Plunkett, Oakland/LA Raiders

PASS RECEIVING

Most Receptions
Career: 20 Roger Craig, San Francisco
Game: 11 Dan Ross, Cincinnati v San Francisco, 1982
11 Jerry Rice, San Francisco v Cincinnati, 1989
Most Yards Gained
Career: 364 Lynn Swann, Pittsburgh
Game: 215 Jerry Rice, San Francisco v Cincinnati, 1989
Most Touchdowns
Career: 4 Jerry Rice, San Francisco
Game: 3 Jerry Rice, San Francisco v Denver, 1990
Longest Reception
80 yds, Kenny King (from Jim Plunkett), Oakland v Philadelphia, 1981
80 yds, Ricky Sanders (from Doug Williams), Washington v Denver, 1988

INTERCEPTIONS

Most by
Career: 3 Chuck Howley, Dallas
3 Rod Martin, Oakland
Game: 3 Rod Martin, Oakland v Philadelphia, 1981

PUNTING

Most Punts
Career: 17 Mike Eischied, Oakland/Minnesota
Game: 9 Ron Widby, Dallas v Baltimore
Longest Punt
63 yds, Lee Johnson, Cincinnati v San Francisco, 1989
Average Yards Punting
Career: (Min. 10 punts)
46.5 yds, Jerrel Wilson, Kansas City
Game: (Min. 4 punts)
48.5 yds, Jerrel Wilson, Kansas City v Minnesota, 1970

PUNT RETURNS

Most
Career: 6 Willie Wood, Green Bay
6 Jake Scott, Miami
6 Theo Bell, Pittsburgh
6 Mike Nelms, Washington
6 John Taylor, San Francisco
Game: 6 Mike Nelms, Washington v Miami, 1983
Most Yards Gained
Career: 94 John Taylor, San Francisco
Game: 56 John Taylor, San Francisco v Cincinnati, 1989
Longest Punt Return
45 yds, John Taylor, San Francisco v Cincinnati, 1989
Highest Average Yards Gained
Career: (Min. 4 returns)
15.7 John Taylor, San Francisco
Game: (Min. 3 returns)
18.7 John Taylor, San Francisco v Cincinnati, 1989

KICK-OFF RETURNS

Most
Career: 10 Ken Bell, Denver
Game: 7 Stephen Starring, New England v Chicago, 1986
Most Yards Gained
Career: 283 Fulton Walker, Miami
Game: 190 Fulton Walker, Miami v Washington, 1983
Longest Kick-off Return
98 yds (for a TD), Fulton Walker, Miami v Washington, 1983
Average Yards Gained from Kick-off Returns
Career: (Min. 4 returns)
35.4 Fulton Walker, Miami
Game: (Min. 3 returns)
47.5 Fulton Walker, Miami v Washington, 1983

FUMBLES

Most by
Career: 5 Roger Staubach, Dallas
Game: 3 Roger Staubach, Dallas v Pittsburgh, 1976
3 Jim Kelly, Buffalo v Washington, 1992

Left *Roger Craig holds the record for pass receptions in Super Bowls, 20 in total.*

SCORING

Biggest Winning Margin
45 pts, San Francisco 55 Denver 10, 1990
Most Points in One Game
55 San Francisco v Denver, 1990
Least Points in One Game
3 Miami v Dallas, 1972
Highest Scoring Game (aggregate)
66 pts, Pittsburgh 35 Dallas 31, 1979
Lowest Scoring Game (aggregate)
21 pts, Miami 14 Washington 7, 1973
Most Aggregate Points (all games)
163 San Francisco
Most Points in any single quarter (both teams)
35 (2nd quarter) Washington 35 Denver 0, 1988
Most Points in any single quarter (one team)
35 Washington v Denver, 1988
Most Touchdowns (game)
One Team: 8 San Francisco v Denver, 1990
Both Teams: 9 Pittsburgh (5) v Dallas (4), 1979
9 San Francisco (8) v Denver (1), 1990
Least Touchdowns (game)
One Team: 0 Miami v Dallas, 1972
Both Teams: 2 Baltimore (1) v NY Jets (1), 1969
Most Points after Touchdown (game)
One Team: 7 San Francisco v Denver, 1990
Both Teams: 9 Pittsburgh (5) v Dallas (4), 1979
Most Field Goals Made (game)
One Team: 4 Green Bay v Oakland, 1968
4 San Francisco v Cincinnati, 1982
Both Teams: 5 Cincinnati (3) v San Francisco (2), 1989

TEAM RECORDS

How the current 28 NFL teams have fared in the Super Bowl

	P	W	L	PF	PA
Buffalo Bills	2	0	2	43	57
Chicago Bears	1	1	0	46	10
Cincinnati Bengals	2	0	2	37	46
Dallas Cowboys	5	2	3	112	85
Denver Broncos	4	0	4	50	163
Green Bay Packers	2	2	0	68	24
Indianapolis/Baltimore Colts	2	1	1	23	29
Kansas City Chiefs	2	1	1	33	42
Los Angeles Rams	1	0	1	19	31
Miami Dolphins	5	2	3	74	103
Minnesota Vikings	4	0	4	34	95
New England Patriots	1	0	1	10	46
New York Giants	2	2	0	59	39
New York Jets	1	1	0	16	7
Los Angeles/Oakland Raiders	4	3	1	111	66
Philadelphia Eagles	1	0	1	10	27
Pittsburgh Steelers	4	4	0	103	73
San Francisco 49ers	4	4	0	163	63
Washington Redskins	5	3	2	122	103

The following teams have never appeared in the Super Bowl:
Atlanta Falcons; Cleveland Browns; Detroit Lions; Houston Oilers; New Orleans Saints; Phoenix Cardinals; San Diego Chargers; Seattle Seahawks; Tampa Bay Buccaneers.

YARDS GAINED

Most Net Yards Gained Rushing & Passing (game)
602 Washington v Denver, 1988
Fewest Net Yards Gained Rushing & Passing (game)
119 Minnesota v Pittsburgh, 1975
Most Yards Gained Passing (game)
341 San Francisco v Cincinnati, 1989
Fewest Yards Passing (game)
35 Denver v Dallas, 1978
Most Yards Gained Rushing (game)
280 Washington v Denver, 1988
Fewest Yards Rushing (game)
7 New England v Chicago, 1986

ATTENDANCES

Record Attendance
103 985 at the Rose Bowl, Pasadena to watch the Pittsburgh–Los Angeles game in 1980.
Lowest Attendance
61 946 at the Los Angeles Coliseum to watch Super Bowl I between Green Bay and Kansas City in 1967.

ATLANTA FALCONS

Atlanta-Fulton County Stadium (formerly Atlanta Stadium, 1966–74)
521 Capitol Avenue SW, Atlanta, Georgia
Stadium Capacity: 59 643

After the franchise was given to Atlanta to establish an NFL team in 1965, a local contest to name the team resulted in it being called the Falcons because the falcon was said to be a 'proud bird full of courage and fight'. Well, the Falcons may have shown plenty of courage and fight in their first 25 years but the trophy room has given the club and fans little to be proud of because one divisional championship, in 1980, is all they have had to show for their efforts.

Their appearance in the 1991 play-offs was the first time in eight seasons they had not finished either bottom or next to bottom of the NFC Western Division.

It took the Falcons five seasons to register their first winning season, then in 1974 their performances slumped to an all-time low and attendances dropped by alarming proportions. Their Western Division title in 1980 remains their sole honour and the Falcons' brief 'glory days' of the 1980s coincided with the presence of English kicker Mick Luckhurst in their team. Luckhurst later went on to find fame as a broadcaster with Channel 4 Television and as the American Football correspondent of the *Daily Telegraph*.

RECORD HOLDERS

Career Records

Points	558	Mick Luckhurst, 1981–7
Touchdowns	48	Gerald Riggs, 1982–8
Rushing (Yards)	6631	Gerald Riggs, 1982–8
Passing (Yards)	23 468	Steve Bartkowski, 1975–85
Passing (Touchdowns)	154	Steve Bartkowski, 1975–85
Receiving (No.)	359	Alfred Jenkins, 1975–83
Receiving (Yards)	6257	Alfred Jenkins, 1975–83
Interceptions	39	Rolland Lawrence, 1973–80
Punting (Average)	42.6	Rick Donnelly, 1985–9
Punt Returns (Average)	11.8	Al Dodd, 1973–4
Kick-off Returns (Average)	24.3	Ron Smith, 1966–7
Field Goals	115	Mick Luckhurst, 1981–7

Season Records

Points	114	Mick Luckhurst, 1981
Touchdowns	13	Alfred Jenkins, 1981
	13	Gerald Riggs, 1984
Rushing (Yards)	1719	Gerald Riggs, 1985
Passing (Yards)	3830	Steve Bartkowski, 1981
Passing (Touchdowns)	31	Steve Bartkowski, 1980
Receiving (No.)	82	Andre Rison, 1990
Receiving (Yards)	1358	Alfred Jenkins, 1981
Interceptions	10	Scott Case, 1988
Punting (Average)	44.3	Billy Lothridge, 1968
Punt Returns (Average)	13.9	Gerald Tinker, 1974
Kick-off Returns (Average)	27.5	Sylvester Stamps, 1987
Field Goals	26	Nick Mike-Mayer, 1973

Single Game Records

Points	18	*Many occasions*
Touchdowns	3	*Many occasions*
Rushing (Yards)	202	Gerald Riggs, 2 Sep 1984
Passing (Yards)	416	Steve Bartkowski, 15 Nov 1981
Passing (Touchdowns)	4	Randy Johnson, 16 Nov 1969
	4	Steve Bartkowski, 19 Oct 1980
	4	Steve Bartkowski, 18 Oct 1981
Receiving (No.)	15	William Andrews, 15 Nov 1981
Receiving (Yards)	193	Alfred Jackson, 2 Dec 1984
Interceptions	2	*Many occasions*
Field Goals	5	Nick Mike-Mayer, 4 Nov 1973
	5	Tim Mazzetti, 30 Oct 1978

REGULAR SEASON RECORD

Year	W	L	T	%
1966	3	11	0	.214
1967	1	12	1	.077
1968	2	12	0	.143
1969	6	8	0	.429
1970	4	8	2	.333
1971	7	6	1	.538
1972	7	7	0	.500
1973	9	5	0	.643
1974	3	11	0	.214
1975	4	10	0	.286
1976	4	10	0	.286
1977	7	7	0	.500
1978	9	7	0	.563
1979	6	10	0	.375
1980	12	4	0	.750
1981	7	9	0	.438
1982	5	4	0	.556
1983	7	9	0	.438
1984	4	12	0	.250
1985	4	12	0	.250
1986	7	8	1	.469
1987	3	12	0	.200
1988	5	11	0	.313
1989	3	13	0	.188
1990	5	11	0	.313
1991	10	6	0	.625

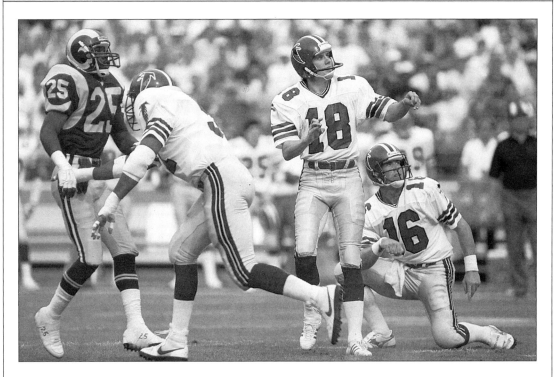

Great Britain's favourite son Mick Luckhurst (18) holds several points and kicking records for Atlanta.

COACHING HISTORY

		W	L	T
1966–8	Norb Hecker	4	26	1
1968–74	Norm Van Brocklin	37	49	3
1974–6	Marion Campbell	6	19	0
1976	Pat Peppler	3	6	0
1977–82	Leeman Bennett	47	44	0
1983–6	Dan Henning	22	41	1
1987–9	Marion Campbell	11	32	0
1989	Jim Hanifan	0	4	0
1990–1	Jerry Glanville	16	18	0

PLAYERS SELECTED AS THE NO. 1 DRAFT CHOICE

Year	Player	Pos	College
1966	Tommy Nobis	LB	Texas
1975	Steve Bartkowski	QB	California
1988	Aundray Bruce	LB	Auburn

ATLANTA HEAD-TO-HEAD AGAINST CURRENT NFL TEAMS

	W	L	T		W	L	T
v Buffalo	3	2	0	v Minnesota	6	12	0
v Chicago	9	7	0	v New England	3	3	0
v Cincinnati	2	5	0	v New Orleans	27	19	0
v Cleveland	1	8	0	v NY Giants	6	6	0
v Dallas	5	10	0	v NY Jets	2	3	0
v Denver	3	4	0	v Philadelphia	7	8	1
v Detroit	5	16	0	v Phoenix	4	10	0
v Green Bay	8	9	0	v Pittsburgh	1	8	0
v Houston	5	2	0	v San Diego	3	1	0
v Indianapolis	0	10	0	v San Francisco	20	29	1
v Kansas City	0	3	0	v Seattle	1	4	0
v LA Raiders	3	4	0	v Tampa Bay	5	5	0
v LA Rams	13	35	2	v Washington	3	12	1
v Miami	1	4	0				

HONOURS

1960–9

NFL Divisional Champions:	None
NFL Champions:	None

1970–92

NFC Divisional Champions:	1980
NFC Champions:	None
Super Bowl – Winners:	None
– Runners-up:	None

FORMER STADIUMS

None

BUFFALO BILLS

Rich Stadium
One Bills Drive, Orchard Park, New York
Stadium Capacity: 80 290

The Bills were formed in 1959 when Ralph C Wilson, a shareholder in the Detroit Lions, was awarded a franchise to set up a team in Buffalo and he named his new outfit after William Cody, alias Buffalo Bill.

Buffalo captured the AFL Championship in 1964 and 1965 but lost to Kansas in the Championship Game in 1966. Heismann Trophy winner OJ Simpson joined the Bills in 1969 and in 1972 he was named the

AFC Player of the Year. He was eventually traded to the 49ers in 1978.

The Bills captured their first divisional title for 14 years in 1980 and in 1988 they captured the first of four consecutive Eastern Division titles. They won the AFC Championship in 1990 and 1991, destroying the Raiders 51–3 in the first of those years. Sadly, they failed to go on and lift the Super Bowl, losing agonisingly by one point to the Giants in 1991.

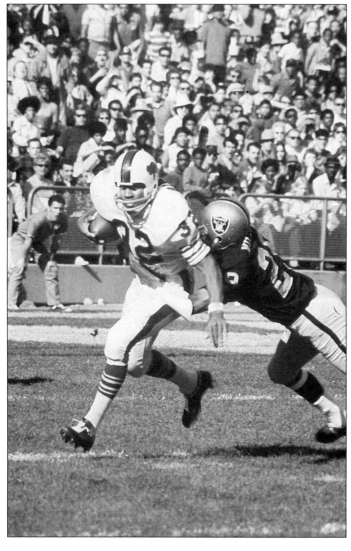

FORMER STADIUMS

1960–72 War Memorial Stadium

REGULAR SEASON RECORD

Year	W	L	T	%
1960	5	8	1	.385
1961	6	8	0	.429
1962	7	6	1	.538
1963	7	6	1	.538
1964	12	2	0	.857
1965	10	3	1	.769
1966	9	4	1	.692
1967	4	10	0	.286
1968	1	12	1	.077
1969	4	10	0	.286
1970	3	10	1	.231
1971	1	13	0	.071
1972	4	9	1	.321
1973	9	5	0	.643
1974	9	5	0	.643
1975	8	6	0	.571
1976	2	12	0	.143
1977	3	11	0	.214
1978	5	11	0	.313
1979	7	9	0	.438
1980	11	5	0	.688
1981	10	6	0	.625
1982	4	5	0	.444
1983	8	8	0	.500
1984	2	14	0	.125
1985	2	14	0	.125
1986	4	12	0	.250
1987	7	8	0	.467
1988	12	4	0	.750
1989	8	8	0	.500
1990	13	3	0	.813
1991	13	3	0	.813

OJ Simpson holds Buffalo's season records for points, rushing and touchdowns.

Green Bay Packers quarterback Bart Starr prepares to throw in the first ever Super Bowl, 1967. Starr was MVP as the Packers defeated the Kansas City Chiefs 35–10.

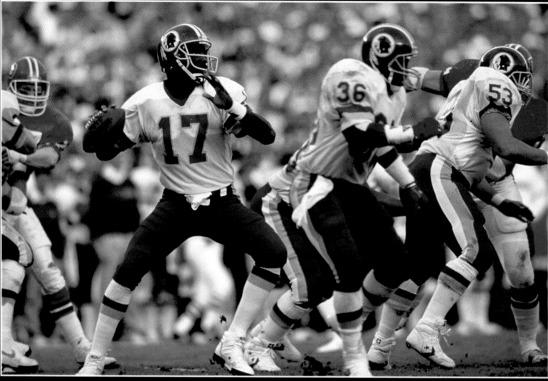

Above *Doug Williams limped back onto the field to destroy the Denver Broncos in Super Bowl XXII in an amazing second quarter: he threw for 228 yards and four touchdowns in an astonishing 15 minutes of football as the Redskins stormed to a 42–10 victory.*

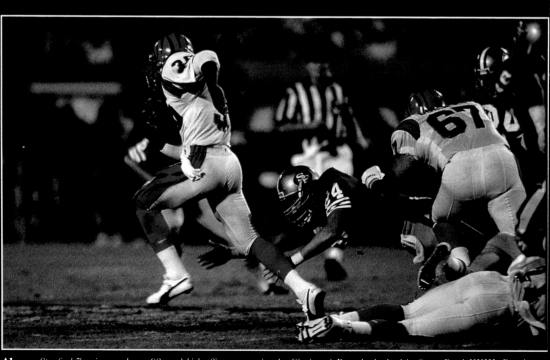

Above *Stanford Jennings makes a 93-yard kick-off return to give the Cincinnati Bengals the lead in Super Bowl XXIII. But the Bengals could not hold their advantage as MVP Joe Montana threw two touchdowns to give the San Francisco 49ers their third Super Bowl victory of the 1980s.*

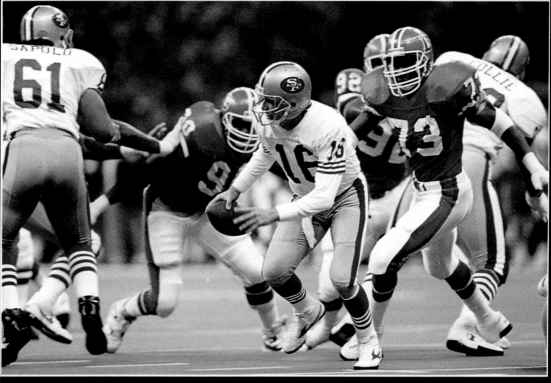

Above *A year later Montana and the 49ers proved far too good for Denver, realising the Broncos fans' worst pre-match fears. San Francisco's 55 10 victory was the biggest margin in Super Bowl history.*

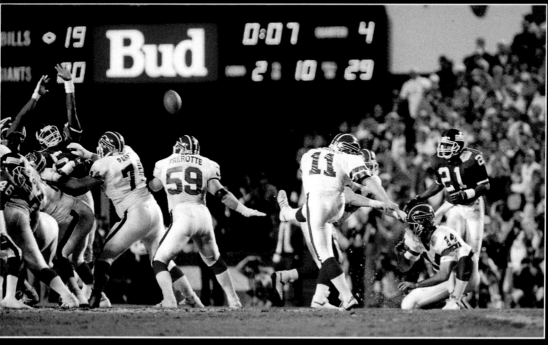

Above *The silver anniversary Super Bowl had an unforgettable finish — the scoreboard shows Scott Norwood's 47-yard field goal attempt coming with just 7 seconds of the game remaining and the Buffalo Bills one point down. But the kick missed and victory belonged to the New York Giants.*

Left *Setting the scene for Super Bowl XXVI in the Hubert H Humphrey Metrodome, Minneapolis.*

Right *Down and out — the Bills quarterback Jim Kelly gets the sack.*

Below *Washington's Brad Edwards is sent flying in spectacular fashion as tight end Keith McKeller makes ground for the Buffalo Bills.*

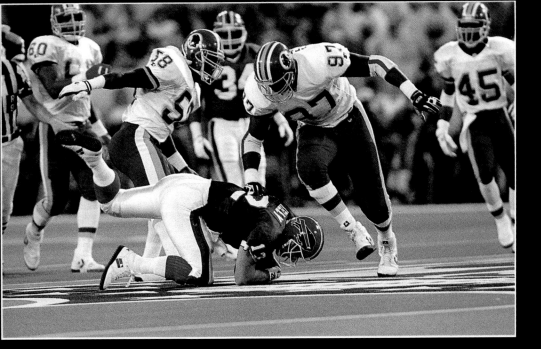

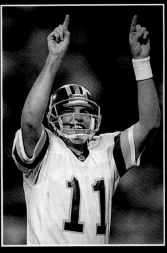

Above *Touchdown Washington . . . quarterback Mark Rypien celebrates. Rypien threw two touchdowns and was the game's MVP.*

Right *Redskins running back Ricky Ervins powers his way through the Buffalo defense. Ervins rushed for 72 yards.*

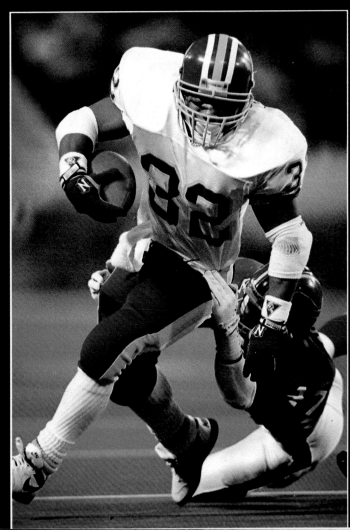

Above *London Monarchs quarterback
Stan Gelbaugh in command at the line
of scrimmage during the first ever
World Bowl, held at Wembley in
1991.*

Left *Jubilant London fans celebrate
their team's success. Over 60 000
attended the game.*

Right *David Smith breaks through for
the Monarchs, winners by 21–0.*

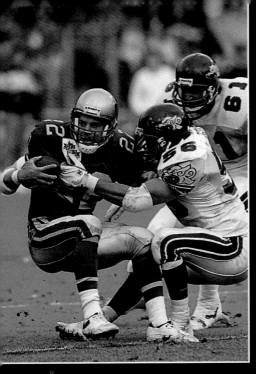

Left *London's Judd Garrett holds onto the ball despite the attentions of Barcelona's Ron Goetz.*

Below *The Monarchs' popular coach Larry Kennan is chaired off by his team. Kennan left the Monarchs to become offensive co-ordinator for the Seattle Seahawks in the NFL.*

NFL action at its most spectacular — Roger Craig leaps in for the San Francisco 49ers against the LA Raiders at Candlestick Park.

COACHING HISTORY

		W	L	T
1960–1	Buster Ramsey	11	16	1
1962–5	Lou Saban	38	18	3
1966–8	Joe Collier	13	17	1
1968	Harvey Johnson	1	10	1
1969–70	John Rauch	7	20	1
1971	Harvey Johnson	1	13	0
1972–6	Lou Saban	32	29	1
1976–7	Jim Ringo	3	20	0
1978–82	Chuck Knox	38	38	0
1983–4	Kay Stephenson	10	26	0
1985–6	Hank Bullough	4	17	0
1986–91	Marv Levy	61	34	0

PLAYERS SELECTED AS THE NO. 1 DRAFT CHOICE

Year	Player	Pos	College
1961	Ken Rice	G	Auburn
1969	OJ Simpson	RB	Southern California
1972	Walt Patulski	DE	Notre Dame
1979	Tom Cousineau	LB	Ohio State
1985	Bruce Smith	DE	Virginia Tech

RECORD HOLDERS

Career Records

Points	670	Scott Norwood, 1985–91
Touchdowns	70	OJ Simpson, 1969–77
Rushing (Yards)	10 183	OJ Simpson, 1969–77
Passing (Yards)	27 590	Joe Ferguson, 1973–84
Passing (Touchdowns)	181	Joe Ferguson, 1973–84
Receiving (No.)	469	Andre Reed, 1985–91
Receiving (Yards)	6466	Andre Reed, 1985–91
Interceptions	40	George Bird, 1964–70
Punting (Average)	42.1	Paul Maguire, 1964–70
Punt Returns (Average)	10.5	Keith Moody, 1976–9
Kick-off Returns (Average)	27.2	Wallace Francis, 1973–4
Field Goals	133	Scott Norwood, 1985–91

Season Records

Points	138	OJ Simpson, 1975
Touchdowns	23	OJ Simpson, 1975
Rushing (Yards)	2003	OJ Simpson, 1973
Passing (Yards)	3844	Jim Kelly, 1991
Passing (Touchdowns)	33	Jim Kelly, 1991
Receiving (No.)	88	Andre Reed, 1989
Receiving (Yards)	1312	Andre Reed 1989
Interceptions	10	Billy Atkins, 1961
	10	Tom Janik, 1967
Punting (Average)	44.5	Billy Atkins, 1961
Punt Returns (Average)	13.1	Keith Moody, 1977
Kick-off Returns (Average)	30.2	Ed Rutkowski, 1963
Field Goals	32	Scott Norwood, 1988

Single Game Records

Points	30	Cookie Gilchrist, 8 Dec 1963
Touchdowns	5	Cookie Gilchrist, 8 Dec 1963
Rushing (Yards)	273	OJ Simpson, 25 Nov 1976
Passing (Yards)	419	Joe Ferguson, 9 Oct 1983
Passing (Touchdowns)	6	Jim Kelly, 8 Sep 1991
Receiving (No.)	13	Greg Bell, 8 Sep 1985
	13	Andre Reed, 18 Sep 1989
Receiving (Yards)	255	Jerry Butler, 23 Sep 1979
Interceptions	3	*Many occasions*
Field Goals	5	Pete Gogolak, 5 Dec 1965
	5	Scott Norwood, 25 Sep 1988

BUFFALO HEAD-TO-HEAD AGAINST CURRENT NFL TEAMS

	W	L	T
v Atlanta	2	3	0
v Chicago	2	3	0
v Cincinnati	7	11	0
v Cleveland	3	8	0
v Dallas	1	3	0
v Denver	16	10	1
v Detroit	1	2	1
v Green Bay	4	1	0
v Houston	12	19	0
v Indianapolis	23	19	1
v Kansas City	16	13	1
v LA Raiders	15	13	0
v LA Rams	2	3	0
v Miami	17	35	1
v Minnesota	2	4	0
v New England	29	34	1
v New Orleans	2	2	0
v NY Giants	3	3	0
v NY Jets	35	28	0
v Philadelphia	2	4	0
v Phoenix	3	3	0
v Pittsburgh	6	6	0
v San Diego	9	17	2
v San Francisco	2	2	0
v Seattle	1	3	0
v Tampa Bay	2	4	0
v Washington	2	5	0

HONOURS

1960–9

AFL Divisional Champions:	1964–6
AFL Champions:	1964–5

1970–92

AFC Divisional Champions:	1980, 1988–91
AFC Champions:	1990–1
Super Bowl – Winners:	None
– Runners-up:	1991–2

CHICAGO BEARS

Soldier Field
425 McFetridge Place, Chicago, Illinois
Stadium Capacity: 66946

The Bears are, along with the Cardinals, the oldest continuous surviving NFL team. The Bears were founded in Decatur, Illinois, by local businessman AE Staley and the team were named the Decatur Staleys. George Halas, a company employee, was put in charge of the team. He was to spend a total of 40 years as head coach to the Bears during which time he became the sport's most successful coach with 325 career wins to his credit.

The Staleys were NFL runners-up in their first year, 1920, but Staley withdrew his sponsorship the following year and Halas became one of the co-owners as the team moved to the Cubs stadium in Chicago and became the Chicago Staleys. Their famous 'T' formation helped them capture their first title. In 1922 they changed their name to the Bears.

Halas stood down as coach (for the first time) in 1930 and two years later, under Ralph Jones, the Bears won their second NFL title. In 1933, with Halas back in charge as head coach, they won the first ever NFL Championship Game when they beat the Giants 23–21. Western Division champions in 1937, they carried off the divisional title again in 1940 and then went on to beat Washington by a staggering 73–0 to win the championship.

With Halas away from football action while serving in the Navy, the Bears won their sixth championship in 1943 when they beat the Redskins again, by 41 points to 21. Halas' return in 1946 coincided with championship number seven. He quit as head coach for a second time in 1955 and the following season 'Paddy' Driscoll guided the Bears to the divisional title but the

Giants trounced them 47–7 in the Championship Game.

Halas returned in 1958 as head coach for his fourth, and last, spell. In 1963 he enjoyed his final honour in the game when he led the Bears to the NFL Championship before eventually retiring, at the age of 71, in 1968. Jim Dooley replaced Halas and in his second season in charge the Bears finished last in their division with their worst ever record since joining the League. Dooley and the Bears parted company in 1971 and that same year they moved to Soldier Field.

Successive coaches Abe Gibron, Jack Pardee and Neil Armstrong could not bring former glories back to the Bears but following the appointment of Mike Ditka as head coach in 1982 their fortunes made a turn for the better and in 1984 they won their first divisional title for 21 years. The following year they beat the Rams 24–0 to win the NFC Championship and went on to trounce the New England Patriots 46–10 in a one-sided Super Bowl.

HONOURS

1921–59

NFL Divisional Champions:	1933–4, 1937, 1940–3, 1946, 1956
NFL Champions:	1921, 1932, 1933, 1940–1, 1943, 1946

1960–9

NFL Divisional Champions:	1963
NFL Champions:	1963

1970–92

NFC Divisional Champions:	1984–8, 1990
NFC Champions:	1985
Super Bowl – Winners:	1986
– Runners-up:	None

COACHING HISTORY

		W	L	T
1920–9	George Halas	84	31	19
1930–2	Ralph Jones	24	10	7
1933–42	George Halas	89	24	4
1942–5	Hunk Anderson/ Luke Johnson	18	11	2
1946–55	George Halas	76	43	2
1956–57	John 'Paddy' Driscoll	14	10	1
1958–67	George Halas	76	53	6
1968–71	Jim Dooley	20	36	0
1972–4	Abe Gibron	11	30	1
1975–7	Jack Pardee	20	23	0
1978–81	Neil Armstrong	30	35	0
1982–91	Mike Ditka	107	57	0

PLAYERS SELECTED AS THE NO. 1 DRAFT

CHOICE

Year	Player	Pos	College
1941	Tom Harmon	HB	Michigan
1947	Bob Fenimore	HB	Oklahoma A & M

Right Chicago finally found a worthy successor to George Halas in Mike Ditka, a brooding presence on the Bears sideline.

RECORD HOLDERS

Career Records

Points	750	Walter Payton, 1975–87
Touchdowns	125	Walter Payton, 1975–87
Rushing (Yards)	16 726	Walter Payton, 1975–87
Passing (Yards)	14 686	Sid Luckman, 1939–50
Passing (Touchdowns)	137	Sid Luckman, 1939–50
Receiving (No.)	492	Walter Payton, 1975–87
Receiving (Yards)	5059	Johnny Morris, 1958–67
Interceptions	38	Gary Fencik, 1976–87
Punting (Average)	44.5	George Gulyanics, 1947–52
Punt Returns (Average)	14.8	Ray McLean, 1940–7
Kick-off Returns (Average)	30.6	Gale Sayers, 1965–71
Field Goals	153	Kevin Butler, 1985–91

Season Records

Points	144	Kevin Butler, 1985
Touchdowns	22	Gale Sayers, 1965
Rushing (Yards)	1852	Walter Payton, 1977
Passing (Yards)	3172	Bill Wade, 1962
Passing (Touchdowns)	28	Sid Luckman, 1943
Receiving (No.)	93	Johnny Morris, 1964
Receiving (Yards)	1200	Johnny Morris, 1964
Interceptions	10	Mark Carrier, 1990
Punting (Average)	46.5	Bobby Joe Green, 1963
Punt Returns (Average)	15.8	Harry Clark, 1943
Kick-off Returns (Average)	37.7	Gale Sayers, 1967
Field Goals	31	Kevin Butler, 1985

Single Game Records

Points	36	Gale Sayers, 12 Dec 1965
Touchdowns	6	Gale Sayers, 12 Dec 1965
Rushing (Yards)	275	Walter Payton, 20 Nov 1977
Passing (Yards)	468	Johnny Lujack, 11 Dec 1949
Passing (Touchdowns)	7	Sid Luckman, 14 Nov 1943
Receiving (No.)	14	Jim Keane, 23 Oct 1949
Receiving (Yards)	214	Harlon Hill, 31 Oct 1954
Interceptions	3	*Many occasions*
Field Goals	5	Roger LeClerc, 3 Dec 1961
	5	Mac Percival, 20 Oct 1968

REGULAR SEASON RECORD

Year	W	L	T	%
1920	10	1	2	.909
1921	9	1	1	.900
1922	9	3	0	.750
1923	9	2	1	.818
1924	6	1	4	.857
1925	9	5	3	.643
1926	12	1	3	.923
1927	9	3	2	.750
1928	7	5	1	.583
1929	4	9	2	.308
1930	9	4	1	.692
1931	8	5	0	.615
1932	7	1	6	.875
1933	10	2	1	.833
1934	13	0	0	1.000
1935	6	4	2	.600
1936	9	3	0	.750
1937	9	1	1	.900
1938	6	5	0	.545
1939	8	3	0	.727
1940	8	3	0	.727
1941	10	1	0	.909
1942	11	0	0	1.000
1943	8	1	1	.889
1944	6	3	1	.667
1945	3	7	0	.300
1946	8	2	1	.800
1947	8	4	0	.667
1948	10	2	0	.833
1949	9	3	0	.750
1950	9	3	0	.750
1951	7	5	0	.583
1952	5	7	0	.417
1953	3	8	1	.273
1954	8	4	0	.667
1955	8	4	0	.667
1956	9	2	1	.818
1957	5	7	0	.417
1958	8	4	0	.667
1959	8	4	0	.667
1960	5	6	1	.455
1961	8	6	0	.571
1962	9	5	0	.643
1963	11	1	2	.917
1964	5	9	0	.357
1965	9	5	0	.643
1966	5	7	2	.417
1967	7	6	1	.538
1968	7	7	0	.500
1969	1	13	0	.071
1970	6	8	0	.429
1971	6	8	0	.429
1972	4	9	1	.321
1973	3	11	0	.214
1974	4	10	0	.286
1975	4	10	0	.286
1976	7	7	0	.500
1977	9	5	0	.643
1978	7	9	0	.438
1979	10	6	0	.625
1980	7	9	0	.438
1981	6	10	0	.375
1982	3	6	0	.333
1983	8	8	0	.500
1984	10	6	0	.625
1985	15	1	0	.938
1986	14	2	0	.875
1987	11	4	0	.733
1988	12	4	0	.750
1989	6	10	0	.375
1990	11	5	0	.688
1991	11	5	0	.688

FORMER STADIUMS

1920	Staley Field (Decatur, Illinois)
1921–70	Wrigley Field *(formerly Cubs Park, 1921–5)*

CHICAGO HEAD-TO-HEAD AGAINST CURRENT NFL TEAMS

	W	L	T								
v Atlanta	7	9	0	v Indianapolis	16	21	0	v NY Jets	3	1	0
v Buffalo	3	2	0	v Kansas City	3	2	0	v Philadelphia	23	4	1
v Cincinnati	2	2	0	v LA Raiders	3	4	0	v Phoenix	51	25	6
v Cleveland	3	7	0	v LA Rams	45	29	3	v Pittsburgh	15	4	1
v Dallas	6	9	0	v Miami	1	5	0	v San Diego	1	4	0
v Denver	5	4	0	v Minnesota	29	30	2	v San Francisco	25	27	1
v Detroit	72	47	5	v New England	3	3	0	v Seattle	2	4	0
v Green Bay	80	57	6	v New Orleans	9	5	0	v Tampa Bay	22	6	0
v Houston	2	3	0	v NY Giants	29	17	2	v Washington	21	16	1

CINCINNATI BENGALS

Riverfront Stadium, Cincinnati, Ohio
Stadium Capacity: 60 389

One of the NFL's newest teams, the Cincinnati franchise was started in 1967 by a group headed by the former head coach of the Cleveland Browns, Paul Brown. He named the new team the Bengals because there had existed a team of the same name in Cincinnati in the 1920s and 30s.

After seven games of the 1970 season the Bengals were bottom of their division but they went on to take the divisional title. Two years after replacing Homer Rice as head coach, Forrest Gregg guided the Bengals to their first AFC Championship in 1981 but they lost narrowly to the 49ers in the Super Bowl. They were Conference champions for a second time in 1988 but another narrow defeat followed in the Super Bowl when they were beaten 20–16, again by San Francisco.

REGULAR SEASON RECORD

Year	W	L	T	%
1968	3	11	0	.214
1969	4	9	1	.308
1970	8	6	0	.571
1971	4	10	0	.286
1972	8	6	0	.571
1973	10	4	0	.714
1974	7	7	0	.500
1975	11	3	0	.786
1976	10	4	0	.714
1977	8	6	0	.571
1978	4	12	0	.250
1979	4	12	0	.250
1980	6	10	0	.375
1981	12	4	0	.750
1982	7	2	0	.778
1983	7	9	0	.438
1984	8	8	0	.500
1985	7	9	0	.438
1986	10	6	0	.625
1987	4	11	0	.267
1988	12	4	0	.750
1989	8	8	0	.500
1990	9	7	0	.563
1991	3	13	0	.188

HONOURS

1960–9
NFL Divisional Champions:	None
NFL Champions:	None

1970–92
AFC Divisional Champions:	1970, 1973, 1981, 1988, 1990
AFC Champions:	1981, 1988
Super Bowl – Winners:	None
– Runners-up:	1982, 1989

COACHING HISTORY

		W	L	T
1968–75	Paul Brown	55	59	1
1976–8	Bill Johnson	18	15	0
1978–9	Homer Rice	8	19	0
1980–3	Forrest Gregg	34	27	0
1984–91	Sam Wyche	64	68	0

FORMER STADIUMS

1968–9   Nippert Stadium (University of Cincinnati)

PLAYERS SELECTED AS THE NO. 1 DRAFT CHOICE

Cincinnati have never had the first pick in the Draft

RECORD HOLDERS

Career Records

Points	875	Jim Breech, 1980–9
Touchdowns	70	Pete Johnson, 1977–83
Rushing (Yards)	6176	James Brooks, 1984–91
Passing (Yards)	32838	Ken Anderson, 1971–86
Passing (Touchdowns)	197	Ken Anderson, 1971–86
Receiving (No.)	420	Isaac Curtis, 1973–84
Receiving (Yards)	7106	Isaac Curtis, 1973–84
Interceptions	63	Ken Riley, 1969–83
Punting (Average)	43.9	Dave Lewis, 1970–3
Punt Returns (Average)	9.9	Mike Martin, 1983–9
Kick-off Returns (Average)	24.7	Lemar Parrish, 1970–8
Field Goals	184	Jim Breech, 1980–9

Season Records

Points	120	Jim Breech, 1985
Touchdowns	16	Pete Johnson, 1981
Rushing (Yards)	1239	James Brooks, 1989
Passing (Yards)	3959	Boomer Esiason, 1986
Passing (Touchdowns)	29	Ken Anderson, 1981
Receiving (No.)	71	Dan Ross, 1981
Receiving (Yards)	1273	Eddie Brown, 1988
Interceptions	9	Ken Riley, 1976
Punting (Average)	46.2	Dave Lewis, 1970
Punt Returns (Average)	15.7	Mike Martin, 1984
Kick-off Returns (Average)	30.2	Lemar Parrish, 1980
Field Goals	27	Horst Muhlmann, 1972

Single Game Records

Points	24	Larry Kinnebrew, 28 Oct 1984
Touchdowns	4	Larry Kinnebrew, 28 Oct 1984
Rushing (Yards)	201	James Brooks, 23 Oct 1990
Passing (Yards)	490	Boomer Esiason, 7 Dec 1990
Passing (Touchdowns)	5	Boomer Esiason, 21 Dec 1986
Receiving (No.)	11	Tim McGee, 9 Nov 1989
Receiving (Yards)	216	Eddie Brown, 6 Nov 1988
Interceptions	3	*Many occasions*
Field Goals	5	Horst Muhlmann, 8 Nov 1970
	5	Horst Muhlmann, 24 Sep 1972
	5	Jim Breech, 1 Nov 1987

CINCINNATI HEAD-TO-HEAD AGAINST CURRENT NFL TEAMS

	W	L	T
v Atlanta	5	2	0
v Buffalo	11	7	0
v Chicago	2	2	0
v Cleveland	23	20	0
v Dallas	2	3	0
v Denver	6	10	0
v Detroit	3	2	0
v Green Bay	4	2	0
v Houston	25	21	1
v Indianapolis	5	7	0
v Kansas City	9	10	0
v LA Raiders	5	16	0
v LA Rams	4	2	0
v Miami	3	10	0
v Minnesota	3	3	0
v New England	6	7	0
v New Orleans	3	4	0
v NY Giants	4	0	0
v NY Jets	6	8	0
v Philadelphia	5	1	0
v Phoenix	3	1	0
v Pittsburgh	21	22	0
v San Diego	9	11	0
v San Francisco	1	7	0
v Seattle	6	5	0
v Tampa Bay	3	1	0
v Washington	2	4	0

CLEVELAND BROWNS

Cleveland Stadium (formerly Municipal Stadium, 1932–74)
West 3rd Street, Cleveland, Ohio
Stadium Capacity: 80 098

'Mickey' McBride was granted a franchise for a team in Cleveland by the newly launched All-America Football Conference. Paul Brown was appointed head coach and when a poll to choose the team's name came up with the Panthers he rejected it on the grounds that there had pre-viously been a team called the Panthers in Cleveland and so dismal was their record that he did not want to adopt the name a second time. The next most popular name in the poll was 'Browns' after the new coach himself. Initially he did not like the idea of the team being named after him but he eventually changed his mind and Cleveland is therefore the only team to be named after its coach.

The Browns captured the AAFC championship in their first year, 1946, and retained the title in the next three years as well. Invincible, they joined the NFL in 1950 and carried on where they had left off by taking the championship, defeating the Rams 30–28 in a close final. They were Eastern Division champions seven times between 1950 and 1957, and were the NFL champions three times during that period. In 1954 they captured the title by beating

Detroit 56–10. Otto Graham, the man who helped make famous the Browns' 'T' formation, bowed out of the game after beating the Rams in the 1955 Championship Game.

Paul Brown was sacked as head coach after 17 years in 1963 when his relationship with many players was on the decline and he was blamed for the team's lack of success. Brown's assistant Blanton Collier took over and he brought success back to the team, winning the

Quarterback Otto Graham pictured in action for the Browns at Cleveland Stadium against Philadelphia in the early 1950s.

NFL Championship in 1964. The Browns retained the Eastern Conference title the following year, when one of the game's great running backs, Jim Brown, quit the game.

Central Division champions in the AFC in 1971, Cleveland suffered their first losing season for 18 years in 1974 and it was not until 1980 that they cap-

tured another divisional title. But the 1980s saw a return to the glory days with four more divisional titles, although they could not quite manage to capture the AFC Championship. In 1986 they lost in overtime to Denver in the Championship Game and the following year they were beaten again by Denver, 38–33.

HONOURS

1921–59

NFL Divisional Champions:	1950–5, 1957
NFL Champions:	1950, 1954–5

1960–9

NFL Divisional Champions:	1964–5, 1967–9
NFL Champions:	1964

1970–92

AFC Divisional Champions:	1971, 1980, 1985–7, 1989
AFC Champions:	None
Super Bowl – Winners:	None
– Runners-up:	None

FORMER STADIUMS

None

COACHING HISTORY

		W	L	T
1950–62	Paul Brown	115	49	5
1963–70	Blanton Collier	79	38	2
1971–4	Nick Skorich	30	26	2
1975–7	Forrest Gregg	18	23	0
1977	Dick Modzelewski	0	1	0
1978–84	Sam Rutigliano	47	52	0
1984–8	Marty Schottenheimer	46	31	0
1989–90	Bud Carson	12	14	1
1990	Jim Shofner	1	6	0
1991	Bill Belichick	6	10	0

PLAYERS SELECTED AS THE NO. 1 DRAFT CHOICE

Year	Player	Pos	College
1954	Bobby Garrett	QB	Stanford

RECORD HOLDERS

Career Records

Points	1349	Lou Groza, 1950–9, 1961–7
Touchdowns	126	Jim Brown 1957–65
Rushing (Yards)	12312	Jim Brown, 1957–65
Passing (Yards)	23713	Brian Sipe, 1974–83
Passing (Touchdowns)	154	Brian Sipe, 1974–83
Receiving (No.)	662	Ozzie Newsome, 1978–90
Receiving (Yards)	7980	Ozzie Newsome, 1978–90
Interceptions	45	Thom Darden, 1972–74, 1976–81
Punting (Average)	43.8	Horace Gillom, 1950–6
Punt Returns (Average)	11.8	Greg Pruitt, 1973–81
Kick-off Returns (Average)	26.3	Greg Pruitt, 1973–81
Field Goals	234	Lou Groza, 1950–9, 1961–7

Season Records

Points	126	Jim Brown, 1965
Touchdowns	21	Jim Brown, 1965
Rushing (Yards)	1863	Jim Brown, 1963
Passing (Yards)	4132	Brian Sipe, 1980
Passing (Touchdowns)	30	Brian Sipe, 1980
Receiving (No.)	89	Ozzie Newsome, 1983
	89	Ozzie Newsome, 1984
Receiving (Yards)	1236	Webster Slaughter, 1989
Interceptions	10	Thom Darden, 1978
Punting (Average)	46.7	Gary Collins, 1965
Punt Returns (Average)	15.6	Leroy Kelly, 1965
Kick-off Returns (Average)	29.5	Billy Reynolds, 1954
Field Goals	24	Matt Bahr, 1984
	24	Matt Bahr, 1988

Single Game Records

Points	36	Dub Jones, 25 Nov 1951
Touchdowns	6	Dub Jones, 25 Nov 1951
Rushing (Yards)	237	Jim Brown, 24 Nov 1957
	237	Jim Brown, 19 Nov 1961
Passing (Yards)	489	Bernie Kosar, 3 Jan 1987
Passing (Touchdowns)	5	Frank Ryan, 12 Dec 1964
	5	Bill Nelson, 2 Nov 1969
	5	Brian Sipe, 7 Oct 1979
Receiving (No.)	14	Ozzie Newsome, 14 Oct 1984
Receiving (Yards)	191	Ozzie Newsome, 14 Oct 1984
Interceptions	3	*Many occasions*
Field Goals	5	Don Cockcroft, 19 Oct 1975

REGULAR SEASON RECORD

Year	W	L	T	%
1950	10	2	0	.833
1951	11	1	0	.917
1952	8	4	0	.667
1953	11	1	0	.917
1954	9	3	0	.750
1955	9	2	1	.818
1956	5	7	0	.417
1957	9	2	1	.818
1958	9	3	0	.750
1959	7	5	0	.583
1960	8	3	1	.727
1961	8	5	1	.615
1962	7	6	1	.538
1963	10	4	0	.714
1964	10	3	1	.769
1965	11	3	0	.786
1966	9	5	0	.643
1967	9	5	0	.643
1968	10	4	0	.714
1969	10	3	1	.769
1970	7	7	0	.500
1971	9	5	0	.643
1972	10	4	0	.714
1973	7	5	2	.571
1974	4	10	0	.286
1975	3	11	0	.214
1976	9	5	0	.643
1977	6	8	0	.429
1978	8	8	0	.500
1979	9	7	0	.563
1980	11	5	0	.688
1981	5	11	0	.313
1982	4	5	0	.444
1983	9	7	0	.563
1984	5	11	0	.313
1985	8	8	0	.500
1986	12	4	0	.750
1987	10	5	0	.667
1988	10	6	0	.625
1989	9	6	1	.594
1990	3	13	0	.188
1991	6	10	0	.375

CLEVELAND HEAD-TO-HEAD AGAINST CURRENT NFL TEAMS

	W	L	T								
v Atlanta	8	1	0	v Indianapolis	14	7	0	v NY Jets	9	6	0
v Buffalo	8	3	0	v Kansas City	7	6	2	v Philadelphia	30	12	1
v Chicago	7	3	0	v LA Raiders	2	10	0	v Phoenix	31	10	3
v Cincinnati	20	23	0	v LA Rams	9	8	0	v Pittsburgh	50	34	0
v Dallas	16	10	0	v Miami	4	6	0	v San Diego	6	7	1
v Denver	5	13	0	v Minnesota	3	7	0	v San Francisco	8	6	0
v Detroit	4	13	0	v New England	8	2	0	v Seattle	3	8	0
v Green Bay	5	8	0	v New Orleans	8	3	0	v Tampa Bay	4	0	0
v Houston	26	18	0	v NY Giants	26	17	2	v Washington	32	9	1

DALLAS COWBOYS

Texas Stadium, Irving, Texas
Stadium Capacity: 65024

The Cowboys were formed in 1960 and used the Cotton Bowl as their home stadium. Tom Landry was the first head coach and it was not until 29 years later that the Cowboys replaced him. Landry became one of the sport's most successful coaches and during his time in charge he guided Dallas to five Super Bowls, two of which resulted in victory.

Eastern Division champions four years in succession from 1966 to 1969, Dallas could not manage to win the NFL Championship. They were beaten on both Championship Game appearances by the Packers, the 1966 game being one of the most exciting in NFL history. They eventually won their first Championship by beating the 49ers for the NFC title in 1970 but disappointment followed in the Super Bowl when they were beaten 16–13 by the Baltimore Colts. However, after a move to their new home at the Texas Stadium in 1971, they retained their NFC title and then beat the Dolphins 24–3 in Super Bowl VI.

A third Super Bowl appearance in 1976 saw then lose 21–17 to the Steelers but they returned two years later and took their second title by beating the Denver Broncos 27–10. Twelve months later, the Steelers repeated their 1976 Super Bowl triumph by beating the Cowboys 35–31.

After losing three consecutive NFC Championship Games in the early 1980s, Dallas failed to make the play-offs for the first time in ten years in 1984 but bounced back to take the Eastern Division in 1985. Lean times followed and Landry was fired after 29 years in 1989. He was replaced by Jimmy Johnson who, in his third season, got the Cowboys into the play-offs for the first time in seven years.

REGULAR SEASON RECORD

Year	W	L	T	%	Year	W	L	T	%	Year	W	L	T	%
1960	0	11	1	.000	1974	8	6	0	.571	1988	3	13	0	.188
1961	4	9	1	.308	1975	10	4	0	.714	1989	1	15	0	.063
1962	5	8	1	.385	1976	11	3	0	.786	1990	7	9	0	.438
1963	4	10	0	.286	1977	12	2	0	.857	1991	11	5	0	.688
1964	5	8	1	.385	1978	12	4	0	.750					
1965	7	7	0	.500	1979	11	5	0	.688					
1966	9	5	0	.643	1980	12	4	0	.750					
1967	9	5	0	.643	1981	12	4	0	.750					
1968	12	2	0	.857	1982	6	3	0	.667					
1969	11	2	1	.846	1983	12	4	0	.750					
1970	10	4	0	.714	1984	9	7	0	.563					
1971	11	3	0	.786	1985	10	6	0	.625					
1972	10	4	0	.714	1986	7	9	0	.438					
1973	10	4	0	.714	1987	7	8	0	.467					

HONOURS

1960–9
NFL Divisional Champions:	1966–9
NFL Champions:	None

1970–92
NFC Divisional Champions:	1970–1, 1973, 1976–9, 1981, 1985
NFC Champions:	1970–1, 1975, 1977–8
Super Bowl – Winners:	1972, 1978
– Runners-up:	1971, 1976, 1979

FORMER STADIUMS

1960–70 Cotton Bowl

COACHING HISTORY

		W	L	T
1960–88	Tom Landry	270	178	6
1989–91	Jimmy Johnson	20	30	0

PLAYERS SELECTED AS THE NO. 1 DRAFT CHOICE

Year	Player	Pos	College
1974	Ed Jones	DE	Tennessee State
1989	Troy Aikman	QB	UCLA
1991	Russell Maryland	DT	Miami

Quarterback Roger Staubach led the Cowboys through their most successful years in the NFL, passing for a career total of over 22 000 yards.

DALLAS HEAD-TO-HEAD AGAINST CURRENT NFL TEAMS

	W	L	T
v Atlanta	10	5	0
v Buffalo	3	1	0
v Chicago	9	6	0
v Cincinnati	3	2	0
v Cleveland	10	16	0
v Denver	3	2	0
v Detroit	7	6	0
v Green Bay	6	10	0
v Houston	4	3	0
v Indianapolis	6	3	0
v Kansas City	2	2	0
v LA Raiders	1	3	0
v LA Rams	12	12	0
v Miami	2	5	0
v Minnesota	10	7	0
v New England	6	0	0
v New Orleans	13	3	0
v NY Giants	36	21	2
v NY Jets	4	1	0
v Philadelphia	37	26	0
v Phoenix	36	22	1
v Pittsburgh	12	13	0
v San Diego	4	1	0
v San Francisco	8	10	1
v Seattle	3	1	0
v Tampa Bay	8	0	0
v Washington	35	27	2

RECORD HOLDERS

Career Records

Points	874	Rafael Septien, 1978–86
Touchdowns	86	Tony Dorsett, 1977–87
Rushing (Yards)	12 036	Tony Dorsett, 1977–87
Passing (Yards)	22 700	Roger Staubach, 1969–79
Passing (Touchdowns)	155	Danny White, 1976–88
Receiving (No.)	489	Drew Pearson, 1973–83
Receiving (Yards)	7988	Tony Hill, 1977–86
Interceptions	52	Mel Renfro, 1964–77
Punting (Average)	41.4	Mike Saxon, 1985–91
Punt Returns (Average)	11.1	Bob Hayes, 1965–74
Kick-off Returns (Average)	26.4	Mel Renfro, 1964–77
Field Goals	162	Rafael Septien, 1978–86

Season Records

Points	123	Rafael Septien, 1983
Touchdowns	16	Dan Reeves, 1966
Rushing (Yards)	1646	Tony Dorsett, 1981
Passing (Yards)	3980	Danny White, 1983
Passing (Touchdowns)	29	Danny White, 1983
Receiving (No.)	93	Michael Irvin, 1991
Receiving (Yards)	1523	Michael Irvin, 1991
Interceptions	11	Everson Walls, 1981
Punting (Average)	45.4	Sam Baker, 1962
Punt Returns (Average)	20.8	Bob Hayes, 1968
Kick-off Returns (Average)	30.0	Mal Renfro, 1965
Field Goals	27	Rafael Septien, 1981
	27	Ken Willis, 1991

Single Game Records

Points	24	*Many occasions*
Touchdowns	4	*Many occasions*
Rushing (Yards)	206	Tony Dorsett, 4 Dec 1977
Passing (Yards)	460	Don Meredith, 10 Nov 1963
Passing (Touchdowns)	5	*Many occasions*
Receiving (No.)	13	Lance Rentzel, 19 Nov 1967
Receiving (Yards)	246	Bob Hayes, 13 Nov 1966
Interceptions	3	Herb Adderley, 26 Sep 1971
	3	Lee Roy Jordan, 4 Nov 1973
	3	Dennis Thurman, 13 Dec 1981
Field Goals	5	Roger Ruzek, 21 Dec 1987

DENVER BRONCOS

Denver Mile High Stadium (formerly Bears Stadium, 1960–66)
1900 West Eliot, Denver, Colorado
Stadium Capacity: 76273

The Broncos were founder members of the AFC in 1960. Frank Filchock was the team's first head coach but he was fired after the first two seasons produced just seven wins from 28 games. Jack Faulkner took over as coach and immediately set about changing the team's image by getting rid of the old kit and replacing it with the orange, blue and white of today. Perhaps psychologically it worked because Denver ended the season with a 7–7–0 record. However, there was a decline and Faulkner went the same way as Filchock.

The team nearly moved to Atlanta in 1965 after it was sold to the Cox Broadcasting Corporation, but they decided to stay put in Denver. In 1967 their stadium, originally called the Bears Stadium, underwent a facelift, capacity was increased and its name changed to the Denver Mile High Stadium. Under their eighth coach, Robert 'Red' Miller, the Broncos had their first success in his first season in charge when they were Conference champions in 1977 but the Dallas Cowboys spoilt their first Super Bowl with a 27–10 win.

Dan Reeves was appointed head coach in 1980 and in 1983 the Broncos acquired quarterback John Elway in a trade. It

cost the Broncos $6 million for Elway's five-year contract. His arrival coincided with the start of the Broncos' best ever spell in the NFL. Divisional champions five times after Elway's arrival, they won the AFC Championship three times but sadly they

Denver's famous Mile High Stadium packed as ever with over 75 000 of the NFL's noisiest fans.

lost all three Super Bowl appearances, losing heavily to the Giants (39–20) in 1987, to the Redskins (42–10) in 1988 and two years later being on the receiving end of the biggest rout in Super Bowl history when San Francisco beat them 55–10.

HONOURS

1960–9

AFL Divisional Champions:	None
AFL Champions:	None

1970–92

AFC Divisional Champions:	1977–8, 1984, 1986–7, 1989, 1991
AFC Champions:	1977, 1986–7, 1989
Super Bowl – Winners:	None
– Runners-up:	1978, 1987–8, 1990

COACHING HISTORY

		W	L	T
1960–1	Frank Filchock	7	20	1
1962–4	Jack Faulkner	9	22	1
1964–6	Mac Speedie	6	19	1
1966	Ray Malavasi	4	8	0
1967–71	Lou Saban	20	42	3
1971	Jerry Smith	2	3	0
1972–6	John Ralston	34	33	3
1977–80	Robert 'Red' Miller	42	25	0
1981–91	Dan Reeves	109	71	0

FORMER STADIUMS

None

PLAYERS SELECTED AS THE NO. 1 DRAFT CHOICE

Denver have never had the first pick in the draft

RECORD HOLDERS

Career Records

Points	742	Jim Turner, 1971–9
Touchdowns	54	Floyd Little, 1967–75
Rushing (Yards)	6323	Floyd Little, 1967–75
Passing (Yards)	27974	John Elway, 1983–91
Passing (Touchdowns)	148	John Elway, 1983–91
Receiving (No.)	543	Lionel Taylor, 1960–6
Receiving (Yards)	6872	Lionel Taylor, 1960–6
Interceptions	44	Steve Foley, 1976–86
Punting (Average)	45.2	Jim Fraser, 1962–4
Punt Returns (Average)	12.1	Rick Upchurch, 1975–83
Kick-off Returns (Average)	26.3	Abner Haynes, 1965–6
Field Goals	151	Jim Turner, 1971–9

Season Records

Points	137	Gene Mingo, 1962
Touchdowns	14	Sammy Winder, 1986
Rushing (Yards)	1407	Otis Armstrong, 1974
Passing (Yards)	3891	John Elway, 1985
Passing (Touchdowns)	24	Frank Tripucka, 1960
Receiving (No.)	100	Lionel Taylor, 1961
Receiving (Yards)	1244	Steve Watson, 1981
Interceptions	11	Goose Gonsoulin, 1960
Punting (Average)	46.1	Jim Fraser, 1963
Punt Returns (Average)	16.9	Floyd Little, 1967
Kick-off Returns (Average)	28.5	Bill Thompson, 1969
Field Goals	27	Gene Mingo, 1962
	27	David Treadwell, 1989, 1991

Single Game Records

Points	21	Gene Mingo, 10 Dec 1960
Touchdowns	3	*Many occasions*
Rushing (Yards)	183	Otis Armstorng, 8 Dec 1974
Passing (Yards)	447	Frank Tripucka, 15 Sep 1962
Passing (Touchdowns)	5	Frank Tripucka, 28 Oct 1962
	5	John Elway, 18 Nov 1984
Receiving (No.)	13	Lionel Taylor, 29 Nov 1964
	13	Bobby Anderson, 30 Sep 1973
Receiving (Yards)	199	Lionel Taylor, 27 Nov 1960
Interceptions	4	Goose Gonsoulin, 18 Sep 1960
	4	Willie Brown, 15 Nov 1964
Field Goals	5	Gene Mingo, 6 Oct 1963
	5	Rich Karlis, 20 Nov 1983

REGULAR SEASON RECORD

Year	W	L	T	%
1960	4	9	1	.308
1961	3	11	0	.214
1962	7	7	0	.500
1963	2	11	1	.154
1964	2	11	1	.154
1965	4	10	0	.286
1966	4	10	0	.286
1967	3	11	0	.214
1968	5	9	0	.357
1969	5	8	1	.385
1970	5	8	1	.385
1971	4	9	1	.308
1972	5	9	0	.357
1973	7	5	2	.571
1974	7	6	1	.536
1975	6	8	0	.429
1976	9	5	0	.643
1977	12	2	0	.857
1978	10	6	0	.625
1979	10	6	0	.625
1980	8	8	0	.500
1981	10	6	0	.625
1982	2	7	0	.222
1983	9	7	0	.563
1984	13	3	0	.813
1985	11	5	0	.688
1986	11	5	0	.688
1987	10	4	1	.700
1988	8	8	0	.500
1989	11	5	0	.688
1990	5	11	0	.313
1991	12	4	0	.750

DENVER HEAD-TO-HEAD AGAINST CURRENT NFL TEAMS

	W	L	T		W	L	T		W	L	T
v Atlanta	4	3	0	v Indianapolis	8	2	0	v NY Jets	10	11	1
v Buffalo	10	16	1	v Kansas City	27	36	0	v Philadelphia	2	4	0
v Chicago	4	5	0	v LA Raiders	19	43	2	v Phoenix	3	0	1
v Cincinnati	10	6	0	v LA Rams	3	3	0	v Pittsburgh	11	7	1
v Cleveland	13	5	0	v Miami	2	5	1	v San Diego	33	30	1
v Dallas	2	3	0	v Minnesota	3	4	0	v San Francisco	4	3	0
v Detroit	4	3	0	v New England	17	12	0	v Seattle	17	13	0
v Green Bay	4	1	1	v New Orleans	4	1	0	v Tampa Bay	2	0	0
v Houston	12	20	1	v NY Giants	2	4	0	v Washington	3	3	0

Left *Denver gambled on the talents of quarterback John Elway and have been rewarded with three AFC Championships – but no Super Bowl triumph.*

DETROIT LIONS

Pontiac Silverdome (formerly Pontiac Metropolitan Stadium, 1975)
1200 Featherstone Road, Pontiac, Michigan
Stadium Capacity: 80500

The Lions were formed in 1934 when radio station owner George Richards bought the Portsmouth Spartans team of Ohio and moved the headquarters to Detroit. Their second season at Detroit saw them win the Western Division and go on to beat the New York Giants in the Championship Game. But that was to be the Lions' only moment of glory for nearly 20 years. They slumped dramatically and in 1942 lost all 11 regular season games.

The appointment of 'Buddy' Parker as head coach in 1951 revived the Lions' fortunes and in 1952 they were NFL champions after beating Cleveland 17–7. They repeated the success the following year when they again beat Cleveland, but with just one point to spare this time. However, their third successive appearance in the Championship Game in 1954 resulted in Cleveland gaining ample revenge with a 56–10 win.

When Detroit won their next championship, in 1957, Parker had quit and been replaced as head coach by George Wilson. Wilson's appointment looked like being a shrewd one, particularly after the 59–14 trouncing of Cleveland in the 1957 Championship Game. He guided the Lions to their best season in 1962 when they won a club record 11 games in one season. But little success has come Detroit's way since Wilson's departure in 1965. The Lions have had eight further coaches and the best any could achieve was the Central Division title in 1983 and 1991 under Monte Clark and Wayne Fontes respectively.

HONOURS

1921–59

NFL Divisional Champions:	1935, 1952–4, 1957
NFL Champions:	1935, 1952–3, 1957

1960–9

NFL Divisional Champions:	None
NFL Champions:	None

1970–92

NFC Divisional Champions:	1983, 1991
NFC Champions:	None
Super Bowl – Winners:	None
– Runners-up:	None

Above *Pat Studstill, a versatile punt and kick-off returner for the Lions, under pressure from the LA Rams defense in 1962.*
Left *Detroit's Pontiac Silverdome, the largest indoor arena in the NFL, which hosted some impressive Lions performances in 1991.*

RECORD HOLDERS

Career Records

Points	943	Eddie Murray, 1980–9
Touchdowns	47	Billy Sims, 1980–4
Rushing (Yards)	5106	Billy Sims, 1980–4
Passing (Yards)	15710	Bobby Layne, 1950–8
Passing (Touchdowns)	118	Bobby Layne, 1950–8
Receiving (No.)	336	Charlie Sanders, 1968–77
Receiving (Yards)	5220	Gail Cogdill, 1960–8
Interceptions	62	Dick LeBeau, 1959–72
Punting (Average)	44.3	Yale Lary, 1952–3, 1956–64
Punt Returns (Average)	12.8	Jack Christiansen, 1951–8
Kick-off Returns (Average)	25.7	Pat Studstill, 1961–7
Field Goals	212	Eddie Murray, 1980–9

Season Records

Points	128	Doak Walker, 1950
Touchdowns	17	Barry Sanders, 1991
Rushing (Yards)	1548	Barry Sanders, 1991
Passing (Yards)	3223	Gary Danielson, 1980
Passing (Touchdowns)	26	Bobby Layne, 1951
Receiving (No.)	77	James Jones, 1984
Receiving (Yards)	1266	Pat Studstill, 1966
Interceptions	12	Don Doll, 1950
	12	Jack Christiansen, 1953
Punting (Average)	48.9	Yale Lary, 1963
Punt Returns (Average)	21.5	Jack Christiansen, 1952
Kick-off Returns (Average)	34.4	Tom Watkins, 1965
Field Goals	27	Eddie Murray, 1980

Single Game Records

Points	24	Cloyce Box, 3 Dec 1950
Touchdowns	4	Cloyce Box, 3 Dec 1950
Rushing (Yards)	198	Bob Hoernschemeyer, 23 Nov 1950
Passing (Yards)	374	Bobby Layne, 5 Nov 1950
Passing (Touchdowns)	5	Gary Danielsen, 9 Dec 1978
Receiving (No.)	12	Cloyce Box, 3 Dec 1950
	12	James Jones, 28 Sep 1986
Receiving (Yards)	302	Cloyce Box, 3 Dec 1950
Interceptions	4	Don Doll, 23 Oct 1949
Field Goals	6	Garo Yepremian, 13 Nov 1966

DETROIT HEAD-TO-HEAD AGAINST CURRENT NFL TEAMS

	W	L	T
v Atlanta	16	5	0
v Buffalo	2	1	1
v Chicago	47	72	5
v Cincinnati	2	3	0
v Cleveland	13	4	0
v Dallas	6	7	0
v Denver	3	4	0
v Green Bay	55	61	7
v Houston	2	3	0
v Indianapolis	17	17	2
v Kansas City	3	4	0
v LA Raiders	2	5	0
v LA Rams	35	39	1
v Miami	2	2	0
v Minnesota	21	38	0
v New England	2	2	0
v New Orleans	6	5	1
v NY Giants	18	15	1
v NY Jets	3	3	0
v Philadelphia	12	9	2
v Phoenix	25	16	5
v Pittsburgh	13	10	1
v San Diego	3	2	0
v San Francisco	26	25	1
v Seattle	1	4	0
v Tampa Bay	14	14	0
v Washington	8	23	0

COACHING HISTORY

		W	L	T
1930	Hal 'Tubby' Griffen	5	6	3
1931–6	George 'Potsy' Clark	49	20	6
1937–8	Earl 'Dutch' Clark	14	8	0
1939	Elmer 'Gus' Henderson	6	5	0
1940	George 'Potsy' Clark	5	5	1
1941–2	Bill Edwards	4	9	1
1942	John Karcis	0	8	0
1943–7	Charles 'Gus' Dorais	20	31	2
1948–50	Alvin 'Bo' McMillin	12	24	0
1951–6	Raymond 'Buddy' Parker	50	24	2

		W	L	T
1957–64	George Wilson	55	45	6
1965–6	Harry Gilmer	10	16	2
1967–72	Joe Schmidt	43	35	7
1973	Don McCafferty	6	7	1
1974–6	Rick Forzano	15	17	0
1976–7	Tommy Hudspeth	11	13	0
1978–84	Monte Clark	43	63	1
1985–8	Darryl Rogers	18	40	0
1988–91	Wayne Fontes	28	27	0

FORMER STADIUMS

1930–3	Spartan Stadium (Portsmouth, Ohio)
1934–7	University of Detroit Stadium
1938–74	Tiger Stadium (formerly Briggs Stadium, 1938–60)

PLAYERS SELECTED AS THE NO. 1 DRAFT CHOICE

Year	Player	Pos	College
1943	Frank Sinkwich	HB	Georgia
1950	Leon Hart	E	Notre Dame
1980	Billy Sims	RB	Oklahoma

REGULAR SEASON RECORD

Year	W	L	T	%	Year	W	L	T	%	Year	W	L	T	%
1930	5	6	3	.455	1951	7	4	1	.636	1972	8	5	1	.607
1931	11	3	0	.786	1952	9	3	0	.750	1973	6	7	1	.464
1932	6	2	4	.750	1953	10	2	0	.833	1974	7	7	0	.500
1933	6	5	0	.545	1954	9	2	1	.818	1975	7	7	0	.500
1934	10	3	0	.769	1955	3	9	0	.250	1976	6	8	0	.429
1935	7	3	2	.700	1956	9	3	0	.750	1977	6	8	0	.429
1936	8	4	0	.667	1957	8	4	0	.667	1978	7	9	0	.438
1937	7	4	0	.636	1958	4	7	1	.364	1979	2	14	0	.125
1938	7	4	0	.636	1959	3	8	1	.273	1980	9	7	0	.563
1939	6	5	0	.545	1960	7	5	0	.583	1981	8	8	0	.500
1940	5	5	1	.500	1961	8	5	1	.615	1982	4	5	0	.444
1941	4	6	1	.400	1962	11	3	0	.786	1983	9	7	0	.563
1942	0	11	0	.000	1963	5	8	1	.385	1984	4	11	1	.281
1943	3	6	1	.333	1964	7	5	2	.583	1985	7	9	0	.438
1944	6	3	1	.667	1965	6	7	1	.462	1986	5	11	0	.313
1945	7	3	0	.700	1966	4	9	1	.308	1987	4	11	0	.267
1946	1	10	0	.091	1967	5	7	2	.417	1988	4	12	0	.250
1947	3	9	0	.250	1968	4	8	2	.333	1989	7	9	0	.438
1948	2	10	0	.167	1969	9	4	1	.692	1990	6	10	0	.375
1949	4	8	0	.333	1970	10	4	0	.714	1991	12	4	0	.750
1950	6	6	0	.500	1971	7	6	1	.538					

GREEN BAY PACKERS

(1) Lambeau Field (formerly City Stadium II, 1957–64)
165 Lombardi Avenue, Green Bay, Wisconsin
Stadium Capacity: 59 543
(2) Milwaukee County Stadium,
Highway 1–94, Milwaukee, Wisconsin
Stadium Capacity: 56 051

In the 1960s the Green Bay Packers were the NFL's most successful team and in 1967 they made history by winning Super Bowl I. They repeated the success the following year but since then the fortunes of one of the NFL's founder members have waned dramatically and they no longer figure as one of the top teams.

The Packers were formed when 'Curly' Lambeau obtained $500 from his employers, the Indian Packing Company, to start a football team in 1919. Two years later the American Football Association granted a franchise to the Acme Packing Company and Lambeau became the team's coach, general manager, halfback and everything else you could care to name. He immediately set about building a winning team and in 1929 the Packers went through the season undefeated as they captured their first Championship.

Their unbeaten run continued into 1930 before they were eventually beaten by the St Louis Cardinals after a 22-match winning streak. However, they retained the title in 1930 and again in 1931. Their next title was in 1936 when they beat the Boston Redskins in the Championship Game and three years later they were champions again, this time at the New York Giants' expense. Remarkably, when they won their next title in 1944 the team was made up of a mixture of old players, servicemen and untried youngsters.

Their makeshift team beat the Giants 14–7.

After 31 years Lambeau resigned in 1950 following disputes with the owners. The Packers then spent a decade in the doldrums but that all changed when Vince Lombardi was appointed coach in 1959. He immediately guided Green Bay to their best season for 15 years and in his second season they captured the Western Conference title. Their first Championship for 17 years came in 1961 when they beat the Giants 37–0 with Paul Hornung scoring 19 points. They retained the NFL title the following year, again beating the Giants, and after two barren years the Packers won three consecutive NFL titles beating first Cleveland and then Dallas twice. After capturing the 1966 Championship they then made history as the first winners of the Super Bowl by beating the Kansas City Chiefs 35–10.

Green Bay also won Super Bowl II with a 33–14 win over the Oakland Raiders but then Lombardi made the shock announcement that he was quitting as head coach, but staying on as general manager. The next season he in fact quit the club completely to take over as the Washington Redskins coach but sadly, the man who made the Packers great died in 1970. Those heady days of the 1960s have never returned to Green Bay, who uniquely share their home games between two venues. Their fans did have some cause for optimism in 1972 when they won the Central Division of the NFC – but that was as far as their revival went.

FORMER STADIUMS

Green Bay
1921–2	Hagemeister Brewery Park
1923–4	Bellevue Park
1925–26	City Stadium I

Milwaukee
Since 1933 the Packers have been playing some games each season in Milwaukee.
The following venues were used 1933–52: Bochert Field, State Fair Park & Marquette Stadium.
Since 1952 the County Stadium has been used for the Milwaukee games.

RECORD HOLDERS

Career Records
Points	823	Don Hutson, 1935–45
Touchdowns	105	Don Hutson, 1935–45
Rushing (Yards)	8207	Jim Taylor, 1958–66
Passing (Yards)	23718	Bart Starr, 1956–71
Passing (Touchdowns)	152	Bart Starr, 1956–71
Receiving (No.)	530	James Lofton, 1978–86
Receiving (Yards)	9656	James Lofton, 1978–86
Interceptions	52	Bobby Dillon, 1952–9
Punting (Average)	42.6	Dick Deschaine, 1955–7
Punt Returns (Average)	13.2	Billy Grimes, 1950–2
Kick-off Returns (Average)	26.7	Travis Williams, 1967–70
Field Goals	120	Chester Marcol, 1972–80

Season Records
Points	176	Paul Hornung, 1960
Touchdowns	19	Jim Taylor, 1962
Rushing (Yards)	1407	Jim Taylor, 1962
Passing (Yards)	4458	Lynn Dickey, 1983
Passing (Touchdowns)	32	Lynn Dickey, 1983
Receiving (No.)	90	Sterling Sharpe, 1989
Receiving (Yards)	1423	Sterling Sharpe, 1989
Interceptions	10	Irv Comp, 1943
Punting (Average)	44.7	Jerry Norton, 1963
Punt Returns (Average)	19.1	Billy Grimes, 1950
Kick-off Returns (Average)	41.1	Travis Williams, 1967
Field Goals	33	Chester Marcol, 1972

Single Game Records
Points	33	Paul Hornung, 8 Oct 1961
Touchdowns	5	Paul Hornung, 12 Dec 1965
Rushing (Yards)	186	Jim Taylor, 3 Dec 1961
Passing (Yards)	418	Lynn Dickey, 12 Oct 1980
Passing (Touchdowns)	5	*Many occasions*
Receiving (No.)	14	Don Hutson, 22 Nov 1942
Receiving (Yards)	257	Bill Howton, 21 Oct 1956
Interceptions	4	Bobby Dillon, 26 Nov 1953
	4	Willie Buchanon, 24 Sep 1978
Field Goals	5	Chris Jacke, 11 Nov 1990

HONOURS

1921–59
NFL Divisional Champions:	1936, 1938–9, 1944
NFL Champions:	1929–31, 1936, 1939, 1944

1960–9
NFL Divisional Champions:	1960–2, 1965–7
NFL Champions:	1961–2, 1965–7

1970–92
NFC Divisional Champions:	1972
NFC Champions:	None
Super Bowl – Winners:	1967–8
– Runners-up:	None

PLAYERS SELECTED AS THE NO. 1 DRAFT

CHOICE

Year	Player	Pos	College
1957	Paul Hornung	HB	Notre Dame
1959	Randy Duncan	QB	Iowa

COACHING HISTORY

		W	L	T
1921–49	Earl 'Curly' Lambeau	212	106	21
1950–3	Gene Ronzani	14	31	1
1953	Hugh Devore/	0	2	0
	Ray 'Scooter' McLean			
1954–7	Lisle Blackbourn	17	31	0
1958	Ray 'Scooter' McLean	1	10	1
1959–67	Vince Lombardi	98	30	4
1968–70	Phil Bengtson	20	21	1
1971–4	Dan Devine	25	28	4
1975–83	Bart Starr	53	77	3
1984–7	Forrest Gregg	25	37	1
1988–91	Lindy Infante	24	40	0

Right *The great Vince Lombardi (right) pictured with Bart Starr (left) and Carroll Dale.*

REGULAR SEASON RECORD

Year	W	L	T	%	Year	W	L	T	%	Year	W	L	T	%
1921	3	2	1	.600	1945	6	4	0	.600	1969	8	6	0	.571
1922	4	3	3	.571	1946	6	5	0	.545	1970	6	8	0	.429
1923	7	2	1	.778	1947	6	5	1	.545	1971	4	8	2	.333
1924	7	4	0	.636	1948	3	9	0	.250	1972	10	4	0	.714
1925	8	5	0	.615	1949	2	10	0	.167	1973	5	7	2	.429
1926	7	3	3	.700	1950	3	9	0	.250	1974	6	8	0	.429
1927	7	2	1	.778	1951	3	9	0	.250	1975	4	10	0	.286
1928	6	4	3	.600	1952	6	6	0	.500	1976	5	9	0	.357
1929	12	0	1	1.000	1953	2	9	1	.182	1977	4	10	0	.286
1930	10	3	1	.769	1954	4	8	0	.333	1978	8	7	1	.531
1931	12	2	0	.857	1955	6	6	0	.500	1979	5	11	0	.313
1932	10	3	1	.769	1956	4	8	0	.333	1980	5	10	1	.344
1933	5	7	1	.417	1957	3	9	0	.250	1981	8	8	0	.500
1934	7	6	0	.538	1958	1	10	1	.091	1982	5	3	1	.611
1935	8	4	0	.667	1959	7	5	0	.583	1983	8	8	0	.500
1936	10	1	1	.909	1960	8	4	0	.667	1984	8	8	0	.500
1937	7	4	0	.636	1961	11	3	0	.786	1985	8	8	0	.500
1938	8	3	0	.727	1962	13	1	0	.929	1986	4	12	0	.250
1939	9	2	0	.818	1963	11	2	1	.846	1987	5	9	1	.367
1940	6	4	1	.600	1964	8	5	1	.615	1988	4	12	0	.250
1941	10	1	0	.909	1965	10	3	1	.769	1989	10	6	0	.625
1942	8	2	1	.800	1966	12	2	0	.857	1990	6	10	0	.375
1943	7	2	1	.778	1967	9	4	1	.692	1991	4	12	0	.250
1944	8	2	0	.800	1968	6	7	1	.462					

GREEN BAY HEAD-TO-HEAD AGAINST CURRENT NFL TEAMS

	W	L	T		W	L	T		W	L	T
v Atlanta	9	8	0	v Indianapolis	19	18	1	v NY Jets	1	5	0
v Buffalo	1	4	0	v Kansas City	2	3	1	v Philadelphia	18	7	0
v Chicago	57	80	6	v LA Raiders	2	5	0	v Phoenix	40	21	4
v Cincinnati	2	4	0	v LA Rams	35	42	2	v Pittsburgh	16	11	0
v Cleveland	8	5	0	v Miami	0	7	0	v San Diego	3	1	0
v Dallas	10	6	0	v Minnesota	31	29	1	v San Francisco	21	25	1
v Denver	1	4	1	v New England	2	2	0	v Seattle	3	3	0
v Detroit	61	55	7	v New Orleans	11	4	0	v Tampa Bay	14	11	1
v Houston	2	3	0	v NY Giants	25	20	2	v Washington	14	13	1

HOUSTON OILERS

Astrodome,
Loop 610, Kirby and Fannin Streets, Houston, Texas
Stadium Capacity: 60502

Founder members of the AFL in 1960, the Oilers were the new League's first champions and the following year they beat San Diego to retain the title. Divisional champions in 1962 and again in 1967, Houston certainly enjoyed a successful start to their NFL career, but that was the end of any success until 1991 when they won the Central Division of the AFC.

The team was founded by 'Bud' Adams who named the new team the Oilers for 'sentimental and social reasons'. One of his first recruits was the veteran George Blanda who came out of retirement to play for the Oilers in their first season. When they retained their title in 1961 they did so after losing four of their first five games. However, when coach Lou Rymkus was replaced by his assistant Wally Lemm they proceeded to win ten games in succession and became the first team to top 500 points in a season. Then in 1962 under 'Pop' Ivy, their third coach in three years, they were beaten in the AFL Championship Game by the Dallas Texans after two periods of overtime were required to decide the outcome; the Texans eventually won 20–17.

After a succession of coaches (ten since 1960) 'Bum' Phillips took the Oilers to successive AFC Championship Games in 1978 and 1979 after wild card entries, but on each occasion they were beaten by Pittsburgh. It was four coaches and ten years later when Houston next reached the play-offs and it was under their 15th coach, Jack Pardee, that they won their first divisional title for 24 years in 1991.

FORMER STADIUMS

1960–4 Jeppesen Stadium
1965–7 Rice Stadium (Rice University)

Houston take on their Texas rivals the Dallas Cowboys at the Astrodome in the early 1970s.

HOUSTON HEAD-TO-HEAD AGAINST CURRENT NFL TEAMS

	W	L	T		W	L	T		W	L	T
v Atlanta	2	5	0	v Indianapolis	6	6	0	v NY Jets	17	12	1
v Buffalo	19	12	0	v Kansas City	15	22	0	v Philadelphia	0	5	0
v Chicago	3	2	0	v LA Raiders	13	22	0	v Phoenix	2	3	0
v Cincinnati	21	25	1	v LA Rams	2	4	0	v Pittsburgh	16	30	0
v Cleveland	18	26	0	v Miami	12	10	0	v San Diego	15	17	1
v Dallas	3	4	0	v Minnesota	2	3	0	v San Francisco	2	5	0
v Denver	20	12	1	v New England	14	17	1	v Seattle	4	4	0
v Detroit	3	2	0	v New Orleans	3	3	1	v Tampa Bay	3	1	0
v Green Bay	3	2	0	v NY Giants	0	4	0	v Washington	3	3	0

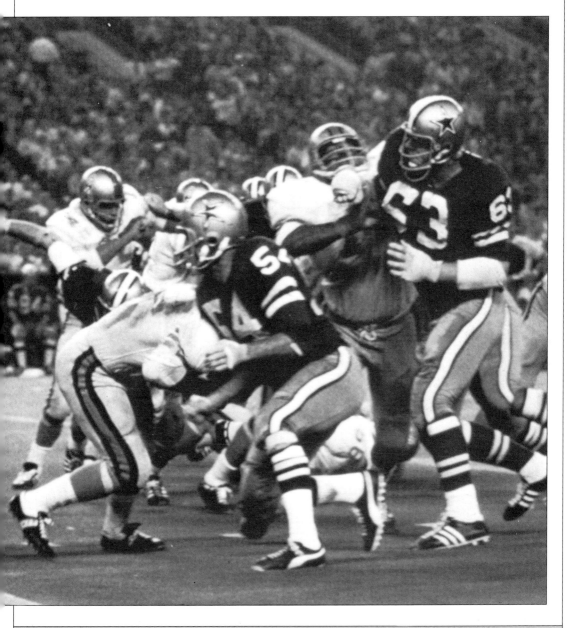

HONOURS

1960–9

AFL Divisional Champions:	1960–2, 1967
AFL Champions:	1960–1

1970–92

AFC Divisional Champions:	1991
AFC Champions:	None
Super Bowl – Winners:	None
– Runners-up:	None

PLAYERS SELECTED AS THE NO. 1 DRAFT CHOICE

Year	Player	Pos	College
1965	Lawrence Elkins	E	Baylor
1973	John Matuszak	DE	Tampa
1978	Earl Campbell	RB	Texas

COACHING HISTORY

		W	L	T
1960–1	Lou Rymkus	12	7	1
1961	Wally Lemm	10	0	0
1962–3	Frank 'Pop' Ivy	17	12	0
1964	Sammy Baugh	4	10	0
1965	Hugh Taylor	4	10	0
1966–70	Wally Lemm	28	40	4
1971	Ed Hughes	4	9	1
1972–3	Bill Peterson	1	18	0
1973–4	Sid Gillman	8	15	0
1975–80	OA 'Bum' Phillips	59	38	0
1981–3	Ed Biles	8	23	0
1983	Chuck Studley	2	8	0
1984–5	Hugh Campbell	8	22	0
1985–9	Jerry Glanville	35	35	0
1990–1	Jack Pardee	21	14	0

RECORD HOLDERS

Career Records

Points	596	George Blanda, 1960–6
Touchdowns	73	Earl Campbell, 1978–84
Rushing (Yards)	8574	Earl Campbell, 1978–84
Passing (Yards)	27 679	Warren Moon, 1984–91
Passing (Touchdowns)	165	George Blanda, 1960–6
Receiving (No.)	480	Drew Hill, 1985–91
Receiving (Yards)	7477	Drew Hill, 1985–91
Interceptions	45	Jim Norton, 1960–8
Punting (Average)	42.3	Jim Norton, 1960–8
	42.3	Greg Montgomery, 1988–91
Punt Returns (Average)	13.2	Billy Johnson, 1974–80
Kick-off Returns (Average)	26.4	Bobby Jancik, 1962–7
Field Goals	117	Tony Zendejas, 1985–90

Season Records

Points	115	George Blanda, 1960
	115	Tony Zendejas, 1989
Touchdowns	19	Earl Campbell, 1979
Rushing (Yards)	1934	Earl Campbell, 1980
Passing (Yards)	4690	Warren Moon, 1991
Passing (Touchdowns)	36	George Blanda, 1961
Receiving (No.)	101	Charley Hennigan, 1964
Receiving (Yards)	1746	Charley Hennigan, 1961
Interceptions	12	Fred Glick, 1963
	12	Mike Reinfeldt, 1979
Punting (Average)	45.0	Greg Montgomery, 1990
Punt Returns (Average)	15.4	Billy Johnson, 1977
Kick-off Returns (Average)	31.2	Ken Hall, 1960
Field Goals	25	Tony Zendejas, 1989

Single Game Records

Points	30	Billy Cannon, 10 Dec 1961
Touchdowns	5	Billy Cannon, 10 Dec 1961
Rushing (Yards)	216	Billy Cannon, 10 Dec 1961
Passing (Yards)	527	Warren Moon, 16 Dec 1991
Passing (Touchdowns)	7	George Blanda, 19 Nov 1961
Receiving (No.)	13	Charley Hennigan, 13 Oct 1961
Receiving (Yards)	272	Charley Hennigan, 13 Oct 1961
Interceptions	3	Many occasions
Field Goals	6	Skip Butler, 12 Oct 1975

REGULAR SEASON RECORD

Year	W	L	T	%
1960	10	4	0	.714
1961	10	3	1	.769
1962	11	3	0	.786
1963	6	8	0	.429
1964	4	10	0	.286
1965	4	10	0	.286
1966	3	11	0	.214
1967	9	4	1	.692
1968	7	7	0	.500
1969	6	6	2	.500
1970	3	10	1	.231
1971	4	9	1	.308
1972	1	13	0	.071
1973	1	13	0	.071
1974	7	7	0	.500
1975	10	4	0	.714
1976	5	9	0	.357
1977	8	6	0	.571
1978	10	6	0	.625
1979	11	5	0	.688
1980	11	5	0	.688
1981	7	9	0	.438
1982	1	8	0	.111
1983	2	14	0	.125
1984	3	13	0	.188
1985	5	11	0	.313
1986	5	11	0	.313
1987	9	6	0	.600
1988	10	6	0	.625
1989	9	7	0	.563
1990	9	7	0	.563
1991	11	5	0	.688

INDIANAPOLIS COLTS

Hoosier Dome
100 South Capitol Avenue, Indianapolis, Indiana
Stadium Capacity: 60 129

Following the folding of the Baltimore Colts team in 1950, pro football returned to the city when the NFL gave permission for the Dallas Texans to transfer to Baltimore, provided they could sell 15 000 season tickets within six weeks – they did so with ten days to spare. They readopted the name Baltimore Colts and made their debut in the 1953 season.

After one season as head coach Keith Molesworth was replaced by Weeb Ewbank. He promised the fans a championship-winning team within five years, and he gave it to them. In 1958, after capturing the Western Conference, the Colts went on to beat the Giants in the Championship Game. Twelve months later there was a repeat performance, the Colts again beating the Giants for the Championship. Ewbank was replaced as coach by 33-year-old Don Shula in 1963 and it was under the new coach that the Colts went on to capture their next championship, in 1968, when they beat Cleveland before going on to lose to the Jets in Super Bowl III. Ironically, New York were coached by Ewbank.

The Colts were moved to the newly formed American Conference in 1970 but were without Don Shula who moved to the Dolphins. However, under new coach Don McCafferty the Colts were the AFC's first champions and this time they produced winning form to beat the Cowboys 16–13 in the Super Bowl thanks to a field goal by Jim O'Brien with just five seconds of the match remaining. Johnny Unitas, one of the Colts best-known players, left the club in 1973 in a move that took him to the San Diego Chargers.

The Baltimore franchise moved to Indianapolis in 1984 under their seventh coach since Shula's departure. Rod Dowhower became coach number 12 in 1986 and after the arrival of running back Eric Dickerson, traded to the Colts from the Rams in 1987, the Colts went on to win the AFC Eastern Division title, their last to date.

FORMER STADIUMS

1953–83 Memorial Stadium (Baltimore)

RECORD HOLDERS

Career Records

Points	678	Lenny Moore, 1956–67
Touchdowns	113	Lenny Moore, 1956–67
Rushing (Yards)	5487	Lydell Mitchell, 1972–7
Passing (Yards)	39 768	Johnny Unitas, 1956–72
Passing (Touchdowns)	287	Johnny Unitas, 1956–72
Receiving (No.)	631	Raymond Berry, 1955–67
Receiving (Yards)	9275	Raymond Berry, 1955–67
Interceptions	57	Bob Boyd, 1960–68
Punting (Average)	43.9	Rohn Stark, 1982–91
Punt Returns (Average)	12.6	Wendell Harris, 1964
Kick-off Returns (Average)	32.5	Jim Duncan, 1969–71
Field Goals	107	Lou Michaels, 1964–9

Season Records

Points	120	Lenny Moore, 1964
Touchdowns	20	Lenny Moore, 1964
Rushing (Yards)	1659	Eric Dickerson, 1988
Passing (Yards)	3481	Johnny Unitas, 1963
Passing (Touchdowns)	32	Johnny Unitas, 1959
Receiving (No.)	82	Joe Washington, 1979
Receiving (Yards)	1298	Raymond Berry, 1960
Interceptions	11	Tom Keane, 1953
Punting (Average)	45.9	Rohn Stark, 1985
Punt Returns (Average)	12.9	Clarence Verdin, 1989
Kick-off Returns (Average)	35.4	Jim Duncan, 1970
Field Goals	30	Raul Allegre, 1983

Single Game Records

Points	24	*Many occasions*
Touchdowns	4	*Many occasions*
Rushing (Yards)	198	Norm Bulaich, 19 Sep 1971
Passing (Yards)	401	Johnny Unitas, 17 Sep 1967
Passing (Touchdowns)	5	Gary Cuozzo, 14 Nov 1965
	5	Gary Hogeboom, 4 Oct 1987
Receiving (No.)	13	Lydell Mitchell, 15 Dec 1974
	13	Joe Washington, 2 Sep 1979
Receiving (Yards)	224	Raymond Berry, 10 Nov 1957
Interceptions	3	*Many occasions*
Field Goals	5	*Many occasions*

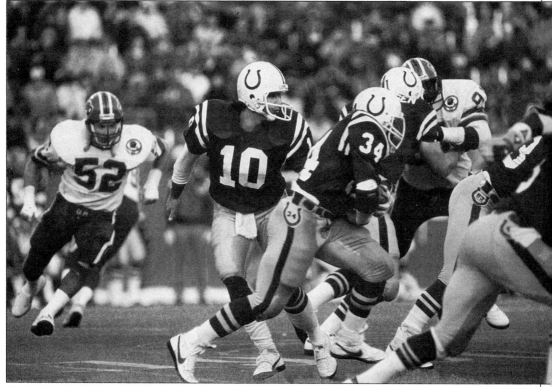

Quarterback Art Schlichter (10) in the thick of the action during the Colts debut season in Indianapolis.

HONOURS

1921–59
NFL Divisional Champions: 1958–9
NFL Champions: 1958–9
1960–9
NFL Divisional Champions: 1964, 1968
NFL Champions: 1968
1970–92
AFC Divisional Champions: 1970, 1975–7, 1987
AFC Champions: 1970
Super Bowl – Winners: 1971
      – Runners-up: 1969

COACHING HISTORY

Year	Coach	W	L	T
1953	Ken Molesworth	3	9	0
1954–62	Weeb Ewbank	61	52	1
1963–9	Don Shula	73	26	4
1970–2	Don McCafferty	26	11	1
1972	John Sandusky	4	5	0
1973–4	Howard Schnellenberger	4	13	0
1974	Joe Thomas	2	9	0
1975–9	Ted Marchibroda	41	36	0
1980–1	Mike McCormack	9	23	0
1982–4	Frank Kush	11	28	1
1984	Hal Hunter	0	1	0
1985–6	Rod Dowhower	5	24	0
1986–91	Ron Meyer	36	36	0
1991	Rick Venturi	1	10	0

PLAYERS SELECTED AS THE NO. 1 DRAFT CHOICE

Year	Player	Pos	College
1955	George Shaw	QB	Oregon
1967	Bubba Smith	DT	Michigan State
1983	John Elway	QB	Stanford
1990	Jeff George	QB	Illinois

REGULAR SEASON RECORD

Year	W	L	T	%	Year	W	L	T	%	Year	W	L	T	%
1953	3	9	0	.250	1966	9	5	0	.643	1979	5	11	0	.313
1954	3	9	0	.250	1967	11	1	2	.917	1980	7	9	0	.438
1955	5	6	1	.455	1968	13	1	0	.929	1981	2	14	0	.125
1956	5	7	0	.417	1969	8	5	1	.615	1982	0	8	1	.056
1957	7	5	0	.583	1970	11	2	1	.846	1983	7	9	0	.438
1958	9	3	0	.750	1971	10	4	0	.714	1984	4	12	0	.250
1959	9	3	0	.750	1972	5	9	0	.357	1985	5	11	0	.313
1960	6	6	0	.500	1973	4	10	0	.286	1986	3	13	0	.188
1961	8	6	0	.571	1974	2	12	0	.143	1987	9	6	0	.600
1962	7	7	0	.500	1975	10	4	0	.714	1988	9	7	0	.563
1963	8	6	0	.571	1976	11	3	0	.786	1989	8	8	0	.500
1964	12	2	0	.857	1977	10	4	0	.714	1990	7	9	0	.438
1965	10	3	1	.769	1978	5	11	0	.313	1991	1	15	0	.063

INDIANAPOLIS HEAD-TO-HEAD AGAINST CURRENT NFL TEAMS

	W	L	T		W	L	T		W	L	T
v Atlanta	10	0	0	v Houston	6	6	0	v NY Jets	24	20	0
v Buffalo	19	23	1	v Kansas City	4	6	0	v Philadelphia	6	5	0
v Chicago	21	16	0	v LA Raiders	3	5	0	v Phoenix	4	6	0
v Cincinnati	7	5	0	v LA Rams	20	16	2	v Pittsburgh	4	11	0
v Cleveland	7	14	0	v Miami	13	32	0	v San Diego	5	6	0
v Dallas	3	6	0	v Minnesota	12	6	1	v San Francisco	21	16	0
v Denver	2	8	0	v New England	18	25	0	v Seattle	2	1	0
v Detroit	17	17	2	v New Orleans	3	2	0	v Tampa Bay	4	2	0
v Green Bay	18	19	1	v NY Giants	7	4	0	v Washington	16	6	0

KANSAS CITY CHIEFS

Arrowhead Stadium
One Arrowhead Drive, Kansas City, Missouri
Stadium Capacity: 78067

When Lamar Hunt, a Texas millionaire, failed to get permission for an NFL franchise in Texas he formed the AFL in 1959 and installed his own team, the Dallas Texans, as founder members. Shortly afterwards the NFL granted a franchise to the Dallas Cowboys. (Hunt's 'Texans' were no relation to them or to the Dallas Texans team which spawned the Indianapolis Colts.)

In their third season in the AFL the Texans captured the championship by beating Houston 20–17. It was their last season in Texas because the Mayor of Kansas City promised Hunt increased ticket sales and offered to enlarge the Municipal Stadium if he moved his franchise to the City, which he duly did. At the same time he renamed the team 'The Chiefs'.

After a dramatic decline in attendances things picked up when the Chiefs recruited Heisman Trophy winner Mike Garrett in 1966 and they went on to win the AFL Championship for the second time. They then met Green Bay in the first ever Super Bowl but the NFL champions ran out 35–10 winners. A second Super Bowl appearance followed three years later after they had beaten Oakland for the AFL title, and this time it was glory for Kansas City as they beat the Minnesota Vikings 23–7.

Garrett was traded to the San Diego Chargers shortly after the Super Bowl triumph when his relationship with coach Hank Stram became strained. Stram was dismissed in 1974 after 15 years as the club's first and only coach. Since then six men have been at the helm but none has, as yet, been able to achieve a return to those glory days of Stram and Garrett.

Lamar Hunt, Chiefs owner and founder of the AFL.

HONOURS

1960–9

AFL Divisional Champions:	1962, 1966
AFL Champions:	1962, 1966, 1969

1970–92

AFC Divisional Champions:	1971
AFC Champions:	None
Super Bowl – *Winners:*	1970
– *Runners-up:*	1967

COACHING HISTORY

		W	L	T
1960–74	Hank Stram	129	79	10
1975–7	Paul Wiggin	11	24	0
1977	Tom Bettis	1	6	0
1978–82	Marv Levy	31	42	0
1983–6	John Mackovic	30	35	0
1987–8	Frank Gansz	8	22	1
1989–91	Marty Schottenheimer	30	20	1

FORMER STADIUMS

1960–2	Cotton Bowl (Dallas)
1963–71	Municipal Stadium

PLAYERS SELECTED AS THE NO. 1 DRAFT CHOICE

Year	Player	Pos	College
1963	Buck Buchanan	DT	Grambling

RECORD HOLDERS

Career Records

Points	1268	Nick Lowery, 1979–91
Touchdowns	60	Otis Taylor, 1965–75
Rushing (Yards)	4451	Ed Podolak, 1969–77
Passing (Yards)	28 507	Len Dawson, 1962–75
Passing (Touchdowns)	237	Len Dawson, 1962–75
Receiving (No.)	416	Harry Marshall, 1976–87
Receiving (Yards)	7306	Otis Taylor, 1965–75
Interceptions	58	Emmitt Thomas, 1966–78
Punting (Average)	43.5	Jerrel Wilson, 1963–77
Punt Returns (Average)	10.6	JT Smith, 1979–84
Kick-off Returns (Average)	26.8	Noland Smith, 1967–69
Field Goals	279	Jan Stenerud, 1967–79

Season Records

Points	139	Nick Lowery, 1990
Touchdowns	19	Abner Haynes, 1962
Rushing (Yards)	1480	Christian Okoye, 1989
Passing (Yards)	4348	Bill Kenney, 1983
Passing (Touchdowns)	30	Len Dawson, 1964
Receiving (No.)	80	Carlos Carson, 1983
Receiving (Yards)	1351	Carlos Carson, 1983
Interceptions	12	Emmitt Thomas, 1974
Punting (Average)	46.0	Jerrel Wilson, 1965
Punt Returns (Average)	15.4	Abner Haynes, 1960
Kick-off Returns (Average)	29.7	Dave Grayson, 1962
Field Goals	34	Nick Lowery, 1990

Single Game Records

Points	30	Abner Haynes, 26 Nov 1961
Touchdowns	5	Abner Haynes, 26 Nov 1961
Rushing (Yards)	200	Barry Word, 14 Oct 1990
Passing (Yards)	435	Len Dawson, 1 Nov 1964
Passing (Touchdowns)	6	Len Dawson, 1 Nov 1964
Receiving (No.)	12	Ed Podolak, 7 Oct 1973
Receiving (Yards)	309	Stephone Paige, 22 Dec 1985
Interceptions	4	Bobby Ply, 16 Dec 1962
	4	Bobby Hunt, 4 Dec 1964
	4	Deron Cherry, 29 Sep 1985
Field Goals	5	*Many occasions*

REGULAR SEASON RECORD

Year	W	L	T	%
1960	8	6	0	.571
1961	6	8	0	.429
1962	11	3	0	.786
1963	5	7	2	.417
1964	7	7	0	.500
1965	7	5	2	.583
1966	11	2	1	.846
1967	9	5	0	.643
1968	12	2	0	.857
1969	11	3	0	.786
1970	7	5	2	.583
1971	10	3	1	.769
1972	8	6	0	.571
1973	7	5	2	.571
1974	5	9	0	.357
1975	5	9	0	.357
1976	5	9	0	.357
1977	2	12	0	.143
1978	4	12	0	.250
1979	7	9	0	.438
1980	8	8	0	.500
1981	9	7	0	.563
1982	3	6	0	.333
1983	6	10	0	.375
1984	8	8	0	.500
1985	6	10	0	.375
1986	10	6	0	.625
1987	4	11	0	.267
1988	4	11	1	.281
1989	8	7	1	.531
1990	11	5	0	.688
1991	10	6	0	.625

KANSAS CITY HEAD-TO-HEAD AGAINST CURRENT NFL TEAMS

	W	L	T		W	L	T		W	L	T
v Atlanta	3	0	0	v Houston	22	15	0	v NY Jets	14	13	1
v Buffalo	13	16	1	v Indianapolis	6	4	0	v Philadelphia	0	1	0
v Chicago	2	3	0	v LA Raiders	29	35	2	v Phoenix	3	1	1
v Cincinnati	10	9	0	v LA Rams	1	3	0	v Pittsburgh	5	12	0
v Cleveland	6	7	2	v Miami	10	8	0	v San Diego	31	31	1
v Dallas	2	2	0	v Minnesota	3	2	0	v San Francisco	1	5	0
v Denver	36	27	0	v New England	12	7	3	v Seattle	15	12	0
v Detroit	4	3	0	v New Orleans	2	3	0	v Tampa Bay	4	2	0
v Green Bay	3	2	1	v NY Giants	1	5	0	v Washington	2	1	0

LOS ANGELES RAIDERS

Memorial Coliseum
3911 South Figueroa Street, Los Angeles, California
Stadium Capacity: 92 488

When the Raiders were formed in 1960 the franchise was given to Oakland, but they had to share the ground of NFL rivals San Francisco because the University of Southern California refused the Raiders permission to use their stadium. After only one season sharing the Kezar Stadium they moved to Candle-stick Park but it heralded a disastrous season which resulted in just two wins. The Raiders lost 55–0 and 44–0 in their first two games and a 13-game losing streak followed in 1962.

It was after Al Davis took over as head coach in 1963 that the Raiders at last found winning ways and he guided them to their first winning season with a 10–4–0 record. Davis left in 1966 to become the AFL commissioner but by then the Raiders were no longer a team of also-rans. They moved into the Oakland–Alameda County Coliseum in 1966 and in 1967, under new coach John Rauch, they captured the AFL Championship by beating Houston, but in the Super Bowl they were beaten by the Packers.

The Raiders won AFL divisional titles in 1968 and 1969 and when the AFC was formed in 1970 they won the Western Division title no fewer than six times in seven years but could only once, in 1976, go on to win

The home of the Raiders – the Memorial Coliseum in Los Angeles, holding over 90 000 fans.

the Championship, beating the Pittsburgh Steelers. This time their Super Bowl appearance was more successful as they beat the Minnesota Vikings 32–14.

After ten seasons, coach John Madden, the youngest ever NFL coach when appointed at the age of 32 in 1969, retired, with former Raiders quarterback Tom Flores replacing him in 1979. Success soon returned for

the new coach and the AFC Championship was followed by a second Super Bowl triumph in 1981 when the Raiders beat the Philadelphia Eagles 27–10.

After the Rams moved from the Los Angeles Coliseum into the Anaheim Stadium, the Raiders applied to move into the Coliseum but were originally refused permission. However, after legal action they eventu-

ally made the move in 1982 and became known as the Los Angeles Raiders. Their end-of-season game against the Rams attracted the first $1 million gate in NFL history. A third Super Bowl victory followed in 1984 when they comprehensively beat the Redskins 38–9. They have not won the AFC Championship since then but have twice won divisional titles.

Bo Jackson (34) in action against Denver. He holds the record for rushing yardage in a single game.

HONOURS

1960–9

AFL Divisional Champions: 1967–9
AFL Champions: 1967

1970–92

AFC Divisional Champions: 1970, 1972–6, 1983, 1985,
                             1990
AFC Champions: 1976, 1980, 1983
Super Bowl – Winners: 1977, 1981, 1984
          – Runners-up: 1968

COACHING HISTORY

		W	L	T
1960–1	Eddie Erdelatz	6	10	0
1961–2	Marty Feldman	2	15	0
1962	Red Conkright	1	8	0
1963–5	Al Davis	23	16	3
1966–8	John Rauch	35	10	1
1969–78	John Madden	112	39	7
1979–87	Tom Flores	91	56	0
1988–9	Mike Shanahan	8	12	0
1989–91	Art Shell	29	18	0

PLAYERS SELECTED AS THE NO. 1 DRAFT CHOICE

Year	Player	Pos	College
1962	Roman Gabriel	QB	North Carolina State

RECORD HOLDERS

Career Records

Points	863	George Blanda, 1967–75
Touchdowns	95	Marcus Allen, 1982–91
Rushing (Yards)	8244	Marcus Allen, 1982–91
Passing (Yards)	19078	Ken Stabler, 1970–9
Passing (Touchdowns)	150	Ken Stabler, 1970–9
Receiving (No.)	589	Fred Biletnikoff, 1965–78
Receiving (Yards)	8974	Fred Biletnikoff, 1965–78
Interceptions	39	Willie Brown, 1967–78
	39	Lester Hayes, 1977–86
Punting (Average)	42.5	Ray Guy, 1973–86
Punt Returns (Average)	12.6	Claude Gibson, 1963–5
Kick-off Returns (Average)	28.4	Jack Larscheid, 1960–1
Field Goals	156	George Blanda, 1967–75

Season Records

Points	117	George Blanda, 1968
Touchdowns	18	Marcus Allen, 1984
Rushing (Yards)	1759	Marcus Allen, 1985
Passing (Yards)	3615	Ken Stabler, 1979
Passing (Touchdowns)	34	Daryle Lamonica, 1969
Receiving (No.)	95	Todd Christensen, 1986
Receiving (Yards)	1361	Art Powell, 1964
Interceptions	13	Lester Hayes, 1980
Punting (Average)	45.3	Ray Guy, 1973
Punt Returns (Average)	14.4	Claude Gibson, 1964
Kick-off Returns (Average)	30.5	Harold Hart, 1975
Field Goals	29	Jeff Jaeger, 1991

Single Game Records

Points	24	Art Powell, 22 Dec 1963
	24	Marcus Allen, 24 Sep 1984
Touchdowns	4	Art Powell, 22 Dec 1963
	4	Marcus Allen, 24 Sep 1984
Rushing (Yards)	221	Bo Jackson, 30 Nov 1987
Passing (Yards)	427	Cotton Davidson, 25 Oct 1964
Passing (Touchdowns)	6	Tom Flores, 22 Dec 1963
	6	Daryle Lamonica, 19 Oct 1969
Receiving (No.)	12	Dave Casper, 3 Oct 1976
Receiving (Yards)	247	Art Powell, 22 Dec 1963
Interceptions	3	*Many occasions*
Field Goals	4	*Many occasions*

REGULAR SEASON RECORD

Year	W	L	T	%	Year	W	L	T	%	Year	W	L	T	%
1960	6	8	0	.429	1971	8	4	2	.667	1982	8	1	0	.889
1961	2	12	0	.143	1972	10	3	1	.750	1983	12	4	0	.750
1962	1	13	0	.071	1973	9	4	1	.679	1984	11	5	0	.688
1963	10	4	0	.714	1974	4	10	0	.286	1985	12	4	0	.750
1964	5	7	2	.417	1975	11	3	0	.786	1986	8	8	0	.500
1965	8	5	1	.615	1976	13	1	0	.929	1987	5	10	0	.333
1966	8	5	1	.615	1977	11	3	0	.786	1988	7	9	0	.438
1967	13	1	0	.929	1978	9	7	0	.563	1989	8	8	0	.500
1968	12	2	0	.857	1979	9	7	0	.563	1990	12	4	0	.750
1969	12	1	1	.923	1980	11	5	0	.688	1991	9	7	0	.563
1970	8	4	2	.667	1981	7	9	0	.438					

RAIDERS HEAD-TO-HEAD AGAINST CURRENT NFL TEAMS

	W	L	T		W	L	T		W	L	T
v Atlanta	4	3	0	v Houston	22	13	0	v NY Jets	13	11	2
v Buffalo	13	15	0	v Indianapolis	5	3	0	v Philadelphia	3	3	0
v Chicago	4	3	0	v Kansas City	35	29	2	v Phoenix	2	1	0
v Cincinnati	16	5	0	v LA Rams	5	2	0	v Pittsburgh	10	6	0
v Cleveland	10	2	0	v Miami	16	4	1	v San Diego	41	22	2
v Dallas	3	1	0	v Minnesota	6	2	0	v San Francisco	5	2	0
v Denver	43	19	2	v New England	13	13	1	v Seattle	15	15	0
v Detroit	5	2	0	v New Orleans	3	2	1	v Tampa Bay	2	0	0
v Green Bay	5	2	0	v NY Giants	3	2	0	v Washington	5	2	0

FORMER STADIUMS

1960 Kezar Stadium (San Francisco)
1961 Candlestick Park
1962–5 Frank Youell Field (Oakland)
1966–81 Oakland–Alameda County Coliseum

LOS ANGELES RAMS

Anaheim Stadium
Anaheim, California
Stadium Capacity: 69 008

The Rams were founded as the Cleveland Rams by Homer Marshman in 1937 and he chose the name because, as he said: 'Wild rams butt heads harder than any other animal.' However, after six seasons in the NFL there hadn't been a lot of heads butted by the Rams because they were perennial 'also-rans' in the Western Division.

New owner Daniel Reeves obtained permission to suspend operations for a year in 1943 because of the war and when the team returned it was another dismal season. But in 1945 they captured their first divisional title before going on to win the championship by beating Washington 15–14. Despite their success on the field, gates were poor and Reeves lost money. A move to Los Angeles was initially thwarted by the NFL but when Reeves threatened to pull out of the sport, they agreed and the Cleveland Rams became the Los Angeles Rams with the Coliseum as their new home.

The Rams won the first of three successive divisional titles in 1949 but only the last, in 1951, saw them go on and win the championship, with a 24–17 win over Cleveland. A fifth divisional title under new coach Sid Gillman followed in 1955 but Cleveland prevented a third championship for the Rams by winning 38–14 in the Coliseum.

Pete Rozelle, who went on to become NFL commissioner, was appointed general manager in 1957 but it was to be another decade before they enjoyed the success of a divisional title again which came a year after the appointment of George Allen as the Rams' ninth coach since their move to Los Angeles. Allen was sacked in 1968 following a difference of opinion with owner Reeves but was reinstated following a public outcry. He eventually left in 1970 after five years as head coach during which time he led the team to two divisional titles.

Reeves died in 1971 and two years later Chuck Knox, one of the game's most celebrated coaches, joined the Rams. He brought instant success, leading the team to the Western Division title in 1973, and again in 1974 when James Harris became the first black quarterback to lead a team to a professional title. The Rams captured the Western Division every year from 1973 to 1979 but only once, in 1979, the year after Knox resigned, did they go on to win the NFC Champion- ship when they beat Tampa Bay 9–0. Their one and only Super Bowl appearance resulted in a 31–19 defeat by Pittsburgh.

Since then the Rams have won just one other divisional title, under coach John Robinson in 1985. Robinson was appointed head coach in 1982 but quit at the end of 1991 after 10 years, which made him the Rams' longest serving coach. He was replaced by the man who had guided them to their successes in the 1970s, Chuck Knox, who quit his post at Seattle.

RECORD HOLDERS

Career Records

Points	789	Mike Lansford, 1982–90
Touchdowns	58	Eric Dickerson, 1983–7
Rushing (Yards)	7245	Eric Dickerson, 1983–7
Passing (Yards)	22 223	Roman Gabriel, 1962–72
Passing (Touchdowns)	154	Roman Gabriel, 1962–72
Receiving (No.)	485	Henry Ellard, 1983–91
Receiving (Yards)	8089	Henry Ellard, 1983–91
Interceptions	46	Ed Meador, 1959–70
Punting (Average)	44.2	Danny Villanueva, 1960–4
Punt Returns (Average)	11.3	Henry Ellard, 1983–90
Kick-off Returns (Average)	27.1	Tom Wilson, 1956–61
Field Goals	158	Mike Lansford, 1982–90

Season Records

Points	130	David Ray, 1973
Touchdowns	20	Eric Dickerson, 1983
Rushing (Yards)	2105	Eric Dickerson, 1984
Passing (Yards)	4310	Jim Everrett, 1989
Passing (Touchdowns)	31	Jim Everrett, 1988
Receiving (No.)	86	Henry Ellard, 1988
Receiving (Yards)	1425	Elroy Hirsch, 1951
Interceptions	14	Dick Lane, 1952
Punting (Average)	45.5	Danny Villanueva, 1962
Punt Returns (Average)	18.5	Woodley Lewis, 1952
Kick-off Returns (Average)	33.7	Verda Smith, 1950
Field Goals	30	David Ray, 1973

Single Game Records

Points	24	Bob Shaw, 11 Dec 1949
	24	Elroy Hirsch, 28 Sep 1951
	24	Harold Jackson, 14 Oct 1973
Touchdowns	4	Bob Shaw, 11 Dec 1949
	4	Elroy Hirsch, 28 Sep 1951
	4	Harold Jackson, 14 Oct 1973
Rushing (Yards)	248	Eric Dickerson, 4 Jan 1986
Passing (Yards)	554	Norm Van Brocklin, 28 Sep 1951
Passing (Touchdowns)	5	Many occasions
Receiving (No.)	18	Tom Fears, 3 Dec 1950
Receiving (Yards)	336	Willie Anderson, 26 Nov 1989
Interceptions	3	Many occasions
Field Goals	5	Bob Waterfield, 9 Dec 1951

REGULAR SEASON RECORD

Year	W	L	T	%
1937	1	10	0	.091
1938	4	7	0	.364
1939	5	5	1	.500
1940	4	6	1	.400
1941	2	9	0	.182
1942	5	6	0	.455
1943	–	–	–	–
1944	4	6	0	.400
1945	9	1	0	.900
1946	6	4	1	.600
1947	6	6	0	.500
1948	6	5	1	.545
1949	8	2	2	.800
1950	9	3	0	.750
1951	8	4	0	.667
1952	9	3	0	.750
1953	8	3	1	.727
1954	6	5	1	.545
1955	8	3	1	.727
1956	4	8	0	.333
1957	6	6	0	.500
1958	8	4	0	.667
1958	2	10	0	.167
1960	4	7	1	.364
1961	4	10	0	.286
1962	1	12	1	.077
1963	5	9	0	.357
1964	5	7	2	.417
1965	4	10	0	.286
1966	8	6	0	.571
1967	11	1	2	.917
1968	10	3	1	.769
1969	11	3	0	.786
1970	9	4	1	.692
1971	8	5	1	.615
1972	6	7	1	.464
1973	12	2	0	.857
1974	10	4	0	.714
1975	12	2	0	.857
1976	10	3	1	.750
1977	10	4	0	.714
1978	12	4	0	.750
1979	9	7	0	.563
1980	11	5	0	.688
1981	6	10	0	.375
1982	2	7	0	.222
1983	9	7	0	.563
1984	10	6	0	.625
1985	11	5	0	.688
1986	10	6	0	.625
1987	6	9	0	.400
1988	10	6	0	.625
1989	11	5	0	.688
1990	5	11	0	.313
1991	3	13	0	.188

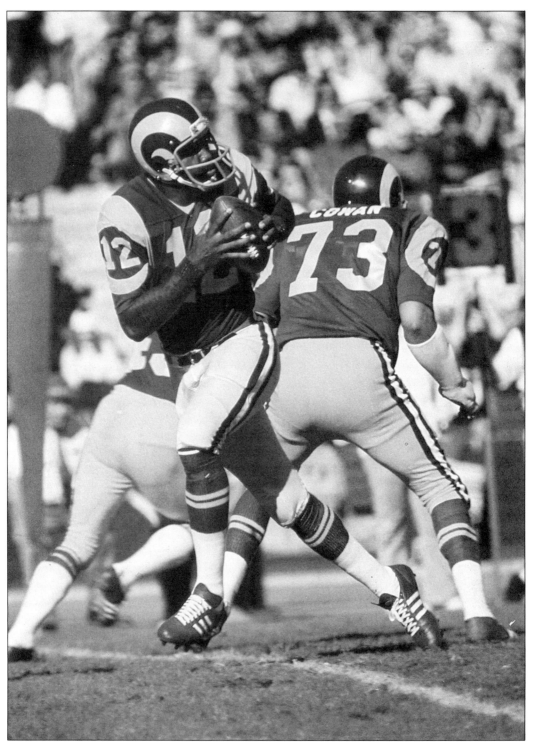

Quarterback James Harris in action for the Rams. Their 1974 divisional success made Harris the first black quarterback to lead his team to a pro title.

HONOURS

1921–59

NFL Divisional Champions: 1945, 1949–51, 1955
NFL Champions: 1945, 1951

1960–9

NFL Divisional Champions: 1967, 1969
NFL Champions: None

1970–92

NFC Divisional Champions: 1973–9, 1985
NFC Champions: 1979
Super Bowl – Winners: None
– Runners-up: 1980

PLAYERS SELECTED AS THE NO. 1 DRAFT

CHOICE

Year	Player	Pos	College
1938	Corbett Davis	FB	Indiana
1952	Bill Wade	QB	Vanderbilt
1960	Billy Cannon	RB	Louisiana State
1963	Terry Baker	QB	Oregon State

COACHING HISTORY

		W	L	T
1937–8	Hugo Bezdek	1	13	0
1938	Art Lewis	4	4	0
1939–42	Earl 'Dutch' Clark	16	26	2
1944	Aldo 'Buff' Donelli	4	6	0
1945–6	Adam Walsh	16	5	1
1947	Bob Snyder	6	6	0
1948–9	Clark Shaughnessy	14	8	3
1950–2	Joe Stydahar	19	9	0
1952–4	Hamp Pool	23	11	2
1955–9	Sid Gillman	28	32	1
1960–2	Bob Waterfield	9	24	1
1962–5	Harland Svare	14	31	3
1966–70	George Allen	49	19	4
1971–2	Tommy Prothro	14	12	2
1973–7	Chuck Knox	57	20	1
1978–82	Ray Malavasi	43	36	0
1983–91	John Robinson	79	74	0

FORMER STADIUMS

1937–45 Municipal Stadium (Cleveland)
1946–79 Memorial Coliseum

RAMS HEAD-TO-HEAD AGAINST CURRENT NFL TEAMS

	W	L	T		W	L	T		W	L	T
v Atlanta	35	13	2	v Houston	4	2	0	v NY Jets	4	2	0
v Buffalo	3	2	0	v Indianapolis	16	20	2	v Philadelphia	16	12	1
v Chicago	29	45	3	v Kansas City	3	1	0	v Phoenix	23	17	2
v Cincinnati	2	4	0	v LA Raiders	2	5	0	v Pittsburgh	13	5	2
v Cleveland	8	9	0	v Miami	1	4	0	v San Diego	3	2	0
v Dallas	12	12	0	v Minnesota	12	19	2	v San Francisco	48	35	2
v Denver	3	3	0	v New England	2	3	0	v Seattle	4	1	0
v Detroit	39	35	1	v New Orleans	26	18	0	v Tampa Bay	8	2	0
v Green Bay	42	35	2	v NY Giants	20	9	0	v Washington	6	16	1

MIAMI DOLPHINS

Joe Robbie Stadium
2269 NW199th Street, Miami, Florida
Stadium Capacity: 73 000

Minneapolis attorney Joe Robbie, along with entertainer Danny Thomas, was responsible for raising the $7.5 million required to take an NFL franchise to Miami in 1965. The team were named the Dolphins after a contest to find a team name – Mrs Swanson of West Miami won the competition for her suggestion and in return she received two lifetime passes to see the team.

George Wilson was appointed as coach, the first of only two the Dolphins have had since joining the NFL, but after four losing seasons Wilson was fired and the former Baltimore Colts coach Don Shula was appointed head coach and vice president. Shula went on to become one of the game's most successful coaches. In his first season in charge, he took the Dolphins into their first play-offs via a wild card entry. The following year they were Eastern Division champions and two years after Shula took over the reins the Dolphins were in the Super Bowl. It ended in defeat by the Dallas Cowboys but the following year they beat the Washington Redskins 14–7 at the end of the first unbeaten and untied record in both regular and post-season games in NFL history. A third successive Super Bowl appearance followed in 1974 and it was win number two as Miami beat the Minnesota Vikings 24–7.

The Dolphins acquired one of the game's great quarterbacks in 1982 when 26 other teams passed up Dan Marino in the draft. Miami took him and in his first season he helped them to the AFC Championship, thanks to two touchdown passes. He then made history by becoming the first 'rookie' quarterback to start in a Super Bowl, but the fairytale ended there because the Dolphins were beaten by the Redskins. The following year Marino became the first quarterback ever to pass for 5000 yards and in 1985 the Dolphins reached their fifth Super Bowl, only for their ambitions to be thwarted again, this time by the 49ers. Shula is still in charge but those winning days of the 1970s and mid-80s seem a long way off as the team tries to get back amongst the honours.

The Joe Robbie Stadium – the home of the Miami Dolphins and also the venue for Super Bowl XXIII.

REGULAR SEASON RECORD

Year	W	L	T	%
1966	3	11	0	.214
1967	4	10	0	.286
1968	5	8	1	.385
1969	3	10	1	.235
1970	10	4	0	.714
1971	10	3	1	.769
1972	14	0	0	1.000
1973	12	2	0	.857
1974	11	3	0	.786
1975	10	4	0	.714
1976	6	8	0	.429
1977	10	4	0	.714
1978	11	5	0	.688
1979	9	7	0	.563
1980	8	8	0	.500
1981	11	4	1	.719
1982	7	2	0	.778
1983	12	4	0	.750
1984	14	2	0	.875
1985	12	4	0	.750
1986	8	8	0	.500
1987	8	7	0	.533
1988	6	10	0	.375
1989	8	8	0	.500
1990	12	4	0	.750
1991	8	8	0	.500

RECORD HOLDERS

Career Records

Points	830	Garo Yepremian, 1970–8
Touchdowns	75	Nat Moore, 1974–86
Rushing (Yards)	6737	Larry Csonka, 1968–74, 1979
Passing (Yards)	35386	Dan Marino, 1983–91
Passing (Touchdowns)	266	Dan Marino, 1983–91
Receiving (No.)	510	Nat Moore, 1974–86
Receiving (Yards)	7547	Nat Moore, 1974–86
Interceptions	35	Jake Scott, 1970–5
Punting (Average)	43.5	Reggie Roby, 1983–91
Punt Returns (Average)	11.4	Freddie Solomon, 1975–7
Kick-off Returns (Average)	26.5	Mercury Morris, 1969–75
Field Goals	165	Garo Yepremian, 1970–8

Season Records

Points	121	Pete Stoyanovich, 1991
Touchdowns	18	Mark Clayton, 1984
Rushing (Yards)	1258	Delvin Williams, 1978
Passing (Yards)	5084	Dan Marino, 1984
Passing (Touchdowns)	48	Dan Marino, 1984
Receiving (No.)	86	Mark Clayton, 1988
Receiving (Yards)	1389	Mark Clayton, 1984
Interceptions	10	Dick Westmoreland, 1967
Punting (Average)	45.7	Reggie Roby, 1991
Punt Returns (Average)	12.3	Freddie Solomon, 1975
Kick-off Returns (Average)	32.9	Duriel Harris, 1976
Field Goals	31	Pete Stoyanovich, 1991

Single Game Records

Points	24	Paul Warfield, 15 Dec 1973
Touchdowns	4	Paul Warfield, 15 Dec 1973
Rushing (Yards)	197	Mercury Morris, 30 Sep 1973
Passing (Yards)	521	Dan Marino, 23 Oct 1988
Passing (Touchdowns)	6	Bob Griese, 24 Nov 1977
	6	Dan Marino, 21 Sep 1986
Receiving (No.)	12	Jim Jensen, 6 Nov 1988
Receiving (Yards)	217	Mark Duper, 10 Nov 1985
Interceptions	4	Dick Anderson, 3 Dec 1973
Field Goals	5	Garo Yepremian, 26 Sep 1971

Joe Robbie (right) pictured with his son Tim.

HONOURS

1960–9

AFL Divisional Champions:	None
AFL Champions:	None

1970–92

AFC Divisional Champions:	1971–4, 1979, 1981, 1983–5
AFC Champions:	1971–3, 1982, 1984
Super Bowl – Winners:	1973–4
– Runners-up:	1972, 1983, 1985

FORMER STADIUMS

1966–86 Orange Bowl

COACHING HISTORY

		W	L	T
1966–9	George Wilson	15	39	2
1970–91	Don Shula	233	119	2

PLAYERS SELECTED AS THE NO. 1 DRAFT CHOICE

Year	Player	Pos	College
1966	Jim Grabowski	RB	Illinois

MIAMI HEAD-TO-HEAD AGAINST CURRENT NFL TEAMS

	W	L	T		W	L	T		W	L	T
v Atlanta	4	1	0	v Houston	10	12	0	v NY Jets	27	25	1
v Buffalo	35	17	1	v Indianapolis	32	13	0	v Philadelphia	5	2	0
v Chicago	5	1	0	v Kansas City	8	10	0	v Phoenix	6	0	0
v Cincinnati	10	3	0	v LA Raiders	4	16	1	v Pittsburgh	9	5	0
v Cleveland	6	4	0	v LA Rams	4	1	0	v San Diego	6	10	0
v Dallas	5	2	0	v Minnesota	5	1	0	v San Francisco	4	2	0
v Denver	5	2	1	v New England	31	21	0	v Seattle	4	2	0
v Detroit	2	2	0	v New Orleans	4	1	0	v Tampa Bay	4	1	0
v Green Bay	7	0	0	v NY Giants	1	1	0	v Washington	5	3	0

MINNESOTA VIKINGS

Hubert H Humphrey Metrodome
50 11th Avenue South, Minneapolis, Minnesota
Stadium Capacity: 63 000

The 'Vikings' were formed in 1960 and it was general manager Bert Rose who came up with the name. The former Rams and Eagles quarterback Norm Van Brocklin was appointed head coach of a team that was made up largely of former NFL players who were past their best. However, in the draft the Vikings picked Fran Tarkenton who went on to become one of the game's most successful quarterbacks. He scored in the Vikings debut game, a shock 37–13 win over Chicago.

The Vikings won their first Central Division title in 1968 under new coach Bud Grant, and after winning it again the following year they went on to capture their first Championship, beating Cleveland 27–7. But their first of four Super Bowl appearances ended in defeat – as indeed all four did – when they were beaten by Kansas City. They were also beaten in Super Bowls VIII and IX by the Miami Dolphins and Pittsburgh Steelers respectively. Grant took the Vikings to their fourth Super Bowl in 1977 after beating the Rams for the NFC Championship, but the Oakland Raiders made it four losses in four Super Bowl appearances.

Fran Tarkenton retired in 1979 and the team had its first losing season for 12 years. Bud Grant ended 17 years as head coach in 1983 but after a disastrous season with Les Steckel in charge, Grant returned for a year before Jerry Burns took over in 1986. In 1989 he took Minnesota to their first divisional title for nine seasons. Burns retired at the end of 1991, handing over to the next man in the Minnesota 'hot seat', Dennis Green.

HONOURS

1960–9

NFL Divisional Champions:	1968–9
NFL Champions:	1969

1970–92

NFC Divisional Champions:	1970–1, 1973–8, 1980, 1989
NFC Champions:	1973–4, 1976
Super Bowl – Winners:	None
– Runners-up:	1970, 1974–5, 1977

FORMER STADIUMS

1961–81   Metropolitan Stadium (Bloomington)

COACHING HISTORY

		W	L	T
1961–6	Norm Van Brocklin	29	51	4
1967–83	Bud Grant	161	99	5
1984	Les Steckel	3	13	0
1985	Bud Grant	7	9	0
1986–91	Jerry Burns	55	46	0

PLAYERS SELECTED AS THE NO. 1 DRAFT CHOICE

Year	Player	Pos	College
1961	Tommy Mason	RB	Tulane
1968	Ron Yary	T	Southern California

MINNESOTA HEAD-TO-HEAD AGAINST CURRENT NFL TEAMS

	W	L	T		W	L	T		W	L	T
v Atlanta	12	6	0	v Houston	3	2	0	v NY Jets	1	3	0
v Buffalo	4	2	0	v Indianapolis	6	12	1	v Philadelphia	10	6	0
v Chicago	30	29	2	v Kansas City	2	3	0	v Phoenix	5	7	0
v Cincinnati	3	3	0	v LA Raiders	2	6	0	v Pittsburgh	6	5	0
v Cleveland	7	3	0	v LA Rams	19	12	2	v San Diego	3	3	0
v Dallas	7	10	0	v Miami	1	5	0	v San Francisco	16	16	1
v Denver	4	3	0	v New England	2	3	0	v Seattle	2	3	0
v Detroit	38	21	2	v New Orleans	12	5	0	v Tampa Bay	20	8	0
v Green Bay	29	31	1	v NY Giants	6	4	0	v Washington	5	7	0

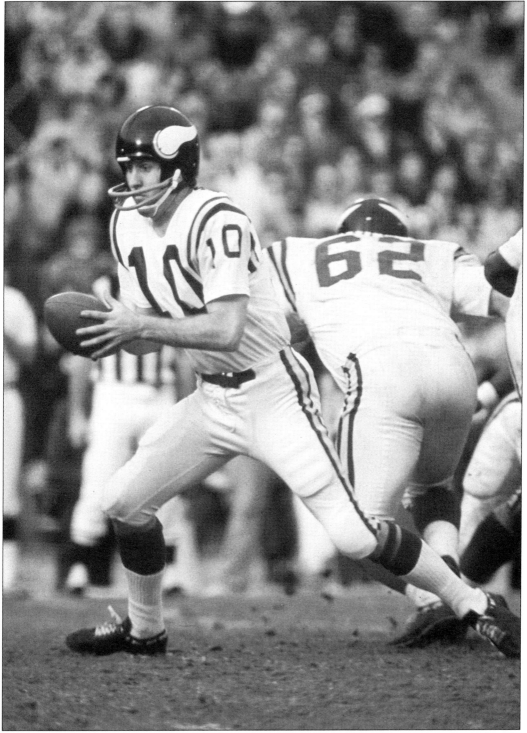

Fran Tarkenton, a draft pick for Minnesota in 1961 who went on to lead the Vikings in two career spells totalling 13 seasons.

REGULAR SEASON RECORD

Year	W	L	T	%
1961	3	11	0	.214
1962	2	11	1	.154
1963	5	8	1	.385
1964	8	5	1	.615
1965	7	7	0	.500
1966	4	9	1	.308
1967	3	8	3	.273
1968	8	6	0	.571
1969	12	2	0	.857
1970	12	2	0	.857
1971	11	3	0	.786
1972	7	7	0	.500
1973	12	2	0	.857
1974	10	4	0	.714
1975	12	2	0	.857
1976	11	2	1	.821
1977	9	5	0	.643
1978	8	7	1	.531
1979	7	9	0	.438
1980	9	7	0	.563
1981	7	9	0	.438
1982	5	4	0	.556
1983	8	8	0	.500
1984	3	13	0	.188
1985	7	9	0	.438
1986	9	7	0	.563
1987	8	7	0	.533
1988	11	5	0	.688
1989	10	6	0	.625
1990	6	10	0	.375
1991	8	8	0	.500

RECORD HOLDERS

Career Records

Points	1365	Fred Cox, 1963–77
Touchdowns	76	Bill Brown, 1962–74
Rushing (Yards)	5879	Chuck Foreman, 1973–9
Passing (Yards)	33 098	Fran Tarkenton, 1961–6, 1972–8
Passing (Touchdowns)	239	Fran Tarkenton, 1961–6, 1972–8
Receiving (No.)	400	Ahmad Rashad, 1976–82
Receiving (Yards)	5925	Sammy White, 1976–85
Interceptions	53	Paul Krause, 1968–79
Punting (Average)	42.9	Bobby Walden, 1964–7
Punt Returns (Average)	10.4	Tommy Mason, 1961–6
Kick-off Returns (Average)	27.1	Bob Reed, 1962–3
Field Goals	282	Fred Cox, 1963–77

Season Records

Points	132	Chuck Foreman, 1975
Touchdowns	22	Chuck Foreman, 1975
Rushing (Yards)	1155	Chuck Foreman, 1976
Passing (Yards)	3912	Tommy Kramer, 1981
Passing (Touchdowns)	26	Tommy Kramer, 1981
Receiving (No.)	88	Rickey Young, 1978
Receiving (Yards)	1225	Anthony Carter, 1988
Interceptions	10	Paul Krause, 1975
Punting (Average)	46.4	Bobby Walden, 1964
Punt Returns (Average)	12.5	Leo Lewis, 1987
Kick-off Returns (Average)	26.3	John Gilliam, 1972
Field Goals	31	Rich Karlis, 1989

Single Game Records

Points	24	Chuck Foreman, 20 Dec 1975
	24	Ahmad Rashad, 2 Sep 1979
Touchdowns	4	Chuck Foreman, 20 Dec 1975
	4	Ahmad Rashad, 2 Sep 1979
Rushing (Yards)	200	Chuck Foreman, 24 Oct 1976
Passing (Yards)	490	Tommy Kramer, 2 Nov 1986
Passing (Touchdowns)	7	Joe Kapp, 28 Sep 1969
Receiving (No.)	15	Rickey Young, 16 Dec 1979
Receiving (Yards)	210	Sammy White, 7 Nov 1976
Interceptions	3	Many occasions
Field Goals	7	Rich Karlis, 5 Nov 1989

NEW ENGLAND PATRIOTS

Foxboro Stadium (formerly Schaefer Stadium, 1971–82, then Sullivan Stadium, 1983–9)
Route 1, Foxboro, Massachusetts
Stadium Capacity: 60 794

Boston was awarded its eighth franchise – but its first for ten years – in 1959 when the Patriots were formed; the name 'Patriots' being taken as a result of a newspaper poll. The club's first season was a disaster with losses of around $350 000 being reported. On the playing side things weren't going too well either and head coach Lou Saban was dismissed part way through the 1961 season and replaced by Mike Holovak.

After three seasons playing at the Boston University field the Patriots moved to Fenway Park in 1963 and won the Eastern Division of the AFL but they were soundly beaten 51–10 by San Diego for the AFL title. Holovak stayed until 1969 when he was replaced by Clive Rush but the team lost the first seven games of the 1969 season and Rush's tenure as head coach lasted a mere season-and-a-half. The team moved out of Boston in 1971 to the Schaefer Stadium at Foxboro, 35 miles away, and subsequently changed their name to the New England Patriots.

Under new coach Chuck Fairbanks, and with Steve

Grogan outstanding at quarterback, the Patriots had their best ever season in 1976, posting an 11–3–0 record and capturing a wild card play-off berth. Two years later they were Eastern Division champions of the AFC. However, it was to be five years – and three coaches – before the Patriots made the play-offs again, when in 1985 as wild card entrants they went on to win the AFC Championship and then met the Chicago Bears in the Super Bowl, where they were overwhelmed 46–10. The Patriots were AFC Eastern Division champions in 1986 but they were eliminated by Western Division champions Denver in the play-offs.

Steve Grogan led the Patriots on their brief run of success in the mid-1980s which included a Super Bowl appearance.

HONOURS

1960–9
AFL Divisional Champions: 1963
AFL Champions: None
1970–92
AFC Divisional Champions: 1978, 1986
AFC Champions: 1985
Super Bowl – Winners: None
– Runners-up: 1986

PLAYERS SELECTED AS THE NO. 1 DRAFT CHOICE

Year	Player	Pos	College
1964	Jack Concannon	QB	Boston College
1971	Jim Plunkett	QB	Stanford
1982	Kenneth Sims	DT	Texas
1984	Irving Fryar	WR	Nebraska

RECORD HOLDERS

Career Records

Points	1130	Gino Cappelletti, 1960–70
Touchdowns	68	Stanley Morgan, 1977–89
Rushing (Yards)	5453	Sam Cunningham, 1973–9, 1981–2
Passing (Yards)	26886	Steve Grogan, 1975–90
Passing (Touchdowns)	182	Steve Grogan, 1975–90
Receiving (No.)	534	Stanley Morgan, 1977–89
Receiving (Yards)	10352	Stanley Morgan, 1977–89
Interceptions	36	Raymond Clayborn, 1977–89
Punting (Average)	42.6	Rich Camarillo, 1981–7
Punt Returns (Average)	12.0	Mack Herron, 1973–5
Kick-off Returns (Average)	27.6	Horace Ivory, 1977–81
Field Goals	176	Gino Cappelletti, 1960–70

Season Records

Points	155	Gino Cappelletti, 1964
Touchdowns	13	Steve Grogan, 1976
	13	Stanley Morgan, 1979
Rushing (Yards)	1458	Jim Nance, 1966
Passing (Yards)	3465	Vito Parilli, 1964
Passing (Touchdowns)	31	Vito Parilli, 1964
Receiving (No.)	84	Stanley Morgan, 1986
Receiving (Yards)	1491	Stanley Morgan, 1986
Interceptions	11	Ron Hall, 1964
Punting (Average)	44.6	Rich Camarillo, 1983
Punt Returns (Average)	14.8	Mack Herron, 1974
Kick-off Returns (Average)	31.0	Raymond Clayborn, 1977
Field Goals	32	Tony Franklin, 1986

Single Game Records

Points	28	Gino Cappelletti, 18 Dec 1965
Touchdowns	3	*Many occasions*
Rushing (Yards)	212	Tony Collins, 18 Sep 1983
Passing (Yards)	414	Tony Eason, 21 Sep 1986
Passing (Touchdowns)	5	Vito Parilli, 15 Nov 1964
	5	Vito Parilli, 15 Oct 1967
	5	Steve Grogan, 9 Sep 1979
Receiving (No.)	11	Art Graham, 20 Nov 1966
	11	Tony Collins, 29 Nov 1987
Receiving (Yards)	182	Stanley Morgan, 8 Nov 1981
Interceptions	3	*Many occasions*
Field Goals	6	Gino Cappelletti, 4 Oct 1964

COACHING HISTORY

		W	L	T
1960–1	Lou Saban	7	12	0
1961–8	Mike Holovak	53	47	9
1969–70	Clive Rush	5	16	0
1970–2	John Mazur	9	21	0
1972	Phil Bengtson	1	4	0
1973–8	Chuck Fairbanks	46	41	0
1978	Hank Bullough/ Ron Erhardt	0	1	0
1979–81	Ron Erhardt	21	27	0
1982–4	Ron Meyer	18	16	0
1984–9	Raymond Berry	51	41	0
1990	Rod Rust	1	15	0
1991	Dick MacPherson	6	10	0

Bullough and Erhardt were co-coaches for the final regular season game of 1978 after Chuck Fairbanks was suspended

FORMER STADIUMS

1960–2	Nickerson Field (Boston University)
1963–8	Fenway Park
1969	Alumni Stadium (Boston College)
1970	Harvard Stadium

REGULAR SEASON RECORD

Year	W	L	T	%
1960	5	9	0	.357
1961	9	4	1	.692
1962	9	4	1	.692
1963	7	6	1	.538
1964	10	3	1	.769
1965	4	8	2	.333
1966	8	4	2	.677
1967	3	10	1	.231
1968	4	10	0	.286
1969	4	10	0	.286
1970	2	12	0	.143
1971	4	10	0	.286
1972	3	11	0	.214
1973	5	9	0	.357
1974	7	7	0	.500
1975	3	11	0	.214
1976	11	3	0	.786
1977	9	5	0	.643
1978	11	5	0	.688
1979	9	7	0	.563
1980	10	6	0	.625
1981	2	14	0	.125
1982	5	4	0	.556
1983	8	8	0	.500
1984	9	7	0	.563
1985	11	5	0	.688
1986	11	5	0	.688
1987	8	7	0	.533
1988	9	7	0	.563
1989	5	11	0	.313
1990	1	15	0	.063
1991	6	10	0	.375

NEW ENGLAND HEAD-TO-HEAD AGAINST CURRENT NFL TEAMS

	W	L	T		W	L	T		W	L	T
v Atlanta	3	3	0	v Houston	17	14	1	v NY Jets	28	35	1
v Buffalo	34	29	1	v Indianapolis	25	18	0	v Philadelphia	2	5	0
v Chicago	3	3	0	v Kansas City	7	12	3	v Phoenix	1	6	0
v Cincinnati	7	6	0	v LA Raiders	13	13	1	v Pittsburgh	3	8	0
v Cleveland	2	8	0	v LA Rams	3	2	0	v San Diego	13	12	2
v Dallas	0	6	0	v Miami	21	31	0	v San Francisco	1	5	0
v Denver	12	17	0	v Minnesota	3	2	0	v Seattle	6	4	0
v Detroit	2	2	0	v New Orleans	5	1	0	v Tampa Bay	3	0	0
v Green Bay	2	2	0	v NY Giants	1	3	0	v Washington	1	4	0

NEW ORLEANS SAINTS

Louisiana Superdome
1500 Poydras Street, New Orleans, Louisiana
Stadium Capacity: 69065

The New Orleans Saints are one of the NFL's newest teams, formed in 1966 with millionaire racing car enthusiast John W Mecom jnr as the major shareholder. The Saints had to wait 12 years before their first non-losing season, when they ended 1979 with an 8–8–0 record, and they had been in the NFL 20 years before their first winning season (12–3–0) and appearance in the play-offs.

The team was named the Saints after the great Dixieland classic *When the Saints Go Marching In.* One of the franchise's shareholders was the jazz trum-peter Al Hirt and it was one of his favourite records. Their first game was played in front of more than 80000 fans at the Tulane Stadium. It was an encouraging start, even though they lost to the Rams 27–13, but good results were not forthcoming. Even the appointment of former *Apollo XII* astronaut Richard Gordon as executive vice-president in 1972 could not improve results on the ballpark. Nor did a move into the world's largest indoor stadium, the Louisiana Superdome, in 1975 bring about a change in fortunes.

However, under Dick Nolan, their sixth coach since their formation, the Saints had an 8–8–0 season in 1979; it was the first time they had not suffered a losing season. The following year it was 'back to normal' with a 1–15–0 record. With Jim Mora in charge they enjoyed their first winning season in 1987 but Minnesota beat then 44–10 in the first round of the play-offs. Mora's arrival at New Orleans has certainly seen a turnaround in their fortunes. They reached the play-offs again in 1990 and 1991, and in the latter of those years they captured their first title when they were Western Division champions. Atlanta ended their Super Bowl ambitions with a 27–20 win in the play-offs but things are looking encouraging way down yonder in New Orleans.

HONOURS

1960–9
NFL Divisional Champions: None
NFL Champions: None
1970–92
NFC Divisional Champions: 1991
NFC Champions: None
Super Bowl – Winners: None
– Runners-up: None

COACHING HISTORY

		W	L	T
1967–70	Tom Fears	13	34	2
1970–2	JD Roberts	7	25	3
1973–5	John North	11	23	0
1975	Ernie Hefferle	1	7	0
1976–7	Hank Stram	7	21	0
1978–80	Dick Nolan	15	29	0
1980	Dick Stanfel	1	3	0
1981–5	OA 'Bum' Phillips	27	42	0
1985	Wade Phillips	1	3	0
1986–91	Jim Mora	57	41	0

RECORD HOLDERS

Career Records
Points	965	Morten Andersen, 1982–91
Touchdowns	42	Dalton Hilliard, 1986–91
Rushing (Yards)	4267	George Rogers, 1981–4
Passing (Yards)	21 734	Archie Manning, 1971–82
Passing (Touchdowns)	115	Archie Manning, 1971–82
Receiving (No.)	398	Eric Martin, 1985–91
Receiving (Yards)	5863	Eric Martin, 1985–91
Interceptions	37	Dave Waymer, 1980–9
Punting (Average)	42.3	Tom McNeill, 1967–9
	42.3	Tommy Barnhardt, 1986–91
Punt Returns (Average)	13.4	Mel Gray, 1986–8
Kick-off Returns (Average)	26.3	Walter Roberts, 1967
Field Goals	217	Morten Andersen, 1982–91

Season Records
Points	121	Morten Andersen, 1987
Touchdowns	18	Dalton Hilliard, 1989
Rushing (Yards)	1674	George Rogers, 1981
Passing (Yards)	3716	Archie Manning, 1980
Passing (Touchdowns)	23	Archie Manning, 1980
Receiving (No.)	85	Eric Martin, 1988
Receiving (Yards)	1090	Eric Martin, 1989
Interceptions	10	Dave Whitsel, 1967
Punting (Average)	43.8	Brian Hansen, 1984
Punt Returns (Average)	14.7	Mel Gray, 1987
Kick-off Returns (Average)	27.9	Don Shy, 1969
Field Goals	31	Morten Andersen, 1985

Single Game Records
Points	18	*Many occasions*
Touchdowns	3	*Many occasions*
Rushing (Yards)	206	George Rogers, 4 Sep 1983
Passing (Yards)	377	Archie Manning, 7 Dec 1980
Passing (Touchdowns)	6	Billy Kilmer, 2 Nov 1969
Receiving (No.)	14	Tony Galbreath, 10 Sep 1978
Receiving (Yards)	205	Wes Chandler, 2 Sep 1979
Interceptions	3	Tommy Myers, 3 Sep 1978
	3	Dave Waymer, 6 Oct 1985
	3	Reggie Sutton, 18 Oct 1987
Field Goals	5	Morten Andersen, 1 Dec 1985
	5	Morten Andersen, 15 Nov 1987

PLAYERS SELECTED AS THE NO. 1 DRAFT CHOICE

Year	Player	Pos	College
1981	George Rogers	RB	South Carolina

FORMER STADIUMS

1967–74 Tulane Stadium

REGULAR SEASON RECORD

Year	W	L	T	%
1967	3	11	0	.214
1968	4	9	1	.308
1969	5	9	0	.357
1970	2	11	1	.154
1971	4	8	2	.333
1972	2	11	1	.179
1973	5	9	0	.357
1974	5	9	0	.357
1975	2	12	0	.143
1976	4	10	0	.286
1977	3	11	0	.214
1978	7	9	0	.438
1979	8	8	0	.500
1980	1	15	0	.063
1981	4	12	0	.250
1982	4	5	0	.444
1983	8	8	0	.500
1984	7	9	0	.438
1985	5	11	0	.313
1986	7	9	0	.438
1987	12	3	0	.800
1988	10	6	0	.625
1989	9	7	0	.563
1990	8	8	0	.500
1991	11	5	0	.688

NEW ORLEANS HEAD-TO-HEAD AGAINST CURRENT NFL TEAMS

	W	L	T
v Atlanta	19	27	0
v Buffalo	2	2	0
v Chicago	5	9	0
v Cincinnati	4	3	0
v Cleveland	3	8	0
v Dallas	3	13	0
v Denver	1	4	0
v Detroit	5	6	1
v Green Bay	4	11	0
v Houston	3	3	1
v Indianapolis	2	3	0
v Kansas City	3	2	0
v LA Raiders	2	3	1
v LA Rams	18	26	0
v Miami	1	4	0
v Minnesota	5	12	0
v New England	1	5	0
v NY Giants	6	8	0
v NY Jets	2	4	0
v Philadelphia	8	9	0
v Phoenix	7	10	0
v Pittsburgh	5	5	0
v San Diego	1	4	0
v San Francisco	13	30	2
v Seattle	3	2	0
v Tampa Bay	10	4	0
v Washington	4	11	0

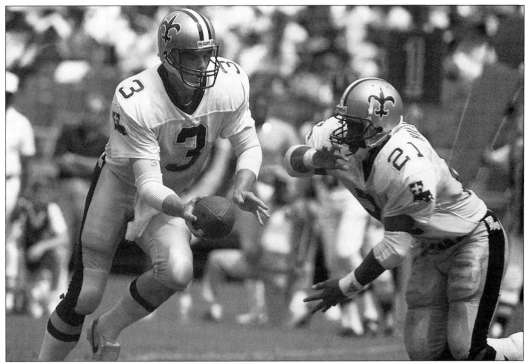

Quarterback Bobby Hebert (3) in action during the Saints' long-awaited first winning season, 1987.

NEW YORK GIANTS

Giants Stadium
East Rutherford, New Jersey
Stadium Capacity: 77311

The Giants are one of the oldest current NFL teams and are also one of the most successful. Formed in 1925, they have been winning honours since they were first champions in 1927. There was a 20-year gap without honours in the 1960s and 70s, but since the mid-80s they have once again been a major NFL force.

The original franchise was acquired for a mere $2500 by Timothy J Mara who took the franchise after abandoning his plans to buy a share in boxer Gene Tunney. Because the gridiron team shared the Polo Grounds with the Giants base-ball team, Mara also named *his* team the Giants. The big attraction in their first year was the 'banned' Olympic champion of 1912, Jim Thorpe, but the Giants found competition for the fans fierce because of the New York Yankees team that played in the rival AFL. However, it was agreed that neither team should play at home at the same time.

In 1927 the Giants captured their first title. They dominated the Eastern Division of the NFL and won the title eight times from 1933 to 1946. However, they only won the NFL championship twice: in 1934 when they beat the Chicago Bears in what became known as 'The Sneakers Game' because the Giants played in basketball shoes to ensure they had more grip on the hard surface, and in 1938 when they beat Green Bay. The Giants had to wait ten years before their next divisional title, but it came at the end of their first season playing in the Yankee Stadium, 1956. They went on to win their fourth NFL title when they beat the Bears 47-7. They remained at the Yankee Stadium until 1973 but never captured the NFL title again, although they were divisional champions on five more occasions.

Something of nomads for a couple of seasons while they were awaiting the completion of the new Giants Stadium, they eventually moved into their new home in 1976. They did not

Giants Stadium, now home to both the New York Giants and their city rivals the Jets.

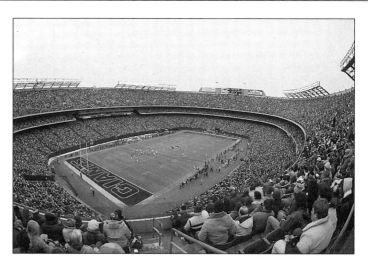

reach the play-offs again until gaining a wild-card entry in 1981, but since then they have appeared regularly in the play-offs and in 1986 they followed up their first divisional title for 23 years by going on to beat Denver 39–20 in the Super Bowl. They captured their second Super Bowl in 1991 with a narrow one-point win over Buffalo, but the following year they failed to make the play-offs.

RECORD HOLDERS

Career Records

Points	646	Pete Gogolak, 1966–74
Touchdowns	78	Frank Gifford, 1952–60, 1962–4
Rushing (Yards)	5296	Joe Morris, 1982–8
Passing (Yards)	29512	Phil Simms, 1979–91
Passing (Touchdowns)	173	Charlie Conerly, 1948–61
Receiving (No.)	395	Joe Morrison, 1959–72
Receiving (Yards)	5434	Frank Gifford, 1952–60, 1962–4
Interceptions	74	Emlen Tunnell, 1948–58
Punting (Average)	43.8	Don Chandler, 1956–64
Punt Returns (Average)	11.4	David Meggett, 1989–91
Kick-off Returns (Average)	27.2	Rocky Thompson, 1971–2
Field Goals	126	Pete Gogolak, 1966–74

Season Records

Points	127	Ali Haji-Sheikh, 1983
Touchdowns	21	Joe Morris, 1985
Rushing (Yards)	1516	Joe Morris, 1986
Passing (Yards)	4044	Phil Simms, 1984
Passing (Touchdowns)	36	YA Tittle, 1963
Receiving (No.)	78	Earnest Gray, 1983
Receiving (Yards)	1209	Homer Jones, 1967
Interceptions	11	Otto Schnellbacher, 1951
	11	Jim Patton, 1958
Punting (Average)	46.6	Don Chandler, 1959
Punt Returns (Average)	15.5	Merle Hapes, 1942
Kick-off Returns (Average)	31.6	John Salscheider, 1949
Field Goals	35	Ali Haji-Sheikh, 1983

Single Game Records

Points	24	Ron Johnson, 2 Oct 1972
	24	Earnest Gray, 7 Sep 1980
Touchdowns	4	Ron Johnson, 2 Oct 1972
	4	Earnest Gray, 7 Sep 1980
Rushing (Yards)	218	Gene Roberts, 12 Nov 1950
Passing (Yards)	513	Phil Simms, 13 Oct 1985
Passing (Touchdowns)	7	YA Tittle, 28 Oct 1962
Receiving (No.)	12	Mark Bavaro, 13 Oct 1985
Receiving (Yards)	269	Del Shofner, 28 Oct 1962
Interceptions	3	*Many occasions*
Field Goals	6	Joe Danelo, 18 Oct 1981

GIANTS HEAD-TO-HEAD AGAINST CURRENT NFL TEAMS

	W	L	T
v Atlanta	6	6	0
v Buffalo	3	3	0
v Chicago	17	29	0
v Cincinnati	0	4	0
v Cleveland	17	26	2
v Dallas	21	36	2
v Denver	4	2	0
v Detroit	15	18	1
v Green Bay	20	25	2
v Houston	4	0	0
v Indianapolis	4	7	0
v Kansas City	5	1	0
v LA Raiders	2	3	0
v LA Rams	9	20	0
v Miami	1	1	0
v Minnesota	4	6	0
v New England	3	1	0
v New Orleans	8	6	0
v NY Jets	3	3	0
v Philadelphia	61	52	2
v Phoenix	63	33	2
v Pittsburgh	42	26	3
v San Diego	4	2	0
v San Francisco	14	11	0
v Seattle	4	2	0
v Tampa Bay	7	3	0
v Washington	67	50	3

Right *Quarterback Phil Simms sidesteps the Raiders defense in 1986. Simms went on to star in the Giants' Super Bowl victory that season.*

HONOURS

1921–59

NFL Divisional Champions:	1933–5, 1938–9, 1941, 1944, 1946, 1956, 1958–9
NFL Champions:	1927, 1934, 1938, 1956

1960–9

NFL Divisional Champions:	1961–3
NFL Champions:	None

1970–92

NFC Divisional Champions:	1986, 1989–90
NFC Champions:	1986, 1990
Super Bowl – Winners:	1987, 1991
– Runners-up:	None

FORMER STADIUMS

1925–55	Polo Grounds II
1956–73	Yankee Stadium I
1973–4	Yale Bowl (New Haven, Connecticut)
1975	Shea Stadium

COACHING HISTORY

		W	L	T
1925	Bob Folwell	8	4	0
1926	Joe Alexander	8	4	1
1927–8	Earl Potteiger	15	8	3
1929–30	LeRoy Andrews	24	5	1
1930	Benny Friedman	2	0	0
1931–53	Steve Owen	153	108	17
1954–60	Jim Lee Howell	54	29	4
1961–8	Allie Sherman	57	54	4
1969–73	Alex Webster	29	40	1
1974–6	Bill Arnsparger	7	28	0
1976–8	John McVay	14	23	0
1979–82	Ray Perkins	24	35	0
1983–90	Bill Parcells	85	52	1
1991	Ray Handley	8	8	0

PLAYERS SELECTED AS THE NO. 1 DRAFT CHOICE

Year	Player	Pos	College
1951	Kyle Rote	HB	Southern Methodist
1965	Tucker Frederickson	RB	Auburn

REGULAR SEASON RECORD

Year	W	L	T	%	Year	W	L	T	%	Year	W	L	T	%
1925	8	4	0	.667	1948	4	8	0	.333	1971	4	10	0	.286
1926	8	4	1	.667	1949	6	6	0	.500	1972	8	6	0	.571
1927	11	1	1	.917	1950	10	2	0	.833	1973	2	11	1	.179
1928	4	7	2	.364	1951	9	2	1	.818	1974	2	12	0	.143
1929	13	1	1	.929	1952	7	5	0	.583	1975	5	9	0	.357
1930	13	4	0	.765	1953	3	9	0	.250	1976	3	11	0	.214
1931	7	6	1	.538	1954	7	5	0	.583	1977	5	9	0	.357
1932	4	6	2	.400	1955	6	5	1	.545	1978	6	10	0	.375
1933	11	3	0	.786	1956	8	3	1	.727	1979	6	10	0	.375
1934	8	5	0	.615	1957	7	5	0	.583	1980	4	12	0	.250
1935	9	3	0	.750	1958	9	3	0	.750	1981	9	7	0	.563
1936	5	6	1	.455	1959	10	2	0	.833	1982	4	5	0	.444
1937	6	3	2	.667	1960	6	4	2	.600	1983	3	12	1	.219
1938	8	2	1	.800	1961	10	3	1	.769	1984	9	7	0	.563
1939	9	1	1	.900	1962	12	2	0	.857	1985	10	6	0	.625
1940	6	4	1	.600	1963	11	3	0	.786	1986	14	2	0	.875
1941	8	3	0	.727	1964	2	10	2	.167	1987	6	9	0	.400
1942	5	5	1	.500	1965	7	7	0	.500	1988	10	6	0	.625
1943	6	3	1	.667	1966	1	12	1	.077	1989	12	4	0	.750
1944	8	1	1	.889	1967	7	7	0	.500	1990	13	3	0	.813
1945	3	6	1	.333	1968	7	7	0	.500	1991	8	8	0	.500
1946	7	3	1	.700	1969	6	8	0	.429					
1947	2	8	2	.200	1970	9	5	0	.643					

NEW YORK JETS

Giants Stadium
East Rutherford, New Jersey
Stadium Capacity: 76891

Success has been limited for the Jets, who were formed as the New York Titans with the Polo Grounds as their home in 1959. After three non-winning seasons, Weeb Ewbank was appointed the team's third coach in 1963 and his arrival brought about the change of name to the Jets. There was an immediate improvement, and when the Jets moved to the Shea Stadium in 1964 attendances increased as well. Then they traded their draft rights to bring University of Alabama quarterback Joe Namath to New York in one of the shrewdest moves in the game's history.

In his first full season Namath threw for more than 2200 yards and for 18 touchdown passes. In 1967, Namath threw for a record 4007 yards and such was his appeal that every Jets home game was a sell-out. They beat Oakland to win the AFL Championship in 1968 and Namath 'guaranteed' that the Jets would go on and win Super Bowl III –

which they did by beating Baltimore 16–7, thus becoming the first AFL team to win the title. They retained the Eastern Division title in 1969 but failed to make the Championship Game.

Namath missed part of the 1970 season after breaking a wrist against the Colts and also part of the 1971 season because of continued knee problems. The fortunes of the Jets declined after that and 1981 represented their first winning season (10–5–1) since 1969, as they reached the play-offs via a wild-card berth. No further glory has come their way, and in 1984 they moved out of the Shea and into the Giants Stadium which is shared with their NFC city rivals.

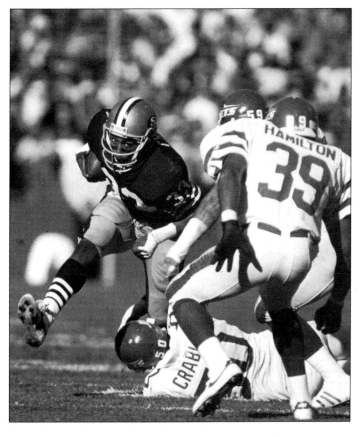

Left *New York Jets defensemen Bob Crable (on ground) and Harry Hamilton combine to stop Roger Craig of the 49ers in 1986, a 10–6 winning season for the Jets.*

HONOURS

1960–9
AFL Divisional Champions: 1968–9
AFL Champions: 1968
1970–92
AFC Divisional Champions: None
AFC Champions: None
Super Bowl – Winners: 1969
       – Runners-up: None

FORMER STADIUMS

1960–3   Polo Grounds
1964–83 Shea Stadium

COACHING HISTORY

		W	L	T
1960–1	Sammy Baugh	14	14	0
1962	Clyde 'Bulldog' Turner	5	9	0
1963–73	Weeb Ewbank	73	78	6
1974–5	Charley Winner	9	14	0
1975	Ken Shipp	1	4	0
1976	Lou Holtz	3	10	0
1976	Mike Holovak	0	1	0
1977–82	Walt Michaels	41	49	1
1983–9	Joe Walton	54	59	1
1990–1	Bruce Coslet	14	19	0

PLAYERS SELECTED AS THE NO. 1 DRAFT CHOICE

New York Jets have never had the first pick in the Draft

RECORD HOLDERS

Career Records
Points	1470	Pat Leahy, 1974–91
Touchdowns	88	Don Maynard, 1960–72
Rushing (Yards)	7904	Freeman McNeil, 1981–91
Passing (Yards)	27 057	Joe Namath, 1965–76
Passing (Touchdowns)	170	Joe Namath, 1965–76
Receiving (No.)	627	Don Maynard, 1960–72
Receiving (Yards)	11 732	Don Maynard, 1960–72
Interceptions	34	Bill Baird, 1963–9
Punting (Average)	42.8	Curley Johnson, 1961–8
Punt Returns (Average)	16.2	Dick Christy, 1961–3
Kick-off Returns (Average)	22.8	Bob Humphery, 1984–9
Field Goals	304	Pat Leahy, 1974–91

Season Records
Points	145	Jim Turner, 1968
Touchdowns	14	Art Powell, 1960
	14	Don Maynard, 1965
	14	Emerson Boozer, 1972
Rushing (Yards)	1331	Freeman McNeil, 1985
Passing (Yards)	4007	Joe Namath, 1967
Passing (Touchdowns)	26	Al Dorow, 1960
	26	Joe Namath, 1967
Receiving (No.)	93	Al Toon, 1988
Receiving (Yards)	1434	Don Maynard, 1967
Interceptions	12	Dainard Paulson, 1964
Punting (Average)	45.3	Curley Johnson, 1965
Punt Returns (Average)	21.3	Dick Christy, 1961
Kick-off Returns (Average)	30.7	Bob Humphery, 1984
Field Goals	34	Jim Turner, 1968

Single Game Records
Points	19	Jim Turner, 3 Nov 1968
	19	Pat Leahy, 16 Sep 1984
Touchdowns	4	Wesley Walker, 21 Sep 1986
Rushing (Yards)	192	Freeman McNeil, 15 Sep 1985
Passing (Yards)	496	Joe Namath, 24 Sep 1972
Passing (Touchdowns)	6	Joe Namath, 24 Sep 1972
Receiving (No.)	17	Clark Gaines, 21 Sep 1980
Receiving (Yards)	228	Don Maynard, 17 Nov 1968
Interceptions	3	Many occasions
Field Goals	6	Jim Turner, 3 Nov 1968
	6	Bobby Howfield, 3 Dec 1972

REGULAR SEASON RECORD

Year	W	L	T	%
1960	7	7	0	.500
1961	7	7	0	.500
1962	5	9	0	.357
1963	5	8	1	.385
1964	5	8	1	.385
1965	5	8	1	.385
1966	6	6	2	.500
1967	8	5	1	.615
1968	7	7	0	.500
1969	6	6	2	.500
1970	4	10	0	.286
1971	6	8	0	.429
1972	7	7	0	.500
1973	4	10	0	.286
1974	7	7	0	.500
1975	3	11	0	.214
1976	3	11	0	.214
1977	3	11	0	.214
1978	8	8	0	.500
1979	8	8	0	.500
1980	4	12	0	.250
1981	10	5	1	.656
1982	6	3	0	.667
1983	7	9	0	.438
1984	7	9	0	.438
1985	11	5	0	.688
1986	10	6	0	.625
1987	6	9	0	.400
1988	8	7	1	.531
1989	4	12	0	.250
1990	6	10	0	.375
1991	8	8	0	.500

JETS HEAD-TO-HEAD AGAINST CURRENT NFL TEAMS

	W	L	T		W	L	T		W	L	T
v Atlanta	3	2	0	v Houston	12	17	1	v NY Giants	3	3	0
v Buffalo	28	35	0	v Indianapolis	20	24	0	v Philadelphia	0	4	0
v Chicago	1	3	0	v Kansas City	13	14	1	v Phoenix	1	2	0
v Cincinnati	8	6	0	v LA Raiders	11	13	2	v Pittsburgh	1	11	0
v Cleveland	6	9	0	v LA Rams	2	4	0	v San Diego	9	16	1
v Dallas	1	4	0	v Miami	25	27	1	v San Francisco	1	5	0
v Denver	11	10	1	v Minnesota	3	1	0	v Seattle	3	8	0
v Detroit	3	3	0	v New England	35	28	1	v Tampa Bay	5	1	0
v Green Bay	5	1	0	v New Orleans	4	2	0	v Washington	0	4	0

PHILADELPHIA EAGLES

Veterans Stadium
Broad Street & Pattison Avenue, Philadelphia, Pennsylvania
Stadium Capacity: 65 356

Bert Bell and Lud Wray bought the franchise of the defunct Frankford Yellowjackets team in 1933 and moved it from the Philadelphia suburb into the city. The team was named the Eagles because the great bird was the symbol of President Roosevelt's National Recovery Administration; though it didn't do a lot for Bell and Wray's team in their first game as they were beaten 56–0 by the Giants.

Wray was the team's first coach, but he was succeeded by Bell in 1936. That same year the Eagles had the first pick in the new draft, which came into being as a result of a suggestion by Bell. Having finished either bottom or second-to-bottom in the Eastern Division every season since their formation, Philadelphia had their first winning season in 1943, but that was only after they merged with the Pittsburgh Steelers to form the Phil-Pitt Steagles. The merger lasted only a year and in 1944 Philadelphia had a first winning season in their own right, finishing second to the Giants in the Eastern Division.

The Eagles won their first divisional title in 1947 when they beat their former 'partners' Pittsburgh in a play-off, but they failed to capture the NFL title, losing 28–21 to the Chicago Cardinals. It was a different

HONOURS

1921–59
NFL Divisional Champions: 1947–9
NFL Champions: 1948–9
1960–9
NFL Divisional Champions: 1960
NFL Champions: 1960
1970–92
NFC Divisional Champions: 1980, 1988
NFC Champions: 1980
Super Bowl – Winners: None
– Runners-up: 1981

PLAYERS SELECTED AS THE NO. 1 DRAFT CHOICE

Year	Player	Pos	College
1936	Jay Berwanger*	HB	Chicago
1937	Sam Francis	FB	Nebraska
1949	Chuck Bednarik	C	Pennsylvania

* The first player ever selected in the Draft

COACHING HISTORY

		W	L	T
1933–5	Lud Wray	9	21	1
1936–40	Bert Bell	10	44	2
1941–50	Earle 'Greasy' Neale	66	44	5
1951	Alvin 'Bo' McMillin	2	0	0
1951	Wayne Millner	2	8	0
1952–5	Jim Trimble	25	20	3
1956–7	Hugh Devore	7	16	1
1958–60	Lawrence 'Buck' Shaw	20	16	1
1961–3	Nick Skorich	15	24	3
1964–8	Joe Kuharich	28	41	1
1969–71	Jerry Williams	7	22	2
1971–2	Ed Khayat	8	15	2
1973–5	Mike McCormack	16	25	1
1976–82	Dick Vermeil	57	51	0
1983–5	Marion Campbell	17	29	1
1985	Fred Bruney	1	0	0
1986–90	Buddy Ryan	43	38	1
1991	Rich Kotite	10	6	0

story the following year as they beat the Cardinals 7–0 to become NFL champions for the first time, and they retained the title in 1949 when they beat the Rams 14–0 in a second successive shutout. Coach and player problems saw a decline in fortunes and by 1956 the Eagles again found themselves languishing at the bottom of the Eastern Division.

Buck Shaw was appointed head coach in 1958 and within two years he had turned Philadelphia into a championship-winning team as they beat Green Bay 17–13 for their third title. But that was to be the Eagles' last honour for 20 years. Troubles off the field affected performances on it and they did not reach the play-offs again until 1978. But the corner had been turned at long last: they reached the play-offs again in 1979 and the following season captured the NFC championship before losing to Oakland in Super Bowl XV at New Orleans. Since then they have won the Eastern Division of the NFC once in 1988 but are still awaiting their second appearance in the Super Bowl.

RECORD HOLDERS

Career Records

Points	881	Bobby Walston, 1951–62
Touchdowns	79	Harold Carmichael, 1971–83
Rushing (Yards)	6538	Wilbert Montgomery, 1977–84
Passing (Yards)	26963	Ron Jaworski, 1977–86
Passing (Touchdowns)	175	Ron Jaworski, 1977–86
Receiving (No.)	589	Harold Carmichael, 1971–83
Receiving (Yards)	8978	Harold Carmichael, 1971–83
Interceptions	34	Bill Bradley, 1969–76
Punting (Average)	42.9	Joe Muha, 1946–50
Punt Returns (Average)	13.9	Steve Van Buren, 1944–51
Kick-off Returns (Average)	26.7	Steve Van Buren, 1944–51
Field Goals	91	Paul McFadden, 1984–7

Season Records

Points	116	Paul McFadden, 1984
Touchdowns	18	Steve Van Buren, 1945
Rushing (Yards)	1512	Wilbert Montgomery, 1979
Passing (Yards)	3808	Randall Cunningham, 1988
Passing (Touchdowns)	32	Sonny Jurgensen, 1961
Receiving (No.)	81	Keith Jackson, 1988
	81	Keith Byars, 1990
Receiving (Yards)	1409	Mike Quick, 1983
Interceptions	11	Bill Bradley, 1971
Punting (Average)	47.2	Joe Muha, 1948
Punt Returns (Average)	15.3	Steve Van Buren, 1944
Kick-off Returns (Average)	29.1	Al Nelson, 1972
Field Goals	30	Paul McFadden, 1984

Single Game Records

Points	25	Bobby Walston, 17 Oct 1954
Touchdowns	4	*Many occasions*
Rushing (Yards)	205	Steve Van Buren, 27 Nov 1949
Passing (Yards)	437	Bobby Thomason, 18 Nov 1953
Passing (Touchdowns)	7	Adrian Burk, 17 Oct 1954
Receiving (No.)	14	Don Looney, 1 Dec 1940
Receiving (Yards)	237	Tommy McDonald, 10 Dec 1960
Interceptions	4	Russ Craft, 24 Sep 1950
Field Goals	6	Tom Dempsey, 12 Nov 1972

REGULAR SEASON RECORD

Year	W	L	T	%
1933	3	5	1	.375
1934	4	7	0	.364
1935	2	9	0	.182
1936	1	11	0	.083
1937	2	8	1	.200
1938	5	6	0	.455
1939	1	9	1	.100
1940	1	10	0	.091
1941	2	8	1	.200
1942	2	9	0	.182
1943*	5	4	1	.556
1944	7	1	2	.875
1945	7	3	0	.700
1946	6	5	0	.545
1947	8	4	0	.667
1948	9	2	1	.818
1949	11	1	0	.917
1950	6	6	0	.500
1951	4	8	0	.333
1952	7	5	0	.583
1953	7	4	1	.636
1954	7	4	1	.636
1955	4	7	1	.364
1956	3	8	1	.273
1957	4	8	0	.333
1958	2	9	1	.182
1959	7	5	0	.583
1960	10	2	0	.833
1961	10	4	0	.714
1962	3	10	1	.231
1963	2	10	2	.167
1964	6	8	0	.429
1965	5	9	0	.357
1966	9	5	0	.643
1967	6	7	1	.462
1968	2	12	0	.143
1969	4	9	1	.308
1970	3	10	1	.231
1971	6	7	1	.462
1972	2	11	1	.179
1973	5	8	1	.393
1974	7	7	0	.500
1975	4	10	0	.286
1976	4	10	0	.286
1977	5	9	0	.357
1978	9	7	0	.563
1979	11	5	0	.688
1980	12	4	0	.750
1981	10	6	0	.625
1982	3	6	0	.333
1983	5	11	0	.313
1984	6	9	1	.406
1985	7	9	0	.438
1986	5	10	1	.344
1987	7	8	0	.467
1988	10	6	0	.625
1989	11	5	0	.688
1990	10	6	0	.625
1991	10	6	0	.625

* Amalgamated Philadelphia and Pittsburgh team who played as Phil–Pitt

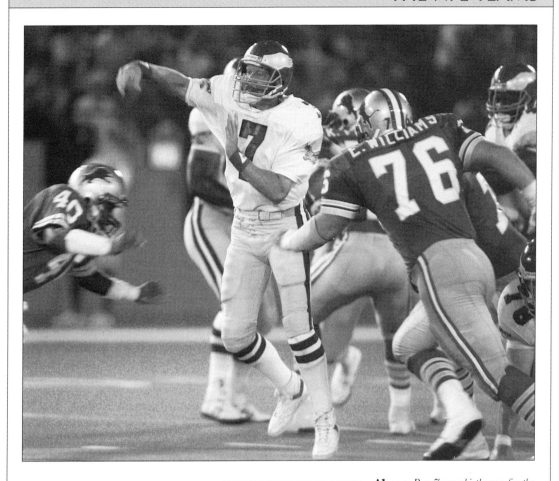

FORMER STADIUMS

1933–5	Baker Bowl
1936–9	Municipal Stadium
1940	Shibe Park
1941	Municipal Stadium
1942	Shibe Park
1943	Forbes Field (Pittsburgh)*
1944–57	Shibe Park *(renamed Connie Mack Stadium in 1953)*
1958–70	Franklin Field (University of Pennsylvania)

* During the Phil–Pitt merger

Above *Ron Jaworski throws for the Eagles against Detroit. He holds the career passing records for Philadelphia.*

PHILADELPHIA HEAD-TO-HEAD AGAINST CURRENT NFL TEAMS

	W	L	T		W	L	T		W	L	T
v Atlanta	8	7	1	v Houston	5	0	0	v NY Giants	52	61	2
v Buffalo	4	2	0	v Indianapolis	5	6	0	v NY Jets	4	0	0
v Chicago	4	23	1	v Kansas City	1	0	0	v Phoenix	41	44	5
v Cincinnati	1	5	0	v LA Raiders	3	3	0	v Pittsburgh	44	25	3
v Cleveland	12	30	1	v LA Rams	12	16	1	v San Diego	2	3	0
v Dallas	26	37	0	v Miami	2	5	0	v San Francisco	4	12	1
v Denver	4	2	0	v Minnesota	6	10	0	v Seattle	3	1	0
v Detroit	9	12	2	v New England	5	2	0	v Tampa Bay	3	2	0
v Green Bay	7	18	0	v New Orleans	9	8	0	v Washington	43	66	5

PHOENIX CARDINALS

Sun Devil Stadium
Fifth Street, Tempe, Arizona
Stadium Capacity: 72 608

Along with the Chicago Bears, the Cardinals are the only founder members of the NFL still in existence. Formed in 1899, they are in fact the oldest of all current NFL teams.

The original team was formed by local painter and decorator Chris O'Brien, whose team played on the South Side of Chicago. They moved to Racine Avenue in the city in 1901 and acquired a used set of equipment from the Univesity of Chicago. Because O'Brien reckoned the colour of the outfit looked 'cardinal', he named his team the Racine Cardinals. There was so little opposition for the Cardinals that O'Brien disbanded the team in 1906, but he reformed them in 1913 and in 1917 they won the Chicago Football league. The war years caused the team to fold again briefly, before O'Brien reformed them once again in 1918 and they became founder members of the NFL's predecessor, the American Professional Football Association.

They became the Chicago Cardinals in 1922, and in 1925 under coach Norman Barry they were NFL champions for the first time with an 11–2–1 record. Yet within a couple of years they were a struggling team as one coach after another failed to get them out of the doldrums. Even persuading Ernie Nevers out of retirement as player-coach failed to have any impact. Perpetually at or near the bottom of the Western Division, fortunes remained unaltered when they merged with Pittsburgh to form

Card–Pitt in 1944 and the 'new' team ended with a 0–10–0 record. The Cardinals were back on their own in 1945 but a 1–9–0 record was nothing to shout about.

The following year, however, the Cardinals had their first winning season (6–5–0) since 1935 and their 'success' coincided with the return of Jimmy Conzelman as head coach. In 1947 he took them to their first championship since 1925 when they beat Philadelphia 28–21. They retained the divisional title the following year but Philadelphia turned the tables and prevented a second successive championship. Conzelman resigned after the game.

With no more successes to their credit the Cardinals were moved to St Louis by the NFL

RECORD HOLDERS

Career Records

Points	1380	Jim Bakken, 1962–78
Touchdowns	70	Roy Green, 1979–90
Rushing (Yards)	7999	Ottis Anderson, 1979–86
Passing (Yards)	34 639	Jim Hart, 1966–83
Passing (Touchdowns)	209	Jim Hart, 1966–83
Receiving (No.)	522	Roy Green, 1979–90
Receiving (Yards)	8497	Roy Green, 1979–90
Interceptions	52	Larry Wilson, 1960–72
Punting (Average)	44.9	Jerry Norton, 1959–61
Punt Returns (Average)	13.7	Charley Trippi, 1947–55
Kick-off Returns (Average)	28.5	Ollie Matson, 1952, 1954–8
Field Goals	282	Jim Bakken, 1962–78

Season Records

Points	117	Jim Bakken, 1967
	117	Neil O'Donoghue, 1984
Touchdowns	17	John David Crow, 1962
Rushing (Yards)	1605	Ottis Anderson, 1979
Passing (Yards)	4614	Neil Lomax, 1984
Passing (Touchdowns)	28	Charley Johnson, 1963
	28	Neil Lomax, 1984
Receiving (No.)	91	JT Smith, 1987
Receiving (Yards)	1555	Roy Green, 1984
Interceptions	12	Bob Nussbaumer, 1949
Punting (Average)	45.6	Jerry Norton, 1960
Punt Returns (Average)	20.9	John Cochran, 1949
Kick-off Returns (Average)	35.5	Ollie Matson, 1958
Field Goals	27	Jim Bakken, 1967

Single Game Records

Points	40	Ernie Nevers, 28 Nov 1929
Touchdowns	6	Ernie Nevers, 28 Nov 1929
Rushing (Yards)	203	John David Crow, 18 Dec 1960
Passing (Yards)	468	Neil Lomax, 16 Dec 1984
Passing (Touchdowns)	6	Jim Hardy, 2 Oct 1950
	6	Charley Johnson, 26 Sep 1965
	6	Charley Johnson, 2 Nov 1969
Receiving (No.)	16	Sonny Randle, 4 Nov 1962
Receiving (Yards)	256	Sonny Randle, 4 Nov 1962
Interceptions	4	Bob Nussbaumer, 13 Nov 1949
	4	Jerry Norton, 20 Nov 1960
Field Goals	7	Jim Bakken, 24 Sep 1967

in 1960 to prevent the newly formed AFL setting up a franchise in the city; there they shared the Busch Stadium with the Cardinals baseball team. But honours still eluded them and it was only after the appointment of Don Coryell as the team's 26th coach in 1973 that they returned to winning ways. They were Eastern Division champions the following year and again in 1975, but Minnesota and Los Angeles respectively ended their hopes in the play-offs. Apart from in the strike-reduced 1982 season, St Louis never made the play-offs again. The franchise was moved to Phoenix in 1988; as yet, the new Cardinals have not made the play-offs.

Ottis Anderson (32), now with the New York Giants, still holds career and season rushing records for the Cardinals. Here he makes ground against the Bengals in 1985.

HONOURS

1921–59
NFL Divisional Champions: 1947–8
NFL Champions: 1925, 1947
1960–9
NFL Divisional Champions: None
NFL Champions: None
1970–92
NFC Divisional Champions: 1974–5
NFC Champions: None
Super Bowl – Winners: None
– Runners-up: None

PLAYERS SELECTED AS THE NO. 1 DRAFT CHOICE

Year	Player	Pos	College
1939	Ki Aldrich	C	Texas Christians
1940	George Cafego	HB	Tennessee
1945	Charley Trippi	HB	Georgia
1958	King Hill	QB	Rice

COACHING HISTORY

		W	L	T			W	L	T
1920–2	John 'Paddy' Driscoll	17	8	4	1951	Phil Handler/	1	1	0
1923–4	Arnold Horween	13	8	1		Cecil Isbell			
1925–6	Norman Barry	16	8	2	1952	Joe Kuharich	4	8	0
1927	Guy Chamberlin	3	7	1	1953–4	Joe Stydahar	3	20	1
1928	Fred Gillies	1	5	0	1955–7	Ray Richards	14	21	1
1929	Dewey Scanlon	6	6	1	1958–61	Frank 'Pop' Ivy	17	29	2
1930	Ernie Nevers	5	6	2	1961	Chuck Drulis, Ray Wilsey			
1931	LeRoy Andrews	0	1	0		& Ray Prochaska	2	0	0
1931	Ernie Nevers	5	3	0	1962–5	Wally Lemm	27	26	3
1932	Jack Chevigny	2	6	2	1966–70	Charley Winner	35	30	5
1933–4	Paul Schissler	6	15	1	1971–2	Bob Hollway	8	18	2
1935–8	Milan Creighton	16	26	4	1973–7	Don Coryell	42	29	1
1939	Ernie Nevers	1	10	0	1978–9	Bud Wilkinson	9	20	0
1940–2	Jimmy Conzelman	8	22	3	1979	Larry Wilson	2	1	0
1943–5	Phil Handler	1	29	0	1980–5	Jim Hanifan	39	50	1
1947–8	Jimmy Conzelman	27	10	0	1986–9	Gene Stallings	23	34	1
1949	Phil Handler/	2	4	0	1989	Hank Kuhlmann	0	5	0
	Raymond 'Buddy' Parker				1990–1	Joe Bugel	9	23	0
1949	Raymond 'Buddy' Parker	4	1	1					
1950–1	Earl 'Curly' Lambeau	7	15	0					

PHOENIX HEAD-TO-HEAD AGAINST CURRENT NFL TEAMS

	W	L	T		W	L	T
v Atlanta	10	4	0	v Miami	0	6	0
v Buffalo	3	3	0	v Minnesota	7	5	0
v Chicago	25	51	6	v New England	6	1	0
v Cincinnati	1	3	0	v New Orleans	10	7	0
v Cleveland	10	31	3	v NY Giants	33	63	2
v Dallas	22	36	1	v NY Jets	2	1	0
v Denver	0	3	1	v Philadelphia	44	41	5
v Detroit	16	25	5	v Pittsburgh	21	29	3
v Green Bay	21	40	4	v San Diego	1	4	0
v Houston	3	2	0	v San Francisco	8	9	0
v Indianapolis	6	4	0	v Seattle	3	0	0
v Kansas City	1	3	1	v Tampa Bay	6	4	0
v LA Raiders	1	2	0	v Washington	33	60	2
v LA Rams	17	23	2				

FORMER STADIUMS

1920–1	Normal Field (Chicago)
1922–5	Comiskey Park (Chicago)
1926–8	Normal Field
1929–59	Comiskey Park
1960–87	Busch Stadium (St Louis)
	(Known as the Busch Memorial Stadium 1966–82)

REGULAR SEASON RECORD

Year	W	L	T	%	Year	W	L	T	%	Year	W	L	T	%
1920	6	2	2	.750	1944*	0	10	0	.000	1968	9	4	1	.692
1921	3	3	2	.500	1945	1	9	0	.100	1969	4	9	1	.308
1922	8	3	0	.727	1946	6	5	0	.545	1970	8	5	1	.615
1923	8	4	0	.667	1947	9	3	0	.750	1971	4	9	1	.308
1924	5	4	1	.556	1948	11	1	0	.917	1972	4	9	1	.321
1925	11	2	1	.846	1949	6	5	1	.545	1973	4	9	1	.321
1926	5	6	1	.455	1950	5	7	0	.417	1974	10	4	0	.714
1927	3	7	1	.300	1951	3	9	0	.250	1975	11	3	0	.786
1928	1	5	0	.167	1952	4	8	0	.333	1976	10	4	0	.714
1929	6	6	1	.500	1953	1	10	1	.091	1977	7	7	0	.500
1930	5	6	2	.455	1954	2	10	0	.167	1978	6	10	0	.375
1931	5	4	0	.556	1955	4	7	1	.364	1979	5	11	0	.313
1932	2	6	2	.250	1956	7	5	0	.583	1980	5	11	0	.313
1933	1	9	1	.100	1957	3	9	0	.250	1981	7	9	0	.438
1934	5	6	0	.455	1958	2	9	1	.182	1982	5	4	0	.556
1935	6	4	2	.600	1959	2	10	0	.167	1983	8	7	1	.531
1936	3	8	1	.273	1960	6	5	1	.545	1984	9	7	0	.563
1937	5	5	1	.500	1961	7	7	0	.500	1985	5	11	0	.313
1938	2	9	0	.182	1962	4	9	1	.308	1986	4	11	1	.281
1939	1	10	0	.091	1963	9	5	0	.643	1987	7	8	0	.467
1940	2	7	2	.222	1964	9	3	2	.750	1988	7	9	0	.438
1941	3	7	1	.300	1965	5	9	0	.357	1989	5	11	0	.313
1942	3	8	0	.273	1966	8	5	1	.615	1990	5	11	0	.313
1943	0	10	0	.000	1967	6	7	1	.462	1991	4	12	0	.250

* Combined Chicago Cardinals/ Pittsburgh Steelers team

PITTSBURGH STEELERS

Three Rivers Stadium
300 Stadium Circle, Pittsburgh, Pennsylvania
Stadium Capacity: 59 492

Success was a long time coming to the Steelers – nearly 40 years – but since capturing the AFC Central Division in 1972 they have gone on to win nine divisional titles, four AFC championships and a record-equalling four Super Bowls.

Former boxer Art Rooney was granted the first franchise in 1933 and he named the team after the city's professional baseball team, the Pirates. Failure on the field season after season resulted in a succession of coaches coming and going, and even Johnny Blood, one of the game's greatest players, could do nothing to change the club's fortunes. A change of name to

the Steelers in 1940 did not immediately help, but in 1942, under their eighth coach in less than ten years, Pittsburgh finally had their first winning season (7–4–0).

During the war the Steelers lost many of their best players and in 1943 they merged with the Philadelphia Eagles to play as Phil–Pitt. The following season they merged with the Chicago Cardinals to become the Card–Pitts. After continual upheavals and disagreements, the Steelers failed to make any impression as a challenging team but all that changed in 1969 when Chuck Noll was hired as the team's 17th head coach.

Noll went on to become one of the game's most successful coaches during his 22 years at the Steelers before eventually retiring at the end of the 1991 season, but his first season was far from impressive: bottom of the division with a 1–13–0 record. However, in the draft the Steelers had first choice and Noll brought quarterback Terry Bradshaw to the club. His arrival sparked off an upturn in the fortunes of the Pittsburgh Steelers and coincided with the move to the Three Rivers Stadium in 1970.

In 1972 Bradshaw, with the help of rookie running-back Franco Harris, took Pittsburgh to their first divisional title in their 39-year history. They lost out to the Dolphins for the AFC Championship but two years later they beat Oakland to capture their first title and then beat the Minnesota Vikings to win the Super Bowl. A run of 11 consecutive victories in 1975 resulted in another divisional title, followed by a second successive AFC Championship and then a second successive Super Bowl when they beat the Dallas Cowboys 21–17. A third successive divisional title followed in 1976, and this after being bottom of the division for eight weeks. But this time Oakland gained revenge for two defeats in the Championship Game by winning 24–7.

After winning their seventh Central Division title in eight years the Steelers went on to capture their third AFC title in 1978 and followed that with their third Super Bowl win when they again beat the Cowboys, 35–31, to become the first team to win three Super Bowls. It was a repeat performance the next year when the Los Angeles Rams succumbed to the Steelers' powerful offense. Bradshaw and Harris retired in 1983 and despite capturing further divisional titles the Steelers have not managed to recapture those glory years of the 1970s.

REGULAR SEASON RECORD

Year	W	L	T	%	Year	W	L	T	%
1933	3	6	2	.333	1963	7	4	3	.636
1934	2	10	0	.167	1964	5	9	0	.357
1935	4	8	0	.333	1965	2	12	0	.143
1936	6	6	0	.500	1966	5	8	1	.385
1937	4	7	0	.364	1967	4	9	1	.308
1938	2	9	0	.182	1968	2	11	1	.154
1939	1	9	1	.100	1969	1	13	0	.071
1940	2	7	2	.222	1970	5	9	0	.357
1941	1	9	1	.100	1971	6	8	0	.429
1942	7	4	0	.636	1972	11	3	0	.786
1943*	5	4	1	.556	1973	10	4	0	.714
1944§	0	10	0	.000	1974	10	3	1	.750
1945	2	8	0	.200	1975	12	2	0	.857
1946	5	5	1	.500	1976	10	4	0	.714
1947	8	4	0	.667	1977	9	5	0	.643
1948	4	8	0	.333	1978	14	2	0	.875
1949	6	5	1	.545	1979	12	4	0	.750
1950	6	6	0	.500	1980	9	7	0	.563
1951	4	7	1	.364	1981	8	8	0	.500
1952	5	7	0	.417	1982	6	3	0	.667
1953	6	6	0	.500	1983	10	6	0	.625
1954	5	7	0	.417	1984	9	7	0	.563
1955	4	8	0	.333	1985	7	9	0	.438
1956	5	7	0	.417	1986	6	10	0	.375
1957	6	6	0	.500	1987	8	7	0	.533
1958	7	4	1	.636	1988	5	11	0	.313
1959	6	5	1	.545	1989	9	7	0	.563
1960	5	6	1	.455	1990	9	7	0	.563
1961	6	8	0	.429	1991	7	9	0	.438
1962	9	5	0	.643					

* Record of amalgamated Philadelphia and Pittsburgh team who played as Phil–Pitt
§ Record of Chicago Cardinals and Pittsburgh team who played as Card–Pitt

HONOURS

1921–59
NFL Divisional Champions:　None
NFL Champions:　None
1960–9
NFL Divisional Champions:　None
NFL Champions:　None
1970–92
AFC Divisional Champions:　1972, 1974–9, 1983–4
AFC Champions:　1974–5, 1978–9
Super Bowl – Winners:　1975–6, 1979–80
　　　　　　– Runners-up:　None

PLAYERS SELECTED AS THE NO. 1 DRAFT
CHOICE

Year	Player	Pos	College
1942	Bill Dudley	HB	Virginia
1956	Gary Glick	DB	Colorado A & M
1970	Terry Bradshaw	QB	Louisiana Tech

COACHING HISTORY

		W	L	T
1933	Forrest 'Jap' Douds	3	6	2
1934	Luby DiMelio	2	10	0
1935–6	Joe Bach	10	14	0
1937–9	Johnny Blood	6	19	0
1939–40	Walt Kiesling	3	13	3
1941	Bert Bell	0	2	0
1941	Aldo 'Buff' Donelli	0	5	0
1941–4	Walt Kiesling	13	20	2
1945	Jim Leonard	2	8	0
1946–7	Jock Sutherland	13	10	1
1948–51	Johnny Michelosen	20	26	2
1952–3	Joe Bach	11	13	0
1954–6	Walt Kiesling	14	22	0
1957–64	Raymond 'Buddy' Parker	51	47	6
1965	Mike Nixon	2	12	0
1966–8	Bill Austin	11	28	3
1969–91	Chuck Noll	209	156	1

During Walt Kiesling's second term as head coach (1941–4) he was co-coach with Earle 'Greasy' Neale in the Phil–Pitt merger of 1943 and with Phil Handler in the Card–Pitt merger of 1944

Pittsburgh complete their Super Bowl hat-trick against Dallas in 1979.

RECORD HOLDERS

Career Records

Points	1010	Gary Anderson, 1982–91
Touchdowns	100	Franco Harris, 1972–83
Rushing (Yards)	11 950	Franco Harris, 1972–83
Passing (Yards)	27 989	Terry Bradshaw, 1970–83
Passing (Touchdowns)	212	Terry Bradshaw, 1970–83
Receiving (No.)	537	John Stallworth, 1974–87
Receiving (Yards)	8723	John Stallworth, 1974–87
Interceptions	57	Mel Blount, 1970–83
Punting (Average)	45.7	Bobby Joe Green, 1960–1
Punt Returns (Average)	14.9	Bobby Gage, 1949–50
Kick-off Returns (Average)	29.6	Lynn Chandois, 1950–56
Field Goals	229	Gary Anderson, 1982–91

Season Records

Points	139	Gary Anderson, 1985
Touchdowns	15	Louis Lipps, 1985
Rushing (Yards)	1246	Franco Harris, 1975
Passing (Yards)	3724	Terry Bradshaw, 1979
Passing (Touchdowns)	28	Terry Bradshaw, 1978
Receiving (No.)	80	John Stallworth, 1984
Receiving (Yards)	1395	John Stallworth, 1984
Interceptions	11	Mel Blount, 1975
Punting (Average)	47.0	Bobby Joe Green, 1961
Punt Returns (Average)	16.0	Bobby Gage, 1949
Kick-off Returns (Average)	35.2	Lynn Chandois, 1952
Field Goals	33	Gary Anderson, 1985

Single Game Records

Points	24	Ray Mathews, 17 Oct 1954
	24	Roy Jefferson, 3 Nov 1968
Touchdowns	4	Ray Mathews, 17 Oct 1954
	4	Roy Jefferson, 3 Nov 1968
Rushing (Yards)	218	John Fuqua, 20 Dec 1970
Passing (Yards)	409	Bobby Layne, 3 Dec 1958
Passing (Touchdowns)	5	Terry Bradshaw, 15 Nov 1981
	5	Mark Malone, 8 Sep 1985
Receiving (No.)	12	JR Wilburn, 22 Oct 1967
Receiving (Yards)	235	Buddy Dial, 22 Oct 1961
Interceptions	4	Jack Butler, 13 Dec 1953
Field Goals	6	Gary Anderson, 23 Oct 1988

PITTSBURGH HEAD-TO-HEAD AGAINST CURRENT NFL TEAMS

	W	L	T
v Atlanta	8	1	0
v Buffalo	6	6	0
v Chicago	4	15	1
v Cincinnati	22	21	0
v Cleveland	34	50	0
v Dallas	13	12	0
v Denver	7	11	1
v Detroit	10	13	1
v Green Bay	11	16	0
v Houston	30	16	0
v Indianapolis	11	4	0
v Kansas City	12	5	0
v LA Raiders	6	10	0
v LA Rams	5	13	2
v Miami	5	9	0
v Minnesota	5	6	0
v New England	8	3	0
v New Orleans	5	5	0
v NY Giants	26	42	3
v NY Jets	11	1	0
v Philadelphia	25	44	3
v Phoenix	29	21	3
v San Diego	12	5	0
v San Francisco	7	7	0
v Seattle	4	4	0
v Tampa Bay	4	0	0
v Washington	27	42	3

FORMER STADIUMS

1933–57	Forbes Field
1958–63	Forbes Field & Pitt Stadium
1964–9	Pitt Stadium

SAN DIEGO CHARGERS

San Diego Jack Murphy Stadium (formerly San Diego Stadium 1967–81)
9449 Friars Road, San Diego, California
Stadium Capacity: 60 835

The Chargers, based at Los Angeles, were one of the six original franchises granted by the new AFL in 1959 and the team's first owner was Barron Hilton, of Hilton Hotel fame. The team were so named because the cry of the University of Southern California football team is 'Chaaaarge!', and a competition to name the new team resulted in 'Chargers' being the winning name.

There was instant success on the field as the Chargers captured the first AFL Western Division before losing to Houston in the Championship play-off, but after losing nearly $1 million Hilton moved the franchise to San Diego in 1961, though retaining the Chargers name. They captured their second divisional title but again Houston dented their Championship hopes. However, under coach Sid Gillman the Chargers captured their first AFL Championship in 1963 when they beat Boston 51–10. Two more divisional titles followed in succession but they were not to progress to the Championship Game.

The team moved into the new San Diego Jack Murphy stadium in 1967. The stadium was named after the sports editor of the *San Diego Union*. Coach Gillman retired through ill-health in 1969 and was succeeded by Charlie Waller, only for the Chargers to have their first losing season since 1962, which resulted in Gillman coming out of retirement for the 1971 season.

Despite a succession of coaches, the Chargers had to wait until 1978 for their first winning season since 1969. It came under Don Coryell and the following season they won their first divisional title since 1965. They successfully retained the Western Division in 1980 and 1981 but could not make it through to their first Super Bowl, Oakland in 1980 and Cincinnati a year later ending their chances in the AFC Championship

HONOURS

1960–9

AFL Divisional Champions:	1960–61, 1963–5
AFL Champions:	1963

1970–92

AFC Divisional Champions:	1979–81
AFC Champions:	None
Super Bowl – Winners:	None
– Runners-up:	None

COACHING HISTORY

		W	L	T
1960–9	Sid Gillman	83	51	6
1969–70	Charlie Waller	9	7	3
1971	Sid Gillman	4	6	0
1971–3	Harland Svare	7	17	2
1973	Ron Waller	1	5	0
1974–8	Tommy Prothro	21	39	0
1978–86	Don Coryell	72	60	0
1986–8	Al Saunders	17	22	0
1989–91	Dan Henning	16	32	0

The Chargers' London-born head coach Al Saunders who led them for three seasons.

FORMER STADIUMS

1960	Memorial Coliseum (Los Angeles)
1961–6	Balboa Stadium

PLAYERS SELECTED AS THE NO. 1 DRAFT CHOICE

San Diego have never had the first pick in the Draft

Game.

Coryell remained as coach until 1986, since when Al Saunders and Dan Henning have tried to put the Chargers back onto winning ways. Henning's failure to do so in 1991 resulted in his sacking and the job now rests in the hands of new coach Bobby Ross.

REGULAR SEASON RECORD

Year	W	L	T	%
1960	10	4	0	.714
1961	12	2	0	.857
1962	4	10	0	.286
1963	11	3	0	.786
1964	8	5	1	.615
1965	9	2	3	.818
1966	7	6	1	.538
1967	8	5	1	.615
1968	9	5	0	.643
1969	8	6	0	.571
1970	5	6	3	.455
1971	6	8	0	.429
1972	4	9	1	.321
1973	2	11	1	.179
1974	5	9	0	.357
1975	2	12	0	.143
1976	6	8	0	.429
1977	7	7	0	.500
1978	9	7	0	.563
1979	12	4	0	.750
1980	11	5	0	.688
1981	10	6	0	.625
1982	6	3	0	.667
1983	6	10	0	.375
1984	7	9	0	.438
1985	8	8	0	.500
1986	4	12	0	.250
1987	8	7	0	.533
1988	6	10	0	.375
1989	6	10	0	.375
1990	6	10	0	.375
1991	4	12	0	.250

RECORD HOLDERS

Career Records

Points	766	Rolf Benirschke, 1977–86
Touchdowns	83	Lance Alworth, 1962–70
Rushing (Yards)	4963	Paul Lowe, 1960–7
Passing (Yards)	43040	Dan Fouts, 1973–87
Passing (Touchdowns)	254	Dan Fouts, 1973–87
Receiving (No.)	586	Charlie Joiner, 1976–86
Receiving (Yards)	9585	Lance Alworth, 1962–70
Interceptions	38	Gill Byrd, 1983–91
Punting (Average)	42.7	Maury Buford, 1982–84
Punt Returns (Average)	12.3	Leslie Duncan, 1964–70
Kick-off Returns (Average)	25.2	Leslie Duncan, 1964–70
Field Goals	146	Rolf Benirschke, 1977–86

Season Records

Points	118	Rolf Benirschke, 1980
Touchdowns	19	Chuck Muncie, 1981
Rushing (Yards)	1225	Marion Butts, 1990
Passing (Yards)	4802	Dan Fouts, 1981
Passing (Touchdowns)	33	Dan Fouts, 1981
Receiving (No.)	89	Kellen Winslow, 1980
Receiving (Yards)	1602	Lance Alworth, 1965
Interceptions	9	Charlie McNeil, 1961
Punting (Average)	44.6	Dennis Partee, 1969
Punt Returns (Average)	15.5	Leslie Duncan, 1965
Kick-off Returns (Average)	28.4	Keith Lincoln, 1962
Field Goals	24	Rolf Benirschke, 1980

Single Game Records

Points	30	Kellen Winslow, 22 Nov 1981
Touchdowns	5	Kellen Winslow, 22 Nov 1981
Rushing (Yards)	217	Gary Anderson, 18 Dec 1988
Passing (Yards)	444	Dan Fouts, 19 Oct 1980
	444	Dan Fouts, 11 Dec 1982
Passing (Touchdowns)	6	Dan Fouts, 22 Nov 1981
Receiving (No.)	15	Kellen Winslow, 7 Oct 1984
Receiving (Yards)	260	Wes Chandler, 20 Dec 1982
Interceptions	3	*Many occasions*
Field Goals	4	*Many occasions*

SAN DIEGO HEAD-TO-HEAD AGAINST CURRENT NFL TEAMS

	W	L	T		W	L	T		W	L	T
v Atlanta	1	3	0	v Houston	17	15	1	v NY Giants	2	4	0
v Buffalo	17	9	2	v Indianapolis	6	5	0	v NY Jets	16	9	1
v Chicago	4	1	0	v Kansas City	31	31	1	v Philadelphia	3	2	0
v Cincinnati	11	9	0	v LA Raiders	22	41	2	v Phoenix	4	1	0
v Cleveland	7	6	1	v LA Rams	2	3	0	v Pittsburgh	5	12	0
v Dallas	1	4	0	v Miami	10	6	0	v San Francisco	3	3	0
v Denver	30	33	1	v Minnesota	3	3	0	v Seattle	12	14	0
v Detroit	2	3	0	v New England	12	13	2	v Tampa Bay	4	0	0
v Green Bay	1	3	0	v New Orleans	4	1	0	v Washington	0	5	0

SAN FRANCISCO 49ERS

Candlestick Park
San Francisco, California
Stadium Capacity: 66455

Having been refused an NFL franchise, Tony Morabito formed the 49ers in 1946 and they became founder members of the new AAFC. The team was named after the gold prospectors who flooded to California in 1849 – they too were know as 'the 49ers'.

'Buck' Shaw was appointed the team's first coach and when they joined the NFL in 1950 he was still in charge. His nine-year reign ended in 1954, despite a winning season every year apart from their NFL debut season, but subsequent coaches failed to turn the 49ers into a team likely to challenge for the Championship.

The appointment of Dick Nolan in 1968 changed that, because two years later he took the team to their first title in the 25 years since their formation when they captured the Western Division title. They lost to Dallas in the NFC Championship game. The 49ers retained the divisional title in 1971, their first season at their new home of Candlestick Park, but they again fell to Dallas in the Championship Game. Dallas dumped them once more in the play-offs in 1972 after they had won their third successive divisional title.

Nolan was replaced by Monte Clark in 1976 and the 49ers had their first winning season since 1972. Clark was replaced in turn by Ken Meyer in 1977, but he lasted just one season and Pete McCulley took over in 1978. He went after nine games with a 1–8–0 record, and Fred O'Connor, who survived until the end of the season, ended up with a 1–6–0 record as the 49ers had their worst ever season.

Bill Walsh, the ex-Stanford University man, was appointed head coach in 1979 and it was Walsh who transformed the San Francisco 49ers into one of the

NFL's top teams of the 1980s. From bottom of the Western Division in 1979 they were champions with a 13–3–0 record in 1981. They went on to beat the Cowboys in the NFC Championship Game and then with the help of star quarterback Joe Montana they captured the Super Bowl by beating Cincinnati 26–21.

Western Division champions again in 1983 and 1984, the 49ers went on to take their second Super Bowl in 1985 when with Montana again starring they beat Miami 38–16 at Stanford. Never failing to miss the play-offs, Walsh led the side to its third NFC title in 1988 and followed that with his and the team's third Super Bowl, when they beat Cincinnati 20–16.

Walsh retired after that success but he had laid the foundations for future San Francisco teams and new head coach George Seifert carried on where Walsh had left off as the 49ers trounced Denver 55–10, the biggest winning margin in Super Bowl history, in 1989. Western Division champions again in 1990, when the 49ers failed to reach the play-offs at the end of the 1991 regular season it was for the first time in ten years.

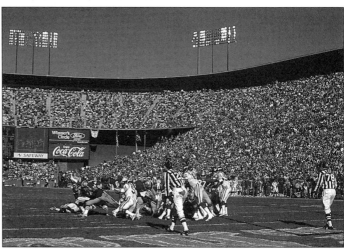

Top left *Coach Bill Walsh with quarterback Joe Montana.*
Bottom left *The 49ers home at Candlestick Park.*
Above *Ray Wersching kicks for goal. He holds San Francisco's career and single game records for field goals.*

FORMER STADIUMS

1950–70 Kezar Stadium

SAN FRANCISCO HEAD-TO-HEAD AGAINST CURRENT NFL TEAMS

	W	L	T		W	L	T		W	L	T
v Atlanta	29	20	1	v Houston	5	2	0	v NY Giants	11	14	0
v Buffalo	2	2	0	v Indianapolis	16	21	0	v NY Jets	5	1	0
v Chicago	27	25	1	v Kansas City	4	1	0	v Philadelphia	12	4	1
v Cincinnati	7	1	0	v LA Raiders	2	5	0	v Phoenix	9	8	0
v Cleveland	6	8	0	v LA Rams	35	48	2	v Pittsburgh	7	7	0
v Dallas	10	8	1	v Miami	2	4	0	v San Diego	3	3	0
v Denver	3	4	0	v Minnesota	16	16	1	v Seattle	4	1	0
v Detroit	25	26	1	v New England	5	1	0	v Tampa Bay	9	1	0
v Green Bay	25	21	1	v New Orleans	30	13	2	v Washington	11	7	1

HONOURS

1921–59

NFL Divisional Champions:	None
NFL Champions:	None

1960–9

NFL Divisional Champions:	None
NFL Champions:	None

1970–92

NFC Divisional Champions:	1970–2, 1981, 1983–4, 1986–90
NFC Champions:	1981, 1984, 1988–9
Super Bowl – *Winners:*	1982, 1985, 1989–90
– *Runners-up:*	None

COACHING HISTORY

		W	L	T
1950–4	Lawrence 'Buck' Shaw	33	25	2
1955	Norman 'Red' Strader	4	8	0
1956–8	Frankie Albert	19	17	1
1959–63	Howard 'Red' Hickey	27	27	1
1963–7	Jack Christiansen	26	38	3
1968–75	Dick Nolan	56	56	5
1976	Monte Clark	8	6	0
1977	Ken Meyer	5	9	0
1978	Pete McCulley	1	8	0
1978	Fred O'Connor	1	6	0
1979–88	Bill Walsh	102	63	1
1989–91	George Seifert	42	11	0

RECORD HOLDERS

Career Records

Points	979	Ray Wersching, 1977–87
Touchdowns	97	Jerry Rice, 1985–91
Rushing (Yards)	7344	Joe Perry, 1950–60, 1963
Passing (Yards)	34 998	Joe Montana, 1979–90
Passing (Touchdowns)	242	Joe Montana, 1979–90
Receiving (No.)	526	Roger Craig, 1983–91
Receiving (Yards)	9072	Jerry Rice, 1985–91
Interceptions	51	Ronnie Lott, 1981–90
Punting (Average)	44.7	Tommy Davis, 1959–69
Punt Returns (Average)	14.7	Manfred Moore, 1974–5
Kick-off Returns (Average)	29.4	Abe Woodson, 1958–64
Field Goals	190	Ray Wersching, 1977–87

Season Records

Points	138	Jerry Rice, 1987
Touchdowns	23	Jerry Rice, 1987
Rushing (Yards)	1502	Roger Craig, 1988
Passing (Yards)	3944	Joe Montana, 1990
Passing (Touchdowns)	31	Joe Montana, 1987
Receiving (No.)	100	Jerry Rice, 1990
Receiving (Yards)	1570	Jerry Rice, 1986
Interceptions	10	Dave Baker, 1960
	10	Ronnie Lott, 1986
Punting (Average)	45.8	Tommy Davis, 1965
Punt Returns (Average)	22.3	Dana McLemore, 1982
Kick-off Returns (Average)	34.4	Joe Arenas, 1953
Field Goals	29	Mike Cofer, 1989

Single Game Records

Points	30	Jerry Rice, 14 Oct 1990
Touchdowns	5	Jerry Rice, 14 Oct 1990
Rushing (Yards)	194	Delvin Williams, 31 Oct 1976
Passing (Yards)	476	Joe Montana, 14 Oct 1990
Passing (Touchdowns)	6	Joe Montana, 14 Oct 1990
Receiving (No.)	13	Jerry Rice, 14 Oct 1990
Receiving (Yards)	286	John Taylor, 11 Dec 1989
Interceptions	4	Dave Baker, 4 Dec 1960
Field Goals	6	Ray Wersching, 16 Oct 1983

PLAYERS SELECTED AS THE NO. 1 DRAFT CHOICE

Year	Player	Pos	College
1953	Harry Babcock	E	Georgia
1964	Dave Parks	E	Texas Tech

REGULAR SEASON RECORD

Year	W	L	T	%
1950	3	9	0	.250
1951	7	4	1	.636
1952	7	5	0	.583
1953	9	3	0	.750
1954	7	4	1	.636
1955	4	8	0	.333
1956	5	6	1	.455
1957	8	4	0	.667
1958	6	6	0	.500
1959	7	5	1	.583
1960	7	5	0	.583
1961	7	6	1	.538
1962	6	8	0	.429
1963	2	12	0	.143
1964	4	10	0	.286
1965	7	6	1	.538
1966	6	6	2	.500
1967	7	7	0	.500
1968	7	6	1	.538
1969	4	8	2	.333
1970	10	3	1	.769
1971	9	5	0	.643
1972	8	5	1	.607
1973	5	9	0	.357
1974	6	8	0	.429
1975	5	9	0	.357
1976	8	6	0	.571
1977	5	9	0	.357
1978	2	14	0	.125
1979	2	14	0	.125
1980	6	10	0	.375
1981	13	3	0	.813
1982	3	6	0	.333
1983	10	6	0	.625
1984	15	1	0	.938
1985	10	6	0	.625
1986	10	5	1	.656
1987	13	2	0	.867
1988	10	6	0	.625
1989	14	2	0	.875
1990	14	2	0	.875
1991	10	6	0	.625

SEATTLE SEAHAWKS

Kingdome
201 South King Street, Seattle, Washington
Stadium Capacity: 64 984

Along with the Tampa Bay Buccaneers, the Seattle Seahawks are the NFL's newest team. They were formed in 1974 when a franchise was awarded to the city. A competition to find the team's name saw more than 20000 entries of which 151 plumped for 'Seahawks'.

Their first campaign in 1976, in the NFC, saw them end the season with a 2–12–0 record. A switch to the AFC in 1977 saw an improvement to 5–9–0, and that was followed by their first winning season, 9–7–0.

Chuck Knox, the former Los Angeles Rams and Buffalo Bills coach, was appointed the Seahawks head coach in 1983 and he guided them to the play-offs, becoming the first man to take three different teams into the play-offs. However, the Raiders beat them in the Championship Game.

Knox guided Seattle to their first divisional title in 1988 but they were then beaten by Cincinnati in the first round of the play-offs. Knox quit as head coach at the end of the 1991 season and was replaced by general manager Tom Flores.

REGULAR SEASON RECORD

Year	W	L	T	%
1976	2	12	0	.143
1977	5	9	0	.357
1978	9	7	0	.563
1979	9	7	0	.563
1980	4	12	0	.250
1981	6	10	0	.375
1982	4	5	0	.444
1983	9	7	0	.563
1984	12	4	0	.750
1985	8	8	0	.500
1986	10	6	0	.625
1987	9	6	0	.600
1988	9	7	0	.563
1989	7	9	0	.438
1990	9	7	0	.563
1991	7	9	0	.438

Dave Krieg led Seattle to their only divisional title in 1988.

HONOURS

1970–92

AFC Divisional Champions:	1988
AFC Champions:	None
Super Bowl – Winners:	None
– Runners-up:	None

COACHING HISTORY

		W	L	T
1976–82	Jack Patera	35	59	0
1982	Mike McCormack	4	3	0
1983–90	Chuck Knox	83	67	0

FORMER STADIUMS

None

PLAYERS SELECTED AS THE NO. 1 DRAFT CHOICE

Seattle have never had the first pick in the Draft

RECORD HOLDERS

Career Records

Points	810	Norm Johnson, 1982–90
Touchdowns	101	Steve Largent, 1976–89
Rushing (Yards)	6705	Curt Warner, 1983–89
Passing (Yards)	26 132	Dave Krieg, 1980–91
Passing (Touchdowns)	195	Dave Krieg, 1980–91
Receiving (No.)	819	Steve Largent, 1976–89
Receiving (Yards)	13 089	Steve Largent, 1976–89
Interceptions	50	Dave Brown, 1976–86
Punting (Average)	43.0	Rick Tuten, 1991
Punt Returns (Average)	11.4	Paul Johns, 1981–4
Kick-off Returns (Average)	22.1	Bobby Joe Edmonds, 1986–8
Field Goals	159	Norm Johnson, 1982–90

Season Records

Points	110	Norm Johnson, 1984
Touchdowns	15	Dave Sims, 1978
	15	Sherman Smith, 1979
	15	Derrick Fenner, 1990
Rushing (Yards)	1481	Curt Warner, 1986
Passing (Yards)	3671	Dave Krieg, 1984
Passing (Touchdowns)	32	Dave Krieg, 1984
Receiving (No.)	79	Steve Largent, 1985
Receiving (Yards)	1287	Steve Largent, 1985
Interceptions	10	John Harris, 1981
	10	Kenny Easley, 1984
Punting (Average)	43.0	Rick Tuten, 1991
Punt Returns (Average)	12.6	Bobby Joe Edmonds, 1987
Kick-off Returns (Average)	24.1	Al Hunter, 1978
Field Goals	25	John Kasay, 1991

Single Game Records

Points	24	Daryl Turner, 15 Sep 1985
	24	Curt Warner, 11 Dec 1988
Touchdowns	4	Daryl Turner, 15 Sep 1985
	4	Curt Warner, 11 Dec 1988
Rushing (Yards)	207	Curt Warner, 27 Nov 1983
Passing (Yards)	418	Dave Krieg, 20 Nov 1983
Passing (Touchdowns)	5	Dave Krieg, 2 Dec 1984
	5	Dave Krieg, 15 Sep 1985
	5	Dave Krieg, 28 Nov 1988
Receiving (No.)	15	Steve Largent, 18 Oct 1987
Receiving (Yards)	261	Steve Largent, 18 Oct 1987
Interceptions	3	Kenny Easley, 3 Sep 1984
Field Goals	5	Norm Johnson, 20 Sep 1987
	5	Norm Johnson, 18 Dec 1988

SEATTLE HEAD-TO-HEAD AGAINST CURRENT NFL TEAMS

	W	L	T
v Atlanta	4	1	0
v Buffalo	3	1	0
v Chicago	4	2	0
v Cincinnati	5	6	0
v Cleveland	8	3	0
v Dallas	1	3	0
v Denver	13	17	0
v Detroit	4	1	0
v Green Bay	3	3	0
v Houston	4	4	0
v Indianapolis	1	2	0
v Kansas City	12	15	0
v LA Raiders	15	15	0
v LA Rams	1	4	0
v Miami	2	4	0
v Minnesota	3	2	0
v New England	4	6	0
v New Orleans	2	3	0
v NY Giants	2	4	0
v NY Jets	8	3	0
v Philadelphia	1	3	0
v Phoenix	0	3	0
v Pittsburgh	4	4	0
v San Diego	14	12	0
v San Francisco	1	4	0
v Tampa Bay	2	0	0
v Washington	1	4	0

TAMPA BAY BUCCANEERS

Tampa Stadium
North Dale Mabry, Tampa, Florida
Stadium Capacity: 74315

A franchise was awarded to Tampa Bay in 1974 with a view to them joining the NFL in 1976, and a poll amongst local people to find the team name came up with the Buccaneers. Unfortunately for everyone who had looked forward to Tampa's first season with such enthusiasm, their debut was a disaster as they became the first team to have a 0–14–0 record, including five shutouts, and were the first team to go through the season without a win since the Dallas Cowboys in 1960.

Having been switched to the National Conference in 1977 they carried on where they had left off in their debut season – by losing their first 12 games. However, they at last enjoyed their first ever NFL success on 11 December 1977 when they beat the New Orleans Saints 33–14. After three seasons at the bottom of their division, they surprised many people by capturing the Central Division of the NFC in 1979 before narrowly losing 9–0 to the Rams in the Championship Game.

Divisional champions again in 1981, they crashed to Dallas 38–0 in the play-offs. That was the last time they made the play-offs apart from in the strike-bound season of 1982.

Running back Ricky Bell makes ground for Tampa during their historic first ever win in the NFL when New Orleans were defeated 33–14.

THE NFL TEAMS

HONOURS

1970–92

NFC Divisional Champions:	1979, 1981
NFC Champions:	None
Super Bowl – Winners:	None
– Runners-up:	None

COACHING HISTORY

		W	L	T
1976–84	John McKay	45	91	1
1985–6	Leeman Bennett	4	28	0
1987–90	Ray Perkins	19	41	0
1990–1	Richard Williamson	4	15	0

RECORD HOLDERS

Career Records

Points	416	Donald Igwebuike, 1985–9
Touchdowns	46	James Wilder, 1981–9
Rushing (Yards)	5957	James Wilder, 1981–9
Passing (Yards)	12648	Doug Williams, 1978–82
Passing (Touchdowns)	73	Doug Williams, 1978–82
Receiving (No.)	430	James Wilder, 1981–9
Receiving (Yards)	4928	Kevin House, 1980–6
Interceptions	29	Cedric Brown, 1977–84
Punting (Average)	41.1	Frank Garcia, 1983–7
Punt Returns (Average)	8.3	Bobby Futrell, 1986–9
Kick-off Returns (Average)	21.9	Isaac Hagins, 1976–80
Field Goals	94	Donald Igwebuike, 1985–9

Season Records

Points	99	Donald Igwebuike, 1989
Touchdowns	13	James Wilder, 1984
Rushing (Yards)	1544	James Wilder, 1984
Passing (Yards)	3563	Doug Williams, 1981
Passing (Touchdowns)	20	Doug Williams, 1980
	20	Vinny Testaverde, 1989
Receiving (No.)	85	James Wilder, 1984
Receiving (Yards)	1176	Kevin House, 1981
Interceptions	9	Cedric Brown, 1981
Punting (Average)	42.7	Larry Swider, 1981
Punt Returns (Average)	11.0	Willie Drewrey, 1989
Kick-off Returns (Average)	23.5	Isaac Hagins, 1977
Field Goals	23	Steve Christie, 1990

Single Game Records

Points	24	Jimmie Giles, 20 Oct 1985
Touchdowns	4	Jimmie Giles, 20 Oct 1985
Rushing (Yards)	219	James Wilder, 6 Nov 1983
Passing (Yards)	486	Doug Williams, 16 Nov 1980
Passing (Touchdowns)	5	Steve DeBerg, 13 Sep 1987
Receiving (No.)	13	James Wilder, 15 Sep 1985
Receiving (Yards)	212	Mark Carrier, 6 Dec 1987
Interceptions	2	*Many occasions*
Field Goals	4	*Many occasions*

FORMER STADIUMS

None

PLAYERS SELECTED AS THE NO. 1 DRAFT CHOICE

Year	Player	Pos	College
1976	Lee Roy Selmon	DE	Oklahoma
1977	Ricky Bell	RB	Southern California
1986	Bo Jackson	RB	Auburn
1987	Vinny Testaverde	QB	Miami

REGULAR SEASON RECORD

Year	W	L	T	%
1976	0	14	0	.000
1977	2	12	0	.143
1978	5	11	0	.313
1979	10	6	0	.625
1980	5	10	1	.344
1981	9	7	0	.563
1982	5	4	0	.556
1983	2	14	0	.125
1984	6	10	0	.375
1985	2	14	0	.125
1986	2	14	0	.125
1987	4	11	0	.267
1988	5	11	0	.313
1989	5	11	0	.313
1990	6	10	0	.375
1991	3	13	0	.188

TAMPA BAY HEAD-TO-HEAD AGAINST CURRENT NFL TEAMS

	W	L	T
v Atlanta	5	5	0
v Buffalo	4	2	0
v Chicago	6	22	0
v Cincinnati	1	3	0
v Cleveland	0	4	0
v Dallas	0	8	0
v Denver	0	2	0
v Detroit	14	14	0
v Green Bay	11	14	1
v Houston	1	3	0
v Indianapolis	2	4	0
v Kansas City	2	4	0
v LA Raiders	0	2	0
v LA Rams	2	8	0
v Miami	1	4	0
v Minnesota	8	20	0
v New England	0	3	0
v New Orleans	4	10	0
v NY Giants	3	7	0
v NY Jets	1	5	0
v Philadelphia	2	3	0
v Phoenix	4	6	0
v Pittsburgh	0	4	0
v San Diego	0	4	0
v San Francisco	1	9	0
v Seattle	0	2	0
v Washington	0	3	0

WASHINGTON REDSKINS

Robert F Kennedy Stadium (formerly DC Stadium, 1961–8)
East Capitol Street, Washington, DC
Stadium Capacity: 55 683

From the time they were formed in 1932, the Redskins enjoyed immediate success up to the war years. Then came a drought, and they had to wait 30 years before the glory days returned, but in recent years they have become one of the NFL's top teams and have won three of their record-equalling five Super Bowl appearances.

The team was founded in Boston and took the name 'Braves' as they shared the Boston Braves baseball team's ground. After a year they moved to Fenway Park, home of the Boston Red Sox, and renamed themselves the Boston Redskins

with Will 'Lone Star' Dietz, a full-blooded Indian, as their head coach. Dietz lasted two years and was replaced by Eddie Casey, who lasted just one year.

It was the next coach, Ray Flaherty, who turned the Redskins into a winning team. They won the Eastern Division in 1936 and moved to Washington the following year with the Griffith Stadium as their home. They captured the NFL title that year for the first time by beating the Chicago Bears 28–21 in the Championship Game. It was the first of 16 seasons with the Redskins for All-American tailback Sammy Baugh.

The Redskins' next appearance in the Championship Game was in 1940 when the Bears gained ample revenge by winning the most one-sided game in NFL history by 73 points to nil. There was some compensation for Washington two years later when they downed the Bears 14–6 to win their second Championship. 'Dutch' Bergman replaced Flaherty as head coach in 1943 and while he led the Redskins to the Eastern Division title it was the Bears who regained the honours by taking the Championship. Cleveland ended the Redskins' Championship hopes in 1945, with Dudley DeGroot now Washington's coach, but that was the nearest the Redskins were to get to becoming NFL champions for 27 years. They slumped to an especially abysmal season in 1961, their first in their present home, when they finished with a 1–12–1 record.

The home of the Washington Redskins, RFK Stadium. In recent seasons it has proved something of an unassailable fortress for visiting teams.

Sonny Jurgensen, the Redskins career best for touchdown passes, outruns the Philadelphia Eagles defense in 1969.

It was not until the arrival of George Allen as head coach in 1971 that the prospects started to look rosy again. In his first season in charge, Allen led the team to its best season since 1942, finishing with a 9–4–1 record. It was enough to make the play-offs but there they lost to San Francisco. The following year, as Eastern Division champions, they went on to beat Dallas for the NFC Championship before losing to Miami in Super Bowl VII.

It was to be another decade until the Redskins' fans could revel in the taste of success and it happened with the arrival of Joe Gibbs as head coach in 1981. The Redskins took the NFC title in 1982 and then went on to beat Miami 27–17 in the Super Bowl. They lost to the Los Angeles Raiders in the Super Bowl the following year, after beating the 49ers 24–21 to take the NFC Championship. They were Eastern Division champions again in 1984, missed a play-off place the following year, then received a wild-card entry in 1986 but lost to the Giants in the Championship Game.

It was Super Bowl triumph number two in 1988 as the Redskins beat Denver 42–10, and they won their third Super Bowl in five appearances in 1992 when they beat the Buffalo Bills 37–24. They had captured the Eastern Division title with a 14–2–0 record as Joe Gibbs confirmed his status as one of the game's top coaches.

HONOURS

1921–59
NFL Divisional Champions:	1936–7, 1940, 1942–3, 1945
NFL Champions:	1937, 1942

1960–9
NFL Divisional Champions:	None
NFL Champions:	None

1970–92
NFC Divisional Champions:	1972, 1983–4, 1987, 1991
NFC Champions:	1972, 1982–3, 1987, 1991
Super Bowl – Winners:	1983, 1988, 1992
– Runners-up:	1973, 1984

PLAYERS SELECTED AS THE NO. 1 DRAFT CHOICE

Year	Player	Pos	College
1948	Harry Gilmer	QB	Alabama
1962	Ernie Davis	RB	Syracuse

FORMER STADIUMS

1932	Braves Field (Boston)
1933–6	Fenway Park (Boston)
1937–60	Griffith Stadium

COACHING HISTORY

Year	Coach	W	L	T	Year	Coach	W	L	T
1932	Lud Wray	4	4	2	1952–3	Earl 'Curly' Lambeau	10	13	1
1933–4	William 'Lone Star' Dietz	11	11	2	1954–8	Joe Kuharich	26	32	2
1935	Eddie Casey	2	8	1	1959–60	Mike Nixon	4	18	2
1936–42	Ray Flaherty	56	23	3	1961–5	Bill McPeak	21	46	3
1943	Arthur 'Dutch' Bergman	7	4	1	1966–8	Otto Graham	17	22	3
1944–5	Dudley DeGroot	14	6	1	1969	Vince Lombardi	7	5	2
1946–8	Glen 'Turk' Edwards	16	18	1	1970	Bill Austin	6	8	0
1949	John Whelchel	3	3	1	1971–7	George Allen	69	35	1
1949–51	Herman Ball	4	16	0	1978–80	Jack Pardee	24	24	0
1951	Dick Todd	5	4	0	1981–91	Joe Gibbs	128	59	0

REGULAR SEASON RECORD

Year	W	L	T	%	Year	W	L	T	%
1932	4	4	2	.500	1962	5	7	2	.417
1933	5	5	2	.500	1963	3	11	0	.214
1934	6	6	0	.500	1964	6	8	0	.429
1935	2	8	1	.200	1965	6	8	0	.429
1936	7	5	0	.583	1966	7	7	0	.500
1937	8	3	0	.727	1967	5	6	3	.455
1938	6	3	2	.667	1968	5	9	0	.357
1939	8	2	1	.800	1969	7	5	2	.583
1940	9	2	0	.818	1970	6	8	0	.429
1941	6	5	0	.545	1971	9	4	1	.692
1942	10	1	0	.909	1972	11	3	0	.786
1943	6	3	1	.667	1973	10	4	0	.714
1944	6	3	1	.667	1974	10	4	0	.714
1945	8	2	0	.800	1975	8	6	0	.571
1946	5	5	1	.500	1976	10	4	0	.714
1947	4	8	0	.333	1977	9	5	0	.643
1948	7	5	0	.583	1978	8	8	0	.500
1949	4	7	1	.364	1979	10	6	0	.625
1950	3	9	0	.250	1980	6	10	0	.375
1951	5	7	0	.417	1981	8	8	0	.500
1952	4	8	0	.333	1982	8	1	0	.889
1953	6	5	1	.545	1983	14	2	0	.875
1954	3	9	0	.250	1984	11	5	0	.688
1955	8	4	0	.667	1985	10	6	0	.625
1956	6	6	0	.500	1986	12	4	0	.750
1957	5	6	1	.455	1987	11	4	0	.733
1958	4	7	1	.364	1988	7	9	0	.438
1959	3	9	0	.250	1989	10	6	0	.625
1960	1	9	2	.100	1990	10	6	0	.625
1961	1	12	1	.077	1991	14	2	0	.875

RECORD HOLDERS

Career Records

Points	1206	Mark Moseley, 1974–86
Touchdowns	90	Charley Taylor, 1964–77
Rushing (Yards)	7472	John Riggins, 1976–9, 1981–5
Passing (Yards)	25 206	Joe Theismann, 1974–85
Passing (Touchdowns)	209	Sonny Jurgensen, 1964–74
Receiving (No.)	801	Art Monk, 1980–91
Receiving (Yards)	10 984	Art Monk, 1980–91
Interceptions	36	Brig Owens, 1966–77
Punting (Average)	45.1	Sammy Baugh, 1937–52
Punt Returns (Average)	12.8	Johnny Williams, 1952–3
Kick-off Returns (Average)	28.5	Bobby Mitchell, 1962–8
Field Goals	263	Mark Moseley, 1974–86

Season Records

Points	161	Mark Moseley, 1983
Touchdowns	24	John Riggins, 1983
Rushing (Yards)	1347	John Riggins, 1983
Passing (Yards)	4109	Jay Schroeder, 1986
Passing (Touchdowns)	31	Sonny Jurgensen, 1967
Receiving (No.)	106	Art Monk, 1984
Receiving (Yards)	1436	Bobby Mitchell, 1963
Interceptions	13	Dan Sandifer, 1948
Punting (Average)	51.4	Sammy Baugh, 1940
Punt Returns (Average)	15.3	Johnny Williams, 1952
Kick-off Returns (Average)	29.7	Mike Nelms, 1981
Field Goals	33	Mark Moseley, 1983

Single Game Records

Points	24	Dick James, 17 Dec 1961
	24	Larry Brown, 4 Dec 1973
Touchdowns	4	Dick James, 17 Dec 1961
	4	Larry Brown, 4 Dec 1973
Rushing (Yards)	221	Gerald Riggs, 17 Sep 1989
Passing (Yards)	446	Sammy Baugh, 31 Oct 1943
Passing (Touchdowns)	6	Sammy Baugh, 31 Oct 1943
	6	Sammy Baugh, 23 Nov 1947
Receiving (No.)	13	Art Monk, 15 Dec 1985
	13	Kelvin Bryant, 7 Dec 1986
	13	Art Monk, 4 Nov 1990
Receiving (Yards)	255	Anthony Allen, 4 Oct 1987
Interceptions	4	Sammy Baugh, 14 Nov 1943
	4	Don Sandifer, 31 Oct 1948
Field Goals	5	*Many occasions*

WASHINGTON HEAD-TO-HEAD AGAINST CURRENT NFL TEAMS

	W	L	T
v Atlanta	12	3	1
v Buffalo	5	2	0
v Chicago	16	21	1
v Cincinnati	4	2	0
v Cleveland	9	32	1
v Dallas	27	35	2
v Denver	3	3	0
v Detroit	23	8	0
v Green Bay	13	14	1
v Houston	3	3	0
v Indianapolis	6	16	0
v Kansas City	1	2	0
v LA Raiders	2	5	0
v LA Rams	16	6	1
v Miami	3	5	0
v Minnesota	7	5	0
v New England	4	1	0
v New Orleans	11	4	0
v NY Giants	50	67	3
v NY Jets	4	0	0
v Philadelphia	66	43	5
v Phoenix	60	33	2
v Pittsburgh	42	27	3
v San Diego	5	0	0
v San Francisco	7	11	1
v Seattle	4	1	0
v Tampa Bay	3	0	0

DEFUNCT TEAMS

The following teams have all appeared in the NFL at some time or other but are no longer current members. Some may have had the same or similar names to existing franchises but are not associated with them in any way.

DEFUNCT TEAMS

Team	Years in the League
Akron Indians	1923–5
Akron Pros	1920, 1926
Baltimore Colts	1950
Boston Bulldogs	1929
Boston Yanks	1944–7
Brooklyn Dodgers	1930–43
Brooklyn Lions	1926
Brooklyn Tigers	1944–5
Buffalo All-Americans	1920–3
Buffalo Bisons	1924–5, 1927, 1929
Buffalo Rangers	1926
Canton Bulldogs	1920–3(a)
Canton Bulldogs	1925–6(b)
Card–Pitt	1944(c)

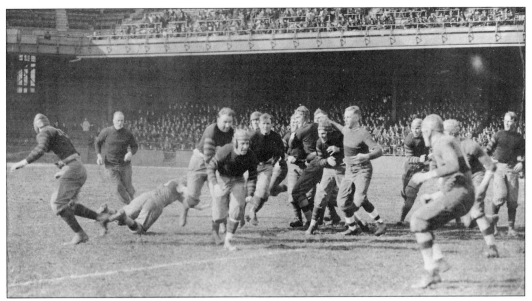

The Colombus Panhandles face the Cleveland Indians at League Park in November 1916.

Team	Years in the League
Chicago Tigers	1920
Cincinnati Celts	1921
Cincinnati Reds	1933–4
Cleveland Bulldogs	1924–5, 1927
Cleveland Indians	1923, 1931
Cleveland Tigers	1920
Columbus Panhandles	1920–2
Columbus Tigers	1923–6
Dallas Texans	1952
Dayton Triangles	1920–9
Detroit Heralds	1920–1
Detroit Panthers	1925–6
Detroit Wolverines	1928
Duluth Eskimos	1926–7
Duluth Kelleys	1923–5
Evansville Crimson Giants	1921–2
Frankford Yellowjackets	1924–31
Hammond Pros	1920–6
Hartford Blues	1926
Kansas City Blues	1924
Kansas City Cowboys	1925
Kenosha Maroons	1924
Los Angeles Buccaneers	1926
Louisville Brecks	1921–3
Louisville Colonels	1926
Milwaukee Braves	1922
Milwaukee Badgers	1923–6
Minneapolis Marines	1921–4
Minneapolis Red Jackets	1929–30
Muncie Flyers	1920–1
New York Bulldogs	1949
New York Yankees	1927–8
New York Yanks	1950–1
Newark Tornadoes	1930

Team	Years in the League
Oorang Indians	1922–3
Orange Tornadoes	1929
Phil–Pitt	1943(d)
Posville Maroons	1925–8
Providence Steamroller	1925–31
Racine Legion	1922–4
Racine Tornadoes	1926
Rochester Jeffersons	1920–5
Rock Island Independents	1920–5
St Louis All Stars	1923
St Louis Gunners	1934
Straten Island Stapletons	1929–32
Toledo Maroons	1922–3
Tonawanda Kardex	1921
Washington Senators	1921

(a) *Became Cleveland Bulldogs in 1924. No relation to the Canton Bulldogs team formed in 1925*
(b) *No relation to the Canton Bulldogs team of 1920–3*
(c) *A merger between the present-day teams Phoenix Cardinals (then Chicago Cardinals) and Pittsburgh Steelers*
(d) *A merger between the present-day teams Philadelphia Eagles and Pittsburgh Steelers*

Winners of the NFL Championship
Canton Bulldogs, 1922–3
Cleveland Bulldogs (formerly Canton Bulldogs), 1924
Frankford Yellowjackets, 1926
Providence Steamroller, 1928

THE DRAFT

The draft was introduced in 1936 at the suggestion of Bert Bell, the League's second commissioner and co-owner of the Philadelphia Eagles. He proposed that pro teams should have the pick of the college players each year, with the team finishing bottom of the League having first pick, and so on. Prior to the draft system, it was a free-for-all at the end of each college season with the teams with the most money getting hold of the best players.

Coincidentally, it was Bell's Philadelphia team who had the first pick in the inaugural draft! They picked Jay Berwanger, a halfback from the University of Chicago. The Eagles traded his rights to the Chicago Bears, but Berwanger never went on to play pro football.

The draft is held each spring with each pro team having 12 picks of the players eligible, i.e. those who have graduated from college. And Bell's original system of the lowest team having the first pick still remains in force.

Strict rules are laid down for draft day, and teams are allowed a maximum of 15 minutes to make their selection of player in the first and second rounds. But in the other ten rounds they are allowed only five minutes to make their minds up whom to select.

The draft takes place in a New York hotel with all teams linked up from their headquarters by telephone. Players who remain unselected at the end of the draft become free agents and can offer their services to any clubs willing to take them. Quite often, clubs will trade their draft picks for current players of opposing teams.

Jeff George, number one draft pick in 1990, pictured on his NFL debut for the Colts against Buffalo in week 1.

Year	No. 1 Draft Pick	College	Selected by	Pos
1936	Jay Berwanger	Chicago	Philadelphia Eagles	HB
1937	Sam Francis	Nebraska	Philadelphia Eagles	FB
1938	Corbett Davis	Indiana	Cleveland Rams	FB
1939	Ki Aldrich	Texas Christian	Chicago Cardinals	C
1940	George Cafego	Tennessee	Chicago Cardinals	HB
1941	Tom Harmon	Michigan	Chicago Bears	HB
1942	Bill Dudley	Virginia	Pittsburgh Steelers	HB
1943	Frank Sinkwich	Georgia	Detroit Lions	HB
1944	Angelo Bartelli	Notre Dame	Boston Yanks	QB
1945	Charley Trippi	Georgia	Chicago Cardinals	HB
1946	Frank Dancewicz	Notre Dame	Boston Yanks	QB
1947	Bob Fenimore	Oklahoma A & M	Chicago Bears	HB
1948	Harry Gilmer	Alabama	Washington Redskins	QB
1949	Chuck Bednarik	Pennsylvania	Philadelphia Eagles	C
1950	Leon Hart	Notre Dame	Detroit Lions	E
1951	Kyle Rote	Southern Methodist	New York Giants	HB
1952	Bill Wade	Vanderbilt	Los Angeles Rams	QB
1953	Harry Babcock	Georgia	San Francisco 49ers	E
1954	Bobby Garrett	Stanford	Cleveland Browns	QB
1955	George Shaw	Oregon	Baltimore Colts	QB
1956	Gary Glick	Colorado A & M	Pittsburgh Steelers	DB
1957	Paul Hornung	Notre Dame	Green Bay Packers	HB
1958	King Hill	Rice	Chicago Cardinals	QB
1959	Randy Duncan	Iowa	Green Bay Packers	QB
1960	Billy Cannon	Louisiana State	Los Angeles Rams	RB
1961	NFL Tommy Mason	Tulane	Minnesota Vikings	RB
	AFL Ken Rice	Auburn	Buffalo Bills	G
1962	NFL Ernie Davis	Syracuse	Washington Redskins	RB
	AFL Roman Gabriel	North Carolina State	Oakland Raiders	QB
1963	NFL Terry Baker	Oregon State	Los Angeles Rams	QB
	AFL Buck Buchanan	Grambling	Kansas City Chiefs	DT
1964	NFL Dave Parks	Texas Tech	San Francisco 49ers	E
	AFL Jack Concannon	Boston College	Boston Patriots	QB
1965	NFL Tucker Frederickson	Auburn	New York Giants	RB
	AFL Lawrence Elkins	Baylor	Houston Oilers	E
1966	NFL Tommy Nobis	Texas	Atlanta Falcons	LB
	AFL Jim Grabowski	Illinois	Miami Dolphins	RB
1967	Bubba Smith	Michigan State	Baltimore Colts	DT
1968	Ron Yary	Southern California	Minnesota Vikings	T
1969	OJ Simpson	Southern California	Buffalo Bills	RB
1970	Terry Bradshaw	Louisiana Tech	Pittsburgh Steelers	QB
1971	Jim Plunkett	Stanford	New England Patriots	QB
1972	Walt Patulski	Notre Dame	Buffalo Bills	DE
1973	John Matuszak	Tampa	Houston Oilers	DE
1974	Ed Jones	Tennessee State	Dallas Cowboys	DE
1975	Steve Bartkowski	California	Atlanta Falcons	QB
1976	Lee Roy Selmon	Oklahoma	Tampa Bay Buccaneers	DE
1977	Ricky Bell	Southern California	Tampa Bay Buccaneers	RB
1978	Earl Campbell	Texas	Houston Oilers	RB
1979	Tom Cousineau	Ohio State	Buffalo Bills	LB
1980	Billy Sims	Oklahoma	Detroit Lions	RB
1981	George Rogers	South Carolina	New Orleans Saints	RB
1982	Kenneth Sims	Texas	New England Patriots	DT
1983	John Elway	Stanford	Baltimore Colts	QB
1984	Irving Fryar	Nebraska	New England Patriots	WR
1985	Bruce Smith	Virginia Tech	Buffalo Bills	DE
1986	Bo Jackson	Auburn	Tampa Bay Buccaneers	RB
1987	Vinny Testaverde	Miami	Tampa Bay Buccaneers	QB
1988	Aundray Bruce	Auburn	Atlanta Falcons	LB
1989	Troy Aikman	UCLA	Dallas Cowboys	QB
1990	Jeff George	Illinois	Indianapolis Colts	QB
1991	Russell Maryland	Miami	Dallas Cowboys	DT

NFL RECORDS & RECORD HOLDERS

ALL-TIME RECORDS

APPEARANCES

Longest Career (Seasons)
26 George Blanda, Chicago Bears, Baltimore Colts, Houston Oilers, Oakland Raiders, 1949–75
Most Seasons with One Club
19 Jim Marshall, Minnesota Vikings, 1961–79
Most Games Played
340 George Blanda, *as above*
Most Consecutive Games Played
282 Jim Marshall, Cleveland Browns/Minnesota Vikings, 1960–79

Paul Hornung holds the points record for a season, 176 for Green Bay in 1960.

SCORING

Most Points
Career 2002 George Blanda, Chicago Bears, Baltimore Colts, Houston Oilers, Oakland Raiders, 1949–75
Season 176 Paul Hornung, Green Bay Packers, 1960
Game 40 Ernie Nevers, Chicago Cardinals v Chicago Bears, 28 Nov 1929
Most Consecutive Games Scoring
181 Jim Breech, Oakland Raiders/Cincinnati Bengals, 1979–91
Most Touchdowns
Career 126 Jim Brown, Cleveland Browns, 1957–65
Season 24 John Riggins, Washington Redskins, 1983
Game 6 Ernie Nevers, Chicago Cardinals v Chicago Bears, 28 Nov 1929; Dub Jones, Cleveland Browns v Chicago Bears, 25 Nov 1951; Gale Sayers, Chicago Bears v San Francisco 49ers, 12 Dec 1965
Most Points After Touchdown Attempted
Career 959 George Blanda, *as above*
Season 70 Uwe von Schamann, Miami Dolphins, 1984
Game 10 Charlie Gogolak, Washington Redskins v New York Giants, 27 Nov 1966
Most Points After Touchdown Made
Career 943 George Blanda, *as above*
Season 66 Uwe von Schamann, *as above*
Game 9 Pat Harder, Chicago Cardinals v New York Giants, 17 October 1948; Bob Waterfield, Los Angeles Rams v Baltimore Colts, 22 Oct 1950; Charlie Gogolak, *as above*
Most Field Goals Attempted
Career 638 George Blanda, *as above*
Season 49 Bruce Gossett, Los Angeles Rams, 1966; Curt Knight, Washington Redskins, 1971
Game 9 Jim Bakken, St Louis Cardinals v Pittsburgh Steelers, 24 Sep 1967
Most Field Goals Made
Career 373 Jan Stenerud, Kansas City Chiefs, Green Bay Packers, Minnesota Vikings, 1969–85
Season 35 Ali Haji-Sheikh, New York Giants, 1983
Game 7 Jim Bakken, *as above*; Rich Karlis, Minnesota Vikings v Los Angeles Rams, 5 Nov 1989
Longest Field Goals
63 yards Tom Dempsey, New Orleans Saints v Detroit Lions, 8 Nov 1970

The great George Blanda pictured in action for the last of his four teams, the Oakland Raiders, towards the end of his 27-year career.

RUSHING

Most Attempts

Career   **3838** Walter Payton, Chicago Bears, 1975–87
Season   **407** James Wilder, Tampa Bay Buccaneers, 1984
Game   **45** Jamie Morris, Washington Redskins v Cincinnati Bengals, 17 Dec 1988

Most Yards Gained

Career   **16 726** Walter Payton, *as above*
Season   **2105** Eric Dickerson, Los Angeles Rams, 1984
Game   **275** Walter Payton, Chicago Bears v Minnesota Vikings, 20 Nov 1977

Most Touchdowns (Rushing)

Career   **110** Walter Payton, *as above*
Season   **24** John Riggins, Washington Redskins, 1983
Game   **6** Ernie Nevers, Chicago Cardinals v Chicago Bears, 28 Nov 1929

> Ernie Nevers' records for the most points in a game (40) and most touchdowns rushing (8), for Chicago Cardinals against the Chicago Bears on 28 Nov 1929, are the NFL's oldest records.

PASSING

Most Passes Attempted

Career   **6467** Fran Tarkenton, Minnesota Vikings, New York Giants, 1961–78
Season   **731** Warren Moon, Houston Oilers, 1991
Game   **68** George Blanda, Houston Oilers v Buffalo Bills, 1 Nov 1964

Most Passes Completed

Career   **3686** Fran Tarkenton, *as above*
Season   **459** Warren Moon, *as above*
Game   **42** Richard Todd, New York Jets v San Francisco 49ers, 21 Sep 1980

Most Yards Gained

Career   **47 003** Fran Tarkenton, *as above*
Season   **5084** Dan Marino, Miami Dolphins, 1984
Game   **554** Norm Van Brocklin, Los Angeles Rams v New York Yanks, 28 Sep 1951

Most Touchdown Passes

Career   **342** Fran Tarkenton, *as above*
Season   **48** Dan Marino, *as above*
Game   **7** Sid Luckman, Chicago Bears v New York Giants, 14 Nov 1943; Adrian Burk, Philadelphia Eagles v Washington Redskins, 17 Oct 1954; George Blanda, Houston Oilers v New York Titans, 19 Nov 1961; YA Tittle, New York Giants v Washington Redskins, 28 Oct 1962; Joe Kapp, Minnesota Vikings v Baltimore Colts, 28 Sep 1969

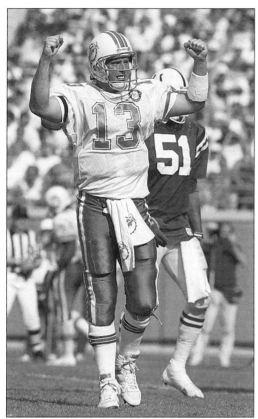

Above *Dan Marino broke 5000 yards passing for the Miami Dolphins in 1984.*

Left *Eric Dickerson's 2000 yards in the 1984 season for the Los Angeles Rams led to a big trade to Indianapolis.*

PASS RECEIVING

Most Receptions
Career **819** Steve Largent, Seattle Seahawks, 1976–89
Season **106** Art Monk, Washington Redskins, 1984
Game **18** Tom Fears, Los Angeles Rams v Green Bay Packers, 3 Dec 1950

Most Yards Gained
Career **13 089** Steve Largent, *as above*
Season **1746** Charley Hennigan, Houston Oilers, 1961
Game **336** Willie Anderson, Los Angeles Rams v New Orleans Saints, 26 Nov 1989

Most Reception Touchdowns
Career **100** Steve Largent, *as above*
Season **22** Jerry Rice, San Francisco 49ers, 1987
Game **5** Bob Shaw, Chicago Cardinals v Baltimore Colts, 2 Oct 1950; Kellen Winslow, San Diego Chargers v Oakland Raiders, 22 Nov 1981; Jerry Rice, San Francisco 49ers v Atlanta Falcons, 14 Oct 1990

INTERCEPTIONS BY

Career **81** Paul Krause, Washington Redskins, Minnesota Vikings, 1964–79
Season **14** Dick Lane, Los Angeles Rams, 1952
Game **4** *by many players*

Yards Gained
Career **1282** Emlen Tunnell, New York Giants, Green Bay Packers, 1948–61
Season **349** Charlie McNeil, San Diego Chargers, 1961
Game **177** Charlie McNeil, San Diego Chargers v Houston Oilers, 24 Sep 1961

Most Touchdowns from Interceptions
Career **9** Ken Houston, Houston Oilers, Washington Redskins, 1967–80
Season **4** Ken Houston, Houston Oilers, 1971
Jim Kearney, Kansas City Chiefs, 1972
Game **2** *by many players*

PUNTING

Most Punts
Career **1154** Dave Jennings, New York Giants, New York Jets, 1974–87
Season **114** Bob Parsons, Chicago Bears, 1981
Game **15** John Teltschik, Philadelphia Eagles v New York Giants, 6 Dec 1987

Longest Punt
98 yards Steve O'Neal, New York Jets v Denver Broncos, 21 Sep 1969

Most Punt Returns
Career **282** Billy Johnson, Houston Oilers, Atlanta Falcons, Washington Redskins, 1974–88
Season **70** Danny Reece, Tampa Bay Buccaneers, 1979
Game **11** Eddie Brown, Washington Redskins v Tampa Bay Buccaneers, 9 Oct 1977

Most Yards Gained
Career **3317** Billy Johnson, *as above*
Season **692** Fulton Walker, Miami Dolphins/Los Angeles Raiders, 1985
Game **207** LeRoy Irvin, Los Angeles Rams v Atlanta Falcons, 11 Oct 1981

Longest Punt Returns
98 yards Gil LeFebvre, Cincinnati Reds v Brooklyn Dodgers, 3 Dec 1933; Charlie West, Minnesota Vikings v Washington Redskins, 3 Nov 1968; Dennis Morgan, Dallas Cowboys v St Louis Cardinals, 13 Oct 1974; Terance Mathis, New York Jets v Dallas Cowboys, 4 Nov 1990

KICK-OFF RETURNS

Most Kick-off Returns
Career **275** Ron Smith, Chicago Bears, Atlanta Falcons, Los Angeles Rams, San Diego Chargers, Oakland Raiders, 1965–74
Season **60** Drew Hill, Los Angeles Rams, 1981
Game **9** Noland Smith, Kansas City Chiefs v Oakland Raiders, 23 Nov 1967; Dino Hall, Cleveland Browns v Pittsburgh Steelers, 7 Oct 1979; Paul Palmer, Kansas City Chiefs v Seattle Seahawks, 20 Sep 1987

Most Yards Gained

Career   **6922** Ron Smith, *as above*
Season   **1345** Buster Rhymes, Minnesota Vikings, 1985
Game   **294** Wally Triplett, Detroit Lions v Los Angeles
Rams, 29 Oct 1950

Longest Kick-off Return

106 yards Al Carmichael, Green Bay Packers v Chicago
Bears, 7 Oct 1956; Noland Smith, Kansas City Chiefs v
Denver Broncos, 17 Dec 1967; Roy Green, St Louis
Cardinals v Dallas Cowboys, 21 Oct 1979

COACHES

COACHES WITH 100 CAREER WINS

Coach	Team(s)	W	L	T	%
George Halas	Chicago Bears	325	151	31	.672
Don Shula	Baltimore Colts, Miami Dolphins	306	145	6	.676
Tom Landry	Dallas Cowboys	270	178	6	.601
Earl 'Curly' Lambeau	Green Bay Packers, Chicago Cardinals, Washington Redskins	229	134	22	.623
Chuck Noll	Pittsburgh Steelers	209	156	1	.572
Chuck Knox	Los Angeles Rams, Buffalo Bills, Seattle Seahawks	178	125	1	.587
Paul Brown	Cleveland Browns, Cincinnati Bengals	170	108	6	.609
Bud Grant	Minnesota Vikings	168	108	5	.607
Steve Owen	New York Giants	153	108	17	.581
Hank Stram	Kansas City Chiefs, New Orleans Saints	136	100	10	.573
Weeb Ewbank	Baltimore Colts, New York Jets	134	130	7	.507
Sid Gillman	Los Angeles Rams, Los Angeles/San Diego Chargers, Houston Oilers	123	104	7	.541
George Allen	Los Angeles Rams, Washington Redskins	118	54	5	.681
Don Coryell	St Louis Cardinals, San Diego Chargers	114	89	1	.561
Joe Gibbs	Washington Redskins	113	55	0	.673
John Madden	Oakland Raiders	112	39	7	.731
Dan Reeves	Denver Broncos	109	71	1	.605
Mike Ditka	Chicago Bears	107	57	0	.652
Ray 'Buddy' Parker	Chicago Cardinals, Detroit Lions, Pittsburgh Steelers	107	76	9	.581
Vince Lombardi	Green Bay Packers, Washington Redskins	105	35	6	.740
Bill Walsh	San Francisco 49ers	102	63	1	.617

MOST SEASONS AS HEAD COACH

40 George Halas, Chicago Bears, 1920–9, 1933–42, 1946–55, 1958–67

MOST GAMES WON AS HEAD COACH

325 George Halas, Chicago Bears (319 Regular Season, 6 Post Season)

TEAMS

Based on Regular Season matches only unless stated

WINS

Most Games Won in a Season
15 (15–1–0), San Francisco 49ers, 1984
15 (15–1–0), Chicago Bears, 1985
Most Consecutive Wins
Career **17** Chicago Bears, 1933–4
Season **14** Miami Dolphins, 1972
The Dolphins had the only 'perfect' season, winning every game
Most Games Without Defeat
25 Canton Bulldogs, 1921–3 (won 22, tied 3)

TIED GAMES

Most Tied Games in a Season
6 Chicago Bears, 1932 (including a record three consecutive)

POINTS

Most Points in a Season
541 Washington Redskins, 1983
Least Points in a Season (since 1932)
37 Cincinnati Reds/St Louis Gunners, 1934
Most Points in a Game
72 Washington Redskins v New York Giants (41), 27 Nov 1966 (*The Redskins were on the receiving end of the NFL's biggest win when they were beaten 73–0 by the Chicago Bears in the 1940 Championship Game*)
Highest Scoring Game
113 Washington Redskins v New York Giants, *as above*
Biggest Comeback to Win Game
31 pts (from 7–35 to win 38–35) by San Francisco 49ers v New Orleans Saints, 7 Dec 1980 (*Denver Broncos trailed Buffalo Bills 7–38 on 27 Nov 1960 and came back to tie 38–38*)
Most Consecutive Games in Which Points Scored
274 Cleveland Browns, 1950–71

DEFEATS

Most Games Lost in a Season
15 New Orleans Saints, 1980; Dallas Cowboys, 1989; New England Patriots, 1990; Indianapolis Colts, 1991
Most Games Without a Win
26 Tampa Bay Buccaneers, 1976–7 (lost 26)

Most Consecutive Defeats
Career **26** Tampa Bay Buccaneers, 1976–7
Season **14** Tampa Bay Buccaneers, 1976; New Orleans Saints, 1980; Baltimore Colts, 1981; New England Patriots, 1990

TEAMS WHO FINISHED TOP OF THEIR DIVISION THE SEASON AFTER FINISHING LAST

Team	Years	Division
Houston Oilers	1966/7	AFL Eastern
Minnesota Vikings	1967/8	NFL Central
Cincinnati Bengals	1969/70	AFL Western/AFC Central
San Francisco 49ers	1969/70	NFL Coastal/NFC Western
Green Bay Packers	1971/2	NFC Central
Baltimore Colts	1974/5	AFC Eastern
Tampa Bay Buccaneers	1978/9	NFC Central
Cincinnati Bengals	1980/1	AFC Central
Indianapolis Colts	1986/7	AFC Eastern
Cincinnati Bengals	1987/8	AFC Central
Cincinnati Bengals	1989/90	AFC Central
Denver Broncos	1990/1	AFC Western

OVERTIME GAMES

The first overtime game was the pre-season game between Los Angeles Rams and New York Giants at Portland, Oregon, on 28 Aug 1955. The Rams won 23–17.

The first regular season overtime game was on 22 Sep 1974 when Pittsburgh Steelers and Denver Broncos tied 35-all after overtime.

The first regular season overtime game to produce a result was on 10 Nov 1974 when the New York Jets scored an overtime touchdown after 6 minutes 53 seconds to beat the New York Giants 26–20.

MOST APPEARANCES IN THE PLAY-OFFS

22 Cleveland Browns, Los Angeles Rams, New York Giants
New Orleans Saints and Tampa Bay

Buccaneers have appeared in the play-offs the least times – three

ALL-TIME TOP TENS

SCORERS

Pts	Player
2002	George Blanda
1699	Jan Stenerud
1470	Pat Leahy
1439	Jim Turner
1382	Mark Moseley
1380	Jim Bakken
1365	Fred Cox
1349	Lou Groza
1268	Nick Lowery
1213	Chris Bahr

PASSERS

Yards	Player
47003	Fran Tarkenton
43040	Dan Fouts
40239	Johnny Unitas
35386	Dan Marino
34998	Joe Montana
34665	Jim Hart
33513	John Hadl
32838	Ken Anderson
32224	Sonny Jurgensen
31566	Steve DeBerg

PUNTERS

Avge	Player
45.1	Sammy Baugh
44.7	Tommy Davis
44.3	Yale Lary
43.9	Ron Stark
43.8	Jerry Norton
43.8	Horace Gillom
43.5	Don Chandler
43.4	Sean Landeta
43.4	Reggie Roby
43.0	Jerrel Wilson

TOUCHDOWNS

No.	Player
126	Jim Brown
125	Walter Payton
116	John Riggins
113	Lenny Moore
105	Don Hutson
101	Steve Largent
100	Franco Harris
97	Jerry Rice
94	Marcus Allen
93	Jim Taylor

RECEIVERS

No.	Player
819	Steve Largent
816	Art Monk
750	Charlie Joiner
710	James Lofton
662	Ozzie Newsome
649	Charley Taylor
633	Don Maynard
631	Raymond Berry
590	Harold Carmichael
589	Fred Biletnikoff

PUNT RETURNERS

Avge	Player
12.8	Jack Christiansen
12.8	George McAfee
12.6	Claude Gibson
12.4	Mel Gray
12.2	Bill Dudley
12.1	Rick Upchurch
11.8	Billy Johnson
11.7	Mack Herron
11.6	Billy Thompson
11.4	David Meggett

RUSHERS

Yards	Player
16726	Walter Payton
12739	Tony Dorsett
12439	Eric Dickerson
12312	Jim Brown
12120	Franco Harris
11352	John Riggins
11236	OJ Taylor
10242	Ottis Anderson
9407	Earl Campbell
8597	Jim Taylor

INTERCEPTORS

No.	Player
81	Paul Krause
79	Emlen Tunnell
68	Dick Lane
65	Ken Riley
62	Dick LeBeau
62	Dave Brown
59	Ronnie Lott
58	Emmitt Thomas
57	Bobby Boyd
57	Johnny Robinson
57	Mel Blount

KICK-OFF RETURNERS

Avge	Player
30.6	Gale Sayers
29.6	Lynn Chandnois
28.7	Abe Woodson
27.9	Claude Young
27.5	Travis Williams
27.3	Joe Arenas
27.1	Clarence Davis
26.7	Steve Van Buren
26.7	Lenny Lyles
26.5	Eugene Morris
26.5	Bobby Jancik

Right *The great Walter Payton of the Chicago Bears, nearly 4000 career yards clear of his nearest rival for rushing.*

THE PRO BOWL

The first Pro Bowl was held at Wrigley Field, Los Angeles, on 15 January 1939 and was between the 1938 NFL champions, New York Giants, and a Pro All-Star team. The Giants won 13–10.

The idea of the Bowl originally came from Washington Redskins owner George Preston Marshall, *Los Angeles Times* sports editor Bill Henry and promoter Tom Gallery.

It was held again continuously until December 1942 – which was, effectively, the 1943 Pro Bowl – then revived in 1951 as a match between All-Star teams from the American and National Conferences. Between 1954 and 1961 it was a match between East and West All-Star teams; then when the AFL came into being both the AFL and NFL held annual East versus West Bowl games, with the exception of 1966 when the AFL's Pro Bowl was between a league All-Stars team and the champions Buffalo.

It was not until 24 January 1971 that the first Pro Bowl as it is known today, between the AFC and NFC, was played. The NFC won 27–6 and to date they lead the series 13–9.

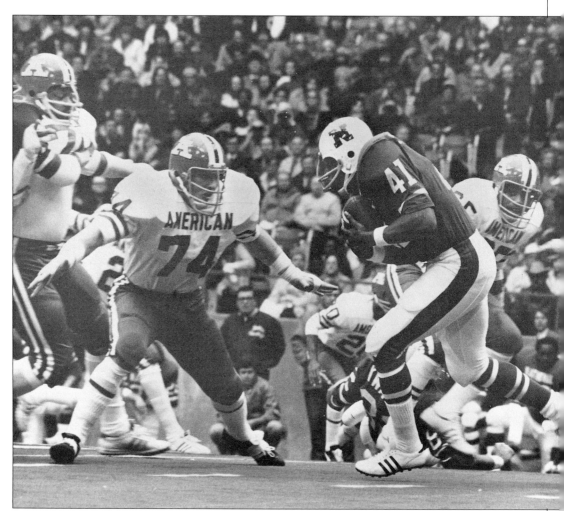

John Brockington (41) of Green Bay scored a record three touchdowns for the NFC in the 1973 Pro Bowl at Texas Stadium.

PRO BOWL RESULTS 1939–70

1939 Jan 15 *Los Angeles 20 000*
NY GIANTS 13 Pro All-Stars 10
1940 Jan 14 *Los Angeles 18 000*
GREEN BAY 16 NFL All-Stars 7
1940 Dec 29 *Los Angeles 21 624*
CHICAGO BEARS 28 NFL All-Stars 14
1942 Jan 4 *New York 17 725*
CHICAGO BEARS 35 NFL All-Stars 24
1942 Dec 27 *Philadelphia 18 671*
NFL ALL-STARS 17 Washington 14
1951 Jan 14 *Los Angeles 53 676*
AMERICAN CONF 28 National Conf 27
1952 Jan 12 *Los Angeles 19 400*
NATIONAL CONF 30 American Conf 13
1953 Jan 10 *Los Angeles 34 208*
NATIONAL CONF 27 American Conf 7
1954 Jan 17 *Los Angeles 44 214*
EAST 20 West 9
1955 Jan 16 *Los Angeles 43 972*
WEST 26 East 19
1956 Jan 15 *Los Angeles 37 867*
EAST 31 West 30
1957 Jan 13 *Los Angeles 44 177*
WEST 19 East 10

1958 Jan 12 *Los Angeles 66 634*
WEST 26 East 7
1959 Jan 11 *Los Angeles 72 250*
EAST 28 West 21
1960 Jan 17 *Los Angeles 56 876*
WEST 38 East 21
1961 Jan 15 *Los Angeles 62 971*
WEST 35 East 31
1962 Jan 7 *San Diego 20 973*
AFL WEST 47 AFL East 27
1962 Jan 14 *Los Angeles 57 409*
NFL WEST 31 NFL East 30
1963 Jan 13 *San Diego 27 641*
AFL WEST 21 AFL East 14
1963 Jan 13 *Los Angeles 61 374*
NFL EAST 30 NFL West 20
1964 Jan 12 *Los Angeles 67 242*
NFL WEST 31 NFL East 17
1964 Jan 19 *San Diego 20 016*
AFL WEST 27 AFL East 24
1965 Jan 10 *Los Angeles 60 598*
NFL WEST 34 NFL East 14
1965 Jan 16 *Houston 15 446*
AFL WEST 38 AFL East 14

1966 Jan 15 *Houston 35 572*
AFL ALL-STARS 30 Buffalo 19
1966 Jan 15 *Los Angeles 60 124*
NFL EAST 36 NFL West 7
1967 Jan 21 *Oakland 18 876*
AFL EAST 30 AFL West 23
1967 Jan 22 *Los Angeles 51 062*
NFL EAST 20 NFL West 10
1968 Jan 21 *Jacksonville 40 103*
AFL EAST 25 AFL West 24
1968 Jan 21 *Los Angeles 53 289*
NFL WEST 38 NFL East 20
1969 Jan 19 *Jacksonville 41 058*
AFL WEST 38 AFL East 25
1969 Jan 19 *Los Angeles 32 050*
NFL WEST 10 NFL East 7
1970 Jan 17 *Houston 30 170*
AFL WEST 26 AFL East 3
1970 Jan 18 *Los Angeles 57 786*
NFL WEST 16 NFL East 13

NFC–AFC PRO BOWL

1971 24 January
Memorial Coliseum, Los Angeles,
48 222
NFC 27
T: Renfro 2, Osborn *FG:* Cox 2
PA: Cox 3
AFC 6
FG: Stenerud 2

1972 23 January
Memorial Coliseum, Los Angeles,
53 647
AFC 26
T: Morin, F Little *FG:* Stenerud 4
PA: Stenerud 2
NFC 13
T: Grim, V Washington *PA:* Knight

1973 21 January
Texas Stadium, Irving, 37 091
AFC 33
T: Simpson, Hubbard, O Taylor, Bell
FG: Gerela 2 *PA:* Gerela 3
NFC 28
T: Brockington 3, Kwalick *PA:* Marcol 4

1974 20 January
Arrowhead Stadium, Kansas City,
66 918
AFC 15
FG: Yepremian 5
NFC 13
T: McCutcheon *FG:* Mike-Mayer 2
PA: Mike-Mayer

1975 20 January
Orange Bowl, Miami, 26 484
NFC 17
T: Gray, Taylor *FG:* Marcol *PA:* Marcol 2
AFC 10
T: Warfield *FG:* Gerela *PA:* Gerela

1976 26 January
Louisiana Superdome, New Orleans,
30 546
NFC 23
T: Foreman, Metcalf, Gray *FG:* Bakken
PA: Bakken 2
AFC 20
T: Burrough, Johnson *FG:* Stenerud 2
PA: Stenerud 2

1977 17 January
Kingdome, Seattle, 64 752
AFC 24
T: Simpson, Joiner, Branch *FG:* Linhart
PA: Linhart 3
NFC 14
T: Thomas, McCutcheon *PA:* Bakken 2

1978 23 January
Tampa Stadium, Tampa, 51 337
NFC 14
T: Metcalf, Payton *PA:* Herrera 2
AFC 13
T: Branch *FG:* Linhart 2 *PA:* Linhart

1979 29 January
Memorial Coliseum, Los Angeles,
46 281
NFC 13
T: Montgomery, T Hill *PA:* Corral
AFC 7
T: Largent *PA:* Yepremian

1980 27 January
Aloha Stadium, Honolulu, 49 800
NFC 37
T: Muncie 2 D Hill, T Hill, Henry
FG: Moseley *PA:* Moseley 4
AFC 27
T: Campbell 2, Pruitt *FG:* Fritsch 2
PA: Fritsch 3

1981 1 February
Aloha Stadium, Honolulu, 50 360
NFC 21
T: Jenkins *FG:* Murray 4 *PA:* Murray *S:* 1
AFC 7
T: Morgan *PA:* J Smith

1982 31 January
Aloha Stadium, Honolulu, 50 402
AFC 16
T: Muncie, Campbell *FG:* Lowery
PA: Lowery
NFC 13
T: Giles, Dorsett *PA:* Septien

1983 6 February
Aloha Stadium, Honolulu, 49 883
NFC 20
T: Andrews, Jefferson *FG:* Moseley 2
PA: Moseley 2
AFC 19
T: Walker, Allen *FG:* Benirschke
PA: Benirschke 2 *S:* 1

1984 29 January
Aloha Stadium, Honolulu, 50 445
NFC 45
T: Andrews 2, Cromwell, Lofton,
Coffman, Dickerson *FG:* Haji-Sheikh
PA: Haji-Sheikh 6
AFC 3
FG: Anderson

1985 27 January
Aloha Stadium, Honolulu, 50 385
AFC 22
T: Allen, Still *FG:* Johnson 2
PA: Johnson 2 *S:* 1
NFC 14
T: Lofton, Payton *PA:* Stenerud 2

1986 2 February
Aloha Stadium, Honolulu, 50 101
NFC 28

T: Browner, Monk, Cosbie, Giles
PA: Andersen 4
AFC 24
T: Allen, Chandler, Lipps *FG:* Anderson
PA: Anderson 3

1987 1 February
Aloha Stadium, Honolulu, 50 101
AFC 10
T: Christensen *FG:* Franklin
PA: Franklin
NFC 6
FG: Andersen 2

1988 7 February
Aloha Stadium, Honolulu, 50 113
AFC 15
T: Kelly *FG:* Biasucci 2
PA: Biasucci *Safety:* 1
NFC 6
FG: Andersen 2

1989 29 January
Aloha Stadium, Honolulu, 50 113
NFC 34
T: Walker 2, Settle, Ellard
FG: Andersen 2 *PA:* Andersen 4
AFC 3
FG: Norwood

1990 4 February
Aloha Stadium, Honolulu, 50 445
NFC 27
T: Meggett, Gray, Millard *FG:* Murray 2
PA: Murray 3
AFC 21
T: Okoye, Edmunds, M Johnson
PA: Treadwell 3

1991 3 February
Aloha Stadium, Honolulu, 50 345
AFC 23
T: Reed, Givins *FG:* Lowery 3
PA: Lowery 2
NFC 21
T: J Johnson 2, Sanders
PA: Andersen 3

1992 2 February
Aloha Stadium, Honolulu, 50 209
NFC 21
T: Irvin, Clark, Rice *PA:* Lohmiller 3
AFC 15
T: Clayton *FG:* Jaeger 2 *PA:* Jaeger
Safety: 1

PRO-BOWL RECORDS

MOST APPEARANCES

10 Lawrence Taylor (New York Giants) NFC 1982–91

RUSHING

Most Attempts
Career: 81 Walter Payton, NFC 1977–81, 1984–7
Game: 19 OJ Simpson, AFC 1974
Most Yards Gained
Career: 368 Walter Payton, *as above*
Game: 112 OJ Simpson, AFC 1973
Longest Run from Scrimmage
Game: 41 yards Lawrence McCutcheon, NFC 1976
Highest Average Gain
Career (min. 20 attempts)
    5.81 yards (209 yards in 36 attempts) Marv
    Hubbard, AFC 1972–4
Game (min. 10 attempts)
    7.00 yards (112 yards in 16 attempts) OJ Simpson,
    AFC 1973
    7.00 yards (70 yards from 10 attempts) Ottis
    Anderson, NFC 1981

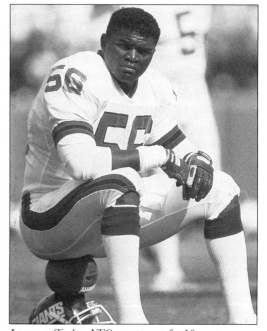

Lawrence Taylor, NFC ever-present for 10 years.

SCORING

Most Points
Career: 30 Jan Stenerud, AFC 1971–2, 1976; NFC 1985
Game: 18 John Brockington, NFC 1973
Most Touchdowns
Career: 3 John Brockington, NFC 1972–4
3 Earl Campbell, AFC 1979–82, 1984
3 Chuck Muncie, NFC 1980, AFC 1982–3
3 William Andrews, NFC 1981–4
3 Marcus Allen, AFC 1983, 1985–6, 1988
*Allen is the only player to score touchdowns in three Pro
Bowls*
Game: 3 John Brockington, NFC 1973
Most Points After Touchdown
Career: 11 Morten Andersen, NFC 1986–9, 1991
Game: 6 Ali Haji-Sheikh, NFC 1984
Most Field Goals Attempted
Career: 15 Jan Stenerud, AFC 1971–2, 1976, NFC 1985
Game: 6 Jan Stenerud, AFC 1972
6 Ed Murray, NFC 1981
6 Mark Moseley, NFC 1983
Most Field Goals Made
Career: 8 Jan Stenerud, AFC 1971–2, 1976, NFC 1985
Game: 5 Garo Yepremian, AFC 1974
Longest Field Goal
51 yards Morten Andersen, NFC 1989

Above *Jan Stenerud kicks for the NFC in 1985, Joe
Montana holds. Stenerud holds several kicking and points
records for the Pro Bowl.*

PASSING

Most Attempts
Career: 120 Dan Fouts, AFC 1980–4, 1986
Game: 32 Bill Kenney, AFC 1984
Completions
Career: 63 Dan Fouts, *as above*
Game: 21 Joe Theismann, NFC 1984
Highest Completion Percentage
Career (min. 40 attempts)
68.9% (31 from 45 attempts) Joe Theismann, NFC
1983–4
Game (min. 10 attempts
90.0% (9 from 10 attempts) Archie Manning, NFC
1980
Most Yards Gained
Career: 890 Dan Fouts, *as above*
Game: 274 Dan Fouts, AFC 1983
Longest Completion
64 yards (for a TD) Dan Pastorini (to Ken
Burrough), AFC 1976

Highest Average Gains

Career: 7.91 yards Randall Cunningham, NFC 1989–91
Game: 15.27 yards Randall Cunningham, NFC 1991

Most Touchdown Passes

Career: 3 Joe Theismann, NFC 1983–4
3 Phil Simms, NFC 1986
3 Joe Montana, NFC 1982, 1984–5, 1988
Game: 3 Joe Theismann, NFC 1984
3 Phil Simms, *as above*

Most Passes Had Intercepted

Career: 8 Dan Fouts, AFC 1980–4, 1986
Game: 5 Jim Hart, NFC 1977

Most Attempts Without an Interception

Game: 27 Joe Theismann, NFC 1984
27 Phil Simms, NFC 1986

Lowest Percentage of Passes Intercepted

Career (min. 40 attempts):
0.00% Joe Theismann, NFC 1983–4

PASS RECEIVING

Most Receptions

Career: 18 Walter Payton, NFC 1977–81, 1984–7
Game: 8 Steve Largent, AFC 1986
8 Michael Irvin, NFC 1992

Most Yards Gained

Career: 236 yards Steve Largent, AFC 1979, 1982, 1985–8
125 yards Michael Irvin, NFC 1992

Longest Reception

64 yards (for TD), Ken Burrough (from Dan Pastorini),
AFC 1976

INTERCEPTIONS BY

Most

Career: 4 Everson Walls, NFC 1982–4, 1986
Game: 2 Mel Blount, AFC 1977
2 Everson Walls (twice), NFC 1982, 1983
2 LeRoy Irvin, NFC 1986
2 David Fulcher, AFC 1990

PUNTING

Most Punts

Career: 33 Ray Guy, AFC 1974–9, 1981
Game: 10 Reggie Roby, AFC 1985

Longest Punt

64 yards, Tom Wittum, NFC 1974

Average Yards Punting

Career (min. 10 punts):
45.25 Jerrel Wilson, AFC 1971–3
Game (min. 4 punts):
49.57 Jim Arnold, NFC 1988

FUMBLES

Most

Career: 6 Dan Fouts, AFC 1980–4, 1986
Game: 4 Jay Schroeder, NFC 1987

PUNT RETURNS

Most

Career: 13 Rick Upchurch, AFC 1977, 1979–80, 1983
Game: 7 Vai Sikahema, AFC 1987

Most Yards Gained

Career: 183 Billy Johnson, AFC 1976, 1978, NFC 1984
Game: 159 Billy Johnson, AFC 1976

Longest Punt Return

90 yards (TD), Billy Johnson, AFC 1976

KICK-OFF RETURNS

Most

Career: 10 Rick Upchurch, AFC 1977, 1979–80, 1983
10 Greg Pruitt, AFC 1974–5, 1977–8, 1984
Game: 6 Greg Pruitt, AFC 1984

Most Yards Gained

Career: 309 Greg Pruitt, *as above*
Game: 192 Greg Pruitt, AFC 1984

Longest Kick-off Return

62 yards, Greg Pruitt, AFC 1984

SACKS

Records kept only since 1983

Most

Career: 7 Mark Gastineau, AFC 1983–6
7 Reggie White, NFC 1987–91
7 Howie Long, AFC 1984–8, 1990
Game: 4 Mark Gastineau, AFC 1985
4 Reggie White, NFC 1987

TEAM RECORDS

Wins

13 NFC, 9 AFC

Biggest Winning Margin

42 pts: NFC 45 AFC 3, 1984

Most Points One Game

45 NFC, 1984

Least Points One Game

3 AFC, *as above*

Highest Scoring Game (aggregate)

64 pts: NFC 37 AFC 27, 1980

Lowest Scoring Game (aggregate)

16 pts: AFC 10 NFC 6, 1987

Aggregate Points (all games)

455 NFC, 359 AFC

Most Touchdowns

All Games: 56 NFC (AFC total 35)
*The NFC have scored a touchdown in all but two of the 22
Pro Bowls. They did not score one in 1987 and 1988.*
Single Game: 6, NFC, 1984

Most Points after Touchdown

All Games: 51, NFC (AFC total 33)
Single Game: 5, AFC, 1974

Most Field Goals

All Games: 36, AFC (NFC total 22)
Single Game: 5, AFC, 1974

Most Net Yards Gained Rushing and Passing in a Game

466, AFC, 1983

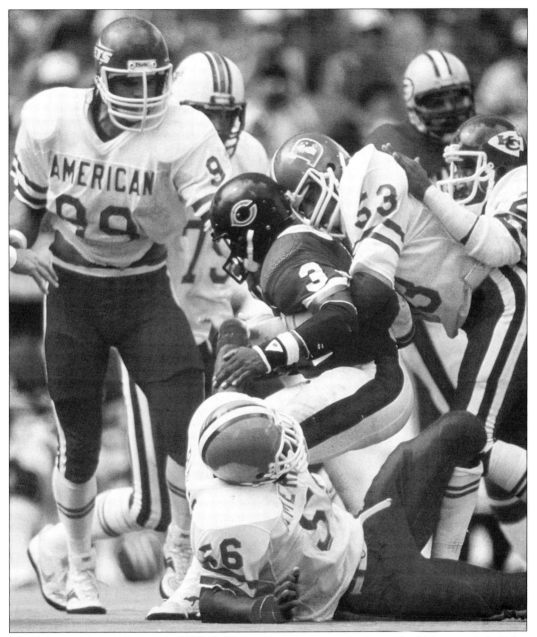

The NFC trounced the AFC 45–3 in 1984, the biggest ever win in the game, and a match which set records for highest and lowest points totals.

Most Yards Gained Passing in a Game
387, AFC, 1983

Most Yards Gained Rushing in a Game
224, NFC, 1976

Most Points in Any Single Quarter (both teams)
27 pts: NFC 14, AFC 13, 4th quarter, 1973
27 pts: NFC 20, AFC 7, 2nd quarter, 1980

Most Points in Any Single Quarter (one team)
20 pts, NFC, as above
*The 1980 Pro Bowl was the only one in which **both** teams scored points in every quarter.*

Record Attendance
66 918, Arrowhead Stadium, Kansas City, 1974

THE HALL OF FAME

The Professional Football Hall of Fame was inaugurated at a meeting on 27 April 1961. Canton, Ohio, venue of the first ever meeting of what became the National Football League in 1920, was chosen as the Hall of Fame's site.

Canton residents and local businesses, industries and foundations donated around $400 000 for the building of the centre which has since undergone several expansion programmes to meet the demands of pro football fans from all over the world who visit the centre each year. Since its opening more than five million fans have visited the Hall of Fame.

The first players, 17 in all, were inducted into the Hall of Fame in 1963 and the five inductees in 1991 took the total to 160 players, coaches, owners and administrators whose contribution to the game has been recognised with membership.

Nominees are discussed at a 31-strong meeting each year, and between four and seven new inductees are admitted annually. To be accepted, a nominee must receive at least 80 per cent approval of the selection committee which is made up of media representatives from every city with an NFL team and a representative of the Pro Football Writers of America.

A person may be nominated simply by a fan writing to the Pro Football Hall of Fame with his nominee. However, a player can only be nominated if retired five years. A coach must also be retired before being nominated, although there is no specification as to his period of retirement. Administrators, owners etc can be nominated whilst still in office.

Jim Thorpe

Don Hutson

THE INDUCTEES

1963 Sammy Baugh; Bert Ball (b); Joe Carr (c); Earl (Dutch) Clark; Harold (Red) Grange; George Hallas; Mel Hein; Wilbur (Pete) Henry: Cal Hubbard; Don Hutson; Earl (Curly) Lambeau (a); Johnny Blood (McNally); Tim Mara (b); George Preston Marshall (b); Bronko Nagurski; Ernie Nevers; Jim Thorpe

1964 Jimmy Conzelman; Ed Healey; Clarke Hinkle; Roy (Link) Lyman; Mike Michalske; Art Rooney (b); George Trafton

1965 Guy Chamberlin; John (Paddy) Driscoll; Dan Fortman; Otto Graham; Sid Luckman; Steve Van Buren; Bob Waterfield

1966 Bill Dudley; Joe Guyon; Arnie Herber; Walt Kiesling; George McAfee; Steve Owen; Hugh (Shorty) Ray (c); Clyde (Bulldog) Turner

1967 Chuck Bednarik; Charles W Bidwell Snr (b); Paul Brown (a); Bobby Layne; Dan Reeves (b); Ken Strong; Joe Stydahar; Emlen Tunnell

1968 Cliff Battles; Art Donovan; Elroy (Crazylegs) Hirsch; Wayne Millner; Marion Motley; Charley Trippi; Alex Wojciechowicz

1969 Glen (Turk) Edwards; Earle (Greasy) Neale (a); Leo Nomellini; Joe Perry; Ernie Stautner

1970 Jack Christiansen; Tom Fears; Hugh McElhenny; Pete Pihos

1971 Jim Brown; Bill Hewitt; Frank (Bruiser) Kinard; Vince Lombardi (a); Andy Robustelli; YA Tittle; Norm Van Brocklin

1972 Lamar Hunt (b); Gino Marchetti; Ollie Matson; Clarence (Ace) Parker

1973 Raymond Berry; Jim Parker; Joe Schmidt

1974 Tony Canadeo; Bill George; Lou Groza; Dick (Night Train) Lane

1975 Roosevelt Brown; George Connor; Dante Lavelli; Lenny Moore

1976 Ray Flaherty; Len Ford; Jim Taylor

1977 Frank Gifford; Forrest Gregg; Gale Sayers; Bart Starr; Bill Willis

1978 Lance Alworth; Weeb Ewbank (a); Alphones (Tuffy) Leemans; Ray Nitschke; Larry Wilson

1979 Dick Butkus; Yale Lary; Ron Mix; Johnny Unitas

1980 Herb Adderley; David (Deacon) Jones; Bob Lilly; Jim Otto

1981 Morris (Red) Badgro; George Blanda; Willie Davis; Jim Ringo

1982 Doug Atkins; Sam Huff; George Musso; Merlin Olsen

1983 Bobby Bell; Sid Gillman (a); Sonny Jurgensen; Bobby Mitchell; Paul Warfield

1984 Willie Brown; Mike McCormack; Charley Taylor; Arnie Weinmeister

George Halas

Ernie Nevers

THE HALL OF FAME

1985 Frank Gatski; Joe Namath; Pete Rozelle (c); OJ Simpson; Roger Staubach

1986 Paul Hornung; Ken Houston; Willie Lanier; Fran Tarkenton; Doak Walker

1987 Larry Csonka; Len Dawson; Joe Greene; John Henry Johnson; Jim Langer; Don Maynard; Gene Upshaw

1988 Fred Biletnikoff; Mike Ditka; Jack Ham; Alan Page

1989 Mel Blount; Terry Bradshaw; Art Shell; Willie Wood

1990 Buck Buchanan; Bob Griese; Franco Harris; Ted Hendricks; Jack Lambert; Tom Landry (a); Bob St Clair

1991 Earl Campbell; John Hannah; Stan Jones; Tex Schramm (b); Jan Stenerud

All members are former players except those marked (a), (b) or (c).

(a) Indicates the member was a former coach

(b) Indicates a team owner or president

(c) Administrators: Joe Carr – NFL President; Hugh (Shorty) Ray – Supervisor of NFL Officials; Pete Rozelle – NFL Commissioner

Since the inaugural 17 inductees in 1963, the most inducted in any one year is eight in 1966 and 1967. The least new inductees was in 1973 and 1976 when only three men were admitted.

Above *YA Tittle*

Top left *Johnny Blood (McNally)*

Bottom left *Elroy Hirsch*

WORLD LEAGUE OF AMERICAN FOOTBALL

The World League of American Football (WLAF) started during the weekend of 23–25 March 1991. Unlike many rival leagues over the years, the WLAF received the full backing of the NFL. Furthermore it received financial support from 26 of the NFL's 28 teams.

The League's aim was to spread the game across the Atlantic and into Europe, and so ten teams, six from the United States, one from Canada, and one each from England, Spain and Germany, formed the first World League.

While all teams used NFL players as the nucleus of their squad, there were exceptions – the London, Barcelona and Frankfurt teams produced some 'home-grown' players. The 'stars' of the NFL were missing, of course, but the World League would not have been viable if they had played: part of its success was the limiting of base salaries for competing players. The estimated payroll of $1.1 million per team was less than the salary of 34 individual NFL players in 1990.

The London Monarchs were the best-supported team in 1991 and they were the World League's first champions. The best attendances in 1992 were in Frankfurt and Barcelona but the World Bowl was an all-American affair, Sacramento defeating Orlando 21–17.

Week 1 of the new World League of American Football – David Smith of the London Monarchs in action during their win over Frankfurt Galaxy.

TEAMS AND THEIR HOME VENUES

European Division

Barcelona Dragons	Montjuich Stadium
Frankfurt Galaxy	Waldstadion
London Monarchs	Wembley Stadium

North American Western Division

Birmingham Fire	Legion Field
Sacramento Surge	Hughes Stadium
San Antonio Riders	Alamo Stadium

North American East Division

Montreal Machine	Olympic Stadium
New York-New Jersey Knights	Giants Stadium
Orlando Thunder	Florida Citrus Bowl
(1991) Raleigh-Durham Skyhawks	Carter-Finley Stadium
(1992) Ohio Glory	Ohio Stadium

1991 RESULTS

Home teams are first named, winners in CAPITALS

Week 1

BARCELONA	19	New York-New Jersey	7
Birmingham	5	MONTREAL	20
Frankfurt	11	LONDON	24
ORLANDO	35	San Antonio	34
SACRAMENTO	9	Raleigh-Durham	3

Week 2

BIRMINGHAM	17	Sacramento	10
LONDON	22	New York-New Jersey	18
Montreal	10	BARCELONA	34
ORLANDO	58	Raleigh-Durham	20
San Antonio	3	FRANKFURT	10

Week 3

LONDON	35	Orlando	12
MONTREAL	23	Birmingham	10
New York-New Jersey	17	FRANKFURT	27
Raleigh-Durham	14	BARCELONA	26
SAN ANTONIO	10	Sacramento	3

Week 4

BARCELONA	33	Orlando	13
Birmingham	0	LONDON	27
Montreal	0	NEW YORK-NEW JERSEY	44
Raleigh-Durham	15	SAN ANTONIO	37
SACRAMENTO	16	Frankfurt	10

Week 5

FRANKFURT	30	Raleigh-Durham	28
LONDON	45	Montreal	7
NEW YORK-NEW JERSEY	28	Sacramento	20
Orlando	6	BIRMINGHAM	31
SAN ANTONIO	22	Barcelona	14

Week 6

BIRMINGHAM	16	San Antonio	12
FRANKFURT	17	Montreal	7
LONDON	35	Raleigh-Durham	10
NEW YORK-NEW JERSEY	42	Orlando	6
Sacramento	20	BARCELONA	29

Week 7

BARCELONA	11	Birmingham	6
Orlando	14	FRANKFURT	17
Raleigh-Durham	6	NEW YORK-NEW JERSEY	42
Sacramento	23	MONTREAL	26*
San Antonio	15	LONDON	38

Week 8

BARCELONA	14	San Antonio	7
FRANKFURT	10	Birmingham	3
MONTREAL	15	Raleigh-Durham	6
New York-New Jersey	7	LONDON	22
ORLANDO	45	Sacramento	33

Week 9

Barcelona	3	FRANKFURT	10
BIRMINGHAM	24	New York-New Jersey	14
Raleigh-Durham	14	ORLANDO	20
Sacramento	21	LONDON	45
SAN ANTONIO	27	Montreal	10

Week 10

Frankfurt	13	SACRAMENTO	24
London	17	BARCELONA	20
Montreal	27	ORLANDO	33*
NEW YORK-NEW JERSEY	38	San Antonio	9
Raleigh-Durham	7	BIRMINGHAM	28

* In Overtime

FINAL STANDINGS

	W	L	T	Pct	PF	PA
European Division						
London Monarchs	9	1	0	.900	310	121
Barcelona Dragons*	8	2	0	.800	206	126
Frankfurt Galaxy	7	3	0	.700	155	139
North American East Division						
New York-New Jersey Knights	5	5	0	.500	257	155
Orlando Thunder	5	5	0	.500	242	286
Montreal Machine	4	6	0	.400	145	244
Raleigh-Durham Skyhawks	0	10	0	.000	123	300
North American West Division						
Birmingham Fire	5	5	0	.500	140	140
San Antonio Riders	4	6	0	.400	176	196
Sacramento Surge	3	7	0	.300	179	226

*Indicates wild card entry into play-offs

PLAY-OFFS

New York-New Jersey	26	LONDON	42
Birmingham	3	BARCELONA	10

WORLD BOWL 1991

Wembley Stadium, 9 Jun, 61 108

LONDON	7	14	0	0	–	21

T: Horton, Crossman, Garrett
PA: P Alexander 3

Barcelona	0	0	0	0	–	0

Most Valuable Player: Dan Crossman (London)

1992 RESULTS

Week 1

Barcelona	0	FRANKFURT	17
SACRAMENTO	20	Birmingham	6
SAN ANTONIO	17	Montreal	16
ORLANDO	13	Ohio	9
LONDON	26	New York–New Jersey	20*

Week 2

BARCELONA	15	New York–New Jersey	14
BIRMINGHAM	17	San Antonio	10
Ohio	6	SACRAMENTO	17
MONTREAL	31	Orlando	29
London	28	FRANKFURT	31

Week 3

BARCELONA	13	London	7
Frankfurt	7	BIRMINGHAM	17
New York–New Jersey	3	SAN ANTONIO	9
SACRAMENTO	14	Montreal	7
Ohio	3	ORLANDO	28

Week 4

Frankfurt	17	BARCELONA	20
London	17	Birmingham	17*
Sacramento	20	SAN ANTONIO	23*
ORLANDO	39	New York–New Jersey	21
MONTREAL	31	Ohio	20

Week 5

London	0	BARCELONA	9
BIRMINGHAM	28	Sacramento	14
SAN ANTONIO	17	Ohio	8
ORLANDO	16	Montreal	8
NEW YORK–NEW JERSEY	24	Frankfurt	21

* In overtime

Week 6

BARCELONA	20	Ohio	19
SAN ANTONIO	17	Birmingham	14
London	26	SACRAMENTO	31
Frankfurt	0	ORLANDO	38
NEW YORK–NEW JERSEY	34	Montreal	11

Week 7

BIRMINGHAM	19	Barcelona	17
San Antonio	21	ORLANDO	39
Montreal	21	SACRAMENTO	35
OHIO	20	Frankfurt	17
NEW YORK–NEW JERSEY	41	London	13

Week 8

Barcelona	0	SAN ANTONIO	17
BIRMINGHAM	23	Montreal	16*
SACRAMENTO	51	Frankfurt	7
ORLANDO	9	London	0
Ohio	33	NEW YORK–NEW JERSEY	39

Week 9

NEW YORK–NEW JERSEY	47	Barcelona	0
BIRMINGHAM	24	Orlando	23
Frankfurt	14	SAN ANTONIO	43
SACRAMENTO	21	Ohio	7
Montreal	13	LONDON	45

Week 10

ORLANDO	13	Barcelona	10
Ohio	24	BIRMINGHAM	27
San Antonio	21	SACRAMENTO	27
FRANKFURT	19	London	16
NEW YORK–NEW JERSEY	41	Montreal	21

FINAL STANDINGS

European Division	W	L	T	Pct	PF	PA
Barcelona Dragons	5	5	0	.500	104	161
Frankfurt Galaxy	3	7	0	.300	150	257
London Monarchs	2	7	1	.250	178	203
North American East Division						
Orlando Thunder	8	2	0	.800	247	127
New York–New Jersey Knights	6	4	0	.600	284	188
Montreal Machine	2	8	0	.200	175	274
Ohio Glory	1	9	0	.100	132	230
North American West Division						
Sacramento Surge	8	2	0	.800	250	152
Birmingham Fire*	7	2	1	.750	192	165
San Antonio Raiders	7	3	0	.700	195	150

* Indicates wild card entry into play-offs

PLAY-OFFS

ORLANDO	45	Birmingham	7
SACRAMENTO	17	Barcelona	15

WORLD BOWL 1992

Olympic Stadium, Montreal, 6 Jun, 43789

SACRAMENTO	0	6	0	15	–	**21**

T: Green, Brown PA: Blanchard FG: Blanchard 2

Orlando	7	10	0	0	–	**17**

T: Ford, Davis PA: Bennett 2 FG: Bennett
MVP: David Archer (Sacramento)